Deviance, Conformity, and Social Control in Canada

Tami M. Bereska

Grant MacEwan College

Toronto

National Library of Canada Cataloguing in Publication

Bereska, Tami M. (Tami Marie), 1968–
Deviance, conformity, and social control in Canada / Tami M. Bereska.

Includes bibliographical references and index.
ISBN 0-13-035518-6

1. Deviant behavior. 2. Social control. 3. Canada—Social conditions. I. Title.

HM811.B47 2004 302.5′42′0971 C2003-907161-8

0-13-035518-6

Vice President, Editorial Director: Michael J. Young
Executive Acquisitions Editor: Jessica Mosher
Associate Editor: Patti Altridge
Senior Marketing Manager: Judith Allen
Signing Representatives: Andy Wellner
Production Editor: Richard di Santo
Copy Editor: John Firth
Proofreader: Anne Borden
Production Manager: Anita Heyna
Page Layout: Heidi Palfrey
Permissions Manager: Susan Wallace-Cox
Photo Researcher: Sandy Cooke
Art Director: Julia Hall
Interior and Cover Design: Monica Kompter
Cover Image: Getty Images

2 3 4 5 08 07 06 05

Printed and bound in Canada.

Contents

Preface

Introduction

The sociology of deviance is a diverse field of study, and this diversity is reflected in the content of Canadian textbooks that are available. Some books are based on theory, with separate chapters on each category of deviance theory, and use specific deviance examples to illustrate components of those theories. These theory books provide a thorough description and critical analysis of a wide range of theories, but if there is one way to make a fascinating subject like deviance rather dull in the eyes of students (as they have repeatedly pointed out to me), it is to bombard them with theory for the sake of theory. In contrast, this textbook reviews theories of deviance in two chapters, but the remaining chapters focus on substantive issues.

Other books have a criminological focus, and contain extensive discussions of topics like prostitution, white-collar crime, police deviance, and sexual assault; these are all very important topics for students to be familiar with. However, students who take separate courses in criminology and in deviance frequently experience too much overlap between the course materials. In contrast, this textbook is specifically intended for courses in deviance or social control. There will still be a small amount of overlap for students taking both criminology courses and deviance courses, but that overlap is minimal. Furthermore, the material that might overlap is presented within a context very different from what students will have in criminology courses.

Some textbooks contain collections of readings that are based upon a similar theoretical approach, such as social constructionism. These collections have the benefit of providing students with original readings; however, they lack a cohesive context to enhance student learning. This book is the kind of single-authored textbook that many professors (and students) prefer.

Finally, some books are characterized by what Ben-Yehuda (1990, p. 5) calls "radical phenomenalism," where countless numbers of isolated, specific phenomena (e.g. call girls, transsexualism, marijuana use) are described in tremendous detail, but without reference to a broader social and historical structure. These phenomena are usually quite interesting to read about, but, without a wider context, the logic of including the various specific phenomena is unclear. To the reader, it can feel somewhat like randomly grabbing items in an all-you-can-eat buffet rather than sitting down to a four-course Italian meal, where the different courses are designed to complement each other. In contrast, within this textbook, there is a method to the madness; the specific topics and issues addressed within each chapter were selected to be part of a cohesive whole. Each individual topic covered is placed within a sociocultural context, and contributes to a bigger picture.

Features

The features of this textbook include the following:

- *Pedagogical aids for students* are interspersed throughout every chapter. Students are asked to engage with the material as they read it. *"Ask Yourself"* sections ask students to think about certain questions, their own lives, or their own points of view prior to reading the next body of material. *"Exercise Your Mind"* sections recommend that students go beyond the textbook material to explore particular issues in more detail, such as looking for critiques of theories, or renting certain movies that demonstrate a topic being discussed. *"An Internet Moment"* sections direct students to specific Internet sites related to the material; these sections also indicate to students what they should be looking for on those sites, or what questions they should keep in mind while on the site. *"Time To Review"* sections ask students review questions at regular intervals throughout the chapters.
- *Objective and subjective approaches* to deviance are integrated within the textbook, rather than focusing on only one or the other. They are presented as complementary rather than contradictory.
- *Two theory chapters* review those theories that are utilized within more objective approaches (Chapter 2) and more subjective approaches (Chapter 3).
- The topics of the substantive chapters are *relevant to students' lives*—sexuality, youth, voluntary and involuntary physical appearance, mental disorders, religious belief systems, and scientific belief systems. The topics were selected to illustrate to students that the social typing and social control of deviance is occurring everywhere around them each day of their lives; they have experienced it, and they participate in it.
- Each of the substantive chapters incorporates material on *social typing and social control*.
- Each of the substantive chapters reveals the *"deviance dance."* That is, each chapter demonstrates how the social typing of deviance is not a uniform process, but rather is characterized by *disagreement, debate, and resistance*, even for the most taken-for-granted issues (e.g. pedophilia).
- Each of the substantive chapters *tells a cohesive story*. Students are not bombarded with an assortment of cafeteria-style facts, but rather learn about the sociocultural context within which particular forms of deviance are socially typed and socially controlled.
- Within the "story" told in each chapter, both *criminal and non-criminal* forms of deviance are explored in relation to the topic at hand.
- The vital role of *power* in determining and controlling deviance is discussed within each chapter.

Organization

The first three chapters in the book provide students with the foundation they need for a course in deviance. Chapter 1 looks at the various ways that academics, laypersons, and activists have defined deviance; these definitions are embedded within a wider discussion of the objective/subjective dichotomy as it has traditionally been presented. From the objective perspective, various definitions are reviewed, illustrated with numerous examples, and critiqued from the point of view of statistical rarity, normative violation, social harm, and societal reaction. From the subjective perspective, deviance is described as "anything that enough important people say it is"; this is embedded within a discussion of social construction. After presenting the traditional objective and subjective points of view, the dichotomy or dualism is questioned, and material is presented showing how there is now more of a blending of the two perspectives in the work of many deviance scholars. Students are introduced to the concept of the social typing process, the different forms of social control, and the role of power in society. The notion of the "deviance dance," that is, the negotiations over deviance—disagreement, debate, and resistance—is introduced.

Chapter 2 explains that, because scholars with more objective and more subjective leanings shine their analytical spotlights on different aspects of deviance, different theories are more useful to each. The remainder of Chapter 2 reviews the positivist theories that are of most use to more objective researchers. This is not an exhaustive theoretical analysis, but rather reviews those theories that have been the most influential in the study of deviance. The section on functionalist theories includes Durkheim, Merton's strain theory, Cloward and Ohlin's differential opportunity theory, Agnew's general strain theory, and Cohen's status frustration theory. The section on learning theories includes Sutherland's differential association theory, Sykes and Matza's neutralization theory, and social learning theory. The section on social control theories reviews Hirschi's social bonds theory, and Gottfredson and Hirschi's general theory of crime.

Chapter 3 reviews the interpretive and critical theories that are of most use to more subjective-leaning scholars. The section on symbolic interactionism addresses the perspective more generally, and then discusses the work of Tannenbaum, Becker, Lemert, and Goffman. The section on critical theories reviews conflict theories, power-reflexive (or critical poststructuralist) theories, feminist theories, and postmodern theories.

The remaining chapters in the book focus on substantive issues. Chapter 4 explores sexuality. An historical and cross-cultural analysis reveals that sexual cultures are society- and time-specific, and precisely what is considered to be "deviant" varies accordingly. The chapter begins with an analysis of the sexual culture of 5th century B.C. Athens, and then moves on to the Sambia of New Guinea. The sexuality of traditional Aboriginal cultures in North America is addressed, and the way that European colonization changed that sexual culture is discussed. The section on how sexual cultures in Canada and the United States have changed from the 16th century through the 20th century is particularly effective in demonstrating how conceptions of sexual deviance vary. Moving into the present day, although there is certainly more sexual freedom than in the past, freedom is not unlimited. We continue to use certain criteria for evaluating people's sexuality as "deviant" or "normal." The criteria include issues of consent, selection of the partner, and the nature of the sexual act; extensive contemporary examples are used to illustrate these criteria, and the means of social control for each of the criteria is discussed as well.

Chapter 5 focuses on youth. The first section of the chapter addresses "deviant" youth—youth crime, gangs, and substance abusers (including binge drinking among college students). Then the concept of "at-risk" youth is introduced and explored; the criticism that the concept of "at-risk" has rapidly expanded so that now it can potentially include all youth in society leads to the second half of the chapter. Here, the following question is asked: "Aren't all youth deviant?" That is, the issue of whether adolescence is an inherently deviant time in the life cycle is explored.

In Chapter 6, voluntary and involuntary physical appearance is explored. The chapter begins with a small discussion of intentional aspects of appearance, such as those embedded within particular lifestyles (e.g., goths). But the emphasis of the chapter is on body size—"too fat," "too thin," and "ideal." The way that these criteria are determined medically is reviewed, as are medical forms of social control. Then the social standards by which these labels are attached are discussed. The culturally ideal body size has become increasingly thinner over the last fifty years, to the point of it now being alarmingly thin. In comparison to this ideal, almost everyone is "too fat." The various means of control through the media, commercial industry, government, and medicine are reviewed, and resistance to the deviantization of "too fat" is addressed. "Too thin" is a label that is attached much less frequently, although recently the media has begun talking about the "Lollipop heads" on television. There is a brief discussion of the extreme of "too thin," that is, anorexia. Social control of "too thin," and even resistance to the "too thin" label, are reviewed.

Chapter 7 is about mental illness. The chapter explores what mental illness is, its prevalence, and the individual and societal costs associated with mental illness. The way mental illness has been socially controlled historically and in the present day is discussed, including issues of mental health policy and funding, and stigmatization. The impact of the deinstitutionalization movement is presented as well. Then the chapter moves to the more subjective interest in how mental illness is determined. Criticisms of the *DSM* and the process by which it is created are presented. Rosenhan's study, "Being Sane in Insane Places," is reviewed, and then the social factors that influence diagnosis and treatment today are presented.

In Chapter 8, religious belief systems are addressed. There are two sections to this chapter. The first section explores "deviant religions." Various churches, sects, and cults are analyzed, and the way that sects and cults are controlled in society is discussed. Then the traditional distinction between churches, sects, and cults is questioned, and students are presented with material demonstrating that all religious groups have been seen as deviant and made subject to social control at some time and in some society. The alleged violations of religious freedoms in various countries in the world are reviewed, such as China and France. The second section of the chapter explores "religion as a social typer of deviance"; that is, the way that religious belief systems dictate what is "deviant." Various instances of the blurring of boundaries between religious and political belief systems are presented—the witch persecutions, European colonization and residential schooling, and the more contemporary concerns about the Christian Coalition's alleged control of the Republican Party in the United States.

In Chapter 9, scientific belief systems are analyzed. The first section looks at "deviance in science," such as fraudulent research, scientific hoaxes, and ethical violations. Laura Schlessinger and John Gray are discussed in the context of the criticisms that have been launched against them for "misusing" their scientific credentials. The second section explores "deviant sciences," that is, pseudo-sciences like astrology; the discussion includes how such sciences are controlled, and how what is seen as a pseudo-science changes over time. The third section of the chapter looks at "science as a social typer of deviance." Scientists are granted the most legitimacy in our society, such that when they make claims to "truth," most of us lend credence to those claims. In this way science helps many of us, but at the same time, historically the credibility lent to scientific claims has resulted in negative consequences. We can see this in the context of the social Darwinism that influenced government policies regarding Aboriginal peoples, and the eugenics movement that swept through the Western world and reached its apex in Nazi Germany. Today, some people suggest that the new science of genetic testing and manipulation is nothing more than eugenics in 21st-century clothing. The claims to "truth" being made by genetic scientists and by their critics are explored, and worldwide efforts to control genetic science are reviewed.

Chapter 10 brings students full circle. The chapter reminds readers of the key themes that were introduced in Chapter 1 and then reflected within each of the substantive chapters—the objective-subjective continuum; social typing, social control, and power; and the "deviance dance." Examples from the various chapters are reiterated to demonstrate these themes. Because of the role of subjectivity in determining and controlling deviance, some students may be left with the question of whether that means "anything goes." That is, they may wonder if no one and nothing can ever be accurately socially typed as deviant. The notion of human rights is introduced as a possible starting point for thinking about when it is, and is not, appropriate to attach a deviant label and subject someone to measures of social control. Key human rights themes that are brought forward are human dignity, freedom from discrimination, and security of person and property.

Supplements

Supplements to this textbook include the following:

- Test Bank
- Instructor's Manual
- PowerPoint slides

These supplements can be downloaded from Pearson Education Canada's protected Instructor Central websites, at **www.pearsoned.ca/instructor.**

Acknowledgements

Not only does it take a village to raise a child, it also takes a village to write a book. I would like to take a moment to thank my "village." Special thanks go to Jessica Mosher from Pearson Education for believing in this project. Thanks also to Patti Altridge from Pearson Education for her advice, her suggestions, her gentle reminders, and her ability to keep everything in order; academics are not easy people to work with, and I have the utmost respect for people who work with us anyway. My summer research assistant, Theresa Vladicka, was a godsend! I have no doubt that there are wonderful things in store for her future. The reviewers of my manuscript provided some wonderful suggestions, and, even more importantly, stimulated my thinking, so thank you to them. Thanks to my colleagues at Grant MacEwan College for commiserating with me when I needed that, and for getting me back on track when I needed that—Diane and Russ, thank you. If academics are hard to work with, they are probably even harder to live with (especially when a deadline is approaching), so special thanks to my husband.

CHAPTER 1

Determining Deviance

Learning Objectives

After reading this chapter, you should be able to:

- Describe the objective/subjective dichotomy.
- Describe four definitions of deviance traditionally associated with the objective side of the objective/subjective dichotomy, and explain their limitations.
- Describe the definitions of deviance traditionally associated with the subjective side of the objective/subjective dichotomy, and summarize the concept of social construction.
- Explain how the study of deviance is influenced by how the researcher defines it. Depict the role of change, negotiation, opposition, and diversity in the "deviance dance" in Canadian society.
- Outline the three components of the social typing process through which someone is defined as "deviant." Explain the role of power, and identify who holds this power in Canadian society.

"Conformity makes everything easier, if you can still breathe." (Mason Cooley)[1]

"You have to be deviant if you're going to do anything new." (David Lee)[2]

The two above quotations both make some very pointed claims about the nature of **deviance** and **conformity**. The first quotation makes the claim that our lives will run more smoothly if we conform; however, it also makes the claim that conformity will constrict and limit us. The second quotation makes a related claim, that doing something or thinking in a new way is necessarily deviant; although "thinking outside the box" is a popular corporate phrase today, the source of this quotation suggests that only "deviants" will actually do so.

Taken together, the claims made within these quotations raise questions about deviance and conformity. Who are the conformists in our society and in our world? Is life easier for them? Are their thoughts, behaviours, and identities limited by their conformity? Who are the deviants? Are they really the innovators of our world, or do they represent some sort of problem that we need to control? What is it that differentiates a "deviant" from a "conformist"? How can we distinguish between them? These are the kinds of questions that will guide us through this textbook.

Ask Yourself:

Before going on, take out your notebook and make a list of types of people whom you consider to be deviant. Remember, no one will see your list, so just write down whatever comes into your mind. We will come back to your list in a little while.

Who Is Deviant?

Who is deviant? One way to try to answer this question is by looking at the topics covered in deviance textbooks. Historically, certain themes have prevailed—what have been referred to as "nuts, sluts, [and] perverts" (Liazos, 1972, p. 103). Criminality has also dominated the topics covered in some deviance textbooks, particularly those written by criminologists who focus their attention on criminalized forms of deviance. However, a growing number of recent books have moved away from these tendencies, and towards broader notions of deviance—welfare recipients (Doherty, 2000), smokers (Tuggle & Holmes, 2003), overweight people (Degher & Hughes, 1991), and motherhood (Wachholz, 2000) have all been analyzed in the context of deviance. A second way to try to answer the question of who is deviant is to ask people. Just as many other deviance professors have done (e.g. Goode, 1997), over several years of teaching I have conducted polls of students in my classes. Certain responses have predominated, and may bear a striking resemblance to the list you created above: People who commit crimes, especially violent crimes (such as serial murderers and rapists), are thought of as deviant by large numbers of students. There is also considerable consensus that those who glaringly perpetuate injustice, such as racists and people who engage in emotional abuse, are deviant as well. However, while there is considerable consensus among students about the top three or four types of people that are deviant, once going beyond the top few, perceptions of deviance become as diverse as the students making those lists. Anyone the student dislikes or is annoyed by is added to the list—classmates who twirl their hair, people who will not hold the door open for you when you are carrying a heavy bag, country singers, and professors who wear too much beige are just some of the hundreds of unique responses students have given. This raises the question of whether deviance refers to a label that each of us can attach to those particular people whom we disapprove of and/or are annoyed by, or whether it refers to something at the level of social processes that goes beyond each of our own personal pet peeves. In answer to that question, although using the term "deviance" in reference to our own individual opinions may be common practice, the concept of deviance transcends the individual level and instead exists at the societal level. That is, deviance is not about people whom I personally disapprove of, but rather is about characteristics of the broader society and sociocultural processes. In other words, just because I personally might not like country singers does not mean that country singers are deviant in Canadian society. Although each of us (along with our individual opinions) is an important participant in the social processes that occur in Canadian society, social processes constitute more than the sum of their parts, more than the sum of each of our personal points of view. Thus, studying deviance requires moving beyond individual belief, and instead analyzing the broader social processes that occur in the society you live in, regardless of whether those processes correspond to your individual beliefs or challenge them.

In addition to focusing analytical attention on social processes rather than on personal points of view, understanding deviance also requires an exploration of its absence. What is the absence of deviance? The quotation by Mason Cooley that opened this chapter utilizes the term "conformity," which is commonly used to refer to the absence of deviance; in fact, some courses in deviance are titled

Ask Yourself:

Look back at your personal list of "deviant" people. Which people on your list are there primarily because you personally do not approve of them or are annoyed by them? Are there people on your list who you think may go beyond the level of personal dislike and instead point to processes occurring at the societal level?

Ask Yourself:

Now that we have looked at whom you consider to be "deviant," write down your answer to another question–whom do you consider to be "normal"?

Ask Yourself:

Go back to the list you made of people whom you consider to be deviant. Take a look at the list. What do all of the people on your list have in common? That is, is there a characteristic that all of them share, which might point to how deviance can be defined or how we can recognize a deviant when we see one? This issue will be addressed in the next section of the chapter.

"Deviance and Conformity." However, the term "**normal**" also serves as an antonym to "deviant," and refers to something or someone who conforms (Merriam-Webster, 2002). Thus, either of these words may be used to refer to the absence of deviance.

If you found this to be a more difficult question to answer, you are not alone. My own students have had considerable difficulty in formulating answers to this question. This is, however, just as important of a question to ask. Perceptions of normalcy, in the eyes of my students, are usually based on the absence of deviance—they do not focus on what normal is, but on what it is not. Lianos (with Douglas, 2000) suggests that "deviance has become a backwards definition of normality..." (p. 261); however, it may be that normality has become a backwards definition of deviance—if you are *not* a deviant, then you are normal. Whether normality is a backwards definition of deviance, or vice versa, one thing is clear—what is considered deviant exists only in conjunction with what is seen as normal or conforming. But how is it that some people come to be seen as deviant while others are perceived as normal?

TIME TO REVIEW:

- What does it mean when someone says that the concept of deviance exists at the societal level rather than the individual level?
- What concepts serve as the opposite of "deviance"?
- What is the relationship between the way some college students have defined "deviance" and the way they have defined "normality"?

How Can We Recognize Deviance When We See It?

Asking the question of how we are able to determine who is deviant and who is normal brings us to the issue of definitions. The dictionary, our culture's institutionalized resource for the meanings of the words we use, tells us the following:

Deviant: "deviating [straying] from an accepted norm." Synonyms: "abnormal, atypical, aberrant, unrepresentative." Contrasted words: "normal, natural." (Merriam-Webster, 2002)

At first glance, the dictionary seems to make the concept of deviance quite clear. Deviance involves violating norms that have been accepted in society, and apparently this is quite serious, because doing so makes one abnormal and unnatural. Clearly, breaking the rules has significant consequences. Perhaps Mason Cooley, quoted at the beginning of this chapter, was correct in saying that conformity makes one's life easier.

We could stop with the dictionary definition of deviance, and let that serve as the foundation for our exploration through the remainder of this book. However, the ways that the word "deviance" is used in academic research and in common usage often differ from the dictionary definition—defining deviance is not as straightforward as the dictionary implies. In the academic realm, the study of deviance has historically been characterized by considerable disagreement over the concept of deviance, and this "problem of definition" (Ben-Yehuda, 1990, p. 4) continues to the present day. That is, even deviance specialists cannot entirely agree on what deviance is. Although contradictory definitions of deviance have co-existed for many decades, some researchers suggest that a broader shift in definitions has become evident over time (Hathaway & Atkinson, 2001). This shift is from older definitions that suggested there is an *objective* way of determining what is deviant to more recent definitions that suggest there is no objective way of defining deviance, and instead point out that deviance is necessarily *subjective*. **Objective** views of deviance claim that the presence of certain characteristics defines deviance—behaviours or people that have those characteristics are "deviant," and those lacking such characteristics are "normal." By looking for these characteristics, we can all identify deviance. In contrast, **subjective** views of deviance claim that there is no shared, observable characteristic that can clearly tell us who or what is "deviant," and who or what is "normal"—instead, we must be told by someone else who it is that is deviant in Canadian society. Both the objective and subjective ways of defining deviance will be outlined and explored in more detail as the chapter progresses.

Proposing that there has been a shift from objective to subjective ways of defining deviance implies certain underlying assumptions. The core underlying assumption is that there is an unmistakable distinction between objective and subjective definitions of deviance, so that an objective definition can be clearly differentiated from a subjective definition. The distinction between objective and subjective is typically described as a dualism, or dichotomy, wherein objective and subjective represent two oppositional and mutually exclusive categories (e.g. Ben-Yehuda, 1990; Adler & Adler, 2003). However, the recent shifts in definitions of deviance often go beyond this notion that objective and subjective are mutually exclusive categories, and instead combine components of both. And if it is possible to combine objective and subjective notions of deviance, this raises the question of whether the objective/subjective dichotomy that has been so frequently referred to is even a useful one to talk about in contemporary deviance research. In the following sections, the traditional objective/subjective distinction will be explored. We will look at the different objective definitions of deviance that have been utilized in the academic arena as well as in common usage. Subjective definitions of deviance will also be reviewed. Finally, we will look at how these two different types of definitions may not be so different after all, and how many contemporary ways of looking at deviance are blends of both objective and subjective. Although this section of the chapter began with what looked like a very clear dictionary definition of deviance, when you finish reading the following sections of the chapter you will see that the subject of this book—deviance—is a far more complex and multifaceted phenomenon than what the dictionary definition suggests.

TIME TO REVIEW:

- What does the "problem of definition" (Ben-Yehuda, 1990, p.4) refer to?
- What is the nature of the shift that has occurred in definitions of deviance, according to some deviance specialists? What assumption lies at the foundation of this proposed shift?

The Objective/Subjective Dichotomy

Objectivism: Deviance as an Act

Looking at the objective side of the dichotomy, as it has typically been depicted, emphasizes the assumption that there is something inherent in a person, behaviour, or characteristic that makes it deviant. There is something that "deviants" have in common that enables us to recognize them when we see them; however, precisely what that shared trait is appears to be a matter of debate. The traits that have been most frequently postulated include statistical rarity, harm, a negative societal reaction, and normative violation (e.g. Deutschmann, 2002; Sacco, 1992). Each of these traits is differentially emphasized by diverse deviance researchers, as well as by various laypersons. Each of these traits, when used as a defining characteristic of deviance, has also been subject to criticism by other deviance specialists, particularly those working from a subjective approach.

Statistical Rarity. One of the definitions of deviance that has been associated with the objective side of the objective/subjective dualism is based on **statistical rarity**. Although this is a definition that is not commonly utilized in a direct way within academic research, it is a definition that is "often heard in everyday conversation" (Clinard & Meier, 2001, p. 7); as a result of its popular usage, it is an important conception of deviance to analyze (Becker, 1963; Ward, Carter, & Perrin, 1994). According to this definition, if something is not typical, it is deviant. Thus, smokers may be thought of as deviant in contemporary Canada, because only 24% of Canadians over the age of 15 smoke (Canadian Medical Association, 2001). Ex-cons may be thought of as deviant because most people have not been in prison. People with green, spiked hair or tattoos on their faces may be thought of as deviant because most people do not have those characteristics. Because most people are heterosexual (Bagley & Tremblay, 1998), homosexuals may be thought of as deviant.

While this definition of deviance has popular credibility, and although there are particular instances where statistical rarity can be observed, postulating statistical rarity as the defining characteristic of deviance has its limitations. First of all, how we define "rare" presents a problem. Is something rare if its prevalence is less than 50%? Or does it have to be less than 30%? Health Canada (1999) has found that 40% of Canadian adolescents in grade 10 have used marijuana. Approximately 40% of college students engage in binge drinking (Keeling, 2000). Are these behaviours rare? The difficulty in determining the criterion for rarity illustrates one of the limitations of this definition of deviance.

Another limitation of utilizing the concept of statistical rarity as the basis for defining deviance is that what we think is rare might not be. For example, many adult Canadians do not realize that as many as 57% of students in grade 9, and 74% of those in Grade 11, have participated in "heavy petting" (i.e., manual genital stimulation of a partner) (Alberta Medical Association, 1991). Accordingly, although laypersons often use statistical rarity as a conception of deviance, this raises the question of the accuracy of their knowledge of what actually is or is not rare in Canadian society. This logically leads us to the next limitation of using statistical rarity as the defining characteristic of deviance: even though the above behaviour is not statistically rare, we as a society still initiate efforts to control and reduce it. In other words, things that are statistically common are not always perceived as being acceptable within the broader society

Finally, we must also consider that there are many rare things that are not considered deviant in Canadian society. Left-handed people are statistically rare, but they are not treated as though they are deviant.[3] Sports prodigies (like Wayne Gretzky) are statistically rare. People who do not drink alcohol are uncommon (Canadian Medical Association, 1999). Health Canada (1999) finds that high school students who are happy, feel healthy, or eat raw vegetables are all uncommon amid their peers. And yet few of us would say that any of the above people are perceived as being deviant in our society. Rarity is not always seen as deviant, nor is commonness always seen as non-deviant; thus, defining deviance on the basis of statistical rarity has limitations. The significance of these limitations is such that this definition has been of little use to deviance researchers.

TIME TO REVIEW:

- What is the core assumption underlying the objective side of the objective/subjective dichotomy?
- Describe the definition of deviance that focuses on statistical rarity, and give some examples.
- What are the limitations of defining deviance this way? Give examples of each limitation.
- Is the definition of deviance based on statistical rarity utilized to a greater extent among deviance specialists or among laypersons?

Harm. Another definition of deviance commonly associated with the objective side of the objective/subjective dichotomy is based on the concept of **social harm** (Deutschmann, 2002; Sacco, 1992). That is, if something/someone causes harm, then it is deviant. The most obvious type of harm is *physical harm*. Thus, if someone harms someone else, such as through assault, drunk driving, or exposing others to second-hand smoke, then the perpetrator of that harm is deviant. Physical harm can also be done to oneself; for example, smoking may be considered deviant because of the physical harm caused to the smoker, in the form of increased risks of heart disease and various types of cancer.

Harm may also be directed not at a human being, but at society itself; that is, certain behaviours or people may interfere with the smooth running of society as a whole. In this context, criminals can be considered deviant because they threaten the safety of the population at large, and the social order as a whole. If everyone committed crimes, then anarchy would rule. Recently, anti-globalization "anarchists" have been portrayed by politicians and the media as deviant because of the harm they do to the social order, the economy, foreign affairs, and the peaceful conducting of international conferences (Ford, 2001; Thomson & Reid, 2001).

Finally, harm may be directed at something far more abstract and ethereal than a person, or a society; harm may occur in the form of a threat to the way we understand the world and our place in it. Historically, religious belief systems have frequently provided us with this means of abstract understanding on a large scale. Even in contemporary societies, religious belief systems provide many people with a fundamental way of understanding existence. With the example of religion, we can see many examples of this more abstract notion of harm. For example, Joan of Arc was seen as deviant (Brower, 1999), in part, because she claimed that she did not need the fathers of the church as a pipeline of communication to God; this violated the dominant religious-based belief system of the time, which claimed only the fathers of the church were able to communicate with God (Read, Armstrong, Pettigrew, & Johansson, 1994). In contemporary society, Muslim women who do not wear head scarves may be seen by some other Muslims who hold a particular interpretation of their religious doctrine as threatening the fundamental assumptions upon which the religious belief system is based (Fernea, 1998; Todd, 2001).

At first glance, notions of physical or emotional harm to someone, harm to the social order, and harm to abstract world views appear to be useful in recognizing and defining deviance. Many different forms of deviance, from murder and smoking to anti-globalization activity and the behaviour of persecuted historical figures like Joan of Arc, can be seen as causing harm to someone or something. And perceptions of harm frequently do galvanize social action, such as in creating non-smoking bylaws. However, a more critical look at the idea of harm is useful.

Even the idea of physical harm is not as clear as it might initially appear. Claims of physical harm can be, and have been, disputed. For many years, the tobacco industry claimed that smoking did not cause the harm that anti-smoking activists suggested it did. In the past, some claims of physical harm were greatly exaggerated. A century ago, doctors argued that masturbation caused hairy palms, acne, and outright insanity. For example, look at the following excerpt by 19th century health reformer Sylvester Graham: "This general mental decay…continues with the continued abuses [of masturbation], till the wretched transgressor sinks into a miserable fatuity, and finally becomes a confirmed and degraded idiot, whose deeply sunken and vacant glassy eye, and livid, shriveled countenance, and ulcerous, toothless gums, and fetid breath, and feeble broken voice, and emaciated and dwarfish and crooked body, and almost hairless head—covered, perhaps, with suppurating blisters and running sores—denote a premature old age—a blighted body—and a mined soul" (cited in Whorton, 2001, p. 3).

Elaborate measures were taken to produce devices that would curb masturbation in children located in orphanages, hospitals, boarding schools, and middle-class homes (see Photo 1.1 and Box 1.1).

Exaggerated claims about the dangers of marijuana use were also common in the past. In the years leading up to the criminalization of marijuana in 1923, social activists, community leaders, and law enforcement officials spoke out about the physical harm it caused. As can be seen in Box 1.2, marijuana use was alleged to cause horrific violent crimes, murder, idiocy, and ultimately complete insanity and even death. Today, such claims are perceived as greatly exaggerated; however, debates over the physical harm caused by marijuana use continue, and are fundamental to discussions of the issues of decriminalization and legalization.

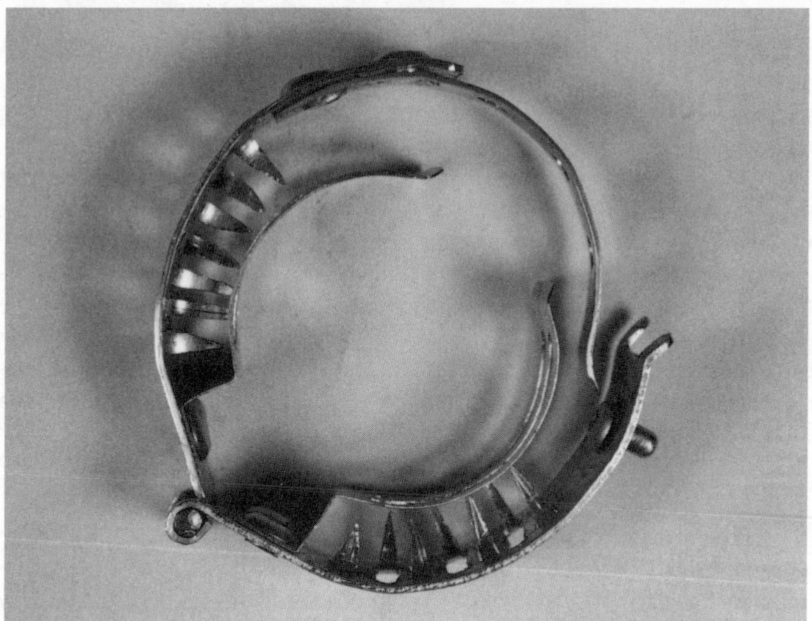

A variety of anti-masturbation devices were used on children during the Victorian era and the early 20th century, because of the harm that the behaviour was thought to cause.

Box 1.1 Preventing Masturbation

The following illustrates the degree to which masturbation was viewed as deviant and harmful behaviour in Western society during the 19th and early 20th centuries. The harms caused by masturbation were thought to be so severe that prevention was prescribed on several different levels. At an informal level, parents, boarding school teachers, hospital workers, and workers in orphanages were advised to increase surveillance of children in situations where they would be alone, particularly at night (Hunt, 1998). Behavioural advice was given as well: "Robert Bullen, who was secretary of the Social Purity Alliance...recommended 'Eight Rules for Daily Life': (1) cold bath every day; (2) regular and vigorous exercise; (3) sleep on a hard bed; (4) moderation in eating and drinking; (5) avoid all 'unhealthy excitement'; (6) never consult doctors who advertise; (7) be regular in prayer; and (8) perform an act of kindness for another every day" (Hunt, 1998, p. 601).

Finally, a wide range of anti-masturbation devices was marketed. Bondage would prevent children from touching themselves at night. The Stephenson Spermatic Truss prevented erections from occurring. The Bowen Device would pull on the wearer's pubic hair if an erection occurred. Steel armor was padlocked shut at night, and a key was required to allow trips to the bathroom. Penis-cooling devices splashed cold water on the genitals if an erection occurred.

Box 1.2 Emily Murphy's Marijuana Campaign

Emily Murphy, the first female judge in the British Empire and a leading Canadian suffragist in the early 20th century, was dismayed at what she saw as the horrors of Canada's drug trade. After interviewing both drug users and law enforcement officials from across North America, in 1922 she wrote the book *The Black Candle* about drug use. One chapter focuses specifically on the harms caused by marijuana use, quoting police officials: "[Marijuana] has the effect of driving the [user] completely insane. The addict loses all sense of moral responsibility. Addicts to this drug, while under its influence, are immune to pain.... While in this condition they become raving maniacs and are liable to kill or indulge in any form of violence to other persons, using the most savage methods of cruelty.... They are dispossessed of their natural and normal will power, and their mentality is that of idiots. If this drug is indulged in to any great extent, it ends in the untimely death of its addict" (Murphy, 1973 [1922], pp. 332-333).

The claims she makes in this chapter, although somewhat humorous to today's reader, had a significant influence on changing drug laws for years to come.

When it comes to the idea of interfering with the current social order, or threatening a belief system or worldview, the limitations of defining deviance by virtue of harm become more evident. First, whether or not society, or a belief system, is being *harmed* can be subjective. Are Muslim women who do not wear headscarves actually a threat to the belief system contained within Islam? While some people

Ask Yourself:

What are some of the controversial or hotly debated issues that are occurring within your community or within the larger society at the present time? Are you aware of any current debates over whether certain forms of behaviour or certain groups of people should be subjected to measures of control? Are notions of "harm" being utilized in any of these debates?

would say so, these women themselves often say there is nothing in the belief system itself that requires the headscarf. During the 20th century, there were several times when women in North America were accused of harming the social order, or abstract belief systems, or both. Early feminists who fought for the right of women to vote faced such accusations, as did later groups of women in the 1960s and 1970s as they questioned the "natural" role of women as homemakers and moved outside the home into paid employment. Were these women causing harm to society or to beliefs? Because the word *harm* implies a negative impact, many would say that these women were not *harming* society, they were simply *changing* society. Others would say that by changing society, they were having a negative impact on the social order of the time, and thus were technically causing harm, but that it was a social order that needed to be changed—it needed to be dismantled.

All of the above limitations of defining deviance on the basis of harm illustrate the necessity of going beyond the idea of harm in seeking the defining characteristic of deviance. The nature of these limitations is such that this definition of deviance is rarely used within academic literature, although it does enjoy popular usage among laypersons, politicians, and social activists.

In your responses to the above questions, perhaps you referred to debates over anti-smoking bylaws (i.e., whether smokers cause harm to the people around them), abortion (i.e., whether a "life" is being harmed), war (i.e., whether a certain country should be attacked in warfare because of the danger it poses to the rest of the world), or early parole for child molesters (i.e., whether they pose a continuing threat to children in the community). In all of these instances, the concept of harm forms the key to social and political debate.

Despite the fact that academic literature rarely suggests that harm is the defining characteristic of deviance, some literature does acknowledge that harm, or something similar to harm (i.e., threat or dangerousness), is *one of* the characteristics of deviance. For example, Stebbins (1996) suggests that perceived threat is central to perceptions of deviance, and that the level of threat that is perceived determines the categorization of that deviance. Hathaway and Atkinson (2001) also incorporate the level of perceived threat into their analysis of societal responses to recreational marijuana use and illegal ticket-scalping in Canada. Lianos (with Douglas, 2000) proposes that what is most significant to the study of deviance is not whether someone actually causes harm or is actually dangerous, but rather whether someone *seems* dangerous. Deviance specialists from the subjective side of the objective/subjective dualism suggest that this requires looking at the social processes that result in someone being seen as potentially dangerous, regardless of whether that person actually is dangerous. Later on in this chapter the use of the notion of perceived danger by subjective researchers will be addressed.

TIME TO REVIEW:

- Describe the definition of deviance that focuses on harm.
- What are the three different types of harm that may occur? Give examples of each.
- What are the limitations of postulating that harm is the defining characteristic of deviance? Give both contemporary and historical examples.
- Do deviance specialists on the subjective side of the objective/subjective dichotomy ever utilize the concept of harm?

Societal Reaction. Another one of the definitions of deviance that has been associated with the objective side of the objective/subjective dichotomy is based on the nature of **societal reaction**. People may respond to others in a number of different ways. If the responses of society's "masses" are primarily negative (such as dislike, anger, hatred, stigmatization, and teasing) rather than positive (such as like, admiration, envy, or tolerance), then the person or act being responded to is deviant. It is seeing this negative evaluation by society that enables us to determine who or what is deviant.

Indeed, as we will see shortly, even those researchers who claim that there is no objective way of recognizing deviance usually agree that a negative evaluation, of some sort, is one of the necessary components of the social processes of deviance; if there is not some type of negative reaction, then there is no deviance (Adler & Adler, 2003; Rubington & Weinberg, 1999; Evans, 2001). However, focusing on a negative societal reaction as *the* defining characteristic of deviance raises many questions. Why does society react negatively against some things and not others? Whose reaction counts? Does my reaction, as a college professor, count more than your reaction, as a student? Does the Prime Minister's reaction count more than mine? How many individual negative reactions must exist before we can say that "society" is reacting negatively?

For example, a recent study by the Canadian Centre on Substance Abuse found that two-thirds of adult Canadians oppose the continued criminalization of marijuana (cited in Hathaway & Atkinson, 2001). Is this a sufficient proportion of society's masses to change the laws? Another survey finds that 75% of Canadians feel that homosexuals deserve the same rights as everyone else, and 53% believe that homosexuals should be allowed to adopt children (cited in *The Edmonton Journal*, July 16, 2001). Angus Reid finds that 53% of Canadians support legal gay and lesbian marriages, and 63% agree that gays and lesbians should receive spousal benefits. These surveys suggest that most Canadians are *not* reacting negatively to issues of gay rights, and yet such rights continue to be denied to a large extent—why? What else, besides societal reaction, is involved?

These types of diverse survey results also reveal that societal reactions are not uniform, and different groups of people react in various ways to the same behaviour or issue. Thus, we can see that societal responses to a particular behaviour or characteristic can include patterns of *inclusion* as well as *exclusion*, patterns of *acceptance* as well as *rejection* (Bogdan & Taylor, 1987). That is, different groups of people will react in different ways to the very same behaviour. Many deviance specialists tend to focus solely on the rejection and exclusion of particular people, behaviours, or characteristics. By doing so, they frequently fail to recognize the complexity of societal reaction, and have oversimplified the social processes involved with deviance.

TIME TO REVIEW:

- Describe the definition of deviance that focuses on societal reaction.
- What are the limitations of defining deviance on the basis of a negative societal reaction? Give some examples.

Normative Violation. The dictionary (as cited on page 4), as well as many deviance specialists, suggests that recognizing deviance is quite straightforward—something is deviant if it violates norms. The "general statement that deviance is focused around the violation of norms" (Ben-Yehuda, 1990, p. 4) is shared extensively among deviance specialists from both the objective and subjective sides of the objective/subjective dichotomy, as well as those who transcend this traditional dualism. However, the manner in which **normative violation** is integrated into a definition of deviance varies among deviance specialists working within the various approaches.

Among deviance specialists working within the objective side of the dichotomy, the violation of norms has been proposed to be *the* defining characteristic of deviance. Indeed, the dictionary definition of deviance makes this point quite clearly as well. Yet even among those recognized as objectivists, the nature of the normative violation seen as constituting deviance has changed. Early objectivists utilized what may be considered an "absolutist" (Adler & Adler, 2003, p. 2) or a value-based (Clinard & Meier, 2001) conception of normative violation, wherein a particular behaviour or characteristic was perceived as being inherently deviant, and universally so (Ward, Carter, & Perrin, 1994; Adler & Adler, 2003; Clinard & Meier, 2001). According to this view, there are certain immutable norms and values that should be held in all cultures and at all times—norms and values that emerge from an "absolute moral order" (Adler & Adler, 2003, p. 3) based upon the word of God, the laws of nature, or some other immutable source. Because of that absolute moral order, what is considered wrong in one place should be considered wrong everywhere; cross-cultural and trans-historical norms prohibiting incest, murder, and lying are perceived as evidence of this absolute moral order.

The simplistic view of norms within the absolutist view, along with difficulties in finding universal norms having identical content, led many objectivists to abandon the absolutist view. However, still working from within the objective side of the objective/subjective dualism, another view of normative violation has developed. Among these more modern objectivists, norms are perceived as being culturally specific rather than universal—based on a given society's moral code rather than on any type of absolute moral order (Ward, Carter & Perrin, 1994). This perspective is still identified as objective, in that someone who violates the norms of the society they live in is seen as deviant. From birth, we are socialized into the norms that govern our society; we learn the standards or the expectations of the society we live in. In Canadian society, as we grow up we are taught to share with others, to be polite, to work hard, to listen to our teachers—in essence, most of us are taught by our parents, teachers, community leaders, and religious leaders to follow the rules. We learn what behaviours will be rewarded (like arriving at work on time) and what behaviours will be punished (like breaking the law). Knowing these expectations, if we then go on to violate the norms, we are "deviant."

Ask Yourself:

On a sheet of paper, write down the norms that are being violated by each of the following people: an obese person; a "free-rider" in a classroom group assignment; someone on social assistance; a drug addict or alcoholic; a thief. Remember, norms refer to standards or expectations of behaviour, so ask yourself what expectations each of these people are not living up to–what "rules" of society are they breaking?

Thus, the obese person may be thought of as deviant for presumably violating the norms of self-control and care for one's appearance. The "free-rider" in a classroom group exercise may be thought of as deviant for violating the norms of hard work, cooperation, and teamwork. The person on social assistance may be thought of as deviant for violating the norms of hard work and self-sufficiency. The drug addict or alcoholic may be thought of as violating the norms of self-control and reliability. The thief has violated norms so central in our society that she or he may end up in prison as a result—our parents, the Criminal Code, and even the world's major religions tell us that stealing is wrong.

Of course, looking at the examples described above, one can see that not all norms are the same. While violating some norms may result in prison (as for the thief), violating other norms has different (and some might say less severe) consequences. The obese person, alcoholic, social assistance recipient, or "free-rider" will not be entered into the criminal justice system for their normative violations. These differential outcomes of normative violation emerge from the existence of various types of norms, ranging from *folkways*, to *morés*, to *laws* (Kendall, Murray, & Linden, 2000; Stebbins, 1996). Norms, as standards or expectations of behaviour, can refer to informal, everyday behaviours, such as rules of etiquette, choice of clothing, and behaviour in the college classroom; these kinds of informal norms are called **folkways**, and if you violate these norms, you might be thought of as odd (Adler & Adler, 2003), rude, or a troublemaker. Other norms are taken more seriously. **Morés** are those standards that are often seen as the foundation of morality within a culture, such as prohibitions of incest or homosexuality; if you violate these norms, you may be thought of as immoral (Adler & Adler, 2003) or even evil. Finally, some norms are considered to be so central to the smooth running of society that they are enshrined within the legal system, for example, in Canada's Criminal Code; if you violate the Criminal Code, you will be thought of as a criminal. At times, the legal system integrates morés (e.g. incest is included in the Criminal Code of Canada, and until 2003 homosexual activities were criminal offences in several American states); however, other acts that are not perceived as the foundation for morality in our culture (e.g., marijuana possession) are also integrated into the legal system.

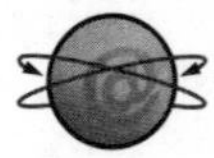

AN INTERNET MOMENT:

You can find a copy of the Criminal Code of Canada at http://www.efc.ca/pages/law/cc/cc.html (or alternatively, you may find a copy in your college or university library). Look at the Table of Contents to see the kinds of normative violations that have been enshrined within Canada's legal system. You might find it particularly interesting to look at the behaviours that are prohibited in the section on Offences Against the Person (which includes assault, hate crimes, and bigamy) and the section on Sexual Offences, Public Morals, and Disorderly Conduct. What, if anything, do all of the norms that are being supported in this document have in common, such that they are considered important enough to enshrine within our criminal justice system?

The way that norms are integrated into objectivist definitions of deviance presumes a certain level of consensus (McCaghy, Capron, & Jamieson, 2003; Miller, Wright, & Dannels, 2001; Ward, Carter, & Perrin, 1994). Although cross-cultural variations in norms are acknowledged, it is assumed that, within a given society, the majority of citizens agree upon the norms. That is, most of us concur about what the rules of our society are. However, deviance specialists working from within the subjective side of the objective/subjective dualism critique this non-problematic view of social norms. Some have reservations about the presumption of normative consensus, asking the question of the extent to which a given expectation must be shared in order to be considered a "norm" and then used as an objective standard against which deviance is judged (Ward, Carter, & Perrin, 1994). Some deviance specialists even question whether it is possible to determine the level of consensus that does or does not exist for a given expectation. They point out that there are countless numbers of groups in society, having innumerable different sets of rules; even a given individual belongs to multiple groups having varying sets of expectations. Given the multiplicity of individuals, groups, and sets of expectations that coexist within a society, normative consensus is difficult to determine (Adler & Adler, 2003; Becker, 1963). How do we determine the level of consensus that exists in society for a given norm (such as obeying authority), if individuals within society may simultaneously belong to social groups that reproduce that norm and social groups that promote an opposing norm (such as questioning the status quo)? In fact, given all of the different expectations that exist in society simultaneously, which expectations are the ones that constitute society's "norms" that are then used to judge deviance and normality?

In response to these critiques, some deviance specialists have elected to focus on those norms that they suggest are characterized by some consensus, "assuming that the agreed-upon norms of a society can be found in its criminal law" (McCaghy, Capron, & Jamieson, 2003, p. 8). Following this chain of logic, deviance becomes equated with criminality, and the forms of deviance studied include prostitution, drug use, white-collar crime, gang behaviour, and other forms of law-violating behaviour. The practice among some deviance specialists of equating deviance with criminality has resulted in an academic debate over what the differences between the fields of criminology and the sociology of deviance are, and whether the sociology of deviance has been subsumed under the umbrella of criminology (Miller, Wright, & Dannels, 2001). Whether focusing on criminal law violations is more illustrative of criminology or the sociology of deviance, the claim that agreed-upon norms can be found in a society's criminal law has itself been questioned.

Some criminologists and some deviance specialists draw our attention to the fact that law creation is a political activity, wherein those norms that are embodied in law do not necessarily reflect the opinion of the majority of citizens (Ward, Carter, & Perrin, 1994). Indeed, the creation of a new law in Canada does not require the support of a majority, nor are the opinions of all Canadians sought prior to its creation. For example, after the September 11, 2001, attack on the United States, the Canadian Parliament passed a bill (C-36) giving police broad new powers of arrest, along with other changes, a move that engendered considerable controversy and debate among Canadians. Whether this new bill reflected the view of the majority of Canadians is unknown, because the government did not seek public opinion prior to passing it. The **consensual view** of law, wherein the law is perceived as arising out of social consensus and is then equally applied to all, is only one of the possible views of crime and law (Siegal & McCormick, 2003).

Criminologists who align themselves with the **conflict view** perceive crime and law very differently. They see the law as a tool used by the ruling class to serve its own interests, and the law is then more likely to be applied to members of the powerless classes in society. For example, some research suggests that young offenders who belong to the lower classes are more likely to be drawn into the justice system than are youth of the middle and upper classes. In Canada, self-report surveys of youth crime show us that middle and upper class youth are underrepresented in official crime statistics; they are, in fact, committing more crimes than is indicated by the criminal justice system (Bell, 2002). Why might this be the case? Howard Becker (1963) suggested that, even given similar behaviours by lower class and middle class youth, police are more likely to enter the former into the justice system, while letting middle class youth go with a warning, or into their parents' custody. Another view of crime, the **interactionist view**, also presents a non-consensual view of criminal law. Within this view, it is suggested that society's powerful define the law at the behest of interest groups, who appeal to those with power in order to rectify a perceived social ill. Again, the criminal law is not seen as emerging out of consensus, but rather out of the interests of certain groups within society. Finally, some criminologists portray a more complex view of criminal law, pointing out the nation's law must attempt to strike some sort of a balance between the interests of the powerful, the opinion of the majority, and the views of special interest groups (Linden, 2000). Looking at these different views, we can see that the criminal law is based on more than a simple consensus over what society's norms are.

The normative objectivity of the law has also been critiqued on the question of the situational applicability of broad social norms. For example, in a rather objective fashion we might say that legal prohibitions against murder reflect normative clarity in society—we know that murder is wrong. However, some deviance specialists point out the many situational characteristics that can modify this abstract norm. Self-defence, capital punishment (in countries where the criminal justice system allows the state to do this), military action in wartime, and euthanasia (in some countries) are all circumstances in which taking a human life may be considered acceptable. So, is taking another human life deviant? Looking at the above, we see that the answer to that question is that taking another human life is deviant at some times but not at other times. In fact, in situations where taking another human life is considered acceptable, the behaviour is called something other than "murder"; for example, during wartime the death of innocent civilians is not "murder," but "collateral damage." Consequently, given the situational variations in which even the most basic norms do or do not apply, some deviance specialists have come to ask whether norms, as reflected in criminal law, are even useful in trying to define deviance (Ward, Carter, & Perrin, 1994).

Thus, although the role of norms in defining deviance initially seems quite straightforward, it appears that normative violation is considerably more complex than the work of objectivist deviance specialists depicts. The limitations that have been proposed regarding traditional objectivist uses of the concept of normative violation have led some researchers to ask, "Given this kind of dilemma, are norms really useful in defining deviance?...The answer depends upon the way one conceptualizes norms." (Ward, Carter, & Perrin, p. 5). That is, even some subjectivist deviance specialists suggest that normative violation *can* be used as a definition of deviance *if* the definition of norm being used is not predicated on consensus, and instead acknowledges that something a statistical minority in society has the power to endorse can be referred to as a norm.

Some deviance specialists step into this debate over the degree of consensus involved in social norms by proposing that there are some norms that do have higher levels of consensus. For example, despite the situational variations in prohibitions against taking another human life, it is likely that most (if not all)

Canadians support the inclusion of homicide in the Criminal Code; the same can also likely be said for auto theft, sexual assault, and break-and-enter. Even Howard Becker (1963), recognized as one of the founders of the subjectivist approach to defining deviance, points out that there *are* some rules about which there is considerable agreement in society. Thio (1983) utilizes the concepts of **high-consensus deviance** and **low-consensus deviance** to distinguish between forms of deviance that have differential levels of support within the broader society. The norms reflected in criminal law are characterized by relatively more consensus than are society's non-legislative norms (such as norms governing physical appearance).

TIME TO REVIEW:

- Describe the definition of deviance that focuses on normative violation, and give a few examples.
- How has the objectivist use of normative violation changed over time?
- Describe the various aspects of the debates over the issue of consensus regarding society's norms.
- What are the different views of the role of consensus in the development of criminal law?
- What are critics referring to when they question the situational applicability of norms? Give an example.
- In what way do some subjectivists utilize the concept of norms?

Subjectivism: Deviance as a Label

Having looked at the objective side of the traditional objective/subjective dichotomy, we now turn our attention to the subjective side. From this point of view, there is a very different answer to the question "How can we recognize deviance when we see it?" While objectivists suggest that deviance can be recognized by the presence of a particular characteristic, subjectivists say that we cannot recognize deviance when we see it; someone has to tell us that someone or something is deviant. Howard Becker (1963) was one of the first sociologists to suggest that deviance is subjective in nature—that there is no singular trait or characteristic that is shared by all deviant people throughout history and across cultures, other than the fact that people with some influence on society have said they are deviant.

Just as the nature of objective conceptions of deviance have changed over time, so have subjective conceptions of deviance. Early subjectivism focused primarily on the process of labelling—deviance is anything that is labelled as such. This form of subjectivism has a negative reaction as its foundation, with Becker (1963) saying that if there is no negative reaction, there is no deviance; in other words, deviance lies within the reaction rather than within the act. The distinction between the ways the concept of "negative reaction" is used by these early subjectivists and the way it is used by objectivists (as discussed earlier in the chapter) is somewhat hazy. The objective use of negative reaction focuses on a *societal* reaction—particular things *are* deviant in our society, and we can see that they are deviant by the negative societal reaction that occurs. In contrast, the early subjective use of negative reaction is more vague, pointing to the reaction as being almost arbitrary—anything may be reacted to negatively, such that we can never know how a particular act will be responded to. The vague way that early subjectivists used the concept of negative reaction has been subject to criticism, particularly for ignoring the act that stimulated a negative reaction in the first place (Ward, Carter, & Perrin, 1994). The reaction itself does not create the initial act that people are reacting to; in other words, people are reacting to a specific act for a reason, rather than out of a purely arbitrary process.

Later deviance specialists working within the subjective side of the objective/subjective dichotomy moved beyond this simple notion of labelling, and toward more complex conceptions of deviance based on social patterns and social construction. These more contemporary deviance specialists emphasize that *social patterns* determine deviance; "deviance exists only when it is created by society" (Adler & Adler, 1997, p. 14) through a "process of definition" (Adler & Adler, 1997, p. 71). This process of definition creates a hierarchy of deviance based upon a combination of social factors, such as how many people condemn a behaviour, the level of power held by those people doing the condemning, and the intensity of their disapproval (Goode, 1997). In other words, not all things are equally likely to be perceived and treated as deviant in society. In our interactions with others, we quickly categorize each other (e.g., "woman," "skinhead," "fat") and then act accordingly. When the labels we use to categorize each other are of a negative nature given societal standards of the time, they stigmatize those to whom the label has been applied, and serve as a way to differentiate "Us" from "Them." The more the perceptions of these categories are shared among people in society, the greater the reaction or consequences for those who have been categorized (Rubington & Weinberg, 2002). Furthermore, the greater the power of the people who share those perceptions, the greater the consequences are likely to be. Thus, those things that are disapproved of by large numbers of powerful people are more likely to be considered deviant than those things that are disapproved of by small numbers of powerless people (Goode, 1997). In fact, the role of power is so central that the approval or disapproval of a few powerful people is likely to take precedence over the approval or disapproval of large numbers of powerless people. The "**dominant moral codes**" (Goode, 1997, p. 29) of a society serve as the foundation for determining who or what is deviant—and a society's dominant moral codes are shaped by the interests and the actions of groups that hold some level of power.

Contemporary subjective deviance specialists point to the complex nature of power relations. Social processes involve far more than simply the powerful controlling and oppressing the powerless. The use and legitimization of power interacts with negotiations about moral boundaries, negotiations that the less powerful groups in society are also able to participate in. Consequently, "this process does mean that the powerless can resist deviantization" (Ben-Yehuda, 1990, p. 7), rather than simply being at the mercy of the interests of the powerful. Continual negotiations are occurring between members of different **symbolic-moral universes** (i.e., groups proposing a specific set of moral boundaries and a particular moral code), and among members of the same symbolic-moral universe, such that the social construction of deviance and normality/conformity is in a constant state of flux (Ben-Yehuda, 1990).

TIME TO REVIEW:

- What is the core assumption of definitions of deviance on the subjective side of the objective/subjective dichotomy?
- How have subjective definitions of deviance changed over time?
- What role does power play in deviance, according to subjective definitions?
- Compare the use of "negative reaction" in objective and subjective definitions of deviance.
- What role do "dominant moral codes" play in deviance, according to subjective definitions of deviance?

Subjectivity and the "Social Construction" of Deviance

Referring to the subjective nature of deviance means focusing on the idea of *social construction*. In other words, there is nothing inherent in a behaviour or a characteristic that makes it deviant; a particular behaviour or characteristic is deviant only if the dominant moral codes of a specific society at a certain time in history say that behaviour is deviant. Similarly, what is considered to be normal is also socially constructed, given that notions of deviance and normality exist only in relation to each other (Freud, 1999). **Social constructionism** refers to the perspective that suggests social characteristics (such as the labels of "deviant" and "normal") can only be understood within the context of a particular society at a specific time in history; something that is considered "deviant" in one society may be considered "normal" within another society, or at another time in history.

Social constructionism has become a dominant force in the study of deviance today. In fact Goode (1997) suggests, "Most deviance specialists [today] are *constructionists*" (p. 35); that is, most contemporary deviance specialists adhere to the idea of social construction. However, there are different levels, or different types of constructionism. One type of constructionism is labelled **radical** (Goode, 1997) or **strict** (Best, cited in Rubington & Weinberg, 2002) constructionism; the other type is labelled **soft** or **contextual** (Best, cited in Rubington & Weinberg, 2002). Most deviance specialists who practice social constructionism follow its latter form rather than the former. The difference between these two levels or types of constructionism broadly indicates a distinction between social constructionism as a distinct theoretical perspective, and social constructionism as a pragmatic tool for analyzing social processes. Radical constructionists often postulate a distinct theoretical perspective claiming that "there is no essential reality to the social world at all, that if everything and anything is simply looked at in a certain way, that is the way it is" (Goode, 1997, p. 35). However, there is considerable intellectual debate over whether social construction can be considered a distinct theoretical perspective. For example, in her book about theories of deviance, Deutschmann (2002) does not include constructionism as a theoretical perspective. By contrast, Rubington and Weinberg (1995) do include constructionism as one of the seven major theoretical perspectives in studying social problems. For the moment, this intellectual and theoretical debate continues. But regardless of this debate, the practice of soft constructionism grows. In other words, many people practice contextual constructionism, wherein instead of using any sort of formal theory of constructionism, they pragmatically look at the ways that certain social phenomenon (like deviance and normality) are socially constructed—that is, created within a particular society at a particular time in history. In such cases, social construction is addressed in terms of a process rather than a theory.

This use of soft social construction helps to circumvent the problem of endless relativism discussed earlier, which frequently arises when constructionism is used as a theory. Thus, "most [contemporary deviance specialists] are not *radical* constructionists. What I mean by this is that most do *not* believe that *everything* is a matter of definition, that there is *no* essential reality to the social world at all.... Rather, most sociologists of deviance believe that there are 'limits' to social constructionism" (Goode, 1997, p.35). When social construction is used in its soft form, as a process, certain theoretical limitations are lifted. Consequently, a constructionist analysis can be combined with a number of different theoretical approaches, approaches that will be addressed in Chapter 3.

Social construction as a process has as its focus the idea that, while specific behaviours or characteristics might be found throughout the world, the meanings that are attached to those behaviours or characteristics are not universal—they vary across cultures and over time (Kimmel & Messner, 1998). Consequently, using social constructionism as a pragmatic tool implies that what is of sociological significance is not the individual behaviour or characteristic itself, but rather: (a) its place in the social order; (b) the roles assigned to people who exhibit that behaviour or characteristic; and (c) the meanings attached to that behaviour or characteristic. All of these sociological focal points are dependent on the particular culture in question at a specific time in history.

The social construction of deviance emerges from four ongoing multilevel processes (Nelson & Robinson, 1999). First is the *sociocultural* level; beliefs, ideologies, values, and systems of meaning have an influence on the path of social construction. Second is the *institutional* level; the structures of our society, such as the government, the education system, and religion affect social construction. Third is the *interactional* level; our interactions with other people influence the way we think and feel about others, thereby determining the role that each of us plays in social construction. Fourth is the *individual* level; at this level our own identities, concepts of self, and ways of understanding our own existence in the world affect the path of social construction.

Figure 1.1 LEVELS OF SOCIAL CONSTRUCTION

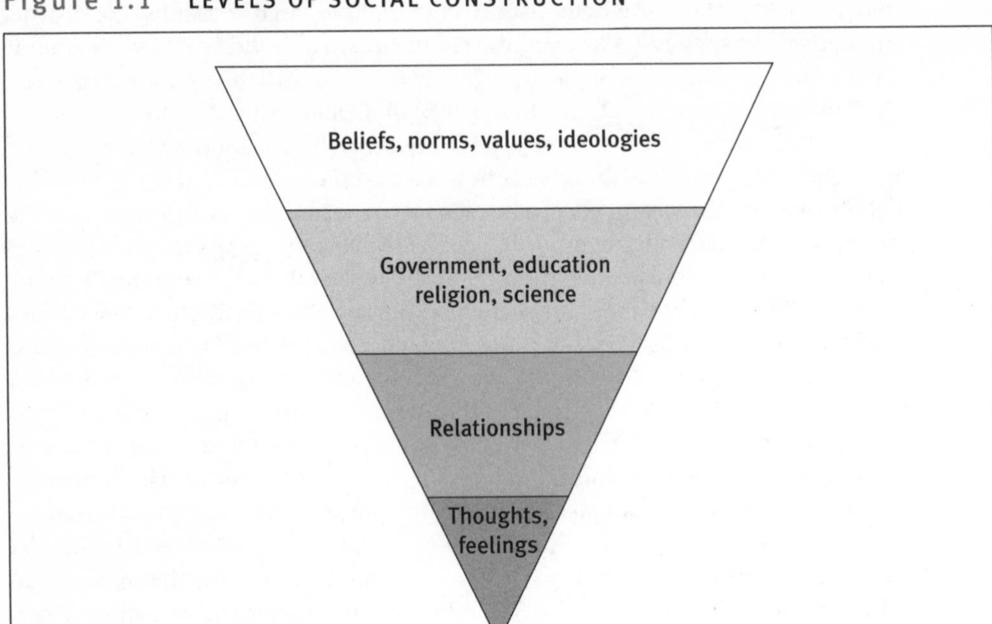

TIME TO REVIEW:

- What does it mean when we say that deviance and normality are socially constructed?
- What are the two different types of social constructionism? How do they differ from each other? What similarities do they share?
- Which type of social constructionism do most deviance specialists today utilize?
- What are the four levels at which the social construction of deviance and normality occurs?

Transcending the Objective/Subjective Dichotomy

The objective and subjective sides of the objective/subjective dichotomy, as it has been traditionally expressed, appear to be considerably distinct. On the objective side of the dualism, deviance specialists claim that there is a shared trait that all deviants have in common, a trait that enables us to recognize deviance when we see it. Although statistical rarity, harm, and a negative societal reaction have each been identified as that shared trait (whether by academics, laypersons, or social activists), the defining characteristic of deviance that is most often identified is that of normative violation. On the subjective side of the dualism, deviance specialists claim that there is no shared trait among deviants; instead, something or someone is deviant if enough important people say so. Through the processes of social construction, which are influenced by power, a dominant moral order emerges that then serves as the standard against which deviance and normality (or conformity) are judged.

The conception of the objective/subjective dichotomy serves as the foundation for the claim that a shift in definitions of deviance has recently occurred, from objective to subjective (e.g. Hathaway & Atkinson, 2001; Goode, 1997). In fact, some deviance specialists suggest that the sociology of deviance, as a distinct field of study, requires the use of the subjective, constructionist view in exploring both legal and illegal norm-violating behavior; if the subjective approach is not used, then the researcher is *not* doing the sociology of deviance (Miller, Wright, & Dannels, 2001). In contrast, the use of the objectivist approach focusing on illegal norm-violating behaviour constitutes criminology rather than the sociology of deviance (Miller, Wright, & Dannels, 2001). However, recent shifts in the study of deviance may, in fact, transcend the objective/subjective dualism, with more objective researchers integrating some level of subjectivity into their analyses, and more subjective researchers integrating some of the traditionally objectivist concepts into their analyses.

We have already seen some evidence of this within the previous discussions of the dualism. For example, we have seen that over time objective deviance specialists have changed their conceptions of norms from that of an absolute moral order to that of a culturally specific moral order. Similarly, over time subjective deviance specialists have acknowledged the role of norms in defining deviance, but in terms of norms that may be socially constructed and determined by processes of power. For example, Evans (2001) suggests that small group-specific normative systems *can* be identified; Evans delineates the set of norms that governs behaviour in Married Life chat rooms, which then serves as the standard against which certain types of chat room behaviour is judged deviant and made subject to a negative reaction by other group members. Tittle and Paternoster (2000) also propose that group-specific normative systems can be identified, and at a larger level; they identify the normative system of middle-class America. Their discussion of norms goes a step further by suggesting that, although this is only one of countless numbers of normative systems in society, it is the one that has come to dominate American society as a whole, through the power that the middle class holds in processes of social construction: "…[T]he middle class dominates US society, both by imposing its standards through the schools, the mass media, and the law and by enjoying a degree of natural hegemony in behavior styles and thinking that flows from the admiration and emulation of those with higher status." (p. 29)

Many contemporary definitions of deviance combine two or more of the following: normative violation, negative reaction, harm, power, and social construction (Hathaway & Atkinson, 2001; Ward, Carter, & Perrin, 1994; McCaghy, Capron, & Jamieson, 2003). For example, Stebbins (1996) defines deviance as normative violation, but goes on to say that the nature of societal reaction depends upon the level of perceived threat the normative violation entails, and that structures and processes of power relations in society influence this entire process. In fact, a retrospective look at work by earlier deviance specialists reveals that the distinction between objective and subjective has always been somewhat blurred. Even Howard Becker (1963), one of the leading proponents of the subjective view of deviance, integrated the notion of harm into his definition of deviance; he stated that deviance is that which is so labelled, but that this process of labelling depends on who has committed the act and who feels harmed by it.

The boundaries of objective and subjective become further blurred when looking at the extent to which the objective traits that have been discussed are present within the content of processes of social construction. The processes by which someone or something is constructed as being deviant frequently refer to statistical rarity, harm, or a negative societal reaction. For instance, interest groups that are opposed to same-sex rights sometimes argue that homosexuality is a statistical rarity, and that laws should be based on the practices of the heterosexual majority rather than the homosexual minority. People who work towards toughening young offender legislation bring arguments of harm into their work. People trying to decriminalize marijuana possession often refer to changing public attitudes that reflect the lack of a negative societal reaction to the issue of marijuana use.

Examining the complexities of the work of both past and present deviance specialists indicates that perhaps the traditional objective/subjective dualism that has served as the foundation for discussing definitions of deviance within the field has always been something of an oversimplification. The actual nature of the work done by sociologists of deviance frequently transcends the dichotomy, blending aspects of both objective and subjective, leading to the question of the extent to which this traditional distinction is useful in discussing deviance. Rather than being embedded within a dichotomy, definitions of deviance and research on deviance may actually fall along more of a continuum, with more objective assumptions lying at one end of the continuum and more subjective assumptions lying at the other end of the continuum (see Figure 1.2).

At the extreme objective end of the continuum lie those deviance specialists who have proposed an absolute moral order as the standard for determining

Figure 1.2 THE OBJECTIVE-SUBJECTIVE CONTINUUM

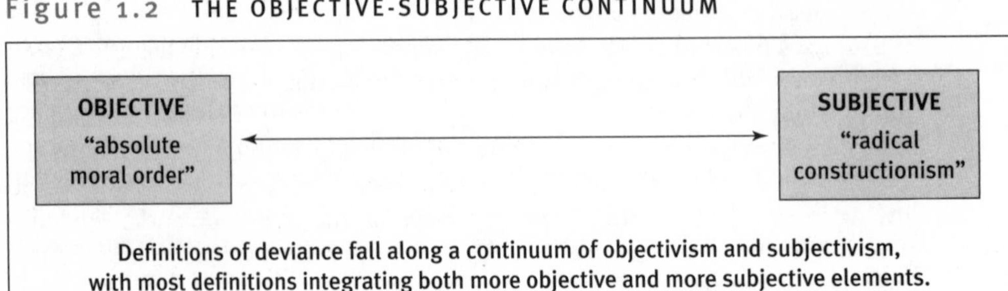

Definitions of deviance fall along a continuum of objectivism and subjectivism, with most definitions integrating both more objective and more subjective elements.

deviance; at the extreme subjective end lie the most radical constructionists, who suggest that there is no reality outside of individual perception. The definitions and analyses of each deviance specialist fall somewhere along this continuum, with some being more objective in nature and some being more subjective in nature. Those researchers who lean towards objectivism may be more likely to study those forms of deviance that Thio (1983) referred to as high-consensus forms of deviance, such as homicide, gang membership, white-collar crime, police corruption, and prostitution. Those researchers who lean towards subjectivism may be more likely to study those forms of deviance that Thio referred to as low-consensus forms of deviance, such as marijuana use, pornography, swinging, gambling, and aspects of physical appearance (e.g., tattoos, body piercing, punk rockers, goths, being overweight).

TIME TO REVIEW:

- How do some deviance specialists differentiate between "criminology" and the "sociology of deviance"?
- In what different ways has the work of some researchers of deviance transcended the traditional objective/subjective dichotomy? Give examples.
- Describe the idea that objective and subjective constitute the extreme ends of a continuum. How would Thio's distinction between high-consensus deviance and low-consensus deviance correspond with research along this continuum?

Studying Deviance

The way that deviance is defined along the objective-subjective continuum has implications for the way deviance is studied. That is, deviance specialists who lean more towards objectivism will study deviance in ways that those who lean more towards subjectivism will not (and vice versa).

Studying the Act: Why People Behave the Way They Do

Those who perceive more objectivity in deviance shine their analytical spotlight on the particular act or characteristic in question. The deviant nature of these behaviours/characteristics is, to some extent, taken for granted (because, after all, they *are* violating norms, or *are* causing harm, et cetera), and then the details of the deviance are studied—who the people are, how they became deviant, what their lives are like (Richardson, Best, & Bromley, 1991; Rubington & Weinberg, 2002). In essence, the interest lies in explaining the person, behaviour, or characteristic in question.

Studying Social Processes: The "Deviance Dance"

Deviance specialists who focus more on the subjective aspects of deviance are less interested in shining their analytical spotlight on the "deviant," and more interested in shining it on society and social processes—the perception of and reaction to the act, as well as the role of power in that perception and reaction. The focus becomes the "**deviance dance**"—the participants in this "dance" have various points of view on the debates, disagreements, and perspectives mentioned above, and each participant takes certain "steps" in order to move the dance in the direction they desire, whether that direction is the creation of a new law, the legalization of something previously illegal, achieving public recognition of a new social problem or one previously ignored, or changing public perceptions that will reduce the prejudices faced by certain groups. In some cases this "dance" may be characterized by considerable cooperation among the participants in achieving a consensual goal—analogous to a country line dance in which everyone does precisely the same steps. In other cases, it is characterized by participants taking opposing steps, but still moving together in their negotiation over the outcome—analogous to something like a waltz, where one partner moves backward and the other forward as they set their course across the dance floor. And in some cases the "dance" may look more like a mosh pit at a heavy metal or punk rock concert—each participant moving independently of the others, in varying and often opposing directions, intentionally pushing, shoving, and ramming into other participants in order to move in their own individually desired direction.

Studying struggles and debates over deviance requires going beyond the problem of "radical phenomenalism" (Ben-Yehuda, 1990, p. 5) that some researchers see as plaguing the sociology of deviance, wherein countless numbers of specific phenomena (e.g. call girls, drug users, swingers) have been studied in tremendous detail, but without paying attention to larger social structures. Ben-Yehuda (1990) suggests that the "study of deviance should be reframed…within general societal processes [of change and stability], in a dynamic historical and political perspective" (p.5). Along this vein, understanding an act of deviance requires understanding its larger context within the society's value systems or moral universes, and understanding the configuration of power relationships that influences the negotiation of moral boundaries among different groups of people.

Studying Acts and Social Processes

Both the more objective and the more subjective approaches to studying deviance lend to our understanding. The most comprehensive knowledge emerges from combining an analysis of the social processes involved in the "deviance dance" and an explication of the act or characteristic in question. For example, information about why people become overweight can be combined with knowledge of the processes by which certain people come to be perceived as "too fat" and are then made subject to various measures of social control. Similarly, an understanding

Prohibitionist Carry A. Nation was known for going into saloons and swinging her hatchet in order to bring down the walls (and anyone else who might get in her way)!

of why people engage in certain sexual behaviours can be combined with knowledge of the processes by which certain sexual behaviours are typed as deviant and made subject to measures of social control, while other sexual behaviours are labelled as conforming and thereby become the standard against which other behaviours are judged. Each of these levels of understanding paints an important part of the picture of deviance that will be integrated into this textbook—that is, at various points we will analyze acts/characteristics, perceptions of and reactions to those acts, and the role played by power in these perceptions and reactions.

The Role of Powerful People

Who are the "important" people who are able to influence the dominant moral codes of society, from which emerge standards of deviance and normality? In Canadian society, some of the most powerful groups involved in this process are politicians/government, scientists, religious institutions, the media, and commercial enterprise. Each of these groups of people may act as, or have a relationship with, **moral entrepreneurs**. Becker (1963) coined this term to describe those individuals and groups who take action to try and influence or change the development and enforcement of society's moral codes. For example, participants in the temperance movement, the abolitionist movement, and the "child-savers" movement all acted as moral entrepreneurs during the Victorian era. Throughout North America and Great Britain, members of church-based groups (frequently women's groups) declared the "demon liquor" a social evil, and sought to reduce alcohol consumption.

In Canada and the United States, groups of people acting as moral entrepreneurs also sought abolition—the eradication of slavery under the law, which occurred considerably sooner in Canada than in the United States. And throughout North America and Western Europe, the "child-savers" influenced child labour laws and encouraged compulsory education for children. All of these groups had substantial influence on society's dominant moral codes, and thereby on perceptions of what was considered deviant. During the 1950s and 1960s, North America's civil rights activists acted as moral entrepreneurs in their efforts to end segregation and gain rights for African-Canadians and African-Americans. And in contemporary society, we continue to see groups of moral entrepreneurs everywhere, as illustrated in the exercise on the left.

Ask Yourself:

Make a list of groups of people that you are aware of who try to influence society's dominant moral codes by seeking to influence our notions of right/wrong, bad/good, deviant/normal, acceptable/unacceptable. At its simplest level, these are groups that you feel are trying to change people's perceptions of a particular behaviour or group of people.

In the above exercise, perhaps you referred to gay rights activists, participants in anti-smoking campaigns, people seeking the legalization of marijuana, groups trying to change the portrayals of overweight characters on TV and in movies, or people wanting to toughen the Youth Criminal Justice Act. All of these are examples of contemporary moral entrepreneurs.

Perhaps the central group in society that acts as or has a relationship with moral entrepreneurs is composed of politicians. Politicians are the people in whom ultimate power, at an overt level, has been invested in modern state systems—the power to invoke new legislation and social policy, revoke existing legislation and social policy, and determine the enforcement of legislation and social policy. Interest groups, acting as moral entrepreneurs who have identified a social ill that they think must be solved in some way, often lobby the government to initiate change.

A second group, comprised of scientists, is able to effectively make claims that influence society's moral codes. The claims made by scientists are backed by what is perhaps the domain granted the highest level of credibility in our society, that of science. As we will see in the chapter on science and deviance later in the textbook, when we are told that scientists say something is true (for example, that the results of the Human Genome Project will bring endless benefits to our lives), many of us will believe those claims simply because scientists say so. When scientists tell us that smoking is harmful, or that having sex too frequently indicates an addiction, or that hearing voices indicates mental illness, or that the genes that play a role in being overweight may be subject to manipulation, they have a persuasive impact on what we see as being "normal." When making such claims, scientists themselves may be acting as moral entrepreneurs; in addition, the claims made by scientists may be used as convincing support for the efforts of other moral entrepreneurs, such as anti-smoking activists.

Religious institutions have also played a central role in the creation of the dominant moral codes that determine deviance and normality. For example, during the Middle Ages and into the early Renaissance, the Christian church was the instigator of the witch persecutions and the Spanish Inquisition, both of which resulted in countless numbers of people being tortured and killed for their deviance. In the present day, the power of religious institutions can be seen in the many nations in which religious-based governments are the source of social order. For instance, the recently displaced Taliban government imposed a particular and extreme interpretation of Islamic beliefs on the people of Afghanistan; other world governments are also sometimes based on certain religious belief systems, although the enforcement of those beliefs on the populace is carried out in varying ways. Contemporary Canadian society is characterized by a separation of church and state; however, the influence of religion on perceptions of deviance and normality maintains its presence in many ways. Fundamentally, Canadian society itself is built upon a Judeo-Christian foundation. For example, two of our national statutory holidays, those days when shopping malls and businesses must close, are Christian holidays—Christmas Day and Easter Sunday. Our criminal law is based on the Judeo-Christian ethic of free will—we are responsible for our own actions, and redemption can occur through punishment (Linden, 2000). At a more individual level, many Canadians adhere to various religious belief systems, including Islam, Hinduism, Judaism, Sikhism, Buddhism, Christianity, and more. The belief systems, in part, provide adherents with moral codes that subsequently affect the role individuals play in larger social processes. For instance, the Victorian prohibitionists, abolitionists, and child-savers described earlier were typically members of various Christian church-based groups. A later chapter in this book looks more closely at the relationship between religious institutions and the "deviance dance."

In our 21st century world, the media serves as the central battleground in the struggles over moral codes. The media is a powerful tool used by a wide range of moral entrepreneurs. When politicians, medical doctors, or interest groups (just to name a few) endeavour to raise awareness of an issue or sway public opinion, they turn to the media. Public service announcements, press conferences, and issue-driven advertisements all appear in the media. For example, the media carried accusations that Alberta Premier Ralph Klein was intoxicated and disorderly during an unannounced visit to a homeless shelter; when Premier Klein then sought to defend himself against these accusations, he also did so through the media. In another example, a recent public service announcement by the Canadian Mental Health Association strived to change perceptions of people with mental illnesses. In this announcement, an attractive man is shown snuggling a cooing baby. The screen fades to black, and a line appears: "This man has a mental illness." Showing the man snuggling the baby again, a voiceover says, "What's really 'sick' is how your perception of him just changed." The media is not just a tool used by moral entrepreneurs, but also acts as a moral entrepreneur itself in terms of the choices made about what will and will not be included on a particular program or in a particular commercial segment. Had the media decided not to show Premier Klein's defence of his behaviour, we might have been left with a very different perception of him, or of politicians more generally.

Finally, in a modern capitalist economy, commercial enterprise has a significant level of power as well, frequently in conjunction with use of the media; in fact, most components of the media itself *are* commercial enterprises driven by a profit motive. Ads, commercials, magazines, television programs, and movies tell us how we are and are not supposed to look—punk rock characters in a movie are the butt of the movie's jokes; magazine articles tell us we will be happier if we can just lose those ten pounds by Labour Day; Rachel and Monica on the television show *Friends* show us the right clothes to wear; parents on a daytime talk show fret over the appearance of their Gothic teenagers. They tell us how we are supposed to act—beer commercials tell us that drinking is the best way to have fun with friends; a fictional television show shows us that "potheads" are losers; a nighttime news program tells us that joining a cult is a bad thing.

Commercial enterprise has power outside of the media as well. For example, Giesbrecht (2000) discusses the power of the alcohol industry over the content and form of alcohol policies created by government. The manner in which alcohol production, marketing, and consumption is controlled in both Canada and the United States is determined, in part, by the influence of the alcohol industry itself. A similar example can be seen in the historical development of the institution of law in modern state systems. It is the law that delineates those actions considered to require the greatest level of control by society; historically, the institution of law developed on the basis of merchant and commercial interests. With the end of feudalism, British kings had much to gain from the wealth of merchants involved in international trade. The feudal lords no longer had the means to finance the nation's warfare and colonial expansion, but the merchants did. It was in the best financial interests of the king, as he oversaw the development and growth of a centralized state, to form it in accordance with commercial interests. These origins serve as the foundation for modern law, wherein most legal infractions by those involved in commercial enterprise are dealt with under the more lenient civil law rather than the more punitive criminal law (Linden, 2000).

This brief discussion of politicians, scientists, religion, media, and commercial enterprise demonstrates the complexity of the notion of power. People are powerful for many different reasons, and their power operates in diverse ways. The moral entrepreneurship of one group of powerful people may contradict or even oppose the moral entrepreneurship of another group of powerful people; for instance, the efforts of commercial enterprise might oppose the efforts of members of a religious-based group. But regardless of whether one group's involvement in social construction contradicts, or conversely coincides with, another group's involvement in social construction, the process through which they operate is the same—that of social typing.

TIME TO REVIEW:

- Differentiate between the ways deviance specialists who lean towards the objective and the subjective sides of the continuum study deviance. What is the "deviance dance" and what role does it play in your preceding answer?
- What are moral entrepreneurs? Give both historical and contemporary examples of moral entrepreneurs.
- What role do politicians, scientists, religion, media, and commercial enterprise play in the development of a society's dominant moral codes? Provide examples of each.

The Social Typing Process

As moral entrepreneurs influence the content and enforcement of society's dominant moral codes, the foundation is laid for the standards that subsequently determine deviance and normality. A closer look at the process by which some people come to be seen as "deviant" and others come to be seen as "normal," reveals what Rubington and Weinberg (2002) label **social typing**. This three-component process has the end result of changing the way people who are typed, or categorized, as "deviant" are treated in society.

The first component of the social typing process is **description**, wherein a label is placed on an individual, or that individual is placed in a particular category, because of an observed or presumed behaviour or characteristic. The exact nature of the label that is applied is dependent on the culture in question (Rubington & Weinberg, 2002); for instance, in contemporary Canada we are unlikely to label someone a heretic or infidel.

The second component of the social typing process is **evaluation**. This occurs when a judgment is attached to the individual by virtue of the label that was previously attached, or the category that individual was placed in, under the description component. If someone is being socially typed as deviant, this judgment is characteristically negative in nature.

The third component of the social typing process is **prescription**. Because of the label that has been given, and the resulting judgment that occurs, the individual is treated in a particular way, a way she or he would not be treated if the initial label had not been applied. In other words, individuals are made subject to a range of social treatments designed to regulate or control their deviance. Just as the larger culture determines the initial label that is used, it also shapes the nature of the prescription that is utilized (Rubington & Weinberg, 2002). For example, a Canadian woman who violates standards of female dress is likely to be teased or stared at, rather than made subject to stoning, as women in Taliban-controlled Afghanistan were. As a society, we decide "what should be done with people who deviate from society's expectations—[such as]...who deserves counseling, who is in need of it, or should be coerced into receiving it" (Freud, 1999, p. 2).

We can illustrate the three components of the social typing process by looking at the example of people who are considered overweight in contemporary Canadian society. Via the description component of the process, they might be labelled "fat." A negative evaluation or judgment is attached; in our society, people who are described as "fat" are frequently judged to be lazy, lacking in self-control, unattractive or inferior. And finally, because these people are "fat" and therefore also lazy or inferior, they are subjected to a wide range of treatments that people who are not "fat" are not subjected to. They are stared at as they walk down the street. A group of teenage boys may snicker as they walk by, or may call out derogatory names. If the "fat" people are children, other children may tease, laugh at, or refuse to play with them. If they people are adults, every magazine they look at tells them to "lose weight," "flatten those abs," or "get slim and sexy by Valentine's Day." Television commercials encourage them to buy pills, powdered drinks, pre-packaged meals, or gym memberships, and tell them that they will be happier if they do. When they go to the doctor for a checkup, the doctor may direct them to take up a walking program, or might list the dangers of being overweight, or may give them the phone number for a medically-supervised weight loss program, or might write them a prescription for a new weight-loss drug. An employer might have weight or fitness requirements that must be adhered to in order to maintain employment.

Exercise Your Mind:

Go through the three components of the social typing process, using the example of someone who belongs to a white supremacist hate group. What description, or label, is given to this person? What judgments or evaluations are attached to this person because of the label you have just given him or her? Finally, how is this person treated in Canadian society by virtue of the label and judgment he or she has received?

The regulation or social control of the person who has been subjected to this social typing process can occur at multiple levels. It may be *formal* or *informal* in nature (Rubington & Weinberg, 2002; Edwards, 1988; Becker, 1963). The informal aspect of the prescription component emerges at the level of patterns of informal social interaction—patterns of interaction with diverse people, such as family members, friends, acquaintances, colleagues, or strangers. As you go about your day seeing many different people, you react to them and interact with them in various ways. You may smile, frown, stare, tease, laugh at, agree with, disagree with, talk to, avoid, ignore, criticize, applaud, and more. These are all means by which informal regulation or social control can occur. You can see one example if you think back to your adolescent years. As you were leaving the house, your parents saw what you were wearing, and clearly disapproved. They may have asked, "What do you think you're wearing?" They may have said, "In those baggy pants you look like a bum!" Or they may have even sent you back to your room to change your clothes. That is informal regulation. Or you may have noticed people staring at you and laughing when you walked down the street. **Informal social controls** can include staring, laughing, frowning, avoiding, shaming, and more (Goode, 1997; Edwards, 1988; Braithwaite, 2000). Informal regulation comprises much of our daily lives today, and in the past, prior to industrialization, served as the dominant way that deviance was controlled (Spector, 1981).

Ask Yourself:

As a student at the college or university you attend, how is your behaviour or appearance informally controlled? In other words, how is your behaviour or appearance controlled at the level of everyday social interaction?

In answering the question at left, perhaps you referred to peer pressure; the desire to fit in with your classmates might have an effect on the clothes you wear to class, or the way you style your hair, or whether you go to the library versus the bar after class. Maybe you recall a time when you were whispering to a friend during class, and two of your classmates gave you a dirty look, or even asked you to keep it down. When you first became a postsecondary student, perhaps an older sibling gave you advice on what it would be like and how you should act. These are all examples of informal control.

The formal aspect of the prescription component involves processing at some type of an organizational or institutional level. Prior to industrialization in the Western world, church prohibitions served as the central means of formal social control. With industrialization and the creation of a centralized government, there was a dramatic increase in organizations and agencies involved in regulation and social control (Spector, 1981). A wide range of types of formal regulation can serve as controls for deviant behaviour—a nation's laws (such as Canada's Criminal Code); a school or work dress code; regulations governing driver's licences or hunting permits; a teacher punishing a student for misbehaviour; the handbook used by psychiatrists that lists the symptoms that constitute various forms of mental illness.

Look at the next "Ask Yourself" question. In answering it, you could have referred to registration requirements—you are only permitted to take Class B if you have already passed Class A. You could have referred to the regulations governing student conduct at your college or university; what behaviours are considered unacceptable, and what are the consequences for those behaviours? Perhaps you referred

Ask Yourself:

As a college or university student, how is your behaviour or appearance formally regulated? How is it controlled at an organizational or institutional level?

to a course syllabus, which tells you what exams and assignments you must complete in order to pass a particular course. Maybe you attend a college that has a student dress code. After an outburst in class, possibly the Chair of the department gave you a written reprimand or made you go see a student counselor. These are all examples of **formal regulation**.

At times, the distinction between formal and informal social control can be ambiguous, and the linkages between them complex. For example, is a magazine article proposing "Thin Thighs in 30 Days" formal or informal regulation? It is an organization that publishes the magazine, and it is an editorial board within that organization that determines the content of the articles in that magazine; this suggests formal regulation. However, the contexts within which that magazine article is seen (such as on a friend's coffee table) or its content transmitted (such as one friend telling another about it) suggest more of an informal level of regulation.

Social control may be *intentional* at times, such as through the creation of rules that must be followed by a child, a student, an employee, or a citizen of the state. At other times regulation might be the result of a more *general influence*; for instance, professionals such as doctors and lawyers have a general influence on their clients' lives (Edwards, 1988). Social control may be either **retroactive** (treating a known deviant in a certain way) or **preventative** (trying to prevent deviance in the first place, such as through socialization) (Edwards, 1988). Social control may be directed at an individual by someone else (e.g., a doctor, parent, or judge), or may occur at the level of **self-regulation** or self-control, where people regulate their own behaviours (such as by dieting to try and conform to an idealized body image, by joining a self-help group to end an addiction, or by avoiding behaviours that they know will be stigmatized) (Foucault, 1995; Gottfredson & Hirschi, 1990).

Of course, because the social construction of deviance and normality are embedded within a bigger "dance," that means a particular behaviour, characteristic, or person is not subjected to only one social typing process at any given moment. Multiple social typing processes may be going on simultaneously, processes that may even contradict each other. One segment of society may socially type someone as "deviant," while another segment of society may claim that same person is "normal." For example, although within some arenas of society someone who is perceived as overweight is labelled "too fat," has negative judgments attached, and is then treated in particular ways as a result, within other arenas of society that person may be seen as "normal" or "healthy."

Even if there is some agreement that someone or something is deviant, there may be differing views on what the appropriate forms of social control are. For example, while some people suggest that addiction is a disease and should be medically regulated, other people disagree and argue that another form of social

Exercise Your Mind:

Go back to the social typing exercise about the member of a white supremacist hate group. You have already explored the processes by which that person may be typed as "deviant," and treated as a result. But now try to apply the idea that different groups in society will label the same behaviour or characteristic in very different ways. What social processes contradict those that type members of white supremacist hate groups as deviant? In other words, are there ways in which this characteristic is perceived as "normal" or okay? Where are these oppositional social processes evident?

control, such as punishment, should be instituted. Thus, within these multiple social typing processes, the claims made by one group often must compete with the claims made by another group; claimsmakers compete with other claimsmakers "in a [deviance] marketplace" (Richardson, Best, & Bromley, 1991, p. 5). But the principal role of power in this process ultimately means that some people's claims count more than other people's claims, and that some people's claims have a greater bearing on the society at large—its norms, its structure, its institutions, and its people.

The consequences of the social typing process, whereby someone or something becomes typed as deviant or, in other words, **deviantized**, are far reaching. Through this process "…description becomes prescription, which is then transformed into a desirable standard of normal behaviour to be upheld and maintained by the educational system, the religious system, the legal system, and of course the psychotherapeutic system, and to which every section of the population has to measure up or be found deficient" (Freud, 1999, p. 2).

TIME TO REVIEW:

- What are the three components of the social typing process? Give an example of each.
- What are the different levels or types of social control or regulation? Give examples.
- Explain how coexisting social typing processes may contradict each other.

Our Journey through this Book

In the process of transcending the objective/subjective dualism, and of integrating analyses of acts, perceptions/reactions, and power relations, many questions will serve as a guide in the remaining chapters of this book:

- Where does a particular act or characteristic come from? That is, how do people come to engage in the behaviours or have the characterics in question?
- What is the nature of the social typing process involved? What are the description, evaluation, and prescription that are being applied to this person, behaviour, or characteristic?
- Who has done the social typing? In most cases it will be several groups of people rather than just one group of people.
- What is the foundation for their arguments? Different groups of social typers may draw upon the same rationale (such as harm, normative violation, societal reaction, or statistical rarity), but different groups may use different rationales.
- How do the social typers benefit from the deviantizing of this behaviour, characteristic, or person? Does the larger society benefit from socially typing this behaviour, characteristic, or person as deviant?
- What larger social conditions support the social typing process?
- How is the "deviance dance" evident? That is, in what way are opposition and resistance to the social typing process evident?

These kinds of questions will guide us in our understanding of deviance in relation to sexuality, youth, physical appearance (voluntary and involuntary), mental disorder, religion, and science. These are all topics that are of utmost relevance to Canadian society, and to the lives of the millions of people who are a part of it. By the end of this book, you will see that you are not an outsider looking in at deviance in society, but instead will see that deviance (and negotiations about deviance) is a part of *your* life every day. The choice of these topics is intended to provide you with critical insight into some of the core processes, as well as the people, that make up the foundation of our society. Such critical insight will be based on both specific structures and processes of deviance as described in the particular topics above, as well as at the level of theoretical understandings and explanations of deviance more generally. These levels of insight correspond to the two sections of this textbook; the chapters in the first section focus on theoretical insights, and the chapters in the second section focus on the specific structures of deviance involved in sexuality, youth, physical appearance, mental disorder, religion, and science.

TIME TO REVIEW:

- What are the six questions that will serve as the guide for exploring and analyzing deviance in this textbook?

CHAPTER SUMMARY

We all can make a list of people that we think are odd, immoral, unacceptable, or annoying. However, this personal list of annoying people is not equivalent to the concept of *deviance*; nor is our personal list of people we like or approve of equivalent to the concept of *normality*. Deviance and normality, concepts that only exist in relation to each other, exist at the level of social processes, not personal opinion.

The study of deviance is characterized by the *problem of definition*, in that there is some disagreement about how deviance should be defined. Some deviance specialists suggest that, within these debates, there has been a general shift in the discipline, from *objective* definitions of deviance to *subjective* definitions of deviance; this assertion is based upon the presumption of an objective/subjective dualism or dichotomy.

The *objective* side of the dualism has traditionally been characterized as suggesting that there is a singular characteristic or trait that all deviant people share, and that distinguishes them from "normal" people. The four different defining traits that laypersons, social activists, politicians, or academics have mentioned are *normative violation* (deviants are those who violate norms), *statistical rarity* (deviants are those people who are rare or atypical), *societal reaction* (deviant are those to whom "the masses" respond negatively), and *harm* (deviants are those who are a threat to themselves, others, the smooth running of the social order, or our basic ways of understanding the world).

However, although one or more of these traits may be present in particular instances of deviance, all people who are considered deviant do not have any one of these traits in common. Consequently, the suggestion has been made that the only thing all deviant people do have in common is that *enough important people have said they are deviant*. This points to the *subjective* side of the objective/subjective dualism. In other words, deviance is a *social construction*.

Social construction can be used in its radical form, as a theory, or it can be used in its soft form, that is, as a way of looking at social processes. Some people suggest that most contemporary deviance specialists are social constructionists, primarily in terms of its softer form.

Looking at deviance from a social constructionist point of view, what is of interest is not a particular behaviour or characteristic itself, but rather the place of that characteristic in the social order, the roles assigned to people who exhibit that characteristic, and the societal meanings attached to that characteristic. All of these vary across cultures and within a single culture over time.

Although deviance specialists have traditionally characterized objectivism and subjectivism as a dichotomy or dualism, recent work may actually transcend the dualism, integrating both objective and subjective components. Thus, objectivism and subjectivism may be thought of as existing along a continuum, with the work of individual deviance specialists falling somewhere along this continuum.

The way that deviance is defined has implications for the way it is studied. Some researchers focus their analyses on the deviant act, while others focus their analyses on the processes involved in the perception of and reaction to the act. Consequently, a more complete understanding emerges from exploring the nature and causes of deviant acts, perceptions of and reactions to those acts, and the role of power in those perceptions and reactions.

The perceptions of *powerful groups* play the central role in the creation of the *dominant moral codes* that underlie the construction of deviance. In our society, powerful groups include politicians, religious institutions, scientists, the media, and commercial enterprise.

Central to issues of deviance are processes of *social typing*, wherein someone is labelled in a particular way, is evaluated or judged on the basis of the label that was given, and has a prescription for treatment applied to him or her as a result of the description and evaluation. Such treatment can occur through various levels of regulation or social control—formal, informal, proactive, retroactive, and via the self.

Recommended Readings

Becker, H. (1963). *Outsiders: Studies in the sociology of deviance*. London: Free Press of Glencoe.

* Note that this book was also reprinted in 1973 in New York by Free Press.

* This book was the first deviance book to introduce and utilize the idea of the subjectivity of deviance. The countercultural era in which it was written results in some fascinating examples and case studies as well.

Edwards, A. R. (1988). *Regulation and repression: The study of social control*. Sydney, Australia: Allen & Unwin.

* This book describes and analyses the multilevel processes of regulation or social control in Western societies.

Endnotes

1 Mason Cooley. Retrieved August 28, 2001, from World Wide Web: **www.bartleby.com**

2 David Lee. Retrieved August 28, 2001, from World Wide Web: **www.quotationspage.com**

3 It is more accurate to say that left-handed people are *no longer* considered deviant. As Barsley (1967) demonstrates, left-handedness has a long history of being associated with bad luck, demonic affiliation, and more.

KEY TERMS

deviance, **p. 2**
conformity, **p. 2**
normal, **p. 4**
objective, **p. 5**
subjective, **p. 5**
statistical rarity, **p. 6**
social harm, **p. 8**
societal reaction, **p. 12**
normative violation, **p. 13**
folkways, **p. 15**
morés, **p. 15**
consensual view of law, **p. 16**
conflict view of law, **p. 16**
interactionist view of law, **p. 17**
high-consensus deviance, **p. 18**
low-consensus deviance, **p. 18**
dominant moral codes, **p. 19**
symbolic-moral universes, **p. 20**
social constructionism, **p. 20**
radical/strict constructionism, **p. 20**
soft/contextual constructionism, **p. 20**
deviance dance, **p. 26**
moral entrepreneurs, **p. 28**
social typing, **p. 31**
description, **p. 31**
evaluation, **p. 31**
prescription, **p. 31**
informal social control/regulation, **p. 33**
formal social control/regulation, **p. 34**
retroactive social control, **p. 34**
preventative social control, **p. 34**
self-regulation, **p. 34**
deviantized, **p. 35**

CHAPTER 2

Explaining Deviance: The Act

Learning Objectives

After reading this chapter, you should be able to:

- Explain how theory is a practical enterprise.
- Explain why different types of theory correspond to objective and subjective views of deviance, and describe the focus of positivist, interpretive, and critical theories in explaining deviance.
- Describe the core assumptions of positivist theories, as well as how deviance is explained by the three types of positivist theories presented in this chapter.
- Describe the core assumptions of functionalist theory, as well as how deviance is explained by (a) Durkheim's anomie theory, (b) Merton's strain theory, (c) differential opportunity theory, (d) general strain theory, and (e) Cohen's concept of status frustration.

- Describe the core assumptions of learning theories, as well as how deviance is explained by (a) differential association theory, (b) neutralization theory, and (c) social learning theory.
- Describe how Hirschi's social bonds theory explains deviance (and the absence of deviance). Describe Gottfredson and Hirschi's more recent general theory of crime.

"There is nothing more practical than a good theory." (Leonid Ilich Breshnev)[1]

Theorizing Deviance

"Theory" is sometimes perceived as the flip side of the coin from "practice"; it is seen as something that only the most esoteric academics in their ivory towers, isolated from the "real world," are interested in. But as the above quote by Leonid Breshnev points out, theory and practice are intimately intertwined and, in fact, theory is quite practical. It is through theory that we come to understand everything around us, the world that we live in. It is through past developments in theory that those of us living in the 21st century can attempt understandings of gravity, nuclear power, and child development. Similarly, it is through theory that we are able to try to understand the way that society works, the reasons why some people are rich and some are poor, why the wives in most marriages are still doing most of the housework while the husbands are doing most of the breadwinning, why people commit crimes, why people get tattoos, and how an underweight body has somehow come to represent the North American cultural ideal. That is, theory provides us with the central means of explaining and understanding deviance—what could be more practical than that?

However, there is some question about whether the sociology of deviance has its own distinct body of theory. Some deviance specialists suggest that, since the mid-1970s, there has been a decline in the sociology of deviance as a distinct discipline, precisely because a correspondingly distinct body of theory is lacking (Sumner, 1994; Miller, Wright, & Dannels, 2001). Instead, they say, the sociology of deviance has been subsumed by the discipline of criminology. And indeed, the overlap between the two areas of study can be seen at both the empirical and theoretical levels. When criminology textbooks and deviance textbooks are compared, a considerable sharing of substantive topics can be seen. One comparison of popular textbooks in the two areas found that seven (out of eleven) topics that were found in two-thirds of the popular deviance textbooks were also found in at least two-thirds of the popular criminology textbooks—rape, white-collar/corporate crime, drug abuse, prostitution, family violence, murder, and property crime (Bader, Becker, & Desmond, 1996). Looking at theory, similar overlaps are evident. A comparison of a popular theory-based deviance textbook (Deutschmann,

2002) and popular criminology textbooks (Linden, 2000; Siegal & McCormick, 2003) illustrates the similarities at the theoretical level—theories covered include the classical, biological, psychological, social disorganization, functionalist, strain, subcultural, social learning, interactionist, social control, and conflict theories, among others. While this degree of similarity has caused some concern that the sociology of deviance has been engulfed by the discipline of criminology, it must be remembered that many "criminological" theories are in reality more general sociological theories that are simply being applied to questions of crime—of those theories listed above, functionalism, interactionism, conflict theory, and social learning theory are all sociological theories rather than specifically criminological theories. Thus, specialists in *all* areas of sociology, and not just deviance and criminology, make use of these bodies of theory. Although the debate over whether there is a distinct body of deviance theory continues, there is no doubt that deviance specialists, whether they focus on criminal or non-criminal forms of deviance, utilize a wide range of theory: general sociological theories (e.g., conflict theory), specifically criminological theories (e.g., strain theory), and interdisciplinary theories (e.g., feminist theories).

Numerous theories exist simultaneously in the social sciences, unlike the natural sciences, where more accurate theories replace older theories that have been disproven. This is frequently one of the first hurdles that students who are new to sociology must overcome—expanding their understanding of what "theory" means to include the possibility of multiple coexisting explanations for the very same phenomenon. The poem "The Six Blind Men and the Elephant" serves as an interesting analogy for this characteristic of sociological theory—I knew you were wondering why there was a drawing of an elephant at the beginning of the chapter (see Box 2.1)!

When American poet John Godfrey Saxe wrote this poem more than a century ago, based on a Hindu fable, would he have guessed what a good analogy it would make for sociological theory? What do blind men and elephants have to do with understanding society and with explaining deviance? Well, just as the blind men's explanations of the nature of the elephant depended wholly on what part of the elephant each focused on, sociologists' explanations of the nature of society depend on what aspect of society each sociological theory focuses on. There are diverse ways of looking at the world around us, and each theoretical perspective has a different view. Each of these ways of looking at society shines a spotlight on a different aspect of the social order—some theories focus on the stability of society, some focus on conflict within society, some focus on interaction. But when a spotlight is directed at one particular location, all other areas necessarily fall into the shadows, just as each blind man's hands resting on one part of the elephant mean that the rest of the elephant's body is going untouched. In other words, because of the area of focus within each sociological theory, it may be able to explain the area being focused on very well, but areas outside of the focal range very poorly; and because of each theory's way of looking at the world, the nature of explanations provided take a particular form. As you will see in this chapter, there are many

Box 2.1 The Six Blind Men and the Elephant

The Six Blind Men and the Elephant

It was six men of Indostan
To learning much inclined
Who went to see the Elephant
(Though all of them were blind),
That each by observation
Might satisfy his mind.

The First approached the Elephant
And happening to fall
Against his broad sturdy side
At once began to bawl:
"Bless me! but the Elephant
Is very like a wall."

The Second, feeling of the tusk,
Cried, "Ho! What have we here,
So very round and smooth and sharp?
To me ' tis mighty clear
This wonder of an Elephant
Is very like a spear."

The Third approached the animal,
And happening to take
The squirming trunk in his hands
Thus boldly up and spake:
"I see," quoth he, "the Elephant
Is very like a snake."

The Fourth reached out his eager hand
And felt about the knee.
"What most this wondrous beast is like
Is mighty plain," quoth he;
"' Tis clear enough the Elephant
Is very like a tree."

The Fifth, who chanced to touch the ear,
Said, "E' en the blindest man
Can tell what this resembles most;
Deny the fact who can,
This marvel of an Elephant
Is very like a fan."

The Sixth no sooner had begun
About the beast to grope
Then, seizing on the swinging tail
That fell within his scope,
"I see," quoth he, "the Elephant
Is very like a rope."

And so these men of Indostan
Disputed loud and long.
Each in his own opinion
Exceeding stiff and strong,
Though each was partly in the right,
And all were in the wrong.

So, oft in theologic wars,
The disputants, I ween,
Rail on in utter ignorance
Of what each other mean,
And prate about an Elephant
Not one of them has seen!

—John Godfrey Saxe (1816–1887)

different theories that try to explain deviance, with each theory concentrating on and trying to explain a particular aspect of deviance; the nature of the explanations provided are based on the way deviance is looked at within each theory.

Is one particular theoretical perspective somehow better than the others? Some sociologists who are strict adherents of specific theoretical perspectives would argue that yes, one theory is superior to the others. And a room filled with these sociologists would look comparable to the group of blind men "disputing loud and long, each in his own opinion, exceeding stiff and strong." But just as with the blind men, each of these sociologists "is partly in the right, and all [are] in the wrong." Each theory provides us with one way of looking at a certain aspect of deviance, but no single theory can explain all of the components that make up deviance as whole. Particular theories may be more useful than others in coming to understand a given issue or aspect of deviance. For example, if you are interested in deviant *acts* (as those deviance specialists who lean toward the objective side of the objective-subjective continuum are), some of the theories of deviance will be more useful to you than others. In contrast, if you are more interested in the *perceptions* of and *reactions* to particular acts, as well as the role that power plays in those perceptions and reactions (as those deviance specialists who lean toward the subjective side of the objective-subjective continuum are), other theories will be of more use to you. Some theories will give you one way of looking at a certain issue, while other theories provide alternative ways of looking at the same issue. But taken together, all sociological theories add to our knowledge and understanding of deviance as a whole.

"Knowledge is not a series of self-consistent theories that converges toward an ideal view; it is rather an ever increasing ocean of mutually incompatible (and perhaps even incommensurable) alternatives, each single theory, each fairy tale, each myth that is part of the collection forcing the others into greater articulation and all of them combining, via this process of competition, to the development of our consciousness." (Paul Feyerabend)[2]

In other words, not only do coexisting theories each add to our knowledge of a different aspect of deviance, but the presence of concomitant theories also stimulates even more theorizing, which can only enhance our level of understanding in the future.

An exhaustive analysis of all of the theoretical perspectives used in the study of deviance is certainly outside the realm of this book; there are whole books that are entirely based on the various different theories used in the study of deviance, bringing in concrete examples to illustrate each theory (e.g., Deutschmann, 2002). In fact, some theories have been the focus of dozens or even hundreds of books in their own right. In this chapter, as well as the next, the core assumptions of the theories that have been most commonly used in the study of deviance will be reviewed.

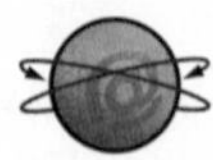

AN INTERNET MOMENT:

Access the catalogue for the library of your own institution, or bigger amalgamations of which your library is a part. Look for a list of all of the books on "social theory" or "sociological theory" to get an indication of how many books have been written that focus only on sociological theories; for example, one library catalogue brings up almost 300 titles. Now search the catalogue using various keywords to indicate specific theoretical perspectives, such as "symbolic interactionism," "functionalism," or "conflict theory."

TIME TO REVIEW:

- In what way is theory "practical"?
- What kinds of theories are used in the sociology of deviance, and how can multiple theories coexist in sociology?
- How can all sociological theories be "partly in the right"? That is, why isn't one theoretical perspective considered better than the others?
- How can all sociological theories be "in the wrong" as well?

The various theories that are used in the study of deviance have been categorized in many different ways, and few (if any) of these ways are necessarily more valid than the others. The format that will be followed in this book is that of Ashley and Orenstein (2001), who propose that all social theories can be classified as *positivist, interpretive,* or *critical*. The different views of deviance that were discussed in the previous chapter, both the more objective approaches and those more subjective, are associated with different ways of theorizing.

In the previous chapter, some relatively more objective ways of recognizing deviance were addressed, including views based on normative violation, statistical rarity, harm, and societal reaction. Each of these definitions of deviance suggests that there is a trait that all deviant people share that differentiates deviants from those who are normal. Emerging from this core idea is the interest in finding out *why* people become deviant—why they violate norms, or engage in behaviours that are atypical, or cause harm, or do something that results in a negative societal reaction. This way of looking at deviance, and the concentration on a particular aspect of deviance (i.e., *why* people act in deviant ways), is intimately linked with particular kinds of theories of deviance, those that might be labelled **positivist** (Ashley & Orenstein, 2001). Positivist theories will be the focus of the remainder of this chapter.

The more subjective ways of looking at deviance suggest that the only thing all deviant people have in common is that enough important people have said they are deviant. Emerging from this core idea is the interest in exploring the social typing process, the process through which deviance and normality are socially constructed. Who becomes typed as deviant? How are they then treated? What are the rationales offered for the deviantizing of someone or something? Do specific groups benefit from categorizing certain people as deviant? Does society as a whole benefit? In what way does power influence societal perceptions of, and reactions to, particular acts that have been defined as deviant? This way of looking at deviance, and the concentration on these aspects of deviance, is intimately linked with a certain set of theories of deviance, those that are labelled **interpretive** and **critical** (Ashley & Orenstein, 2001). Interpretive and critical theories will be the focus of the next chapter.

Although positivist, interpretive, and critical theories will be discussed separately, a significant trend in theorizing is that of theoretical integration—combining aspects of different theories in order to explain a particular phenomenon. Consequently, positivist and interpretive theories may be integrated, as may interpretive and critical theories, and positivist and critical (Ashley & Orenstein, 2001). For example, Victor (1992) combines positivist (i.e., functionalist), interpretive (i.e., social constructionist), and critical (i.e., conflict) theories in a discussion of scapegoating; even aspects of positivist Emile Durkheim's work of more than a century ago have served as a foundation for some interpretive and critical work.

TIME TO REVIEW:

- What ways of looking at deviance presented in the previous chapter are associated with positivist theories? What ways of looking at deviance are associated with interpretive and critical theories?
- What do positivist theories of deviance focus on?
- What do interpretive and critical theories of deviance focus on?
- Can different theories be integrated?

Why Do People Become Deviant? Using Positivist Theories

Positivist sociological theories are fundamentally interested in explaining why people act in particular ways. They are modelled after the approaches to theorizing in the natural sciences, which "seek generalizable, universally applicable laws" (Ashley & Orenstein, 2001, p. 30) that govern the environment. Although positivist sociologists also pursue the rules that govern the social environment, they do not seek the same type of cause-effect relationships as natural scientists do. Instead they look for statistical relationships—those variables that *tend* to be associated with a particular behaviour or outcome (Ashley & Orenstein, 2001). These statistical explanations are less certain than the explanations of the natural sciences, but still have an empiricist foundation in gathering data about an external reality that requires explanation. Although positivist sociological theories are somewhat different from positivist theories of the natural sciences, they are both also based on a technical interest in the mastery of the environment; in the case of positivist sociological theories, this technical interest is in pursuit of planning for a better society (Ashley & Orenstein, 2001). "The interest that positivism exhibits is in methodological, calculating control; and this interest in instrumentalism can be applied to both natural and social environments. Theories of crop management seek to increase the yield of an agricultural product; from a positivistic point of view, theories about the causes of crime should enable agencies of social control to reduce the crime rate" (Ashley & Orenstein, 2001, p. 35).

Thus, seeking to understand why deviant people act that way triggers subsequent attempts to prevent other people from becoming deviant. In that regard, positivist explanations of deviance are inevitably coupled with efforts at social control, efforts you might personally agree with (such as with violent crime), or disagree with (such as with homosexuality). It is important to note that individual theorists may not personally be seeking mastery of the environment or more effective social control of particular behaviours; their interest may be solely in explaining the variability in people's behaviours in society (i.e., why groups of people act in different ways). However, positivist theorizing lays the groundwork for those individuals who are seeking more effective social control or plans for a better society (Ashley & Orenstein, 2001).

In the remainder of this chapter, the positivist theories that will be reviewed are some of those that have been the most commonly utilized in explaining deviant acts, and which have had significant influences on the sociology of deviance as a discipline. These include functionalist theories (including theories of anomie and strain), learning theories, and theories of social control.

Functionalist Theories

Functionalist theories, which in the past were also called *structural functionalist* theories, have their origins in the birth of the discipline of Sociology itself; in fact, this theoretical perspective dominated the discipline until the mid-20th century. Within this perspective, society is seen as being comprised of various structures (e.g., the family; the educational system; the political system), each of which fulfills necessary functions for the smooth running of the social order. Analogous to this perception of society is a pyramidal stack of cans on display in the supermarket; each can is necessary for the display as a whole to keep standing. You may be stricken with fear at the idea of selecting one of those cans to place in your shopping cart, because if you move the wrong can, or if one of the cans is not perfectly in position, the entire display may collapse. Similarly, the smooth running of society is threatened if one of its structures has a poor fit with the other structures that make up society.

One of the core concerns within the functionalist perspective as a whole is the maintenance of the social order. This conservative focus is inherent within the perspective because of the assumption that the rules that make up the social order are consensual, based upon widespread agreement; in other words, the rules exist because we agree that they should exist. And we agree they should exist because they serve a useful function for society. For example, sociologists Talcott Parsons and Robert Bales (1955) suggest that traditional gender roles, wherein men are responsible for instrumental tasks and women are responsible for expressive tasks, are functional for society because they ensure that the division of labour within the family is done efficiently; challenging traditional gender roles may interfere with the social order and threaten the equilibrium of society. Thus, if the rules are typically functional, and if rules exist because we agree they should, we need to figure out why some people do not follow those rules. It may be that breaking certain rules is dysfunctional for society, and we therefore need to determine the causes of such behaviour so that we can restore social order. Alternatively, it may be that something in the structure of society has become dysfunctional, and that is causing people to break the rules.

Within these broad assumptions that are part of the functionalist perspective, individual theorists have taken different paths in applying those assumptions to the study of deviance. In the remainder of this section on functionalist theories, we will look at the different ways that Emile Durkheim, Robert Merton, collaborators Cloward and Ohlin, Robert Agnew, and Albert Cohen have applied functionalist assumptions to an understanding of deviance.

TIME TO REVIEW:

- What are positivist sociological theories and how are they modelled after the natural sciences?
- How are positivist explanations of deviance related to efforts at social control?
- According to functionalist theories, what is society made of?
- Why do functionalist theories focus on the importance of maintaining the social order? How is this concern related to the nature of society's rules?

Durkheim: Anomie

Not only is Emile Durkheim (1933; 1951) recognized as one of the founders of the discipline of sociology, his work also defined the structural functionalist theoretical perspective itself. Durkheim's work focused on the development of a **grand theory**—an overarching theory of society as a whole that attempts to explain a wide range of phenomena. But within this grand theory of structural functionalism, the notion of deviance is addressed in two ways. One way that Durkheim talked about deviance is in the context of how a certain level of deviance is actually functional for society; it serves a useful purpose that helps maintain society's balance or equilibrium. Deviance is functional in that seeing someone break the rules leads the rest of us to realize how important the rules are, and the necessity of following the rules. A certain level of deviance thereby enhances social order, and *increases social solidarity* among those of us who join together in fighting back against those people who break the rules. Deviance is also functional in that it is through observing behaviour and its consequences that *a society determines what its moral boundaries are*, what its rules should be, and what is considered acceptable and unacceptable. Deviance can be functional in that it *tests society's boundaries*, and may demonstrate when certain rules no longer work and need to be changed. Finally, deviance serves as a way of *reducing societal tensions*, which it can do in two ways. First, societal tensions can be reduced when there is some sort of scapegoat that can be blamed for a social problem; by blaming a scapegoat, the pressure is taken off of society at large. The second way that societal tensions can decline is when individuals engage in small acts of minor deviance that act as a safety valve and let off some steam.

Parsons and Smelser (1956) elaborate on this latter function, suggesting that letting off steam through minor acts of deviance subsequently activates social processes that return deviant actors to their acceptable roles in society. The social processes that return people to their acceptable roles include **socialization** (wherein deviant actors who are letting off steam have internalized society's rules sufficiently that they return themselves to their legitimate social roles), **profit** (which teaches citizens that there is a payoff or benefit accorded those who conform to society's rules), **persuasion** (through advertising, the sermons of religious leaders, psychologists' advice, etc.), and **coercion** (punishment for those who do not return to their legitimate social roles).

Several researchers have explored the functionality of deviance in reinforcing moral boundaries, testing social boundaries, increasing social solidarity, and reducing societal tensions. Kai Erikson's (1966) classic analysis of the Puritans of the Massachusetts Bay Colony reveals that acts of deviance helped to reinforce the moral boundaries of the community, reminding its citizens what the rules were. Over a period of time, the punishments for deviance emerged out of the dominant values of the time, illustrating to citizens, for example, the power of the church (through the punishment of witchcraft) or the value of private property (through the punishment of theft). The nature of these punishments also reminded citizens about the norms and values that were considered important by authorities within that community.

The role of deviance in testing society's boundaries and facilitating changes in outdated rules can be seen historically. The actions and influences of activists on behalf of civil rights, women's rights, and disabled rights certainly changed society in significant ways. Their efforts demonstrated to the rest of society that some of its norms were outdated and unjust, and needed to be changed in order to further equality for all groups.

Does deviance increase social solidarity? Liska and Warner's (1991) investigation of whether the presence of crime increases social solidarity, and subsequently decreases the crime rate, led them to uncertain conclusions. They concluded that the fear of robbery does cause people to change their behaviours in ways that subsequently reduce the risk of robbery, but they question whether this consequence is the result of social solidarity. However, Victor's (1992) review of scapegoating in America illustrates the functionality of deviance both in reducing societal tensions and in enhancing social solidarity. He argues that directing hostility toward some type of external enemy temporarily helps to reduce tensions and increase social solidarity. When conflict emerges in society, "when moral values are in dispute, a witchhunt for moral subversives serves the purpose of clarifying, redefining, and strictly enforcing the limits of moral conduct" (Victor, 1992, para. 12). The collective manufacturing of an *evil enemy image* has been directed at heretics and witches during the Middle Ages, Communist subversives in the 1950s, Satanists in the late 1980s and early 1990s, Jewish communities during various anti-Semitic pogroms from the 12th through the 20th centuries, citizens of Japanese extraction during World War II (Victor, 1992), and, since

September 11, 2001, "terrorists." Each of these external "enemies" has served as a way of increasing social solidarity as people join together to fight that enemy, and as a way of clearly illustrating to people the boundaries of acceptable behaviour or characteristics.

Although Durkheim proposed that deviance is functional for society, he pointed out that it remains functional only up to a particular point. Beyond a certain level, deviance no longer enhances the social order, but rather interferes with it. Living in 19th century Europe, Durkheim observed that the processes of industrialization and urbanization, with their growing emphasis on individuality, seemed to result in a much greater prevalence of deviance, wherein deviance exceeded a functional level. He noted, for example, that suicide rates were higher in more individualistic communities. In explaining this apparent increase in deviance, Durkheim focused on the ways that society's structures had changed with industrialization, and the impact this had on people's behaviour, including deviant behaviour. Before industrialization, society's structure was held together by **mechanical solidarity**—society was bonded together by *likeness*, or by a collective commitment to conformity. These societies were characterized by minimal specialization within the division of labour; for example, people who needed a new wagon would either build themselves a new wagon, or barter with someone they knew who was good at building wagons. Interactions between individuals in this type of society were quite personal, and often kin-based; everyone knew, and had a personal relationship with, everyone else. Each person in this society had much in common with every other person.

With industrialization, the bonding mechanism for the social structure was transformed into one of **organic solidarity**—society was bonded together by *difference*, or by interdependence. Industrial societies are characterized by a highly specialized division of labour, analogous to an organic system like the human body. In the human body, the heart fulfills certain specialized functions necessary to survival; the lungs fulfill other specific functions; the brain fulfills yet other particular functions. Each part of the human body is responsible for certain tasks that keep the whole body running smoothly. Similarly, in industrial society the tasks that keep society running smoothly are divided among different parts of society. The education system fulfills certain tasks, while the political system and the medical system fulfill other tasks. Individuals employed within the different parts of society are responsible for unique tasks as well. Interactions between people in this type of society are somewhat impersonal, based primarily on our dependence on others because of the degree of specialization within the division of labour. A collective way of thinking and interacting is replaced by individualism.

Although bonds between people continue to exist in industrialized societies, when social change occurs at too rapid a pace, individualism gets out of control, and bonds between people become weaker than is necessary for the well-being of society. Traditional norms and traditional means of social control deteriorate, creating a situation of normlessness, or **anomie**. The presence of anomie in modern societies opens the door for greater levels of deviance, beyond the degree that is functional for society. Thus, it is the structure of society itself and its impact on individuals that contributes to harmful levels of deviance within society.

Here we have seen one theorist's application of functionalist ideas to an explanation of why deviance occurs, the central concern of both objective ways of defining deviance and the related positivist theoretical perspectives. Robert Merton, a 20th century functionalist theorist, both built upon and moved away from Durkheim's ideas. Looking at Merton's theory shows us another way that functionalist assumptions have been applied to the study of deviance.

TIME TO REVIEW:

- According to Durkheim's functionalist assumptions, what are the ways that deviance can be functional for society? Describe some empirical research studies that have demonstrated these functions.
- How did the structure of society and interactions between people in society change with the transition from mechanical solidarity to organic solidarity?
- According to Durkheim, when is deviance no longer functional for society? Why does this happen?
- Broadly considering Durkheim's use of functionalist assumptions, why do people become deviant?

Merton: Strain Theory

Robert Merton (1938; 1968) applied functionalist assumptions to the study of deviance in two different ways. First, he pointed out that there are multiple ways of fulfilling the same need in society, and that in fulfilling particular needs, a given act of deviance may be functional for some people but dysfunctional for others. A functionalist analysis of deviance and social control contains several steps that integrate those assumptions:

a) Describe the form of deviance or social control being analyzed;
b) point out other patterns of deviance or social control that are being excluded by the pattern being analyzed;
c) explore the meaning of the deviance or social control for the people who are involved in it;
d) determine why people follow one particular pattern rather than another; and,
e) describe patterns that may not be recognized by the participants, but which have significant consequences nonetheless.

Merton also applied functionalist assumptions in the form of his **strain theory**, "the dominant theory in the area of deviance from the early 1950s until about 1970" (Collins, cited in Pfohl, 1994, p. 279). Merton suggested that deviance originates not only from the individual, but also from the structure of society itself, which propels some people into deviance. What is it about the structure of

Ask Yourself:

As a member of Canadian society, what have you been taught that you are supposed to achieve in life in order to be considered "successful"? That is, what does this culture tell us that "success" is? Who are the people that are considered the most "successful" in our society? What characteristics do people who are publicly admired or envied have that make them such objects of admiration? Once you have defined the characteristics of success, think about how you have learned this to be so. Who has taught you this? Where have you learned it? What do you see in the society around you that reinforces your belief that these are, indeed, the criteria for success?

society that creates a greater likelihood that some people, more than others, will become deviant? The exercise on the left will bring you closer to an answer to that question.

The exercise on the left asks you to think about what Merton referred to as **institutionalized goals**. In contemporary capitalist society, these are the goals that are broadly accepted, or are culturally exalted; these are the things that we learn we are *supposed to* want to achieve. Merton said that in North America, the goals we are to aspire to include things like *wealth*, *status/power*, and *prestige*—the qualities that make up the "(North) American Dream." Almost everywhere we look we encounter the message that these are the things we should try to achieve in life. Who are the people who are admired and envied in society? People who are wealthy; these are people who drive Mercedes, Jaguars, or BMWs, who live in houses with indoor swimming pools, who travel to expensive and exotic places several times a year. We admire powerful people, such as Bill Gates. We admire professional athletes (like Wayne Gretzky or Michael Jordan), famous actors (like Meryl Streep, Robert DeNiro, or Julia Roberts), and famous musicians (like Bono, Tony Bennett, or Mick Jagger)—people with prestige. Our society rewards those who attain wealth, power, or prestige; they have the nicest "toys," they win awards (such as the Grammy, the Oscar, or the Playoff MVP), they are interviewed endlessly to share their secrets for success, they have men and women throwing themselves at their feet offering sexual favours, and they have thousands of people wanting to be just like them. The fact that these characteristics are culturally exalted is evident even if you think back to your childhood—it is unlikely that you aspired to grow up and be poor, powerless, and unrecognized. Of course, as adults some of you might not personally admire people who are wealthy or famous, and you might personally aspire to be kind, fulfilled, and balanced. However, even if your personal goals differ from the institutionalized goals Merton referred to, the larger issue is that our society is structured in a way that gives benefit to or rewards those who have attained these institutionalized goals.

Merton suggested that just as our culture is characterized by institutionalized goals, it is also characterized by **legitimate means** of attaining those goals. What are recognized as the legitimate ways of attaining wealth, power, and prestige? We

The "(North) American Dream" serves as the foundation for deviance in society, according to Robert Merton.

Ask Yourself:

Following Merton's assumption that our society's institutionalized goals include wealth, power, and prestige, think about how those goals are achieved. Living in Canadian society today, what do we learn about the ways in which we are supposed to try to achieve these goals? Are the means of achieving wealth, power, and prestige equally available to everyone?

are supposed to get a good education (and probably even a university degree), find a good job, and work hard; alternatively, perhaps you inherited wealth or were born into a powerful family. However, he pointed out that society is structured in a way such that everyone does not have equal access to legitimate opportunities. A child growing up in a middle-class or upper-class neighbourhood with good teachers and good schools, a wide range of extracurricular activities available, a safe house in a safe community, and middle-class or upper-class parents is likely to have assured access to the legitimate means of achieving institutionalized goals. However, consider a child growing up in an impoverished neighbourhood. The dilapidated schools, devoid of library books, have trouble attracting teachers and offer few extracurricular activities. Home is a run-down house in a community where the child looks out the window and sees drug dealers. The parents live in poverty or are chronically on social assistance. Does this child have the same access to legitimate opportunities in life that the middle-class child does? Looking at this in another way, who has a better chance of ending up at a prestigious university, such as Harvard or Cambridge—someone like this impoverished child, or someone born into a wealthy and powerful family?

Merton proposed that, given the inequalities that exist in the structure of society, as illustrated by the above example, some people have access to fewer legitimate opportunities than others do. With this structural gap (or *strain*) between institutionalized goals and the legitimate means of achieving those goals, individuals must find ways to adapt. According to Merton, people can adapt to the gap between goals and means in five different ways, some of which result in deviance (see Table 2.1).

Table 2.1 MERTON'S MODES OF ADAPTATION

MODE OF ADAPTATION	GOALS	MEANS
Conformity	accept	accept
Innovation	accept	reject
Ritualism	reject	accept
Retreatism	reject	reject
Rebellion	new	new

The first possible mode of adaptation is **conformity**. The individual continues to accept both society's institutionalized goals and the legitimate means; this person keeps pursuing wealth, power, or prestige by going to school, finding a good job, and working hard. The second possible mode of adaptation, **innovation**, can result in deviance. The individual accepts the institutionalized goals, but rejects the legitimate means and instead seeks alternative means of achieving those goals. This person wants wealth, power, or prestige, but pursues it through alternative paths such as illegal or unethical activities. For example, if you want to become wealthy, you can do so by pursuing a higher education and training for a high-paying career, or you can do so by selling drugs. The third possible mode of adaptation is **ritualism**. The person engaging in ritualism has rejected or given up on the institutionalized goals, but continues to engage in the legitimate means. This is someone who thinks he or she will never get anywhere in life, but still keeps going through the motions. For example, the television character Drew Carey felt stuck in middle-management at the company he worked for, and had given up hope of ever getting a promotion, a better house, or a nicer car; however, he continued to be a good employee, and in one episode received an award for having never missed a day of work. With this mode of adaptation, people are unlikely to be looked upon as deviant because, to the outside world, they appear to reliably follow the rules. Merton's fourth mode of adaptation is **retreatism**, wherein people reject both the institutionalized goals and the legitimate means. These are people who have given up on the goals, do not even go through the motions anymore, and instead retreat into their own, frequently dismal, worlds; these are often worlds of alcohol abuse or drug addiction. The last mode of adaptation is **rebellion**. As with retreatism, people engaged in rebellion also reject both institutionalized goals and legitimate means; however, unlike retreatists, they substitute new goals and new means. These are people who have a "vision" of a different world, and act to bring that vision to life. For example, in a famous speech American civil rights leader Martin Luther King said he "had a dream," and went on to describe his dream for a society based on equality for all races, religions, and creeds. Nelson Mandela had a vision of a different South African society, and fought for more than 20 years for that vision. In the 1960s and 1970s, the hippie counterculture envisioned a society in which everyone would give up material wealth, including money, and instead seek peace and love; in pursuit of these goals many hippies stopped working, "made love, not war," consumed a wide range of mind-altering drugs, and moved into various types of commune-like settings.

AN INTERNET MOMENT:

Go to the Website for The King Center at *http://www.thekingcenter.com*. Emerging out of Martin Luther King's vision and work, The King Center now carries on that "dream." On this Website you can look at a biography of Martin Luther King (which demonstrates that he was considered "deviant" in much of American society), hear some of his speeches, and see what impact King's "dream" has had on American society. Although the Website emphasizes American society, Martin Luther King served as a vital impetus for civil rights activism in Canada as well.

Thus, according to Merton, the way people adapt to the gap between institutionalized goals and legitimate means leads some people into deviance, whether through rebellion, retreatism, or innovation. And it is the current structure of society that creates this gap, more so for some groups of people in society than for others. This is why some people engage in deviance.

Thus far we have seen two diverse, and highly influential, ways that functionalist assumptions have been used to explain why people engage in deviance. As functionalist theories, both suggest that parts of the structure of society may become dysfunctional in some way, and result in deviant behaviour on the part of some people in society. Durkheim focuses on the problems that emerge when society changes too rapidly, while Merton focuses on the strain that is created for some people because of the gap between goals and means. The next functionalist theorists we will be discussing, collaborators Richard Cloward and Lloyd Ohlin, also point to something about the structure of society leading to deviance for some people.

TIME TO REVIEW:

- According to Merton, what are the characteristics of a functionalist analysis of deviance?
- According to Merton's application of functionalist assumptions, what is it about the structure of society that results in deviance?
- Is everyone in society equally likely to engage in deviance? Why or why not?
- What are the four ways that people might adapt to the strain created by society's structure? Give an example of each.

Cloward and Ohlin: Differential Opportunity Theory

Cloward and Ohlin's (1960) theory extends aspects of Merton's strain theory. Like Merton, they suggest that the way society is structured results in differential access to legitimate opportunities; in other words, the lower-class child living in a poor neighbourhood does not have the same level of access to **legitimate opportunities** that the middle- or upper-class child does. However, Cloward and Ohlin go on to propose that the way society is structured also results in differential access to **illegitimate opportunities**. That is, some people have more access to illegitimate opportunities than other people do. For example, I recently had a conversation with an acquaintance that grew up in an inner city neighbourhood. He spoke of looking out the front window of his home and seeing street gangs fighting in the distance, people selling drugs on one corner, and prostitutes standing on another corner. In contrast, as someone who grew up in a middle-class neighbourhood, I can honestly say that in 21 years of living in the same house while growing up, not once did I see a gang, drug dealer, or prostitute when I looked out my window. Clearly, as a child and then an adolescent, I had much less access to illegitimate opportunities than my friend did; at the same time, I had much more access to legitimate opportunities than he did.

Due to the differential access to both legitimate and illegitimate opportunities that is created by the structure of society, Cloward and Ohlin suggested that some people are more likely to become participants in deviant subcultures. Some people in lower-class neighbourhoods may become part of **criminal gangs**,

Figure 2.1 DIFFERENTIAL OPPORTUNITY THEORY

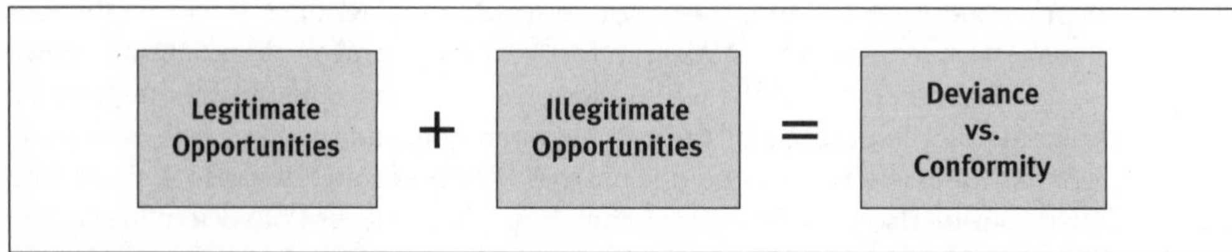

which turn criminal behaviour into something akin to small businesses. Other people may become part of "**retreatist gangs**" (Cloward and Ohlin's rather counterintuitive term) which, reflecting Merton's concept of the retreatist mode of adaptation, consist of groups of people who retreat into substantial drug or alcohol use. Finally, people in these neighbourhoods may join **conflict gangs**, which fight for status and power in the neighbourhood via violence against competitive gangs. All three of these instances are a consequence of what opportunities are available in the community. As children grow up in these neighbourhoods they may see people making their livings through criminal involvement with similar others, or people drinking and taking drugs to excess (and perhaps even trying to sell drugs and alcohol to children in the neighbourhood), or gang violence. Being a part of this environment while growing up makes certain illegitimate opportunities easily available. But as with Durkheim and Merton, the explanation for deviant behaviour lies within society's structure. Robert Agnew, the next theorist to be addressed, also focused on the roles played by structure and by strain in creating deviance.

Agnew: General Strain Theory

Robert Agnew (1998) proposes that strain can be produced by a variety of processes. While strain can occur when we fail to achieve goals (e.g., failing a course), as discussed above, it may also arise when valued stimuli are removed (e.g., the loss of a job, or the dissolution of a marriage), or when negative stimuli are presented (e.g., being teased at school, or living in a conflict-ridden family). However, strain is not sufficient in itself to produce deviance; deviance emerges only when strain is accompanied by **negative affect** (i.e., negative emotions), especially anger. Consequently, if someone has the economic, interpersonal, or psychological resources to effectively deal with strain-producing situations, deviance is unlikely to occur.

Agnew's General Strain Theory has been analyzed for its applicability with different forms of deviance, and with different populations. In one study, White and Agnew (cited by Broidy and Agnew, 1997) found that anger, when combined with low levels of depression, was associated with male delinquency. In another study, purging behaviour among young women was analyzed (Sharp, Terling-Watt, Atkins, & Gilliam, 2001). A negative correlation was found between the successful achievement of goals and purging behaviour; that is, women who were less successful at goal achievement were more likely to engage in purging. Certain negative emotions, particularly depression, served as the mediating factor for this relationship; however, anger was related to purging behaviour only among women who had high levels of depression. Sharp and colleagues conclude that anger, accompanied by high levels of depression, may result in self-destructive forms of deviance such as purging; in contrast, anger that is accompanied by low levels of depression (as found by White & Agnew) may result in externally directed forms of deviance such as delinquency.

The addition of negative emotions to notions of strain is what distinguishes Agnew's general strain theory from Merton's strain theory and from Cloward and Ohlin's differential opportunity theory. The last functionalist theorist we will be addressing is Albert Cohen, whose subcultural theory also integrates structured inequalities as the impetus for deviance.

Cohen: Status Frustration

Albert Cohen (1955) claims that the inequalities in the structure of society are reproduced in the classroom, with the end result of creating delinquent subcultures among lower-class boys; consequently, Cohen's theory is sometimes categorized as a **subcultural theory** rather than a functionalist theory. The middle-class foundation of the school system creates a **middle-class measuring rod** that lower-class boys find difficult to live up to. When they are unable to succeed according to the standards of the classroom, they experience something akin to strain—**status frustration**. As a result, they join together with other lower-class boys who are having the same experience (i.e., **mutual conversion**), and develop a set of oppositional standards that they are able to succeed at (**reaction formation**); thus, if the middle-class standard is to delay gratification, the oppositional standard is to be hedonistic. Nonutilitarian, malicious, negativistic youth gangs are the result. In support of Cohen's theory, many empirical studies have found poor school performance or early school leaving to be associated with criminal behaviour (e.g., Gomme, 1985).

TIME TO REVIEW:

- According to Cloward and Ohlin's application of functionalist assumptions, what is it about the structure of society that results in deviance?
- How is Cloward and Ohlin's theory an extension of Merton's theory?
- What are the three types deviant subcultures that can emerge in society, according to Cloward and Ohlin?
- According to Agnew, when can strain emerge, and what role do negative emotions play?
- According to Cohen, what role does the classroom play in the creation of deviance?
- Why are lower-class boys more likely to become deviant, and what form does their deviance take?

A Closing Look at Functionalist Theories of Deviance

Emile Durkheim, Robert Merton, collaborators Richard Cloward and Lloyd Ohlin, Robert Agnew, and Albert Cohen have each applied functionalist assumptions to an explanation of deviance, although in slightly different ways. Durkheim's grand theory of society includes discussions of how deviance can be functional for society, but can reach dysfunctional levels when social change occurs too rapidly and anomie is created. Merton's theory, which focuses more explicitly on explaining deviance, describes with greater specificity what it is about the structure of modern society that leads some people into deviance; for Merton, this is the gap between institutionalized goals and legitimate means of achieving those goals experienced more by some groups of people in society than others. Cloward and Ohlin's theory narrows the focus by addressing specific types of deviance, those engaged in by subcultures or gangs. Like Merton, they suggest that the structure of society creates differential access to legitimate opportunities, but they extend the notion of differential access to illegitimate opportunities as well. Agnew goes a step further by saying that strain must be accompanied by negative emotions for deviance to be the result. Finally, Cohen suggests the reproduction of structured inequalities within the school system serves as the impetus for deviance among groups of lower-class boys. Despite the slightly different paths that are taken by these various theories, they all make use of functionalist assumptions—society is comprised of structures that fulfill important functions for the maintenance of the social order; something within the structure of society contributes to deviance; and deviance is a threat to society's equilibrium (at least at certain levels).

Functionalist theories have been subject to considerable criticism by deviance specialists. Functionalism in general has been criticized for its **tautological** reasoning, its conservative bias, and its treatment of women. The explanations for behaviour that are offered within functionalist theories are perceived by some as tautological (or circular). That is, if deviance exists, then it must be functional for society; we know deviance is functional for society because if it did not serve any function, then it would not exist. By determining the functions of almost any aspect of social life, functionalists are criticized for ignoring the social and historical circumstances from which those aspects of social life emerge. The presumption of functionality also contributes to the critique of functionalism's conservative bias (Pfohl, 1994; Deutschmann, 2002); for instance, strain theorists only seek to point out the influence of structural inequalities on deviance, they do not seek to modify society's structure in order to reduce inequalities in the distribution of opportunities. Finally, functionalist theories arise from an **androcentric bias**, meaning that women have only been addressed in functionalist theories to a limited extent. When women's experiences have been addressed in functionalist theories, a conservative bias once again becomes evident; for instance, women's traditional gender roles have been identified as serving important functions for society.

Each of the specific theories reviewed thus far have also been subject to particular criticisms. The various strain theories, such as Merton's, Cloward and Ohlin's, and Cohen's, have all been criticized for identifying deviance and criminality as lower-class phenomena. If deviance is acknowledged as a middle- and upper-class phenomenon as well (such as in the form of suburban gangs), then the very foundation of their explanations of deviance (as originating with unequal opportunities) must be questioned (Ward, 1994; Pfohl, 1994; Hackler, 2000; Siegal & McCormick, 2003). Merton's strain theory has been criticized for failing to recognize individual differences, such as gender and cultural differences, in response to strain (Deutschmann, 2002), and for failing to recognize the diversity of values and goals that actually exists in society (Pfohl, 1994). Cohen's theory of status frustration has been criticized for failing to recognize nonutilitarian, negativistic, malicious acts of deviance among middle-class suburban gangs (Kitsuse & Dietrick, 1979). His weak treatment of female deviance has also been critiqued, since Cohen suggests without significant empirical support that female deviance emerges from interpersonal strain rather than economic strain and is therefore more likely to be of a sexual nature (Deutschmann, 2002).

The theorists we have discussed are certainly not the only functionalist theorists who have sought explanations for deviance. They are, however, among the most influential over the last several decades; the influence they have had on discussions and understandings of deviance led to their selection for this chapter. Although functionalist theories no longer dominate the study of deviance, they do continue to maintain a presence (Agnew, 1992; Sharp et. al, 2001; Victor, 1992).

In addition to functionalist theories, other perspectives originate from a positivist understanding of why people act in deviant ways. The next set of positivist theories we will be addressing are those typically labelled learning theories.

TIME TO REVIEW:

- What are some criticisms of the functionalist theories that have been presented?

Learning Theories

Learning theories, like functionalist theories, have been widely used explanations of deviance. As the label suggests, these theories explain deviant behaviour as a result of the learning process. In other words, someone has taught deviant people to be deviant. The precise nature of this learning process is outlined in various learning theories. In this section of the chapter, we will focus on Differential Association Theory, Neutralization Theory, and Social Learning Theory, all of which have had considerable influence on the way deviance has been understood over the last several decades.

Sutherland: Differential Association Theory

Just as we began our exploration of functionalist theories with the foundational work of Emile Durkheim, our exploration of learning theories begins with an influential theorist whose work has served as the foundation for many later learning theories. Edwin Sutherland (1947), beginning with the assumption that deviant behaviour is learned, developed a theory that focuses on explaining the nature of the learning process. Although Sutherland's theory was initially proposed as a theory of crime, it has since been successfully applied to other forms of deviance, particularly adolescent substance use (Aseltine, 1995; Elliot, Huizinga, & Ageton,

1985). Some deviance specialists suggest that his theory of **differential association** is one of the dominant explanations of deviance today (Erickson, Crosnoe, & Dornbusch, 2000; Cullen & Agnew, 1998). Sutherland proposed that deviant behaviour is learned through the very same process by which conforming behaviour, or any other type of behaviour, is learned. Central to the learning process is the direct interaction and communication that occurs within small, intimate groups. Deviant people become that way because that is what they learn through communication within the intimate groups they are a part of; intimacy is crucial to the learning of deviance, such that impersonal agents like music, television, and movies are relatively inconsequential. Within these personal groups, individuals learn both **techniques** (i.e., skills and tools) and **motives** (i.e., reasons, rationalizations) for particular kinds of behaviour. If, in the various group interactions people are involved with in life, they are exposed to more deviant definitions than conforming definitions, they are likely to become deviant themselves; in other words, if they are learning techniques for how to engage in deviance and motives for engaging in deviance more than they are learning techniques for how to be conforming and motives for conforming, they are more likely to engage in deviant behaviour.

This differential exposure to deviant and conforming definitions is further complicated by the fact that not all group interactions have the same impact on our learning processes. First, the extent of group influence varies by *frequency*, in that those groups we interact with more frequently will have more of an influence on our learning. Second, interactions that are of longer *duration* have more of an influence than those of shorter duration. Third, there is a *priority* to our small group interactions; those intimate groups we interact with earlier in life have a greater influence on our learning. Finally, interactions vary in *intensity*, or in how important a particular group is to us; the more important a particular group is to us, the greater its influence on our learning processes. The interaction of frequency, duration, priority, and intensity determine how influential the definitions of behaviour we are exposed to within various groups are on our learning processes.

Sutherland's explanation of the learning process that leads to deviance had a substantial impact on subsequent theorizing about deviance. Gresham Sykes and David Matza's neutralization theory later highlighted and expanded upon one aspect of differential association theory.

Ask Yourself:

Think about your own life and your own experiences while growing up. List the various groups that you interacted with as a child or adolescent. For each group, consider the types of techniques and motives you were exposed to. Did you learn ways to engage in what might be seen as deviant behaviour, and reasons for doing so? Did you learn ways to engage in conforming behaviour, and reasons for doing so? If you consider your childhood and adolescence as a whole, do you think you were exposed to more deviant definitions than conforming definitions, or vice versa?

TIME TO REVIEW:

- According to learning theories, why do people engage in deviance?
- According to Sutherland's theory of differential association, where is deviance learned? How is it learned? What, specifically, is learned?
- What are the four factors that influence the extent of influence a particular group has on our learning processes?

Sykes and Matza: Neutralization Theory

Sykes and Matza (1957), like Sutherland, focused on criminal behaviour in the formulation of their theory, which was later appropriated for understanding the broader issue of deviance. They agreed with Edwin Sutherland's suggestion that deviance emerges as the result of a learning process within group interaction. However, the particular focus of their theory is on the nature of some of the *motives* that Sutherland alluded to. According to Sykes and Matza, the most important motives that are learned through group interaction, which subsequently open the door for deviant behaviour, are **techniques of neutralization**. Part of what deviant people learn are the justifications or rationalizations for the behaviour they engage in; by justifying their behaviour, they can convince themselves that what they are doing is not *really* wrong. One of the techniques of neutralization is the **denial of responsibility**, which shifts the blame or responsibility off of the individual, directing it elsewhere. The blame may be directed at other people, situations, or environments. Statements illustrating this technique of neutralization include: "It's not my fault"; "I didn't know there would be drugs there"; "My father was never there for me when I was growing up"; "There's nothing else to do in a small town!"

The second technique of neutralization is the **denial of injury**. In this situation, the accused deviant expresses the perception that what they have done hurts or harms no one. For example, some people refer to "victimless crimes," such as drug use or prostitution. Similarly, a male cross-dresser or someone who dresses in "rave" style may also say that what they do does not hurt anyone.

The **denial of the victim** is the third neutralization technique, where the perception is that the victim of the deviant's behaviour was somehow deserving of their fate. For example, Robin Hood was seen as a hero for robbing from the rich, who were perceived as corrupt and immoral, and therefore deserved to be robbed. When Matthew Shepard, a young gay man, was murdered simply for being homosexual, protesters at his funeral carried signs saying, "God hates fags"; his murderers and the protesters perceived him as deserving his fate.

The fourth neutralization technique that Sykes and Matza refer to is **condemnation of the condemners**. This technique shifts the focus from the deviants' own behaviour to the deviant behaviour of others, especially people from the social groups that have pointed to this person's deviance. The condemners are accused of being hypocrites who are engaging in other forms of deviance, perhaps secretly. For example, although hippies in the 1960s were frequently accused of being deviant, they turned the tables on their accusers by pointing to all of the negative things that "the establishment" was doing—"You're the ones who are killing babies in Vietnam!"; "You're the ones who are treating money as more important than your own families!"; "You're the ones who are willing to destroy the environment just to earn a profit!"

The final technique of neutralization is **appealing to higher loyalties**, where the deviant behaviour is justified as serving a higher purpose. In this situation, people acknowledge that they have violated norms, but in service of other more important norms. Someone might get into a violent fight in order to protect a friend. Someone might dress in gothic attire in the name of individuality and freedom. Hippies looked the way they looked and acted the way they did in service of wanting to bring peace, love, and equality to the world. A suicide bomber might walk into a shopping mall in order to punish evildoers and achieve spiritual salvation in the afterlife.

These five techniques of neutralization, adopted through the kind of learning processes described earlier in the theory of differential association, are central to explaining why people engage in deviance. Only by being able to justify their actions do people become deviant. Techniques of neutralization have been found to play a central role in the behaviours of deer poachers (Eliason & Dodder, 2000) in fighting, truancy, vandalism, and drug use among male high school students in Ontario (Teevan & Dryburgh, 2000), and in the rationalizations used by mothers of child beauty pageant contestants (Heltsley & Calhoun, 2003) (see Box 2.2).

Box 2.2 Beauty Pageant Moms

Following the 1996 murder of child beauty queen JonBenet Ramsey (which remains unsolved), child beauty pageants were suddenly in the spotlight. The pageants were criticized as dangerous events that sexualize little girls and attract pedophiles. Mothers of child beauty pageant contestants were especially singled out for criticism, for bringing their daughters into that "deviant" world that attracts a sexually "deviant" audience. During an eight-month period of time in 1996 and 1997, Heltsley and Calhoun (2003) interviewed 43 mothers of child beauty pageant contestants to determine whether they used any of the techniques of neutralization suggested by Sykes and Matza (1957). The researchers found that these mothers used four out of five neutralization techniques.

The most commonly used technique (46.5% of the mothers) was *condemnation of the condemners*. In using this neutralization technique, the mothers expressed outrage at the accusation that pageants attract pedophiles. They turned the tables on their accusers, stating that only someone who was really "sick" themselves would suggest that anyone would find these little girls "sexy."

The second neutralization technique used by the pageant mothers was *denial of injury* (25.6% of the mothers). In this way they claimed that not only were beauty pageants not *harming* their daughters, pageants were actually *benefitting* them. The mothers pointed to characteristics like increased confidence and an enhanced ability to concentrate in

school as arising from the experience of competing in pageants.

The third technique used was *denial of responsibility* (13.9% of mothers). With this technique, the mothers indicated that they really did not have any choice but to enter their daughters in these pageants. In some cases, the mothers claimed that pageants were their daughters' ideas in the first place, and that their daughters insisted on continuing in the competitions. In other cases, the mothers stated that pageants were the only way to improve their daughters' delicate self-esteem, to prove to them that they were beautiful, smart, and charming.

The last technique of neutralization used was *appealing to higher loyalties* (13.9% of mothers). Mothers using this technique frequently acknowledged that there were problems with the structure of child beauty pageants and the competition requirements. But at the same time they remained committed to the pageant world for their daughters' sakes, or because their daughters were still interested in competing.

TIME TO REVIEW:

- What are "techniques of neutralization"? Where do they come from?
- What are the five techniques of neutralization, according to Sykes and Matza's neutralization theory? Give an example of each.

Ask Yourself:

As a child, how did your parents respond when you broke the rules, like when you stole a cookie from the cookie jar before dinner, or when you broke curfew as a teenager? How did they respond when you did something they approved of, like cleaning your room or receiving a high grade on a report card?

Social Learning Theory

Social learning theory highlights the role of learning processes not only in deviant behaviour but in behaviour more generally; according to these theorists (e.g., Bandura, 1986), all of our behaviours can be explained in the same way.

In the "Ask Yourself" exercise, you probably talked about your parents punishing you when you broke the rules. Perhaps you had to go to your room, or you were spanked, or you had a privilege taken away, or you were grounded. When you did something they approved of, maybe they praised you, or expressed their pride in you, or gave you a smile that you only got at times like that, or hugged you, or gave you a reward (like $5 for every "A" on your report card). If you responded to the above questions in this way, you are moving toward the essence of social learning theory. Within this theory, it is suggested that all behaviour is the result of reinforcement (i.e., rewards), punishment, and modelling. Social learning theory is related to the behaviourist theory of *instrumental conditioning*, which suggests that we are more likely to engage in behaviours we have been rewarded (or reinforced) for in the past, and we are less likely to engage in behaviours that we have not been rewarded for, or that we have been punished for, in the past. We can see principles of instrumental conditioning being used in parenting all the time; a child who misbehaves is spanked, given a time out, has telephone privileges taken away, or is grounded, while a child who acts in accordance with the parent's wishes is given praise, attention, or perhaps an increase in allowance. In school, children are rewarded for behaving well and for studying by getting good grades and perhaps special privileges (such as getting to help the teacher clean the blackboard after school). Social learning theory goes a step further by saying that, not only are our behaviours influenced by what we personally have been rewarded and punished for in the past, they are influenced by what we see other people being rewarded and punished for, through the process of imitation or modelling. For example, if we hear Dad make a racist joke and all of his friends laugh and show approval, we are more likely to act in similar ways and develop similar views. If Mom is bulimic and we see her being rewarded by everyone complimenting her on how beautiful she is and what a wonderful figure she has, we are more likely to act in similar ways, especially if we are also female (because social learning theorists suggest children are more likely to imitate same-sex role models). Thus, people engage in deviance because they have either been rewarded for it in the past, or they have seen other people being rewarded for it (Bandura, 1986; Akers, 1977).

Ask Yourself:

In the examples of Dad's racist joke, or Mom's bulimic actions, we see the role of modelling behaviours that would be considered deviant. But now consider the role of modelling behaviours that would be considered conforming. Think of some examples of children growing up to imitate conforming behaviours or appearances. You might consider situations where children see people being rewarded for working hard, for being honest, for dressing in a clean-cut way, for studying hard, or for being non-prejudiced; conversely, you might consider situations where children see people being punished for being lazy, dishonest, dressing "weird," not studying, or being racist. For example, in the context of your own life, what role has modelling or seeing other people rewarded/punished played in your decision to become a college or university student?

Akers (2000) has recently modified his version of social learning theory to integrate structural factors as well, factors that learning theorists have been criticized for ignoring. He suggests that dimensions of the social structure create the differential contexts in which learning occurs for different people. These dimensions include *differential social organization* (i.e., a community's demographic characteristics), *differential location in the social structure* (i.e., an individual's defining characteristics such as ethnicity, gender, and educational attainment), *theoretically defined structural variables* (e.g., anomie, conflict, social disorganization), and *differential social location* (i.e., an individual's membership in different social groups, such as peer groups). His recent work is one more example of the trend toward theoretical integration in the sociology of deviance.

A Closing Look at Learning Theories

The principles of social learning theory, as used to explain the acquisition of behaviour, appeal to most of us at a common-sense level; it is fairly easy for us to see reinforcement, punishment, and modelling everywhere around us and in our own lives. It, like neutralization theory and the theory of differential association, draw attention to processes of learning as key to explaining why people engage in deviance. Despite the differences in the way each of these theories explains the learning process that leads to deviance, they all point to learning as the answer to the question of why people act the way they do—why people become deviant. The final set of positivist theories that have been frequently used to explain deviance, *social control theories*, provide yet another way of understanding the origins of deviance based on the objectivist conceptualization of the nature of deviance.

TIME TO REVIEW:

- In what way does social learning theory try to explain all behaviour, and not just deviant behaviour?
- How is social learning theory similar to the notion of instrumental conditioning?
- How is social learning theory different from the notion of instrumental conditioning?
- What are some examples of reinforcement, punishment, and modelling?
- According to social learning theory, why do people become deviant?
- How does Akers (2000) integrate structural dimensions into his learning theory? What are those structural dimensions?

Social Control Theories

Social control theories focus on a different type of question than the other positivist theories do. While other positivist theorists direct their attention to why some people become deviant, social control theorists direct their attention to why all people do not become deviant. They suggest that deviant behaviour is inherently attractive, exciting, and appealing. Given the appeal of deviant behaviour, it is only through higher levels of social controls that some of us do not become deviant.

Hirschi: Social Bonds Theory

The most widely used social control theory in explanations of deviance has been Travis Hirschi's (1969) **social bonds theory**. His argument is that four different types of social bonds rein most of us in, restraining us from deviance.

The first bond is that of **attachment** to parents, teachers, and peers. Hirschi suggested that the greater our level of emotional attachment to others, the more bound we are to conformity. Conversely, a lack of emotional attachments leaves us freer to engage in deviance. The second bond is **commitment** to conformity. Being committed to conventional activities like school, work, organized sports, or childrearing gives us more of a stake in the conventional world; if we were to engage in deviance, we would threaten everything we have invested in conventionality and have too much to lose. In contrast, people who have little invested in conventional activities have less to lose by engaging in deviance. The third social bond is **involvement** in conventional activities. In other words, people who are so highly involved in such activities that the activities take up much of their time simply do not have any time for deviance. On the other hand, someone who has substantial unused time on their hands is more likely to be drawn to the appeal of deviance—"idle hands are the devil's workshop." The last bond is **belief** in the norms, values, and assumptions that comprise the conventional world. Holding such beliefs bonds people to the conventional world, while not holding such beliefs loosens the restraints from deviance. The interaction of these four types of social bonds determines the extent to which individuals will be restrained, or fail to be restrained, from the appeal of the deviant world.

Ask Yourself:

Try to apply social bonds theory to your own life. How many people would you say you have an emotional attachment to? What might you lose from your life if you engaged in deviance? How much of your time is spent engaging in conventional activities?

Social bonds theory has been successfully applied to understandings of substance use, including marijuana, cigarettes, and alcohol (Hawdon, 1996; Massey & Krohn, 1986; Marcos, Bahr, & Johnson, 1986). Erickson, Crosnoe, and Dornbusch (2000) integrate Hirschi's social bonds theory with Sutherland's differential association theory in an analysis of adolescent delinquency and substance use. They conclude that social bonds influence these outcomes via deviant peer associations and susceptibility to deviant peer associations; that is, adolescents who have strong social bonds are less likely to associate with deviant peers, and are less susceptible to peer influence even if they do associate with deviant peers.

Gottfredson and Hirschi: General Theory of Crime

Although Hirschi initially focused on the relationship between social control and deviance, in recent years he has collaborated with Michael Gottfredson on a

General Theory of Crime (Gottfredson & Hirschi, 1990). Here they suggest that **self-control** is central to explaining why some people are predisposed to deviant acts while others are not. Low self-control is the result of ineffective parenting, and although it may be ameliorated by other influences in a child's life, it remains relatively stable throughout life; low levels of self-control predispose the individual to deviant acts.

Although the relatively recent nature of the General Theory of Crime limits the amount of empirical research that has been done utilizing it, research support has been steadily building. LaGrange and Silverman (1999) found that low levels of self-control explained a portion of the gender differences in criminal offence rates among Canadian high school students. Stylianou (2002) found low self-control to be a predictor (albeit a rather weak one) of a wide range of deviant behaviours, including alcohol and marijuana use, tobacco use, traffic offences, and chronically skipping classes.

A Closing Look at Social Control Theories

Social control theories, by asking why we do not all engage in deviance, instead of asking only why some people do engage in deviance, provide us with a unique standpoint from which to study deviance. However, it must be noted that social control theories have thus far been applied primarily to criminal acts of deviance rather than non-criminal acts of deviance, so their utility for the sociology of deviance, broadly speaking, is still to be determined.

TIME TO REVIEW:

- In what way do the questions asked by social control theorists differ from the questions asked by other positivist theorists?
- What are the four social bonds referred to in Hirschi's social bonds theory?
- What kind of empirical research is there to support Hirschi's theory?
- What are the core assumptions of Gottfredson and Hirschi's general theory of crime?

Summarizing Positivist Theories

The diverse positivist theories of deviance that have been addressed in this chapter share similar goals—trying to understand why people act in particular ways. Functionalist theories, such as Durkheim's anomie theory, Merton's strain theory, Cloward and Ohlin's differential opportunity theory, Agnew's general strain theory, and Cohen's theory of status frustration direct their attention to the role that the structure of society itself plays in the emergence of deviance. Learning theories, such as Sutherland's differential association theory, Sykes and Matza's neutralization theory, and social learning theory point to the centrality of learning processes in the emergence of deviance. In other words, people learn to be deviant from others around them. Social control theories, such as Hirschi's social bonds theory, explain why all of us do *not* become deviant—because of social bonds that restrain us from giving in to the appeal of deviance. Gottfredson and Hirschi's general theory of crime addresses the influence that parenting patterns have on the development of social control.

Functional, learning, and social control theories each shine a light on a particular aspect of social life in their efforts to explain deviance. Despite their differential areas of focus, and despite the diversity within each of these bodies of theory, there is something they all have in common. They are all positivist theories that seek to explain why some people act in deviant ways and other people do not.

Positivist theories dominated academic understandings of deviance for many years. However, as more subjective views of deviance developed and become more widespread, different types of theories became useful. Just as certain types of theory correspond with more objective views of deviance, certain kinds of theory correspond with more subjective ways of looking at deviance—interpretive and critical theories. These theories will be addressed in the next chapter.

Exercise Your Mind:

Review the theories that have been addressed in this chapter. For each theory, ask yourself how this theory has helped you understand deviance better; try to think of some examples from your own life or your own observations that illustrate how this theory advances your understanding. Then, for each theory, ask yourself what you still don't know about deviance. In other words, what questions about deviance are you left with after learning about each theory? Try to think of some examples from your own life or your own observations that illustrate the gaps in your understanding after reading about the theory. This might be an interesting topic for discussion with your classmates, either inside or outside of the classroom. To follow up, go to the library and look for some of the critiques of each of these theories to see how they correspond to your own thoughts.

Chapter Summary

Although theory is frequently perceived as distinct from practice, theory actually is quite practical in providing us with the means of understanding the world around us. Many different theories are utilized within the sociology of deviance, corresponding to the various ways one can look at deviance, and different views of what society is made of. With sociological theories, we cannot say that one theory is "right" and the other theories are "wrong"; instead, each theory shines a spotlight on a particular aspect of deviance and provides one way of understanding it.

Different theories will be useful for different purposes. Thus, people who have the more *objective* views of deviance discussed in the last chapter (in terms of normative violation, harm, statistical rarity, or negative societal reaction), and therefore are interested in why deviant people become that way, find *positivist* theories to be the most informative tools. Positivist sociological theories are modelled after the use of theory in the natural sciences as a tool by which the natural or social environment can be mastered.

People who have the more *subjective* views of deviance discussed in the last chapter (in terms of the social construction of deviance) find *interpretive* and *critical* theories to be the most informative tools. Interpretive and critical theories are tools for understanding societal perceptions of and reactions to particular acts, as well as the role played by power in these perceptions and reactions.

Functionalist theories dominated positivist understandings of deviance, and the discipline of sociology itself, for many years. Although many different functionalist theories exist, they share a structural and consensual view of society that points to something gone awry in the social structure that causes some people to become deviant. Emile Durkheim directed his attention to *anomie* as the root cause of deviance, Robert Merton suggested a structural gap between *institutionalized goals* and *legitimate means* as the cause, collaborators Cloward and Ohlin pointed to differential access to *legitimate opportunities* and *illegitimate opportunities*, Robert Agnew emphasized the relationship between strain and *negative affect*, and Albert Cohen focused on *status frustration*.

Learning theories are another body of positivist theories that explain the emergence of deviance as a result of individual learning processes. *Differential association theory* suggests that we learn techniques and motives within intimate groups that lead us either into deviance or into conformity. According to *neutralization theory*, the key learning process that results in deviance is the learning of rationalizations that enable deviant people to think that what they are doing is not *really* wrong. *Social learning theory* points to the importance of being rewarded or punished for past behaviours, and seeing other people being rewarded or punished for behaviours, in determining our own future behaviours.

The last group of positivist theories that were explored in this chapter are *social control theories*. Travis Hirschi's *social bonds theory* has been the most widely appropriated control theory for understanding deviance. Instead of asking why some people become deviant, the question is reversed by asking why all of us do not become deviant. Hirschi's answer lies in the notion of social bonds that rein us in from becoming deviant; people with weak social bonds are freer to engage in deviance. Gottfredson and Hirshi's *general theory of crime* emphasize the role of ineffective parenting in the development of low levels of *self-control*.

Recommended Readings

Durkheim, E. (1951). *The division of labor in society*. New York: Free Press.

* This is one of the theorists who started it all. He defined the functionalist perspective, and he defined the discipline of sociology for many years. This is a classic example of positivist theory, based upon theory in the natural sciences, being used in the study of society.

Sutherland, E.H. (1947). *Principles of criminology*. Philadelphia: J. B. Lippincott.

* This book serves as a good example of one of the early learning theories that was used to understand deviance. It also illustrates the tendency to equate deviance with criminology that existed for many years.

Bandura, A. (1986). *Social foundations of thought and action: A social cognitive theory*. Englewood Cliffs, NJ: Prentice Hall.

* Bandura is one of the most well-known social learning theorists. This book illustrates a more contemporary approach to social learning theory; although discussed as one of the positivist theories, aspects of social learning theory are also appropriated within subjective views of deviance.

Hirschi, T. (1969). *Causes of delinquency*. Berkeley, CA: University of California Press.

* Hirschi's social bonds theory was definitive in the area of social control theories. This theory remains the most cited social control theory in the present day.

Endnotes

1 Leonid Ilich Breshnev. Retrieved November 28, 2002 from World Wide Web: **http://www.tqpage.com**.

2 Paul Feyerabend. Retrieved November 28, 2002 from World Wide Web: **http://www.tqpage.com**.

Key Terms

positivist, **p. 45**
interpretive, **p. 45**
critical, **p. 45**
functionalist theories, **p. 47**
grand theory, **p. 48**
socialization, **p. 49**
profit, **p. 49**
persuasion, **p. 49**
coercion, **p. 49**
mechanical solidarity, **p. 50**
organic solidarity, **p. 50**
anomie, **p. 50**
strain theory, **p. 51**
institutionalized goals, **p. 52**
legitimate means, **p. 52**
conformity, **p. 54**
innovation, **p. 54**
ritualism, **p. 54**

retreatism, **p. 55**
rebellion, **p. 55**
legitimate opportunities, **p. 56**
illegitimate opportunities, **p. 56**
criminal gangs, **p. 56**
retreatist gangs, **p. 57**
conflict gangs, **p. 57**
negative affect, **p. 57**
subcultural theory, **p. 58**
middle-class measuring rod, **p. 58**
status frustration, **p. 58**
mutual conversion, **p. 58**
reaction formation, **p. 58**
tautological, **p. 59**
androcentric bias, **p. 59**
learning theories, **p. 60**
differential association, **p. 61**
techniques, **p. 61**
motives, **p. 61**
techniques of neutralization, **p. 62**
denial of responsibility, **p. 62**
denial of injury, **p. 62**
denial of the victim, **p. 62**
condemnation of the condemners, **p. 62**
appealing to higher loyalties, **p. 63**
social learning theory, **p. 64**
social bonds theory, **p. 67**
attachment, **p. 67**
commitment, **p. 67**
involvement, **p. 67**
belief, **p. 67**
self-control, **p. 68**

CHAPTER 3

Explaining Deviance: The Perception, Reaction, and Power

Learning Objectives

After reading this chapter, you should be able to:

- Explain how interpretive theories approach the topic of deviance, and describe how symbolic interactionism gave rise to other interpretive theories of deviance.
- Describe such concepts as labelling, stigmatization, transition from primary to secondary deviance, the dramatization of evil, deviance as a master status, and the deviant career. Tie each concept to its roots in symbolic interactionist theory, and contrast it with the other concepts.
- Explain how critical theories approach the topic of deviance.
- Describe critical theories like Marxist and pluralist conflict theories, power-reflexive theories, feminist theories, and postmodern theories. Explain what they all share as critical theories, and how they differ from each other.

"There are no moral phenomenon [sic] at all, but only a moral interpretation of phenomena." (Friedrich Nietzsche)[1]

Non-Positivist Theorizing

The above quotation emphasizes *interpretation* as the source of understanding, suggesting that moral codes emerge from a process of interpretation rather than from within any type of absolute morality. This signals a substantial shift away from the positivist approach to theorizing that was addressed in Chapter 2. Positivist theories shine their spotlights on the actor or the act, and try to explain why some people behave in deviant ways while others do not. Affiliated with more objective ways of understanding deviance, positivist theories are based on the assumption that deviance can be identified in some clear-cut way; once identified, an explanation for that outcome is sought. The strengths of positivist theories of deviance lie in their search for causation, which facilitates the identification of the most effective means of achieving fixed ends (Ashley & Orenstein, 2001). For instance, preventing youth crime or treating alcoholism is most effective when based on an understanding of how some people enter criminal activity or begin to abuse alcohol.

However, deviance specialists who are affiliated with more subjective ways of understanding deviance are critical of positivist theories. They suggest that trying to understand why some people act in ways that the rest of us do not takes the concept of deviance for granted. Focusing on individual deviance implies assumptions about what the world *should* be like and how people *should* act, and tries to explain deviations from normative behaviour more than normative behaviour itself. In contrast, the more subjective deviance specialists suggest that normative behaviour must not be assumed to be the way people *should* act. Positivist theories have also been criticized in that, according to some researchers, "nearly all positivist attempts to explain deviance have been disappointing. The expected differences between deviants and nondeviants rarely materialize when the evidence is carefully examined" (McCaghy, Capron, & Jamieson, 2003, p. 17). Of course, positivist-oriented researchers would dispute this claim and, in fact, some of the evidence that supports positivist theories was addressed in the previous chapter. A more moderate critique of positivist theories of deviance claims that positivism has not resulted in the level of predictive value that might be hoped for. Despite some of the critiques of positivism, it is probably true that, "nevertheless, positivism remains the dominant approach among students of deviance" (McCaghy, Capron, & Jamieson, 2003, p. 17), particularly among students of deviance who are embedded within the field of criminology, described in earlier chapters.

Others disagree, claiming that while positivist theories may continue to have a stronghold in the discipline of criminology, most contemporary deviance specialists utilize more subjective views of deviance and their affiliated theories (Goode, 1997). In fact, some sociologists contend that a more subjective, constructionist perspective is the defining feature of the sociology of deviance (Miller, Wright, & Dannels, 2001). Because the more subjective views of deviance claim that we cannot know deviance when we see it, and instead must be told that something is deviant, the associated theories do not look at the violation of social expectations, but rather look at the nature of the social expectations themselves (McCaghy, Capron, & Jamieson, 2003). The interest is not in the act, but in the perceptions of and reactions to the act, as well as the role of power in influencing these perceptions and reactions. Deviance is seen as being constructed through the social typing process, whereby people have descriptive labels attached to them, are evaluated or judged on the basis of those labels, and then are treated in certain ways because of the prior descriptions and evaluations (Rubington & Weinberg, 2002). When it is society rather than deviant people that goes under a microscope—when the interest is in understanding social processes rather than specific people—the positivist interest in explaining the acquisition of deviant behaviour becomes less relevant. In its place, those theories that are often categorized as *interpretive* or *critical* are the ones that can best explain the social construction of deviance.

Most interpretive and critical theories reject the claim that there are certain standards of objectivity that can be recognized in the study of society, and that it is the role of the sociologist to discover what those standards are. Rather, they propose that social processes are the result of culturally and historically specific human social interaction. Social interaction creates those bodies of social rules that then influence our lives. These rules influence all members of society, even though people may frequently be unaware of what those rules are. The role of the sociologist is to examine the processes by which these social rules are created, and the impact those rules subsequently have on individuals.

Interpretive theories explain "something that might be unique and unrepeatable" (Ashley & Orenstein, 2001, p. 31). This stands in contrast to positivist theories that seek to identify generalizable, immutable laws that govern the environment. Interpretive theorists claim that the only "reality" is that which emerges through reciprocal intersubjective understanding between people; their focus thereby becomes the meanings that emerge from interactions between people who are engaged in symbolic dialogue. **Critical theories** have a self-reflective **value-orienting** foundation (Ashley & Orenstein, 2001), that is, an underlying interest in emancipation. Their focus is on the power relations that underlie the creation of social rules. Taken together, critical and interpretive theories are useful in explaining those aspects of deviance that more subjective-oriented deviance specialists are interested in—the social construction of deviance.

A combination of several interpretive and critical theories is associated with the soft or contextual social constructionism that informs more subjective understandings of deviance. One of the most well-known deviance constructionists, Joel Best (2003), claims that labelling theory (which he equates with interpretive theory more generally) and conflict theory (one of the core critical theories) make up the approach referred to as "constructionism." Other researchers suggest that elements of social learning theory (discussed in the previous chapter), symbolic interactionism, ethnomethodology, feminist theories, and postmodernist theories constitute the constructionist approach as well, even though they are all considered distinct theoretical perspectives in themselves (Nelson & Robinson, 1999; Beaman, 2000; Peace, Beaman & Sneddon, 2000). The boundaries among these various interpretive and critical theories are certainly somewhat more ambiguous than is the case with positivist theories, and they can be quite complementary to each other as well. Many contemporary deviance specialists utilize combinations of these theories in their analyses of various aspects of deviance and normality (e.g., McCaghy, Capron, & Jamieson, 2003; Rossol, 2001). It should also be noted that some level of theoretical integration exists beyond interpretive and critical theories. That is, there are some theorists who have combined elements of interpretive or critical theories with positivist theory as well. For example, Karl Marx's conflict theory is positivist in that it seeks universal, generalizable truth, but combines it with a critical agenda based upon the emancipation of society's economically powerless. In a more contemporary example, Ben-Yehuda's (1990) theory of deviance integrates neo-functionalist, non-Marxist conflict theory with interactionism in exploring the social negotiations that influence the boundaries of different symbolic-moral universes that define moral orders.

TIME TO REVIEW:

- What are the strengths and limitations of positivist theories?
- What aspects of deviance do more subjective researchers focus on, and what types of theories are most useful to them in explaining those areas of focus?
- What are the foundational assumptions of interpretive and critical theories?
- What is the range of theories that have been described as comprising the constructionist approach?

Why Are Some Acts Considered Deviant? Using Interpretive and Critical Theories

As we have already noted, a wide range of specific theories are utilized to explain the social construction of deviance and normality. In the remainder of this chapter, the interpretive and critical theories that will be reviewed are some of the most commonly used in explaining the construction of deviance, and those which have had significant influences on the sociology of deviance as a discipline.

Interpretive Theories

Symbolic Interactionism

Symbolic interactionism, or what some people simply refer to as *interactionism*, is the foundation for the range of interpretive theories used to study deviance; in fact, some deviance specialists (e.g., Deutschmann, 2002) equate interactionism with interpretive theories and with constructionism. This section of the chapter will begin with a broad discussion of the core assumptions of symbolic interactionism, and will then progress to a discussion of some more specific components of interpretive theories of deviance—the dramatization of evil, labelling, and stigmatization.

From a symbolic interactionist perspective (Blumer, 1986), society is created by social interaction, which occurs via communication through symbols. In other words, society is made up of people in constant communication with each other, as depicted in this chapter's opening photo; this is the source of all meaning and understanding. All communication is perceived as being symbolic in nature. The symbols that constitute the English alphabet serve as the foundation for written and verbal communication in English. For example, in English, we use the symbols C-A-T to refer to a small furry creature that meows and grabs your toes under the covers when you are trying to sleep; other languages use other symbols to refer to the same creature. Nonverbal communication, through avenues such as gestures and facial expressions, is symbolic as well. For example, when you have cut someone off in traffic, and you are subsequently shown that person's middle finger, you know precisely what message that person is communicating to you. When your boss frowns when you ask if you can leave early, you know what message is being conveyed. Clothing serves as a form of symbolic communication as well. For instance, when you are going to a job interview, do you wear sweatpants and a stained t-shirt? Why not? Do you think that would communicate the wrong message to the interviewer? All of these forms of symbolic communication are what constitute the basic foundation of society, according to symbolic interactionists. Everything else that occurs in society arises from this foundation of symbolic communication.

Via these avenues of communication, we create meaning in our lives and an understanding of the world around us. Because each of us has a distinct set of interactions during the course of our lives, the way each of us understands the world varies to some extent. Thus, for example, my interpretation of a particular movie or novel may be different than your interpretation of that same movie or novel. Both of us may watch the documentary *Bowling for Columbine* and, because of our different interpretations, engage in a resounding debate afterward. The way you choose to act as a student in a college classroom may be different than the way someone else chooses to act in that same environment. Various processes contribute to the meanings and understandings each of us creates. One of these processes is that of **role-taking**. By vicariously placing ourselves in the roles of others, we try to see the world from their points of view, and determine our own attitudes and actions accordingly. In that regard, your professors may try to imagine what it is like being a student today, and what skills you will most benefit from in your future careers, when they are deciding how to teach a course, what assignments to give, and what videos to show. When you are going for a job interview, you may try to imagine the position of the interviewers and what they are looking for in a job candidate when you are deciding what to wear and how to answer their questions. A second process that contributes to the way we develop meaning is through the role of the **looking glass self**. When determining how to look or act and how we feel about ourselves, we imagine how we appear to other people; what we imagine other people think of us influences what we think about ourselves and how we look or act. These "others" may be *significant others* or a *generalized other*. **Significant others** are those people who are important to us, those people whose perceptions and opinions matter to us. What these significant others think about you has a significant impact on your actions—you might think "What would my grandmother/husband/boss/favourite professor say if I did that?!" The **generalized other** refers to "other people" more generally as almost a generic person—"What would people think if I dressed like that?!" Through the influences of role-taking, the looking glass self, significant others, and the generalized other, we come to understand the world in particular ways, understand our places in that world, and choose our appearances and actions.

Ask Yourself:

Think for a few moments about the roles that these processes have played in your own life. In what situations have you tried to understand the world from someone else's point of view? When have you looked to other people to figure out how you should be looking or acting? Have there been times when other people's opinions of you have affected your own opinion about yourself? Who are the specific people in your life whose opinions matter the most to you? How much does what others think about you matter to you?

In the above exercise, perhaps you recalled a time when you imagined what it must be like to be homeless, and consequently gave your spare change to a panhandler. Maybe you look to the media to figure out what constitutes "attractiveness," what clothes you should wear, what your body should look like, or how a "real man" should act. Upon finding yourself at a formal restaurant, perhaps you surreptitiously watch other people in order to know which fork to use first. Maybe after enough people told you that you were stupid, fat, or good-for-nothing, you started to believe it yourself and began to act accordingly. Perhaps last time you missed class due to illness, you were afraid that your favourite professor would think you were skipping, and so brought a medical note to your professor even though you were not required to—you did not want your favourite professor to think poorly of you. Looking at role-taking, the looking glass self, significant others, and the generalized other in the context of your own life makes it quite easy to see the usefulness of symbolic interactionism in understanding processes of social construction and social typing.

As applied to understanding deviance and normality, these processes constitute how we develop a perception of what the social rules are, and decide whether we will live in accordance with those rules or disregard them. It is also through these processes that individuals who share some perceptions come together and form groups based on those shared perceptions; these groups may then attempt to influence the perceptions of deviance and normality held by others. And because meanings and understandings vary among people based on their own interactions and communications, the "deviance dance" emerges—some individuals or groups will try to socially type certain people as deviant, while other individuals or groups will argue that those same people are normal, not deviant. Deviance specialists who hold an interactionist view may focus on many different aspects of this deviance dance. How do people develop particular understandings of deviance? What sociocultural and individual forces influence these understandings? What leads some people to join groups that consist of others with similar understandings? How do participants in the deviance dance understand and attribute meaning to their roles in the social construction process? How do they understand the other participants? What do the people who are the focus of this struggle over deviance and normality think about the whole situation, and how do they understand their own experiences? How do people and groups try to influence the perceptions of other people and groups? The specific questions that can be asked from within this approach are almost endless. However, what they have in common is the foundational assumption of the symbolic interactionist perspective—we develop understanding and attribute meaning to the world around us and to ourselves on the basis of interactions we have had with other people in our lives.

Box 3.1 The Meaning of Being Straightedge

The emphasis on interpretation and meaning that underlies the interactionist approach is vital to researchers who study various subcultures or lifestyle groups. Research done with nudists (Weinberg, 1967), gangs (Jankowski, 1991), and people with tattoos (DeMello, 2000), among others, revolves around interviewing members of those groups to explore what that lifestyle means to them. Recently, the straightedge lifestyle has been the focus of this type of research attention as well (Atkinson, 2003; Irwin, 1999; Wood, 1999; Wood, 2001).

To the outside observer a straightedger may look like any other punk rocker—Doc Martens, shaved heads, Mohican hairstyles, torn clothing. And, indeed, the straightedge movement did emerge from the punk rock scene. However, there are distinct characteristics of straightedgers that make them very different from other punk rockers, and from mainstream society. The lifestyle is referred to as *straight*edge because of its ideological epicentre—a clean, straight, physically pure life. Disturbed by the hedonistic, self-indulgent nature of modern life, straightedgers develop an oppositional value system based on abstaining from alcohol, drugs, and casual (or even premarital) sex. Some members of this lifestyle group abstain from caffeine, prescription drugs, and over-the-counter medication as well. This value system does not come out of any strongly held religious belief system, as you might expect, but rather from their personal observations of where self-indulgence leads people. They have seen how one night of "fun" can ruin people's lives from drug overdoses, drunk driving, sexually transmitted diseases, unwanted pregnancies, and the many other "stupid" things people frequently do while intoxicated. In addition to ruining people's lives, they also perceive these hedonistic behaviours as holding people back from personal fulfillment and self-awareness, as well as having a negative impact on society. Controlling their bodies through physical purity and body modification (such as tattooing) is a form of resistance to the self-indulgent wider society.

There is, however, diversity within straightedge. That is, the meaning of being straightedge varies somewhat among individuals. Within the broader pursuit of physical purity and resistance to mainstream society, some individuals incorporate other behaviours—vegetarianism, anti-racist activism, militant animal rights activism, and violence directed at people who are engaging in the behaviours seen as "deviant" by straightedgers (e.g., consuming drugs). Those straightedgers who engage in violence against others in order to spread their message, or violence in pursuit of militant animal rights activism, face the disdain of other straightedgers; within the straightedge lifestyle itself they are socially typed as "deviant" by those who wish to distance themselves (and the larger straightedge lifestyle) from extremists. Being straightedge means different things to different people, and symbolic interactionist ideas allow us to understand why.

Labelling and Stigmatization. Arising from these core assumptions are a number of specific concepts and theories used to understand the social construction of deviance. One of the most widely used interpretive or interactionist theories in the study of deviance is **labelling theory**. According to labelling theory, deviance is a label that is attached to some people, which then has consequences for how they are treated by others and how they come to identify themselves; this has consequences for their subsequent actions in life. This view of deviance is most often associated with Howard Becker (1963), but other scholars who preceded him also utilized notions of labelling.

Tannenbaum (1938) spoke of the role that **tagging** plays in the **dramatization of evil**. He suggested that we, as observers in society, may initially identify a particular act as deviant or "evil," but soon come to generalize that judgment to the person as a whole—we identify the actor as deviant or "evil." This act of *tagging* the individual results in changes in that person's self-image and identity, whereby the identity comes to be built around the label, and subsequent behaviours correspond to the label and to the new identity.

Lemert (1951) used the term "labelling" rather than the term "tagging" in what is perhaps the most well-known version of labelling theory. Lemert distinguished between **primary deviance** and **secondary deviance**. He suggested that we all engage in little acts of rule-breaking that are seldom noticed and rarely caught by others (i.e., primary deviance). Even though we all engage in occasional rule-breaking, few of us build a lifestyle around it (i.e., secondary deviance).

Getting caught sets into motion a series of processes that result in the transition from primary deviance (i.e., a deviant act) to secondary deviance (i.e., a lifestyle built around deviance). Someone who is not caught in an act of deviance may simply move on to other things in time. For instance, as a child or a teenager you may have shoplifted something of low value from a neighbourhood convenience store, but it is likely that most of you only did that once or twice and eventually grew out of that "phase." However, Lemert suggested that the mere act of being caught changes the way others see you, and subsequently changes the way you see yourself. That is, if you were caught shoplifting, and then arrested, the police saw you as a "thief." If convicted in youth court, you were officially labelled a "thief" and a "delinquent." Your parents may have then considered you to be a "thief." As a result of this process of labelling, you come to see yourself as a "thief" or a "delinquent," and figure you might as well act accordingly.

Howard Becker (1963) elaborated upon the processes involved in the transition to secondary deviance. He suggested that once labelled deviant, that label becomes a **master status**. A master status is a characteristic by which others identify you; for example, you may immediately identify others on the basis of age (e.g., "teenager"), sex (e.g., "girl"), or class (e.g., "rich"). A deviant label assumes the level of master status; if you have been officially given the label of "thief," others will identify you as "that thief" rather than as "Sam." Once a deviant label becomes a master status, implications for the person's daily life emerge. Certain life opportunities will be blocked, in that the legitimate, "normal" world will no longer be as accepting. This is particularly the case if the deviant label is a criminal label, but non-criminal deviant labels result in some blocked opportunities as well. With the conforming world no longer being as accepting, the only place to turn for acceptance may be the deviant world. For example, if you were convicted of theft as a youth, the way you were treated at school may have changed. Perhaps certain peer groups began to exclude you because they did not want to hang out with a "thief." Maybe the girl you were dating broke up with you because she did not want to tarnish her own reputation. The teacher who had offered you a babysitting job on Wednesday nights with her children may have revoked the offer. Soon, you begin to feel like an "outsider" (which happens to be the title of Becker's 1963 book). At that point, it may have been that only other kids who had been labelled "troublemakers" or "delinquents" were willing to spend time with you; that became the only world in which you felt accepted. And before long, you began to see yourself as a "troublemaker"—your identity gradually changed, and your behaviour soon followed. This process of exclusion from the conforming world, and acceptance in the deviant world, is what Becker suggested led to a lifestyle built around deviance, what Lemert (1951) had called *secondary deviance*.

Other deviance specialists have referred to this process of exclusion, of becoming an outsider, as **stigmatization** (Goffman, 1963). A proponent of the sociological school of thought known as **dramaturgy**, Goffman (1959) suggested that social life is analogous to being in the theatre. In our lives, we are all assigned certain "roles" to play—college student, daughter, soccer player, homosexual, smoker. When we

Ask Yourself:

In your own life, has there ever been anything about yourself that you have tried to hide from the outside world because of your fear of stigmatization? For instance, you may have had a run-in with the law when you were a teenager, and you now hope no one will ever find out about it. Or perhaps you had a substance abuse problem in the past, and now when someone offers you a drink you claim that you are allergic to alcohol so that you do not have to explain yourself. Have you ever restricted your interactions to people you knew would be accepting of you, people you knew would be able to understand you? For example, by hanging out only with members of your own religious group, perhaps you feel that you can avoid being stigmatized, teased, or discriminated against because of your religious belief system. Have you ever proudly displayed an aspect of yourself that you know many people in society consider to be deviant? For instance, maybe you have intentionally taken your interest in the music, clothes, movies, and attitudes associated with a Gothic lifestyle to an extreme, by dying your hair black, wearing black lipstick, putting white makeup on your face, and choosing particular kinds of clothes to wear that you know will "advertise" your interests to anyone who sees you.

are in front of certain groups of people, we play our roles in certain ways—we manage the impressions our audience has of us, through bringing out our **front stage selves**. When we leave the front stage and retreat with the select groups of people who are a part of our private lives, we allow our **back stage selves** to emerge; that is, we no longer feel like we have to engage in impression management. If the role others have assigned to us is deviant in nature (i.e., we have had a deviant label attached to us), managing the impressions others have of us is that much more difficult. No matter what we try to do, others will still perceive us as deviant, because we have been *stigmatized*. Once stigmatized, we may continue to try to hide the stigma from the outside world (with varying levels of success), we may retreat to a world of similarly stigmatized others who will understand what we are going through and will accept us, or we may embrace the stigma and proudly show it to the world. For example, some people who are stigmatized because of being homosexual may try to hide their sexual orientation and give the appearance of having a "normal" heterosexual life, by dating members of the opposite sex, getting married, and having children. Others may immerse themselves within a gay or lesbian subculture, so that their social lives are largely limited to similar people from whom they do not have to hide their sexual orientation. And yet others may grab placards and march in a "gay pride" parade, or wear buttons claiming "Gay and Proud." These are all different responses to the same experience, that of being stigmatized.

Although Goffman's work on stigmatization emphasizes the negative impact of stigma, there are potentially positive consequences of stigmatization in certain situations. Braithwaite (2000) postulates **reintegrative shaming** as an effective treatment for criminal behaviour. With reintegrative shaming, the criminal is stigmatized, or shamed, for the criminal act, but it is a temporary stigma; the criminal is shown that leaving criminality behind will result in being fully accepted back into the community. Research with former psychiatric patients has also found that being labelled can have a wide range of positive consequences, including enhancing personal growth, bringing families closer together, and exempting such individuals from some of the demands and responsibilities of daily life (Herman & Miall, 1990).

Early interactionists, and particularly early labelling theorists, frequently painted a picture of the labelled deviant as a powerless, passive recipient of a socially constructed label that subsequently had irreversible consequences of the deviant's life. However, later deviance specialists have emphasized the possibility of resistance to a deviant label. Kitsuse (1980) refers to **tertiary deviance** as a stage that can potentially emerge after the transition from primary to secondary deviance. Some people who have been labelled, and who then develop an identity and a lifestyle based on that label, may resist the idea that the label is a "deviant" one. That is, they may go on to try to change social norms, to show society that whatever behaviour they may have engaged in or whatever characteristic they may have, is not "deviant" at all; they seek to redefine "normal" to include whatever act or characteristic they have been labelled for. For example, some groups of gay and bisexual men who are HIV positive engage in activism to remove the stigma associated with their illness, and to increase acceptance in society (Siegel, Lane, & Meyer, 1998).

Whether we use the terminology of "the dramatization of evil," "tagging," "labelling," or "stigmatization," the processes of deviance being referred to are similar. Being perceived as "deviant" affects the way people treat us, which affects the way we see ourselves, which then affects the way we act in the future. But in addition to studying the processes that occur after being "caught" at deviance, some interactionists are also interested in the **deviant career**.

The Deviant Career. In addition to the work already discussed, Howard Becker (1963) utilized the concept of the "deviant career" to study deviance. He postulated that deviance is something that emerges, progresses, and changes over time; there are stages to involvement in deviance, just as there are stages in the development of a career. Thus, the concept of the "career" refers not to those who make a living out of deviance, but rather the way that deviance unfolds in people's lives. Just as with the traditional notion of a "career," people enter deviance, manage their experiences of deviance, and may quit (or exit) deviance. Becker illustrated this sequential model of deviance with marijuana users, exploring the stages by which they became marijuana users, acted as marijuana users, and stopped using marijuana at some point. Other deviance specialists have utilized the concept of the career to analyze the transition from pre-mental patient to ex-mental patient (Goffman, 1959), and becoming a cocaine dealer (Murphy, Waldorf, & Reinarman, 1990). Particular deviance specialists may focus specifically on the entrance phases, the management phases, or the exit phases of the deviant career. Various **career contingencies**, or what may be seen as significant *turning points*, influence the directions that people take within the deviant career. For example, interactions that lead people to interpret their lives as "lonely" may result in certain deviant behaviours (e.g., substance use), being officially labelled may lead some people to become involved with deviant subcultures (i.e., groups of similar others), and interactions that change self-perceptions may cause some people to exit deviance. The core interactionist concepts and assumptions discussed earlier in the chapter, such as role-taking, meaning, understanding, and communication are applied to the notion of deviant careers.

A Closing Look at Interpretive Theories

Interpretive theories focus on the construction of meaning and understanding within interpersonal interactions, as well as the consequences of people's understandings for how they treat others and how they perceive themselves. These theories draw our attention to various aspects of deviance, such as the processes by which understandings of deviance and normality develop in people's lives, and the processes by which variation in these understandings among individuals and groups materializes. They give us insight into the emergence of the "deviance dance," wherein some people will say that Group X is deviant and can be fixed in a certain way, while other people will agree that Group X is deviant but can be fixed in a different way, and other people will say that Group X is not deviant at all. These theories shine a spotlight on how someone's lifestyle and identity may come to be based on deviance, on the different ways that individuals may react once they are identified as deviant by others, and on how some people may exit deviance. However, interpretive theories in themselves do not help us understand how some people are more able than others to influence what will and will not be given a deviant label in a particular society at a particular time in history. Nor do these theories explain how some people are more able than others to determine the direction that the "deviance dance" will take. Although different people will have varying perceptions of deviance and normality, some people's perceptions have more of an impact on the larger society; in other words, some people's perceptions count more than others. This is where critical theories of deviance step in—exploring the role of *power* in the social construction of deviance.

TIME TO REVIEW:

- According to symbolic interactionism, what is the result of symbolic communication? What do the concepts of role-taking, the looking glass self, significant others, and the generalized other refer to?
- How can the processes described within the symbolic interactionist approach help us understand the concept of the "deviance dance"?
- What are the core assumptions of "labelling theory"? What are some of the different ways that various interpretive deviance specialists have discussed the process of labelling? In answering the latter question, you should refer to (a) tagging and the dramatization of evil, (b) primary and secondary deviance, (c) master status, and (d) stigmatization.

- According to the dramaturgical school of thought, what is social life analogous to? In what ways do we act differently in front of an "audience" compared to in the privacy of our own homes?
- What are different potential responses to being stigmatized? Does being stigmatized always have only negative consequences? Are people always powerless and passive recipients of a stigmatizing label?
- What does the concept of the "deviant career" add to our understanding of deviance?

Critical Theories

The range of theories that have been categorized as **critical theories** of deviance is quite substantial—Marxist theories, non-Marxist conflict theories, non-conflict critical theories, feminist theories, postmodernist theories, discourse theories, anarchist theories, peacemaking theories, radical multicultural theories, and more (Pfohl, 1994; Deutschmann, 2002; Ward, Carter, & Penn, 1994). What these theories have in common is both theoretical and practical in nature. At a theoretical level, these are all theories that analyze "the relationship between human struggles for power in history and the ritual construction, deconstruction, and reconstruction of normative social boundaries" (Pfohl, 1994, p. 404). At a practical level, these are all theories that have an emancipatory interest, that is, an interest in working toward social justice for society's powerless. In the remainder of this chapter, a range of critical theories that have been definitive for the study of deviance will be reviewed—conflict theories, power-reflexive theories, feminist theories, and postmodern theories.

Conflict Theories

Although **conflict theories** themselves are of considerable diversity, they do share some core assumptions (McCaghy, Capron, & Jamieson, 2003). First, they presume that social rules do not emerge out of consensus, but rather out of conflict, and serve the interests of the most influential groups in society. Second, they suggest that members of powerful groups are less likely to break the rules, because the rules were created in order to serve their interests in the first place. Third, conflict theories propose that members of less powerful groups are more likely to act in ways that violate social rules, either because (a) their sense of oppression and alienation causes them to act out in rule-breaking ways, or (b) because social rules have defined the acts of the powerless as deviant in the first place. Precisely which groups are perceived as being in conflict varies among specific conflict theories, but all conflict theories integrate propositions about the structures of inequality that exist in society with the ideologies that are used to maintain the status quo and reproduce the existing structures of inequality (Beaman, 2000).

The origins of conflict theory are typically attributed to Karl Marx, who proposed that society consists of a small group of powerful people at the top, and a

Karl Marx is considered the "father" of conflict theory.

large group of powerless people at the bottom. He ascribed these power differentials to economic factors, specifically the relationship to the means of production. Society's powerful (i.e., the **bourgeoisie**) are those who own the means of production; society's powerless (i.e., the **proletariat**) are the wage earners who work for the people who own the means of production. The sense of alienation experienced by the proletariat due to their working conditions gives rise to deviant behaviour among some people. Later Marxists fell into two general camps, **instrumental Marxists** and **structural Marxists**. Instrumental Marxists (e.g., Quinney, 1977) propose that institutionalized social rules, such as the law, are created by the powerful in order to serve the interests of the powerful, the owners of the means of production. A deviant label thereby becomes an instrument used to control the proletariat and maintain the economic structure in society. Structural Marxists (e.g., Chambliss & Seidman, 1982) propose that institutionalized social rules are created by the powerful in order to protect the capitalist economic system, rather than to protect individual capitalists. The need to maintain the power of the economic system as a whole means that even members of the bourgeoisie may be subject to a deviant label if their behaviour threatens the fundamental principles of capitalism.

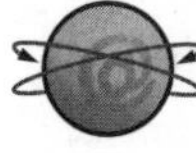

AN INTERNET MOMENT:

A number of contemporary political and social activism groups in Canada have Marxist theory as their foundation. For example, you can go to the Website of the Communist Party of Canada Marxist-Leninist at *http://www.cpcml.ca* to learn more about how Marxist ideas are being applied in Canadian society today. This Website will tell you about the political party itself, but also provides information on a number of social issues in provinces across the country, such as educational funding cuts. The way these issues are addressed on the Website will show you how a Marxist theoretical framework influences the way social issues and events are interpreted.

Although Marxist conflict theories are based upon the presumption of economic structures of inequality, **pluralist conflict theories** focus on multiple axes of inequality that make up the structure of society, based upon conflicts between various economic, religious, ethnic, political, and social groups. Sellin's (1938) **culture conflict theory** claims that, in societies having multiple, diverse cultural groups, there will be multiple sets of norms that may conflict with each other. Dominant cultural groups have the power to impose the norms that comprise their culture on all other cultural groups in society, labelling the norms of conflicting cultural groups as "deviant" and in need of measures of social control. For example, some years ago Sikh RCMP officers were not permitted to wear turbans (even those with the same patterns of coloration and having the same RCMP insignia as the hats that were a part of the uniform), a central component of their religious and cultural belief system; the norms of Euro-Canadian cultural groups had been the ones integrated into the rules governing dress in the RCMP. Tremendous debate emerged among different groups of Canadians. Some groups claimed that the hat that was part of the RCMP uniform was a fundamental symbol of Canadian identity that "foreigners" had no right to tamper with; this side of the debate illustrates the notion of cultural conflict quite nicely. Other groups countered that the RCMP uniform had changed multiple times over the past century, and the hat that was part of the current uniform could not be considered a fundamental part of Canadian identity. Furthermore, they pointed out that the Canadian government had no problem with Sikh men wearing turbans when they were laying their lives on the line as Canadian soldiers during World War II. This counterargument illustrates the idea that rules are constructed by the powerful to serve their own needs at the time.

In **group conflict theory**, George Vold (1958) extended conflict assumptions not just to cultural groups, but a wide range of other groups as well. He suggested that multiple groups are always maneuvering for more power in society, and conflict with each other as a result of their simultaneous struggles for power. The norms or social rules of certain groups gain more legitimacy in society because these groups are able to get authorities on their side more effectively. In situations of conflict, crime and deviance emerge because people will commit acts they do not normally engage in (e.g., vandalism, assault) in pursuit of their higher goal—trying to attain more power for their social groups.

Austin Turk (1969) stated that the core struggle in society is more broadly between *those who are in positions of authority* and *those who are subject to authority*. Those who are in authority try to maintain their authority through convincing society's less powerful groups of the validity of the existing social rules, using as much coercion as necessary if the less powerful groups refuse to be "convinced." Socially typing the norms or actions of conflicting groups as deviant is one of the ways that positions of authority can be maintained.

Whether referring to Marxist theories, the above pluralist conflict theories, or one of the many other criminological conflict theories that have been proposed (e.g., Richard Quinney's radical conflict theory; Left Realism), the theoretical interest in exploring the struggle for power and its role in defining social norms, and the practical interest in emancipation, together define critical theories of deviance. In essence, the various conflict theories postulate that different groups in society have different interests and perceptions of what the rules should be; however, having more power and resources enables groups to pursue their own interests more effectively. Thus, the "rules" as perceived by powerful groups are imposed on all of the groups that make up society as a whole. In this regard, it is society's powerful who are able to construct the dominant moral code by which deviance and normality are defined. Powerful groups are able to maintain their power by socially typing the interests and the perceptions of other social groups as deviant; they are able to quash the competition simply by creating rules that deviantize the competitors' behaviours. Of course, in contemporary democratic societies powerful groups cannot act in ways that would make them look like authoritarian dictators engaged in constant oppression. Instead, they maintain their power by convincing enough of the populace that they are responsive to the interests of the people, and are working in everyone's best interests. Consequently, powerful groups must strike a balance between pursuing their own interests, integrating some of the interests of society's masses, and integrating the desires of vocal interest groups. In the end, "deviance" is a label that justifies the control efforts of powerful groups and thereby helps them to maintain their power.

Convincing society's masses that those in positions of authority in society are working in everyone's best interests involves manufacturing a worldview within which the actions of the powerful seem logical. Marx and other conflict theorists used the term **ideology**, in its broad sense, to refer to the world view of society's powerful groups, a world view based on the interests and needs of the ruling class. This ideology is then taught to citizens as "common-sense" via institutions such as schools and the media. A later school of critical theorists that grew out of the conflict perspective (but developed what came to be known more generally as "critical theory"), the Frankfurt School, focuses much of its work on the idea of **false consciousness** (originally a Marxian concept). When such false consciousness develops among society's repressed, people came to perceive the existing oppressive social system as rational and acceptable. Finally, Antonio Gramsci developed the concept of **hegemony** to refer to the dominant world view, a way of seeing and understanding the world that is intertwined with institutionalized power. The role of ideology, false consciousness, or hegemony is to render any alternative ways of seeing and understanding the world as outside of the realm of possibility in most people's minds—the dominant view becomes "common sense." All of these conflict theorists suggested that change is possible. That is, there will always be some people in society who are able to see the ideological nature of "common sense," and the hidden interests operating in the institutionalized knowledge of society. The goal of theory and action, they suggest, is to enlighten society's masses, so that they too become aware of ideology, false consciousness, or hegemony. Only then can hierarchal structures of power be changed in order to create social justice.

TIME TO REVIEW:

- What are the theoretical interest and the practical interest that are shared among critical theories? What are the three core assumptions shared among various conflict theories?
- What factor did Karl Marx say distinguished the people at the top of society from the people at the bottom of society? What did he label these groups?
- What is the difference between "instrumental Marxists" and "structural Marxists"?
- How are pluralist conflict theories different from Marxist conflict theories? Describe the following pluralist conflict theories: (a) culture conflict theory; (b) group conflict theory; and (c) Turk's theory of conflict and authority.
- Whose rules constitute society's dominant moral code, and why? How do society's powerful groups maintain their power?

Power-Reflexive Theories

Power-reflexive theories, or what Pfohl (1994) calls **critical poststructuralist theories**, are built upon a foundation that emphasizes the intertwining of knowledge and power. Within these theories it is proposed that all claims to knowledge are socially situated, embedded within relations of power. Multiple **discourses** (i.e., bodies of knowledge, or everything that is "known") coexist in society; relations of power determine which claims to knowledge come to be institutionalized, or perceived as "truth" within society as a whole (Foucault, 1980). For example, during the Middle Ages in Europe, the claims made by the Christian church (as a governing body in most European nations) were seen as the "truth." With the Enlightenment and the related development and growth of science, the claims made by "science" were accorded more "truth" than the claims of the Christian church. As we will address in a later chapter, in contemporary society the claims made by science are granted more legitimacy in the eyes of the public than any other claims to truth being made.

Deviance specialists drawing upon a power-reflexive tradition have three tasks (Pfohl, 1994). First, they must make clear how their own claims to knowledge are embedded within larger social situations; that is, they must emphasize how their own position in society affects the way they see the world, the way they do research, and the knowledge claims that result. Second, they must embed their analyses of substantive topics (e.g., mental illness) within simultaneous analyses of the larger society; in other words, they must address what their research tells us about broader power relations in society. Third, they must link their analyses to an emancipatory interest that advances social justice—they must address how they can work toward making the world a better place based on what they have learned from their research.

Power-reflexive researchers frequently link their research results to power relations in society by studying particular discourses that make up accepted social beliefs. For example, Bereska (2003) analyzes discourses of masculinity as integrated in Young Adult novels for boys, from the 1940s to the late 1990s. This analysis reveals that what boys are told about the "right" way to be a Real Man did not change during that time period and, in fact, is virtually identical to how boys living one hundred years earlier were told to behave. An analysis of these results is then embedded within a discussion of the continued presence of patriarchal power relations in society, the limited successes of feminist movements, and the "crisis in American boyhood" observed by other researchers (e.g., Pollack, 1998).

Renowned poststructuralist Michel Foucault, in addition to theorizing about the linkages between power and knowledge, also engaged in substantial theorizing about social control (Foucault, 1995). He proposed that, with the industrialization and bureaucratization of society, numerous mechanisms of social control or regulation were developed to ensure "normal" behaviour and punish or prevent "deviant" behaviour. But the most effective means of social control is self-control or self-regulation. Regulatory mechanisms are so pervasive within the structures and processes of society that eventually most of us do not need to be watched for normative transgressions—we engage in self-surveillance, and regulate our own behaviours. That is, we become our own "Big Brother" and endlessly watch ourselves for transgressions. For example, you may not need an outside comment about your body in order for you to lower your caloric intake or intensify your exercise program; instead, you may carefully inspect your own body and decide that you are "fat" and must improve your diet and exercise program to make your body more acceptable. A power-reflexive researcher would then go on to analyze the processes of power and knowledge creation in society, and the discourses that are present that gave you the knowledge base to judge your own body in the first place.

TIME TO REVIEW:

- What do power-reflexive theories focus on?
- How are claims to knowledge related to power relations? Give an example.
- What are the main tasks of power-reflexive researchers?
- What has Michel Foucault taught us about social control?

Feminist Theories

Although when the word "feminism" is mentioned many people get a stereotypical image of feminism (usually an overweight, unattractive, short-haired, man-hating lesbian vocalizing the evils of *man*-kind), there are multiple forms of **feminist theory** and practice, often quite distinct from each other, and sometimes in intense conflict with each other (Nelson & Robinson, 1999). What the wide range of feminist theories has in common is a focus on the experiences of women in society, and the distinction of their experiences from male experiences. Historically, the discipline of sociology has in large part been a male-oriented enterprise—male sociologists studying and theorizing about male social experiences. Mainstream sociological theories, particularly those dating from the emergence of the discipline until the mid- to late-20th century, have often been guilty of ignoring women altogether (and implicitly or explicitly assuming that the male experience can be generalized to understanding the female experience). They may also treat women in a peripheral fashion, as the Other that stands in contrast to the normative male standard. For example, some social theorists first developed a "theory of society," and then (usually much later), a separate "theory of women," as though women were somehow separate from or outside of "society." (For an analysis of these historical trends, see Rosalind Sydie's 1994 book *Natural Women, Cultured Men: A Feminist Perspective on Sociological Theory*).

In studying deviance, feminist theories in general underscore the fact that the socially constructed norms by which we judge deviance and normality frequently vary for women and men. That is, what are considered "normal" behaviours, appearances, or characteristics for women are quite different than for men. For example, a woman who wants to work in a daycare centre will be viewed very differently than a man who wants to work in a daycare centre; she is far more likely to be perceived as "normal," while he is far more likely to be perceived as "deviant." Similarly, a women who dislikes being around children is more likely to be seen as abnormal than is a man who dislikes being around children. In relation to power, most feminist theories also share the assumption that, historically, society has been structured in ways that serve the interests of males.

But outside of these shared basic assumptions, the feminist analysis of and theorizing about deviance varies tremendously. For example, the causes of prostitution, problems of prostitution, and solutions to prostitution are perceived very differently by radical feminists and liberal feminists, whereby radical feminists see prostitution as one more example of the sexual oppression of women within patriarchy, while liberal feminists are more likely to see it as an occupation in which women need to be given more control over working conditions (Larsen, 2000; Peace, Beaman, & Sneddon, 2000). Other feminists, looking at prostitution, might be more likely to explore why female prostitutes have been more likely to be socially typed as deviant than have their male customers. And yet other feminists might focus on how prostitution came to be socially typed as a deviant activity in the first place.

The complexities of feminist theories and feminist theorizing about deviance are further magnified when we consider the fact that, not only is there a wide range of distinct "feminist theories" (such as radical feminism, cultural feminism, liberal feminism, and maternal feminism), but feminist theorizing is also done from within virtually every theoretical perspective addressed in this book. That is, there are feminist interactionist theories, Marxist feminist theories, feminist functionalist theories, feminist learning theories, and feminist social control theories. Feminist theorizing, in its diversity, is becoming fully integrated into the study of deviance as a whole. Despite the fact that feminist theorizing has been incorporated into the positivist and interpretive theories reviewed in this book (as well as into other types of critical theories), feminist theories are often categorized as inherently critical theories. That is because of their foundation in the theoretical interest in exploring power relations in society, and the practical interest in emancipation—achieving equality for women in society.

TIME TO REVIEW:

- Is there a single "feminist theory"?
- What do feminist theories have in common?
- How can feminist theories be applied to the study of deviance and normality?

Box 3.2 Are There "Masculinist" Theories?

Until well into the 1980s, "gender" was a concept that was equated with "female" in both the public mind and in academic research. To speak of "gender" was to speak of women's experiences in society. However, more recently scholars have recognized that "gender" is a concept that is applicable to both women's and men's lives. During the 1990s, research about various aspects of men and "gender" grew enormously, eventually coming to be seen as a distinct field of study. Groundbreaking books in the development of this field of study include *Manhood in America: A Cultural History* (Kimmel, 1996), *Masculinities* (Connell, 1995), and the anthology *Men's Lives* (Kimmel & Messner, 1989); today, there are also academic journals devoted to research about men and gender, such as *The Journal of Men's Studies*. Research has explored topics as diverse as how the meaning of being a "real man" has changed (or not changed) over time (Kimmel, 1996; Bereska, 2003), the role of organized sports in the development of masculinity in boys (Messner, 1990), how homeless men are able to redefine what "manhood" means (Nonn, 1998), and how *Playboy* magazine shapes the structure of masculinity in its readers (Beggan & Allison, 2003).

Despite the growth in men's studies, as yet there is no cohesive body of theories equivalent to "feminist theories" that can be labelled "masculinist theories" (although there are more generic approaches that can be considered "gender theories"). But just as there are many different feminist theories, there are also diverse approaches used within men's studies. Many men's studies researchers propose that traditional gender roles constrain and negatively impact men's lives, just as they do women's lives (Pollack, 1998). For example, on the popular television talk show *Oprah* in 1999, psychologist William Pollack suggested that the "mask of masculinity," wherein boys are taught that showing emotions (other than anger) will result in a label of "Sissy," has negative psychological consequences for boys. He said that repressed emotions turned inward contribute to depression, suicide, learning disabilities, and poor performance in school among males; repressed emotions turned outward contribute to violence, such as dating violence, physical fights with other males, and mass violence (e.g., public shootings). Just a few weeks after Pollack warned society of the dangers of the unemotional "mask of masculinity," the shootings at Columbine High School in Littleton, Colorado, occurred.

In contrast to those men's studies scholars who point to the negative impact of traditional gender roles on men's lives, others propose the opposite, that the loss of traditional gender roles is the cause of many social problems today. At its most extreme, this approach blames "femi-Nazis" for making white men the most discriminated-against group in society today. These divergent, and even contradictory, approaches within men's studies parallel the diversity within feminist theory; there may not be a body of "masculinist theories" as such, but theory is still the foundation of men's studies.

Postmodern Theories

If discussing "feminist theories" as a cohesive category is difficult and somewhat artificial, discussing **postmodern theories** as a cohesive category is perhaps even more so. In fact, there is limited agreement about precisely what constitutes "postmodern" theorizing, and whether or not it can be included within the category of "critical theories." For instance, postmodernism is sometimes equated with the power-reflexive or critical poststructuralist theories addressed earlier, such as the work of Foucault (e.g., Deutschmann, 2002; Peace, Beaman, & Sneddon, 2000). Postmodern theories are broadly based on the notion of *rejection*—rejection of overarching theories of society (such as structural functionalism or symbolic interactionism), rejection of social categorization (e.g., "man"; "black"; "Christian"), and rejection of the possibility of "truth." At its extreme, postmodern theory is completely solipsistic, postulating that nothing exists outside of the individual mind (and perhaps the individual mind doesn't even exist). At its less extreme, it deconstructs what is seen as "knowledge," master narratives, or overarching theories, and focuses analysis on the local and specific.

Postmodernists claim that advanced capitalist societies faced rapid social change following the end of World War II. Such societies can no longer be considered "industrial" societies, because symbols and culture (rather than products) have taken centre stage in the economy. Capitalism now exists primarily "by selling consumers new needs, new experiences, and new forms of meaning, all of which are defined exclusively by the marketplace" (Ashley & Orenstein, 2001, p. 475). Commercialism is the defining feature of society, with people pursuing "style over substance" (p. 475); even politics has become a commercial activity. People are "consumers" rather than "citizens," becoming politically indifferent, self-absorbed, and hedonistic in their endless pursuit of personal style. Postmodernists speak of the "end of the individual" for this very reason; the individual is nothing more than the style or image being pursued. Any notion of a dominant moral code by which we can judge deviance and normality is gradually being eroded: "The postmodern subject is besieged by an endless jumble of messages, codes, and ideas, most of which are incompatible, inconsistent, and quite infantile. Many people respond to the current cacophony of mostly commercial messages that bombard them daily by abandoning all hope that they ever could attain some kind of rational understanding of the world," becoming "an empty shell that is incapable of exercising any kind of critical judgment." (Ashley & Orenstein, 2001, p. 476).

Although postmodern assumptions, in their purer forms, are rarely used in analyses of deviance, the implications of the lack of a moral code and the creation of subjects that are incapable of critical judgment for the study of deviance are interesting to ponder. Is "deviance" possible if there is no moral code that serves as the foundation for its social construction? Can anyone be socially typed as deviant if people become incapable of critical judgment? Is a populace that is incapable of critical judgment simply more susceptible to the interests and whims of those who are in authority? In the study of deviance, postmodernism raises more questions than it answers.

TIME TO REVIEW:

- In what ways is postmodernism based on rejection?
- According to postmodernists, how have advanced capitalist societies changed since the end of World War II? How have people changed as a result?
- What does the "end of the individual" mean?
- What kinds of questions do postmodern assumptions raise for the study of deviance?

A Closing Look at Critical Theories

Critical theories are defined by a theoretical interest in the power struggles by which normative social boundaries are created, and a practical interest in the pursuit of social justice. Through their analyses, critical theorists try to determine the processes by which the views of certain groups of people, more than other groups of people, come to be applied to society as a whole—how some people's "rules" become society's "rules," and thereby serve as the standard against which deviance and normality are judged. Conflict theories focus on social structures that create an opposition between the powerful and the powerless. Power-reflexive theories emphasize the intertwining of power relations and claims to knowledge (including their own). Feminist theories focus on the gender bias embedded within most sociological knowledge claims of the past, and the historical oppression of women in society. Postmodern theories, which are still rather amorphous and hard to pin down, focus on the "end of the individual" and a rejection of the possibility of "truth"; they represent an important layer of recent theoretical development, although their usefulness for understanding the social construction of deviance is yet to be determined.

Taken together, critical theories and interpretive theories paint a picture of the social construction of deviance. Interpretive theories address the interactions between people by which diverse, and even contradictory, understandings of deviance and normality emerge. They also explore what happens to people once they have been labelled deviant, and how people who are considered deviant attribute meaning to their own life experiences. Interpretive theories draw our attention to the many steps involved in the deviance dance. On the other hand, critical theories address the role that power plays in the social construction of deviance, whereby the understandings of deviance held by more powerful groups in society are the understandings that become institutionalized. They draw our attention to the fact that some people are better able to determine the direction of the deviance dance—some people are allowed to "lead" the dance, and such people may be those of a particular sex, or those with more wealth, or those who control the media, or those whom we consider to be "scientists." Critical theorists look closely at various aspects of power relations, depending upon the particular theory in question, and their relationship to the way that deviance is socially constructed in a particular culture at a certain time in history.

At this point in the book we have explored what "deviance" is, and changing conceptions of deviance. We have also reviewed the dominant theoretical perspectives utilized by deviance specialists who have more objective understandings of deviance (i.e., positivist theories), and those utilized by deviance specialists who have more subjective understandings of deviance (i.e., interpretive and critical theories). Having established this foundation of knowledge about the discipline and how deviance may be studied, in the next section of the book we will turn our attention to an exploration of several substantive topics of deviance and normality—sexuality, youth, voluntary and involuntary physical appearance, mental disorder, science, and religion. As you progress through these substantive topics, the concepts, ideas, and theories that have been reviewed in the first three chapters of the book, for example, normative violation or social typing, will repeatedly emerge. The application of particular concepts and theories within the discussion of concrete situations will make these concepts and theories clearer over time.

Exercise Your Mind:

Review the theories addressed in this chapter. For each of the theories, ask yourself how that theory has helped you understand deviance better. Try to think of examples from your own life or your own observations to illustrate how that theory has facilitated your understanding. Then, for each theory, ask yourself what you still don't know about deviance. That is, what are you left wondering about deviance after learning about that theory? Try to think of examples from your own life to illustrate the gaps in understanding left after reading about each theory. This might be a good topic for discussion with your classmates, either inside or outside of the classroom. To follow up, you may want to go to the library (or hit the academic Internet databases that are available through your university) and find some of the critiques that have been launched at the various interpretive and critical theories we have addressed.

Chapter Summary

The positivist theories described in the previous chapter are the most useful for deviance specialists who have more objective understandings of deviance, and an interest in explaining deviant acts. However, deviance specialists who have more subjective understandings of deviance are not interested in the acts themselves, but rather in the way particular acts are socially constructed as deviant through the social typing process. *Interpretive* and *critical* theories are those theories that more subjective deviance specialists find most useful in understanding the social construction of deviance and normality.

Interpretive theories, with their emphasis on how meaning is created through social interaction and symbolic communication, draw our attention to how each of us comes to understand that certain acts are "deviant" while other acts are "normal." They also draw our attention to how different people develop contrasting understandings of deviance.

Labelling theory explains how the process of getting caught in a deviant act, and subsequently either formally or informally labelled as deviant, serves as the impetus for the transition from *primary* to *secondary* deviance. A deviant label becomes a *master status* that then limits our opportunities in the "normal" world, opens up opportunities in the "deviant" world, and changes a person's self-perception and identity.

Different people may react to being *stigmatized* in various ways, such as by trying to hide the stigma, by immersing oneself in a world of similarly stigmatized others, or by proudly displaying the stigma. Some recent researchers suggest that the effects of stigmatization are not always negative.

The notion of the *deviant career* is another interpretive strategy for exploring people's entrance into, management of, and possible exit from deviant activities.

Critical theories share a theoretical interest in the power struggles that define normative social boundaries, and a practical interest in emancipation. Diverse critical theories exist, including conflict theories, power-reflexive theories, feminist theories, and postmodern theories.

Conflict theories originated with the economic deterministic model of Karl Marx, and have progressed to *pluralist conflict theories* that point out how various axes of inequality create powerful groups who are able to impose their moral order on powerless groups. Successfully imposing their social rules on the rest of society involves convincing society's masses that those rules are in the best interests of everyone. *Ideology, false consciousness,* and *hegemony* are various concepts used to explain this process.

Power-reflexive theories emphasize the intertwining of power relations and claims to knowledge. They propose that all claims to knowledge are socially situated (including their own), embedded within power relations. They seek to clarify the positioning of their own knowledge claims, identify what the results of their specific analyses tell us about power relations in society, and determine how what they have learned can be used to make society a better place. Some power-reflexive theorists (e.g., Foucault, 1980) also analyze structures of surveillance of control, and the creation of self-surveillance, by which we regulate our own behaviours even if no one else is doing so.

Feminist theories are extremely diverse. However, they share an interest in gendered experiences and outcomes in society, the bias of existing mainstream sociological research and theories, and an interest in the emancipation of women and full gender equality. They suggest that deviance and normality are socially constructed in different ways for males and females in society.

Postmodern theories represent a recent theoretical development arising out of the social changes following the end of World War II. Their proponents promulgate the notion of the "end of the individual" in society as people have become consumers rather than citizens. These theorists reject overarching theories of society, and claim that the moral codes which would enable people to rationally understand society have eroded.

Recommended Readings

Lemert, E. (1951). *Social pathology*. New York: McGraw-Hill.

* This book elaborates upon the processes involved in labelling theory.

Goffman, E. (1963). *Stigma: Notes on the management of spoiled identity*. Englewood Cliffs, NJ: Prentice Hall.

* This book describes, in elaborate detail, the interpretive processes by which people seen as deviant become stigmatized in society and find ways to understand that experience. An interesting read; students usually find Goffman's books fascinating.

McHoul, A., & Grace, W. (2000). *A Foucault primer: Discourse, power, and the subject.* Washington Square, NY: New York University Press.

* This book serves as a somewhat understandable introduction to the full range of work of critical poststructuralist Michel Foucault, including his explications of the link between power and knowledge, and the creation of people constantly engaged in self-surveillance, regulating their own behaviours. Reading the English translations of Foucault's own work is an admirable goal, but this primer is a good place to start.

Beaman, L. G. (Ed.) (2000). *New perspectives on deviance: The construction of deviance in everyday life*. Scarborough, ON: Prentice Hall.

* This collection of Canadian research on deviance is based upon the notion of social construction, and illustrates the range of interpretive and critical theories that have been addressed in this chapter. The papers in this collection address diverse topics, including the media, mental illness, marriage breakdown, images of female beauty, and motherhood, among others.

Endnotes

1 Friedrich Nietzsche. Retrieved July 3, 2003 from World Wide Web: **http://www.quotationspage.com**

Key Terms

CHAPTER 4

"Deviant" and "Normal" Sexuality

Learning Objectives

After reading this chapter, you should be able to:

- Describe the sexual culture of Sambian society, contrasting the dominant meaning of sexuality in that culture with that of Canadian society. Explain how the concepts of heterosexuality, homosexuality, and pedophilia are (or are not) recognized by Sambian sexual culture.
- Describe "deviant" and "normal" aristocratic male sexuality in ancient Athens, and explain the role of the hierarchy of power in shaping those judgments.
- Contrast the sexual cultures of traditional Aboriginal societies with that of the colonizing Europeans, and explain how colonization affected Aboriginal sexual cultures.
- Describe how deviant sexuality was defined and regulated from the 17th century through the 20th century, explaining how the changing sexual cultures reinforced class, gender, and racial hierarchies of the times.

- Describe the criteria that we use in determining "deviant" and "normal" sexuality, and describe how the "deviance dance" is evident in sexual cultures, both past and present.

"The only unnatural sexual act is that which you cannot perform." (Alfred Kinsey)[1]

"There is hardly anyone whose sexual life, if it were broadcast, would not fill the world at large with surprise and horror." (W. Somerset Maugham)[2]

What Is Deviant Sexuality?

At first glance, the two quotations above seem contradictory. If, as Alfred Kinsey claims, "the only unnatural sexual act is that which you cannot perform," then why would people's sexual lives fill us "with surprise and horror," as suggested by Somerset Maugham? In fact, these two quotations demonstrate the complexity of sexuality in human societies, and point to the different ways sexuality can be perceived—biologically and sociologically. Kinsey's view of sexuality draws upon biology as the foundation upon which normal and deviant sexuality is defined; normal sexuality is simply that which is physically possible. However, Maugham suggests that we all judge people's sexuality, and that most people's sexual lives, if known, would be judged negatively. Evidently, something more than biology plays a role in how sexuality is perceived, and in the aspects of sexuality that are defined as deviant and normal. There appears to be a substantial difference between what is biologically possible and what is considered socially acceptable.

> ***Ask Yourself:***
>
> In your opinion, what is "normal" sexuality? What is "deviant" sexuality? In your response you might refer to fantasies, behaviours, identities, or more abstract ideals. Now answer a slightly different question. In Canadian society, what do you think is considered to be "normal" and "deviant" sexuality? How similar is this list to the one you made of your own opinions?

If you compared the list you made at left of your own opinions to the list that someone else made, you would see some differences. You might be shocked by something that someone else is not shocked by, and vice versa. In other words, what is considered acceptable varies across individuals. However, as pointed out in the first chapter, a deviant label is not a product of individual perceptions, but rather social processes, processes that you were referring to in answering the above question about Canadian society. Social processes determine what is considered deviant and normal sexuality in society; more objective deviance specialists refer to cultural and historical variations in the norms that are used as the standard against which deviance is judged, and more subjective deviance specialists refer to processes of social construction. Social processes determine who is socially typed as deviant through the processes of *description* (placed in a category because of their sexuality), *evaluation* (judged on the basis of the category into which they have been placed), and *prescription* (made subject to particular measures of regulation or social control). Thus, although similar sexual activities and characteristics may be found throughout much, if not all, of the world, there is variation across cultures and time in where those characteristics get slotted into the social hierarchy, the roles assigned to people who exhibit those characteristics, and the meanings attached to those characteristics. For example, although same-sex activities have been found throughout the world, the judgments placed on people engaging in same-sex activities, the social treatment they receive, the meanings attached to those activities, and issues of sexual identity are all socially embedded, depending upon the culture in question and the particular time in history.

When we look at these sorts of processes, we turn our attention to certain questions about sexuality. What meaning does sexuality have for different groups of people? What kinds of sexuality are perceived as "normal" and "deviant," and why? How is "normal" sexuality encouraged, and "deviant" sexuality discouraged or stopped? How do the answers to the preceding questions change over history and across cultures? Are the answers to the above questions influenced in any way by the perceptions and actions of people with some level of power?

The Cultural and Historical Construction of Sexuality

Even a brief look at cultural and historical variations in sexuality reveals how the perceptions, meanings, and control of sexuality in contemporary Canada represent only a small portion of that which is found throughout the world; one's own perceptions and meanings of sexuality, as revealed in the list you made near the beginning of this chapter, are an even smaller segment of what people in the world think and feel about sexuality. The cultural and historical analysis of sexuality has exploded in recent years, and indeed has become an "acceptable" area of scientific study; however, such analyses were also done long before it was considered "acceptable," in the work of several early anthropologists (Herdt, 1999). Margaret Mead, Ruth Benedict, and Branislaw Malinowski were all early 20th century anthropologists who provide us with a wealth of research that serves as a foundation for contemporary analyses of the influence social processes have on sexuality. Their work, as well as the work of their followers, demonstrated that sexual behaviours and meanings were incredibly diverse across cultures (Herdt, 1999). For example, in her exploration of adolescence in Samoa during the 1920s, Mead found a much more permissive attitude toward premarital sex, suggesting that this was why adolescence seemed to be a much smoother and more stress-free life transition there than in the more sexually-repressive culture of the United States at the time (Mead, 1927). Benedict's research on tribal groups in New Guinea, and Malinowski's work on the Trobriand Islanders, also pointed to the cultural relativism that is involved with social life more generally, of which human sexuality is one part. Because these early anthropologists were constrained by academic and social norms that defined the study of sexuality as a taboo—as a deviant activity itself—they often studied sexuality in an indirect way, through analyses of marriage and procreation (Herdt, 1999). In the late 20th century, the study of sexuality was no longer taboo; this enabled researchers to explicitly and directly study sexuality in cultures around the world, and present their research in academic circles at a level previously forbidden.

In this more permissive academic environment, one anthropologist who has had a substantial influence on understandings of the normative variation, or the social construction, of sexuality is Gilbert Herdt (1984). His research on the Sambia of New Guinea has become what is perhaps the most cited cross-cultural research on sexuality to be found in deviance books today. His analysis reveals cross-cultural variations in what are seen as "normal" sexual behaviours, but, even more significantly, leads us to question the very categories of "heterosexual" and "homosexual" that we take for granted in contemporary Canadian society.

The Sambia of New Guinea

Sambian society, at the time that Herdt studied it, was characterized by both **patriarchy** (i.e., social power was embedded in the males) and **misogyny** (i.e., extreme distrust, and even hatred, of women). It was believed that the presence of females polluted boys and, if uncontrolled, would prevent the development of masculinity, seen as the ability to engage in warfare. In a culture based on a long history of tribal warfare, the masculinity of its potential warriors was considered crucial. To ensure the development of "normal" manhood, when a sufficient number of boys reached the ages of somewhere between 7 and 10 (approximately), they were removed from daily contact with the females in the village and separated into an all-male enclave for the next 10 to 15 years. However, removing boys from the "contamination" of the female presence was not perceived as sufficient for the full development of masculinity. Lacking certain biological and scientific knowledge, Sambians presumed that semen (a fluid that only males, and therefore warriors, have), was the source of masculinity and that it had to be transmitted to boys so that they could also become warriors. Thus, within the all-male enclave to which boys were removed, acts of fellatio occurred between the older males and the boys. As boys progressed through adolescence and were seen as having accumulated sufficient masculine essence, they would move from being the fellator to the fellatee. At marriage, they would move out of the male enclave and begin having sexual intercourse with their wives while continuing same-sex activities with the segregated younger males. When a man's first child was born, he would no longer participate in the same-sex activities except for a short, ritualized period of time when a new group of boys would be moved into the all-male enclave.

As North Americans learning about Sambian society, we are tempted to place these males into categories—homosexual when they are boys, bisexual when they are young men, and heterosexual when they are adults. Furthermore, we also would interpret sexual activities between adult men and boys as "pedophilia." However, there are no similar types of categories in Sambian language or perception. Males are not categorized on the basis of these sexual activities, for the simple reason that all of these activities, in the temporal order described above, are a "normal" part of the life cycle for every male without exception. The behaviours are simply characteristic of being "male," not of being a particular type of male. What comprises "normal" and "deviant" sexuality in Sambian society is quite different from what comprises "normal" and "deviant" sexuality in Canadian society. In Canadian society, many of the activities described above would be perceived as "deviant" and both formally and informally socially controlled. For example, a man who participated in sexual activities with a boy would be dealt with by the criminal justice system, and adults who participate in same-sex activities with other adults are stigmatized in everyday social interaction. But what is considered "deviant" sexuality, subject to formal and informal social control, in Sambia is quite different—a male who does not participate in these rituals; an older male performing fellatio on a younger male, rather than vice versa; a father who continues to participate in same-sex activities in the all-male enclave outside of the short, ritualized periods of time defined within the culture; and the spilling of semen on the ground.

The differences in norms, perceptions, and meanings of sexuality in Canadian and Sambian society go beyond perceptions of "normal" and "deviant," and the categories used to describe particular behaviours. Sexuality itself has a different meaning in the two cultures. In North America, sexuality is often viewed as a distinct part of life; of course, sexuality may overlap with "love," or with marriage, but it also is seen as existing for its own sake. We do not only have sex for the purposes of procreation, but also for the purposes of physical pleasure. In contrast, in Sambian society sexuality does not exist independently outside of social life more generally. The purpose of the same-sex activities that occur within the male enclaves is not the pursuit of physical pleasure (although the activities may feel pleasurable); rather, the purposes are social and religious in nature. These same-sex activities between males are intended to reproduce and perpetuate the society they live in (i.e., the strictly distinct roles of men and women, the patriarchy that characterizes Sambian society, the ability of males to be effective warriors if it becomes necessary), as they believe is prescribed within their spiritual belief system.

Gilbert Herdt's research on sexuality in Sambian culture raises significant questions for those of us living in Canadian society about the way we perceive and categorize particular sexual behaviours, and the way we separate sexuality from most other aspects of social life. It also raises important ethical questions. Because sexual activity between boys and adult men is perceived as "normal" in Sambian society, does that mean it is an "acceptable" behaviour within the world at large? Should the world intervene to protect Sambian boys? Does this culture need to be changed, or not? Should all cultures be accepted for what they are, or are there certain standards that can and should be applied universally? These kinds of complex questions will be addressed in the final chapter of this book, where we will explore the issue of whether the subjective aspects of deviance that are recognized in varying degrees by both more objective and more subjective deviance specialists implies that we should be tolerant of all behaviours (for instance, if deviance is "socially constructed," does that mean "anything goes"?).

TIME TO REVIEW:

- In Sambian society, why are boys separated into all-male enclaves?
- In Sambian society, how do men's sexual behaviours change as they progress through adolescence, when they get married, and when they become fathers? Why?
- Are the concepts of heterosexuality, homosexuality, bisexuality, and pedophilia applied within Sambian culture? Why or why not?
- What sexual behaviours are socially typed as deviant in Sambian society?
- How is the fundamental meaning of sexuality different in Sambian society and Canadian society?

The example of Sambian society illustrates normative variation or the social construction of sexuality in a rather dramatic fashion. However, the dramatic nature of this example can result in the perception of Sambian society as a very "foreign" Other, which can contribute to **ethnocentrism** (i.e., the belief that one's own culture is better than, or superior to, another culture) and to misperceptions about the influence of social processes on norms and perceptions of sexuality. In fact, the social construction of sexuality is everywhere around us, which we can see more clearly by looking at some less sensational examples of cross-cultural variations. We will look at the nature of the sexual cultures among the ancient Greeks, the traditional Aboriginal cultures of North America, and during the process of industrialization.

Ancient Athens

The ancient Greeks are typically looked upon as having created the foundation upon which Western societies are built. Their technology, medicine, philosophy, and political systems each continue to have extensive influences on the lives we live today. Yet despite the similarities between contemporary Canadian society and ancient Greek society, there are also considerable differences, including in the meanings and structures of sexuality. The latter varied even across regions within Greece; thus, we will focus on one area within Greece at one particular time in history, 5th century B.C. Athens (Arkins, 1994).

The relationship between *power* and both "normal" and "deviant" sexuality is quite clear in 5th century B.C. Athens. Aristocratic men were at the highest

Ask Yourself:

Are there any similarities between the way sexuality was socially constructed in 5th century B.C. Athens and Canadian society today? For example, does the way sexuality is constructed in contemporary Canada serve the needs of adult males in particular, or not? Does it serve the needs or interests of any other powerful groups in particular, or does our sexual culture serve the interests of everyone in society equally?

Is "normal" sexuality in Canadian society of considerable range as well, or is it of quite a narrow range? It might be interesting to discuss (or even debate) these questions with other students in your class; you might be surprised at the diverse responses there will be to these questions!

level in the hierarchy of power. Indeed, they were the only people considered to be citizens in Athenian society; slaves, people from outside of Greece, and women were not considered citizens of the state. Thus, the sexual culture of the time was structured such that the needs of these powerful male citizens were satisfied. A wide range of sexual relationships and behaviours were permitted for aristocratic males. They would have sexual relationships with the aristocratic women they married for the purpose of producing male heirs. They could have sexual relationships with other women, slaves, and foreigners, who were expected to sexually service male citizens. Aristocratic males could also form sexual relationships with adolescent aristocratic boys. Thus, "normal" sexuality for male citizens included sexual relationships with a wide range of people, both male and female. There was no distinction made between heterosexual and homosexual; rather, these diverse sexual relationships and activities represented "a single state available to [all] adult male [citizens]" (Arkins, 1994, para. 13). Normality was of considerable range in Athens at this time.

"Looking at the flip side of normality, controlling deviance in the realm of sexuality was an important part of Athenian culture as well, and the social typing process was evident. For example, sex was expected to be a unidirectional relationship between a superior and an inferior, not a mutual relationship between two equals, as illustrated in the following quotation: "In Athens a man would have been regarded as perverted if he sought a relationship with another person equal to him in age and status. For his sexual needs he could use women, slaves, prostitutes, and boys, in any combination, but not another adult male citizen." (Bloch, 2001, para. 6)

Even though sexual activities between male citizens and adolescent boys were viewed as acceptable, there were guidelines to prevent deviance. The state acknowledged that there was the potential for some type of harm to come to adolescent males in their relationships with the more powerful adult citizens; thus, certain laws were instituted, such as prohibiting such sexual activities between dusk and dawn, when the greater level of isolation might enable deviant sexual behaviours to occur. Changes in sexual behaviours were expected during the lifespan. Boys who had been the passive partners with adult males during their youth were expected to make the transition to the dominant sexual role as they grew up, and "…if they persisted in sexually passive ways they were…subject to deep humiliation and shame" (Bloch, 2001, para. 18). Anal intercourse between males was perceived as unacceptable, because it meant that a man was acting like a woman—only women were to be recipients of insertion. If, in his relationship with an adult male, an aristocratic adolescent boy allowed anal intercourse to occur, and furthered that deviant behaviour by taking some type of compensation for it (i.e., prostituted himself), he was forbidden to ever become a citizen of the state; upon reaching adulthood he could not vote or participate in politics. If he attempted to act as a citizen, he would be dealt with by the justice system and possibly lose his life. In 5th century B.C. Athens, the formal and informal social controls of sexuality were widespread in order to prevent and punish deviance.

Thus, by looking at the ways in which sexuality was socially typed in Athens, we can see that, although ancient Greece created the foundation upon which Canadian and other Western societies are built, it had a distinctive sexual culture. What was perceived as "normal" sexuality was of considerable range—marital sex for the purpose of producing male heirs, and sexual relationships with other women, slaves, foreigners, and aristocratic adolescent boys for the purposes of pleasure. But "normal" and "deviant" sexuality were defined on the basis of power—the needs and desires of aristocratic males (Athens' only "citizens"), and the maintenance of the social order.

TIME TO REVIEW:

- What was considered "normal" sexuality in ancient Athens? How was it related to power?
- What types of sexual activities and relationships were considered "deviant"? How were they regulated?

Although we could explore the sexual cultures of countless numbers of other cultures around the world and at different points in history, looking at the Sambia of New Guinea, and Athens in the 5th century B.C. already demonstrates how sexuality varies across time and place. But if we narrow our focus even further by moving geographically much closer to home, we can see the power of normative variation even more clearly.

Traditional Aboriginal Cultures of North America

The arrival of Europeans in what is now the Americas, and their subsequent colonization of that land and its indigenous peoples, had a massive impact on all aspects of Aboriginal societies. For hundreds of years, various facets of Aboriginal cultures were suppressed, facing potential eradication at the hands of political and religious authorities. It has only been in the last few decades that scholars and historians have begun to bring the norms, values, beliefs, and practices of traditional Aboriginal cultures to widespread attention; within this growing body of knowledge, the distinct sexual cultures of these societies are being addressed.

However, before progressing to an exploration of how sexuality was socially constructed in traditional Aboriginal cultures, it is important to point out the diversity among such cultures. At the time of European colonization, there were thousands of distinct Aboriginal cultures in the Americas and, in fact, more than 100 different Aboriginal languages being spoken in Canada alone. Thus, it is imperative that all Aboriginal cultures are not painted with the same brush and presumed to be the same, any more than all European cultures could be.

That said, many Aboriginal societies in what is now Canada did have some similarities in cultural beliefs and practices, particularly in terms of their contrast with the beliefs and practices of the colonizing European cultures. In the realm of sexuality, its construction in Aboriginal cultures and European cultures was so distinct that sexuality became a nexus of conflict and subsequent social control as colonization progressed (Mandell & Momirov, 2000).

In traditional Aboriginal cultures, sexuality was inextricably interwoven with all other aspects of social life (Newhouse, 1998). Life was viewed as consisting of four components—physical, intellectual, emotional, and spiritual. Because life was seen as consisting of these components, so was sexuality; the physical, intellectual, emotional, and spiritual were perceived as existing within sexuality, and sexuality was thought to enhance these four components in the rest of a person's life. As with all else in the world, sexuality was perceived as being a sacred gift from the Creator, intended to be pleasurable—"having sex was to touch the life force within us, and...to touch the life force meant to touch Creation" (Newhouse, 1998, para. 12). In fact, a recent survey of more than 600 Aboriginal people across Ontario reveals that more than half describe sex as "magical" (Newhouse, 1998, para. 10). Sexuality was incorporated into myths and stories, and although all cultures have their own myths and historical stories, the following story illustrates the pleasure-oriented view of sexuality in many traditional Aboriginal cultures:

"One of the Anishnabe teachings tells of the way in which sex is introduced into the world. Men and women lived separately for a long time. The Creator, in his efforts to increase the population of humans, made sex pleasurable so that men and women would desire it, and hence, through acting upon their desire, increase the population. Sex was to be an act of pleasure." (Newhouse, 1998, para. 12)

In many Aboriginal cultures, this pleasure was acceptable between members of the same sex as well. Recognizing more than two sexes and more than two genders, many cultures perceived a wider range of sexualities as "normal" (Nelson & Robinson, 1999). For example, Navajo society included the **nadles**, men who were erotically attracted to other men; they were seen as necessary for the wealth and success of the community. Similarly, Mojave society recognized both male homosexuals (**alyha**), and female homosexuals (**hwame**); such males were viewed as being able to become powerful medicine men, and such females were preferred as wives of chiefs (Newhouse, 1998). But not only were people who were attracted to members of the same sex accepted within these cultures, and given specific roles within the social structure, they were perceived as "normal" and even "necessary." As Newhouse (1998, para. 16) points out, "Mojaves believed that 'from the beginning of the world, it was meant that there should be homosexuals.'" The moral codes of these cultures did not regulate particular types of sexual behaviours specifically, but rather proper types of relationships between people, ones that, within the spiritual belief systems, were necessary to maintain harmony and balance in social life and in the larger society (Newhouse, 1998).

For the colonizing European cultures of the time, sexuality had a very different meaning. Sex was for the sole purpose of reproduction, and even then, notions of pleasure were frowned upon; sexuality was sinful, requiring careful and stringent control. Sexuality was not integrated within social life, but rather isolated from it, almost as a necessary evil, and infused with guilt (Newhouse, 1998; D'Emilio & Freedman, 1997). The only non-deviant sexuality was that which occurred between husband and wife, and even then, only if their sole sexual behaviour was intercourse, if it took place in the "missionary" position, and if they did not enjoy it too much or do it too often. Same-sex activities were unacceptable, and subject to both informal (e.g., community sanction) and formal (e.g., excommunication from the church) sanction (D'Emilio & Freedman, 1997).

Of course, with these considerably divergent sexual cultures, conflict between European and Aboriginal cultures became inevitable. However, during the early years of colonization in Canada, sexual unions between white men and Aboriginal women were common, due to a relative scarcity of white women as well as the usefulness of Aboriginal women because of their skills in trapping, languages, diplomacy, and other areas (Mandell & Momirov, 2000; Das Gupta, 2000; Razack, 2002). The Aboriginal women with whom early European settlers formed relationships were called **les femmes du pays**, or "country wives" (Mandell & Momirov, 2000, p. 22). Such pragmatic concerns led the Hudson's Bay Company to not only allow but encourage these interracial relationships among employees. Even missionaries during the early years did not actively discourage the unions (Razack, 2002). However, as colonization progressed, Aboriginal sexuality became one of the things that the emerging authorities felt the need to regulate—"…missionaries attempted to eradicate 'devilish' practices such as polygamy and cross-dressing, and condemned the 'heathen friskiness' of the natives" (D'Emilio & Freedman, p. 6). Conflicts grew between religious authorities and many Aboriginal women in particular, because of the women's rejection of European ideals of male authority, monogamy, premarital chastity, and marital fidelity (Mandell & Momirov, 2000). Changes in the social perceptions of sexual relationships between Aboriginals and Euro-Canadians occurred as settlement progressed, and as the fur trade was slowly replaced by agriculture as Canada's primary economic activity. Relationships between Euro-Canadian men and Aboriginal women were discouraged as the population of mixed-race women, such as Métis, grew; being half European, these women were perceived as more acceptable partners (Das Gupta, 2000; Mandell & Momirov, 2000). Even in Western Canada, which was settled considerably later, by the mid-19th century "colonial officials and religious authorities began to fear the consequences of this widespread 'race-mixing'" (Razack, 2002, p. 52). Laws were instituted at various times in various parts of Canada as well as the rest of the Americas, prohibiting white/Aboriginal relationships.

Thus, over time we can see Aboriginal sexuality being socially typed: it was described as "heathen friskiness," judged as being "devilish," and made subject to a wide range of prescriptions, including being taught by church fathers the "right" way to have sexual intercourse (hence the phrase, "missionary position"). With such overt attempts to regulate and control Aboriginal sexuality, substantial changes occurred in the sexual cultures of Aboriginal societies as they adopted and integrated many aspects of European sexual culture; as Aboriginal people today regain their cultural traditions, their sexual cultures will continue to evolve as well (Newhouse, 1998).

Sexual cultures are comprised of dynamic and ever-changing processes, regardless of whether we are speaking of Aboriginal cultures or other cultures of the world. As cultures continuously evolve and transform, so does sexuality, as we can see by looking at how the meanings and place of sexuality in the social structure have changed in the dominant culture of North America over the last few centuries. It is by looking at transhistorical changes, that is, changes over time within a single society, that the powerful role of social processes in the creation of sexual cultures and sexual identities becomes acutely evident.

TIME TO REVIEW:

- How was sexuality embedded within social life as a whole in traditional Aboriginal societies?
- How were people who were erotically attracted to members of the same sex perceived in many traditional Aboriginal cultures?
- How was sexuality constructed in the colonizing European cultures? What were the meanings of sexuality? What activities were considered to be "normal" and "deviant"?
- How did the prevalence of sexual relationships between Aboriginal women and Euro-Canadian men change over time, and why?
- Why did conflict emerge between Aboriginal and European cultures regarding sexuality?

North America: From the 17th Century to the 20th Century

The past few hundred years have been a time of immense social change; North America today is a very different place than the North America of 300 or 400 years ago. And as economic, religious, familial, scientific, and other cultural changes have occurred, sexuality has changed as well. Looking at social changes in both Canadian and American history reveals that the meaning of sexuality, its place within the social order, how it is judged, and the agents of its regulation have all fluctuated over time, and been intertwined with racial, class, and gender hierarchies of the broader society (D'Emilio & Freedman, 1997; Valverde, 1991). There is a particular wealth of historical analyses of American sexuality (more so than for Canadian sexuality) that visibly conveys these ideas to us. During the progression from the 17th century (referred to as the *Colonial era* in American society) to the end of the 20th century, the meaning of sexuality was transformed from a primary association with reproduction within a powerful structure of kinship to a primary association with emotional intimacy and physical pleasure for individuals.

The 17th century in Canada was a time of early exploration and settlement, and economic activities revolved around the fur trade. As described previously, sexual relationships between Aboriginal women and white men were common and accepted during this time, despite broader differences between Aboriginal and European sexual cultures. Meanwhile, among the small number of European families who had settled in Eastern Canada, ownership of black slaves also sprang up during this era, continuing until the early 19th century (Das Gupta, 2000). The practice of slavery was closely intertwined with the control of sexuality. Slave owners frequently determined who was permitted to mate with whom for the purposes of reproduction (and when); female slaves were valued in part for their reproductive capacities, and certain male slaves were selected as "studs" to impregnate these females (Das Gupta, 2000). Female slaves were also expected to be continually sexually available for male members of the owner's family. Even the sexuality of free blacks came to be socially controlled, as laws were instituted prohibiting blacks from marrying outside of their race (Das Gupta, 2000).

In the more urbanized United States, sexuality during the Colonial era was channeled into marriage for the purpose of reproduction, although some sexual activity was tolerated within courtship. Sexuality outside of the arenas of courtship and marriage was considered unacceptable, and was both formally and informally controlled by the local Christian church, the courts (which operated in conjunction with the church), the family, and the community. Sexual behaviours viewed as deviant included premarital pregnancy, same-sex activities, activities with farm animals, interracial sexual activities, and marital sexual activities not associated with attempts at reproduction (including oral sex and contraceptive use). Premarital pregnancy would usually result in marriage being enforced, often at the insistence of the young woman's father—the phrase "shotgun wedding" refers to those weddings that occurred, figuratively and sometimes literally, at the barrel end of the father's shotgun once a premarital pregnancy was detected. The young couple usually respected the father's directive because the kinship system was perceived as a legitimate regulator of sexuality and reproduction. The community was also seen as a legitimate regulator of deviance, and it was not uncommon for nosy neighbours to report sexual improprieties to the relevant family members, community leaders, or church leaders; given their perceived legitimacy, they were unlikely to even be viewed as being "nosy" for doing so. Individuals could be excommunicated from the local church for deviant sexuality, and in fact in some regions certain forms of sexual deviance (such as adultery and having sex with farm animals) were considered criminal and sometimes even punishable by death. However, during the Colonial era deviating individuals were more often seen as having made an error in judgment; it was the behaviour that was viewed as deviant rather than the person. Thus, some form of punishment for the unacceptable behaviour was dispensed in order for individuals to learn the error of their ways and thereby be accepted back within the family, the community, and the church:

"Courts...typically sentenced offenders to some form of public humiliation, such as whipping at the post or sitting in the stocks....In New England, public confession and repentance both restored the individual to the congregation and at the same time confirmed the propriety of sexual rules."

(D'Emilio, J., & Freedman, E. B. [1997]. *Intimate Matters: A History of Sexuality in America* [2nd ed.], p. 27. Chicago, IL: University of Chicago Press.)

The specific nature of the punishment dispensed often depended upon the social characteristics of the person involved. For example, the higher the socioeconomic status of the sexual transgressors, the less severe their punishments were likely to be. For instance, in the case of rape, upper-class men were less likely to go to trial and usually received milder penalties if they did, while more severe penalties (such as the death penalty) were dispensed to lower-class men. Women and men regularly received different types of punishment. Men, who often owned property, were more likely to be fined while women, who did not own property, were more likely to be physically punished (such as through whipping); women were also more likely than men to be punished for sexual deviance, such as adultery. In addition to gender, the racial hierarchies embedded within the social structure of the time were also reflected within Colonial society's sexual culture, and its definition and regulation of deviant sexuality. In many American colonies, black men convicted of raping white women (but not black women) were castrated. In contrast, white men convicted of raping either white or black women were not castrated; in most regions it was even unlikely that a white man could be considered as having "raped" a black woman.

"That white men of the planter class could have casual sexual relations with slave women, but reserved the most brutal corporal punishment for black men who slept with white women, clearly illustrates the ways that sexual rules reinforced a system of racial dominance. That enormous scorn was heaped upon a white woman who had sex with a black man—even if they were married—while black women were expected to service the sexual needs of white men, reveals the combined forces of gender and racial hierarchy."

(D'Emilio, J., & Freedman, E. B. [1997]. *Intimate Matters: A History of Sexuality in America* [2nd ed.], p. 37. Chicago, IL: University of Chicago Press.)

The various ways that deviant sexuality was controlled and defined revolved around the dominant meanings of sexuality during the 17th century, which incorporated both pragmatic considerations as well as cultural ideals. In the growing Euro-Canadian and Euro-American cultures, the nature of the definition and control of sexual deviance "served the larger function of reminding the community at large that sexuality belonged within marriage [or marriage-like relationships between European men and Aboriginal women], for the purpose of producing legitimate children" (D'Emilio & Freedman, 1997, p. 28). The definition and control of sexual deviance also reinforced the socioeconomic class, gender, and racial hierarchies through which society was constructed.

TIME TO REVIEW:

- How was sexuality controlled under slavery in Canada?
- During the Colonial era in American history, what was the dominant meaning of sexuality?
- What types of sexuality or sexual activity were considered acceptable? What types were socially typed as deviant?
- In what ways did each of the following agents serve as a regulator of sexual deviance during the 17th century: the family; the community; the Christian church; the state?
- How did the social characteristics of individuals affect the ways in which sexual deviance was regulated? Be sure to address socioeconomic status, gender, and race.

Near the end of the 18th century and throughout the 19th century, Canadian and American society underwent significant changes that affected the way sexuality was perceived (Valverde, 1991; D'Emilio & Freedman, 1997). Urbanization and wage labour outside of the kinship system took hold and progressed at a rapid pace, creating more anonymous lives distanced from extended family members and community surveillance. Religious shifts transferred the responsibility for salvation onto the individual, reducing the role of the church, and subsequently the State, as regulator of morality. In the United States, the Revolutionary War and the expansion of commerce spread the ideology of the "pursuit of happiness," which subsequently infused sexual culture as well; although the "pursuit of happiness" was explicitly voiced in American discourse, similar ideals came to characterize Canadian and British societies as well (Mandell & Momirov, 2000; D'Emilio & Freedman, 1997). Economically based and arranged marriages declined; with people more likely to be marrying for "love," more open expressions of affection emerged. Enlightenment ideology within philosophy and science identified nature (including sexuality) as inherently good. These changes, along with others too numerous to mention, infused the sexual culture of the time, such that the language of sexuality was no longer reproductive, but rather based on *personal intimacy* within marriage. The role of the church in regulating sexuality declined, as did the role of the State; the family was becoming more of an isolated unit in society, recognized as a *private* realm outside of the surveying gaze of many others. However, the role of other social control agents grew—women, the medical profession, social reformers, and the culture industries (D'Emilio & Freedman, 1997; Valverde, 1991).

Women played a larger role in regulating sexuality through their efforts at reducing pregnancy rates. Previously, high infant mortality rates meant that women would have large numbers of babies simply to ensure that a sufficient number of them survived into childhood to contribute to the maintenance of the family. During the 19th century, infant mortality rates declined, but perinatal and postnatal mortality rates of women did not. With the tremendous health risks associated with pregnancy and childbirth, and less of a need for large numbers of children, middle- and upper-class women acted to reduce pregnancy by abstaining from sex with their husbands for extended periods of time and by using contraception (usually with the consent of the husbands).

The use of contraception was aided by the medical profession, which was growing in size, knowledge, and legitimized power. The medical profession came to have a more encompassing role in the regulation of sexuality by "scientifically" defining sexual deviance (such as the "disease" of sodomy), and by conveying medical knowledge to the broader community. For example, medical knowledge at the time described the body as a closed energy system, wherein overindulgence in any activity (including sexual), could be a danger to physical health—*self-control* became a dominant theme in the contributions of science to the sexual culture of the time.

Self-control as a means to avoid illness and energy depletion was perceived as particularly important during this era because of its relevance to commercial expansion. The "self-made man" was idealized in politics, religion, and popular culture; in order to achieve such success in this new industrial and capitalist economy, he had to ensure that he did not waste too much of his bodily energy elsewhere. Thus, controlling his sexual passions would enable him to focus his energies on economic success.

The economic changes that were occurring in society at this time included the emergence of a powerful culture industry—newspapers, magazines, mass-produced books, and more. On one hand, the culture industry contributed to the sexual culture of the era in terms of the spread of the sex industry, such as pornography (in the form of stories, books, drawings, burlesque shows, and early photography). But other facets of the culture industry also contributed to sexual culture in terms of the role it played in the regulation of sexual deviance. For example, young women were viewed as being extremely vulnerable to the sexual appetites of unsavoury young men in the growing cities. In response to this problem, poems and stories in popular publications warned young women of these dangers, as illustrated in the following poem:

Young ladies, now take warning
Since you find young men unjust
It may be your own best lover's hand;
You know not whom to trust
Pearl Bryan died away from home
And in that lovely spot.
My God, my God, believe it girls,
Don't let this be your lot.

(Cited in D'Emilio, J., & Freedman, E. B. [1997]. *Intimate Matters: A History of Sexuality in America* [2nd ed.], p. 70. Chicago, IL: University of Chicago Press.)

The young woman in the above poem dies as a result of being seduced by a man and led into a life of sexual impropriety; in fact, death was a common outcome for the female characters in these didactic poems and stories. The perceived vulnerability of young women contributed to the emergence of **social purity** or **sex hygiene movements**, who believed this susceptibility drew women into the sex industry (e.g., prostitution, nude dancing, etc.). At a broader level, social purity was equated with sexual purity for females and males of all ages; sexuality was seen as the heart of morality, which was defined as the cornerstone of society as a whole. Social purity activism was well established in Canada, the Northeastern United States, and Britain by the late 1800s, and included a number of alcohol temperance groups, such as the Women's Christian Temperance Union (Valverde, 1991). The concerns of these groups included "prostitution, divorce, illegitimacy, 'Indian and Chinese [male immigrants],' public education, suppression of obscene literature, prevention (of prostitution) and rescue of fallen women, and shelters for women and children" (Valverde, 1991, p. 17). The area of the greatest concern changed over time, from masturbation (in the 19th century), to prostitution (in the early 20th century), to premarital sex (by the Depression era). Social purity efforts were directed particularly at the lower classes, which by virtue of simply being lower class were presumed sexually depraved as well.

The specific ways in which sexual deviance was defined and regulated depended upon social characteristics, just as in earlier eras. Racial ideologies continued to infuse sexual culture. Members of the white middle class (society's dominant group at the time) defined their own sexuality as being "civilized," and the sexuality of other classes and races as being "depraved." As Das Gupta (2000) suggests, "the sexuality of people of colour is always a problem for a racist society" (p. 159). Thus, the ideology of self-control served both economic pursuits and racially based ideological purposes as well.

"Within the middle class, [white] gentlemen learned to control their sexual appetites in order to succeed. In nineteenth-century thought, sexual control [also] helped differentiate the middle class from the working class, and whites from other races."

(D'Emilio, J., & Freedman, E. B. [1997], p. 57. *Intimate Matters: A History of Sexuality in America* [2nd ed.]. Chicago, IL: University of Chicago Press.)

Racial ideologies were reflected in law as well. For example, in New Orleans a white woman could be jailed between one and six months for having sex with a black man, and yet black women were expected to be available to sexually service white men. Race interacted with class in that this law was less strictly applied to lower class white women, whose purity was already suspect simply by virtue of these women being members of the lower class. Even with the abolition of slavery, hierarchies of race were embedded within the definition and regulation of sexual deviance, as indicated by the following American analysis:

"Black women's vulnerability to sexual abuse by whites did not disappear with the eradication of slavery. For one, northern soldiers who shared southerners' assumptions about the sexual passions of black women both raped black women and girls and took black concubines. In addition, during Reconstruction southerners unleashed their rage against freed slaves by sexually assaulting black women. Whites, arguing that black men lusted after white women, also used the specter of black sexual violence against whites to terrorize black men and ultimately to justify lynching."

(D'Emilio, J., & Freedman, E. B. [1997]. *Intimate Matters: A History of Sexuality in America* [2nd ed.], p. 105. Chicago, IL: University of Chicago Press.)

Lynching (wherein a black man who was even suspected of having sex with a white woman was captured and hung by an angry crowd that had taken the law into its own hands) dramatically illustrates the embeddedness of sexuality within the larger culture and the power of the social typing process. Black men were defined as

Ask Yourself:

We have explored many different aspects of sexuality in 19th century Canadian and American culture–the roles of women, medicine, the ideology of self-control, the ideology of personal intimacy, the economy, the culture industry, social reformers, race, and class. This might be a good time for you to apply some of the concepts and issues raised in Chapter 1 to the specific topic of sexuality. Considering what you have learned about the way sexuality was socially constructed in Canadian and American culture during the 19th century and into the early 20th century, think about the following questions. Who was doing the social typing of deviant sexuality? What was the foundation for their arguments–that is, did they type certain sexual behaviours as deviant because they thought those behaviours were statistically rare, were harmful, violated norms, or engendered a negative societal reaction? How did the social typers benefit from the social typing of particular people or groups as deviant? Did the larger society benefit, in any way, from the social typing of particular groups of people? What larger social conditions supported the social typing process? Your answers to these questions may integrate some of the main ideas that have been addressed, such as the dominant meaning of sexuality at the time, broader social changes, the ideology of self-control, the growth of the culture industry, the regulation of sexuality, and the reinforcing of social hierarchies.

being passionate and incapable of self-control, their sexuality was evaluated as "depraved," and sexual regulation included laws against sexual relations with white women, and lynching by angry mobs if these men did have sex with white women. The role played by power in the sexual culture of the time was evident, in that the description, evaluation, and regulation of white men's sexuality (even when it involved black women) was of a very different nature. American perceptions and panics over black men's sexuality was having a considerable influence on Canadian society as well. Portrayals of black men's sexuality as dangerous and uncontrollable, making them liable to rape white women, were being spread by Canadian media; in the early 20th century such attitudes would serve as a rationale for Emily Murphy's efforts to regulate immigration (Valverde, 1991).

Not only was black men's sexuality suspect by the end of the 19th century in Canadian society, but so was that of Chinese men. Chinese men, brought to Canada as labourers for the building of the railway, were also perceived as a threat to young white women, who might be easily lured by their seemingly innocent, less "masculine" countenance, and by the opium these men might supply. It was thought that opium had strong sexual qualities, which would result in "the amazing phenomenon of an educated gentlewoman, reared in a refined atmosphere, consorting with the lowest classes of yellow and black men" (Emily Murphy, cited in Valverde, 1991, p. 184).

The 19th century, then, brought considerable transformation to Western sexual culture. The meaning of sexuality changed, and responsibility for controlling sexual deviance was shifted to individuals and their own self-control. The role of the state in regulating sexual deviance declined somewhat in the early part of the 19th century. However, as moral entrepreneurs (in the form of sexual activists, social reformers, and doctors) identified and drew attention to perceived problems such as sexual "diseases" (e.g., sodomy, homosexuality), the sex industry, and what they defined as female sexual exploitation, the state's role in controlling sexual deviance and regulating morality grew once again. Sexual culture is always embedded within the culture as a whole, and the way that sexuality was perceived during this era integrated class, gender, and racial inequalities of the time.

With the dawn of the 20th century and after, the sexual culture of American society continued to transform. The dominant meaning of sexuality eventually shifted from a focus on personal intimacy within marriage to a focus on *personal happiness*, regardless of marriage (D'Emilio & Freedman, 1997). In other words, sexual activity came to be accepted not only within marriage, but also within courtship, casual dating, and even much briefer relationships; pleasure and "fun" were considered sufficient reasons for sexual activity. Sexuality continues to be controlled in many arenas, including the criminal justice system and the culture industry. In the realm of criminal justice, criminal codes regulate sexual deviance by criminalizing particular aspects of sexuality, such as sexual assault and public indecency.

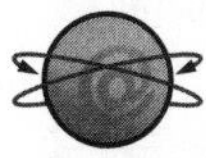

AN INTERNET MOMENT:

Find a copy of the Criminal Code of Canada at the Department of Justice Website (http://laws.justice.gc.ca/en/C-46/index.html) and go to the section on Sexual Offences. Here you can see the aspects of sexuality that are defined as deviant in a criminal sense in Canadian society at the present time. Look at the range of sexual offences that are included, and think about what aspects of sexuality are being regulated in each case. For example, is a particular behaviour being regulated? Is the nature of the relationship the issue that is being controlled? Is a broader issue, such as age, involved? Looking at this material will provide you with a more informed background for the upcoming section on sexuality in contemporary society.

The culture industry grew rapidly during the 20th century, to the dominant force it is today. In contemporary America, the culture industry, through the sex industry (see Box 4.1) and the integration of sexuality into mainstream culture (i.e., television, movies, music, advertising, etc.), is perhaps the predominant single contributor to sexual culture. In fact, with the globalization of American popular culture throughout the world (including Canada), the American culture industry is a significant contributor to the sexual culture of many societies. At the same time, moral entrepreneurs and special interest groups also use the media as a tool for communicating their positions in the deviance dance. For example, public service campaigns promote "safer sex" in magazines, the pharmaceutical industry creates television commercials for the drug Viagra, and gay rights organizations send out press releases about their organizations' activities (such as parades or protests).

Box 4.1 The Sex Industry

What is the "sex industry" worth? It is difficult to say for certain. The "sex industry" includes Internet pornography, adult video sales and rentals, strip clubs, peep shows, pornographic magazines, telephone sex, and more. Despite the difficulty in obtaining numbers, there is considerable consensus that the industry's worth is almost beyond imagination, both within and outside of Canada.

The pornographic video industry alone has a substantial economic worth, in 1999 constituting 18% of Canada's video sales and rental market, for a conservative estimate of $300 million. It is estimated that Canada's sex industry is worth 10 times Canada's music industry (Hoffman, 1999), approximately $1.4 billion (in US dollars) annually (*Montreal Gazette*, 2002). Internet pornography itself is a billion-dollar industry worldwide, and online components of the sex industry generate more income than any other income-generating Websites (Cooper, 2002). There are more online searches for sex-related sites than for sites devoted to education, government, or fine arts (*Network World Canada*, 2002).

Statistics on the sex industry in the United States are even more staggering: "[In 1996] Americans spent more than $8 billion on hardcore videos, peep shows, live sex acts, adult cable programming, sexual devices, computer porn, and sex magazines—an amount much larger than Hollywood's domestic box office receipts and larger than all the revenues generated by rock and country music recordings. Americans now spend more money at strip clubs than at Broadway, off-Broadway, regional, and nonprofit theaters; at the opera, the ballet, and jazz and classical music performances—combined." (Schlosser, 1997)

The economic power of the sex industry makes it a significant contributor to our sexual culture today.

Exercise Your Mind:

For this exercise, I want you to watch American television, go to the movie theatre, and/or rent American movies–yes, you can tell everyone that you are doing this as an exercise in learning for your deviance class. Spending a night (or even better, a few nights) watching American television or movies is a good way to see the role played by the culture industry in the way sexuality is socially constructed in the United States, Canada, and other nations where American popular culture predominates. As you watch these television shows or movies, think about the broader sexual culture involved. What are these television shows or movies saying about sexuality? What meanings of sexuality are they communicating to the audience? What is "acceptable" and "deviant" sexuality according to whatever shows or movies you are watching? Are there conflicting or opposing messages about sexuality being conveyed? If you are interested, and have adequate access, rent some movies or watch some reruns from different time periods to see the ways in which the sexual culture has changed or stayed the same. Movies you might want to choose from include *Gone With the Wind* (1930s), *The Philadelphia Story* (1940s), *The Graduate* (1960s), *Animal House* (1970s), and *Porky's* (1980s). Television shows from different eras that can be easily found include *I Love Lucy, Petticoat Junction, All in the Family, MASH,* and a contemporary comparison, *Friends*.

If you have engaged in the above exercise, you now have some additional insight into the media as one facet of sexual culture, and into how, even when focusing solely on mass media, there have been considerable changes in the way sexuality has been socially constructed during the 20th century. For instance, the messages about sexuality contained in the 1980s movie *Porky's* are very different than those contained in the 1940s movie *The Philadelphia Story*. Seeing the extent of transformation during the relatively short period of time between these two movies gives you some indication of the magnitude of changes in the sexual cultures of North America over the past 400 years, from the 17th century to the 21st century. And if the sexual culture of this small part of the world can change so substantially over time, think about the magnitude of variations that can occur across cultures, as illustrated in the sections on Sambian society, ancient Athens, and traditional Aboriginal cultures of North America. The ways that sexuality is constructed has an almost incomprehensible impact on what we, as people living in a given society at a precise moment in history, think, act, and are treated by others in terms of sexuality.

This brings us to the present moment, and the sexual culture of *our* time. In the following sections of the chapter, we will more closely examine the sexual culture of contemporary Canadian society.

TIME TO REVIEW:

- *What is the dominant meaning of sexuality in the 20th century? Is it still perceived as an avenue to personal intimacy within marriage (as in the 19th century), or has it evolved into something else?*
- *What roles have the criminal justice system and the culture industry played in the creation of the sexual culture of the 20th century?*

Sexual Culture Today

If you participated in the last exercise, you spent some time watching television and/or movies to learn something about sexuality in contemporary society. I asked you to watch American television shows and movies, but the fact that you are able to turn on your television or go to your local video store and access American mass media means that it contributes to the creation of Canada's sexual culture as well. In watching television or movies, you have been able to observe the construction of deviance and normality within those arenas—what is considered acceptable, what is considered deviant, what happens to those who are deviant. These are precisely the issues we will direct our attention to in this section of the chapter. We will explore some of the criteria by which sexual deviance and normality are determined within the sexual culture of our time, and some of the contrasting viewpoints within this deviance dance.

Criteria for Determining Deviance

Ask Yourself:

How can you determine whether someone's sexuality is "deviant" or "normal"? Make a list of the basis upon which you make your judgments about people's sexuality.

A closer look at our contemporary sexual culture reveals a number of criteria that are used to evaluate sexuality as either "deviant" or "normal." Dimensions that have been explored by other deviance specialists include the degree of consent, nature of the sexual partner, nature of the sexual act, setting, frequency, time, age, and number of partners (Wheeler, 1960; Goode, 1997). We will explore consent, nature of the partner, and nature of the act as core criteria by which we determine "deviant" sexuality, and setting and frequency as two of the more peripheral criteria used.

Consent

One of the criteria we use to determine deviance in the realm of sexuality is that of **consent** (Wheeler, 1960; Goode, 1997), and some researchers (e.g., Mackay, 2000) use the concept of consent as the defining characteristic of "normal" sex. Is consent involved in the sexual act in question? Is it even possible for consent to be involved in the sexual act in question? The most obvious use of this criterion is by the criminal justice system in cases of sexual assault; if there is no consent involved, then the act is a criminal one, making it necessarily deviant. In fact, the complete lack of consent leads many people to interpret sexual assault as more of an act of violence than a sexual act. In court cases involving "date rape," that is, a victim sexually assaulted by a date, the issue of consent is usually central to the case. The defence attorney will argue that the victim did consent, or at least that the defendant reasonably thought that consent had been given; the prosecutor will argue that the victim did not consent. In the courtroom, the way that date rape cases are argued elicits the question of whose story is more believable—the defendant's or the victim's.

The question of whether it is possible for consent to be involved is another aspect of this criterion for judging sexual deviance. Beginning in the late 1990s, the use of **date rape drugs** escalated. These drugs, such as Rohypnol (also know as "roofies" or "roopies") and GHB (also known as "G" or "Liquid X"), are odorless and tasteless drugs that when mixed with alcohol cause intense drowsiness (or even passing out) and memory impairment. If someone slips one of these drugs into someone's drink, that person will not know it is there, and may not be able to remember anything that happens in the ensuing hours. These drugs are referred to as "date rape drugs" because of the instances when they have been used in order to have sex with someone without having to get consent (or, more significantly, without the victim being coherent enough to say "no"). These consequences of the drugs have caused them to be labelled as a danger, and formal and informal regulation have emerged. It is likely that the student services organization at your university has had campaigns to raise people's awareness of these drugs and the way they are used; for example, you may have seen posters displayed on your campus that provide information about how to avoid being a victim. When you and friends go to bars or nightclubs, perhaps you do not accept drinks being brought to you by anyone other than the bar server, or maybe when you go to make a phone call you leave your unfinished drink in the protection of a trusted friend (or even take it with you to the phone). The legal system has determined that having sex with someone after giving them these drugs constitutes sexual assault, arguing that in these situations the person is not of a state of mind where giving consent is possible.

Courts have also argued that consent is not possible in situations involving sexual acts between children and adults. Due to level of cognitive development as well as significant power differentials, a child is not considered capable of giving consent, especially to an adult. Thus, sexual acts between children and adults are defined as crimes on the part of the adult. You can see a description of Canada's age-of-consent laws, and their complexities, in Box 4.2.

Box 4.2 Canada's Age-of-Consent Laws

What is the age of consent for sexual activity in Canada? The answer to that question is not as straightforward as one might initially think. Canada's age-of-consent laws are multifaceted and complex. The laws governing sexual behaviour, in which age of consent is an issue, are as follows:

Sexual Assault: A common defence in sexual assault trials is that the accused believed there was consent involved in the sexual activity. However, if the complainant is under the age of 14, the accused cannot make the claim of consent; consent is perceived as not being possible in that instance.

Sexual Interference: This is a crime defined by the sexual touching of the body of someone under the age of 14. The lack of the possibility of consent is what defines this crime.

Invitation to Sexual Touching: This is a crime defined by requesting someone under the age of 14 to sexually touch the accused. Again, the lack of the possibility of consent is what defines this crime.

The above age-of-consent laws are further complicated by the question of the age of the accused. That is, consent *is* considered possible in regard to the above behaviours if (a) the complainant is at least 12 but under the age of 14, *and* (b) the accused is between the ages of 12 and 16, *and* (c) the accused is no more than two years older than the complainant, *and* (d) the accused is not in a position of trust and authority over the complainant.

Bestiality in the Presence of a Child: Bestiality (i.e., sexual activity with an animal) is itself a crime. However, committing an act of bestiality in front of a child under the age of 14, or inciting a child under the age of 14 to commit an act of bestiality, is a specific subsection of that same law.

Sexual Exploitation: Although the age of 14 is highlighted in the age-of-consent laws described above, sexual exploitation involves sexually touching (or inviting sexual touching from) someone between the ages of 14 and 18, *if the accused is in a position of trust or authority over the complainant.*

Some specific examples may be helpful in illustrating the above age-of-consent laws:

Example #1: Someone older than the age of 16 cannot engage in sexual activity with someone under the age of 14.

Example #2: No one, regardless of age, can engage in sexual touching (or invitation to sexual touching) of someone between the ages of 14 and 18, if the accused is in a position of trust or authority.

Example #3: Consent is perceived as being possible between a 12-year-old and a 14-year-old, but not between a 12-year-old and a 15-year-old (because in the latter instance, the age difference is more than two years).

Canada's age-of-consent laws are clearly multifaceted and complex. They are also a dynamic force in Canadian society, being subject to change over time. For instance, recently debates have emerged over whether the age of consent should be increased in order to prevent the potential exploitation of youth over the age of 14, who receive less protection than those under the age of 14 within current age-of-consent laws.

Although sexual interaction between adults and children is necessarily deviant because of it is forbidden by the Criminal Code, social characteristics of the child and the adult may play a role in public perceptions of deviance or normality. The age of the child and the age of the adult may influence public perceptions of whether consent is possible. For example, an 8-year-old may be perceived as much less capable of giving consent than a 13-year-old is. And if a 13-year-old is having sex with her 16-year-old boyfriend, in contrast to her 37-year-old boyfriend, the public may view it as a consensual relationship (even if they disapprove of 13-year-olds being sexually active in general). In interaction with age, gender may affect public perceptions of deviance or normality as well. That is, teenage boys are often seen as being more capable of giving consent to adults than teenage girls are.

This gender discrepancy became evident in the state of Washington in 1997, when Mary Kay Letourneau, a 35-year-old schoolteacher, was convicted of having a sexual relationship with a 12-year-old boy, her former student. When arrested, she was pregnant with the boy's child and subsequently became pregnant a second time after receiving a suspended sentence. Continuing to see the boy was a violation of her suspended sentence, so she was subsequently sentenced to more than seven years in prison. An intense debate ensued within the media. On one side of the debate, people suggested that, while what she had done was rather "odd," she and the boy (who had said he did consent to the sexual relationship) were in love and wanted to spend the rest of their lives together. On the other side of the debate, people pointed out that both as a child and as a former student of Letourneau's, the boy was incapable of giving consent. They argued that if this were the case of a 12-year-old girl who became pregnant as a result of her relationship with a 35-year-old male teacher, there would be no debate over the possibility of consent—everyone would be outraged. At the present time, Letourneau remains in prison, and the boy and his mother are raising the two children born out of the relationship. The young man (who is now on the verge of adulthood) no longer professes his love for Letourneau; he considers himself to be a victim of a child molester who took advantage of her authority over him, and he has launched a lawsuit against the local school board for failing to protect him. Letourneau's husband (who was the one who found out about the relationship and reported it to the police) has divorced her and moved to Alaska with their four children. More recently, a number of similar cases involving female schoolteachers and young males in Canada and Britain have received media attention as well.

Issues of consent are perceived differently across place and time. In many countries, consent is not considered necessary between husband and wife; sexual relations are prescribed as required within the marital relationship. In fact, it was only in 1983 that the Canadian legal system defined sexual assault as possible within marriage. Similarly, it was only in 1987 that our legal system made sexual assault laws gender-neutral, recognizing that it is possible for a man to be raped by either another man or a woman (Nelson & Robinson, 1999). Many societies today continue to define the crime of sexual assault only in terms of a male perpetrator and a female victim. In the historical section of the chapter, we saw that from the 17th century through most of the 19th century, black women were expected to be sexually available to white men (Das Gupta, 2000; Mandell & Momoirov, 2000; D'Emilio & Freedman, 1997). Because of this expectation, white men were unlikely to be charged with raping black women if there was no consent. In fact, if the black woman was a slave and the white man a member of the slave-owner's family, then consent was a non-issue because she was considered a piece of the family's property, to do with as they pleased.

Divergent points of view exist even on the issue of the age at which consent is possible, not only across cultures, but within North America itself today. Historically we saw that in ancient Athens, male youth were perceived (however realistically, given their age and social status) as capable of consenting to sexual relationships with adult aristocratic males. Cross-culturally we saw that, among the Sambia of New Guinea, adult male sexual activities with male children and adolescents is normative, and that the question of consent itself is non-existent. In contemporary North America, the North America Man/Boy Love Association (NAMBLA) argues that teenagers are capable of giving consent in sexual relationships with adults, and some members of NAMBLA suggest that even younger children are capable of giving consent (NAMBLA home page, 2002). Of course, as you may have expected, tremendous opposition exists to NAMBLA's message, and to the organization itself. Afraid of being associated with this organization, gay rights organizations have been especially vocal in their opposition, "deploring NAMBLA and everything it advocates which basically amounts to a push to legitimize child molestation," and arguing that the organization "has no legitimate place in society, Queer or Straight" (The NAMBLA Controversy, para. 1). Obviously, the debate over age-of-consent laws is a highly heated one. By challenging one of society's most firmly held beliefs, organizations like NAMBLA have been socially typed as deviant; they are described as "pedophiles," evaluated in an extremely negative light, and face a tremendous level of public outcry.

TIME TO REVIEW:

- How is consent, as a criterion by which sexuality is judged as "deviant" or "normal," related to sexual assault and date rape? What are "date rape drugs," and why have they been given that label?
- Why does the legal system define children as incapable of consenting to sexual relationships with adults? Give two examples of Canada's age-of-consent laws.
- How do public perceptions regarding age of consent vary, based on (a) the specific age of the child, and (b) the specific age of the adult?
- Give examples of how issues of consent have been perceived differently across time and place, specifically regarding (a) marital status, (b) gender, (c) race, and (d) age.

The issue of consent raises a related issue, that of "appropriate" sexual partners. Someone who does not give consent, or who is not capable of giving consent, is considered an unacceptable sexual partner, both legally and socially. However, the choice of a sexual partner as either "deviant" or "normal" goes beyond the issue of consent alone.

Nature of the Sexual Partner

The historical and cross-cultural variations that were presented earlier in this chapter pointed to the role that the **nature of the sexual partner** plays in determining sexual deviance. In Sambian society, the appropriate sexual partner varies during a male's life, from older males, to younger males, to younger males and wives, and finally to wives alone. In Athens during the 5th century B.C., acceptable sexual partners for aristocratic men included wives, prostitutes, slaves, foreigners, and adolescent males; men of equal social status were defined as inappropriate sexual partners. In the dominant Europeanized culture of North America, from the 17th century to the 20th century marriage gradually lost its monopoly as the only legitimate outlet for sexual behaviour, and a wider range of sexual partners came to be deemed appropriate. However, despite this transition to more freedom in the selection of a sexual partner, there still is not *complete* freedom in the choice of a sexual partner in contemporary North America.

Beginning with the law, we can see particular people being defined as unacceptable sexual partners. We already addressed the issue of age-of-consent laws, making individuals who are under the age of consent inappropriate sexual partners. The Criminal Code also prohibits sexual relationships between close family members—parents, children, grandparents, grandchildren, siblings, and half-siblings. Violating this prohibition between close family members constitutes the crime of *incest*. Bestiality is a crime in Canada, making animals unacceptable sexual partners. Finally, several sexual laws within the Criminal Code (such as "sexual exploitation") define as inappropriate sexual partners anyone over whom the individual is in a position of trust or authority, or anyone who is in a relationship of dependency with the individual.

The nature of the sexual partner is also controlled outside of the legal system. The choice of sexual partners is formally regulated within some places of business, where company policies prohibit intimate relationships between co-workers, or between bosses and employees. Many schools, colleges, and universities prohibit sexual relationships between teachers and students. Within the psychiatric and psychological communities, professional organizations define sexual relationships between therapists and clients as a violation of the professional code of ethics. If the sexual partner in question is an object rather than a person, and if that object is necessary for sexual stimulation to occur, the psychiatric community labels it a *fetish*, for which treatment can be obtained.

At an informal level, particular sexual partners may be perceived as socially unacceptable. For example, although the law does not prohibit sexual relations between first cousins, such relations would still push the boundaries of social acceptability. However, in other cultures, it is quite common for marriages to be arranged between them. And even though some universities and colleges do not have policies prohibiting intimate relationships between students and professors, within the cultural climates of those institutions, such relationships are still frowned upon, and professors who engage in such relationships frequently become stigmatized.

At both formal and informal levels, members of the same sex continue to be defined as inappropriate sexual partners to some extent. There have been significant changes in social attitudes regarding homosexuality over the past several decades, the result of social activism and education; these changes have increased individual freedom to choose a member of the same sex as a sexual partner. For example, sexual orientation has recently begun to be incorporated into Canadian human rights legislation (despite the vocal opposition by some provincial governments). Even the Catholic Church, which historically has strongly condemned homosexuality as an abomination, is beginning to show some change. Formally, Catholic doctrine continues to prohibit homosexuality. Recently, however, a pastoral letter written by US Catholic bishops "advised parents to put love and support for their gay sons and daughters before church doctrine" (Hone-Mcmahan & Schleis, 1998, para. 3), saying that science tells us homosexuality is not a choice, and since it is not a choice, it is not a sin.

However, despite some changes in prevailing social attitudes, gays and lesbians continue to be deviantized for the nature of their sexual partners. Of course, the stigmatization experienced by gays and lesbians in North America may not be as formal and as overt as in some other cultures in the world, such as the eight countries of the world wherein homosexuality is a crime punishable by the death penalty—Afghanistan, Iran, Mauritania, Pakistan, Saudi Arabia, Sudan, United Arab Emirates, and Yemen (Mackay, 2001). But even in the United States several states continued to define homosexual acts as crimes until 2003, and in Canada gays and lesbians are just gaining full equality under marriage and family laws. Throughout North America, various organizations and helping professionals claim that through therapy or prayer they can help people to become "ex-gay" (ABC News, 2001). And many other organizations have weeded out gays and lesbians who are discovered within the organizations, such as the Boy Scouts in the United States and, in the mid-20th century in Canada, the military and federal civil service (Ferguson, 2001).

In the informal realm of everyday interaction, the stigmatization of gays and lesbians is evident as well. A brief search of the Internet reveals thousands of "anti-gay" Websites, many of which express support of physical violence directed at people who are homosexual. Franklin (2000) found, in a survey of college students, that 10% admitted to acts of physical violence or threats of physical violence directed at people whom they *thought* were homosexual. Verbal stigmatization is even more common. Franklin's (2000) survey found that approximately one-quarter of young adults admit to calling people whom they thought were gay various derogatory names. High school students report that they hear anti-gay comments or name-calling an average of 25 times a day (PFLAG, 2001).

The deviantization of gays and lesbians in North America is the most clearly illustrated by the acts of violence directed at them. For example, in Wyoming in 1998 a young gay man, Matthew Shepard, was tied to a fence, beaten, pistol-whipped, tortured, and left to die in the cold—simply because he was gay. He had been beaten twice before in the past two months, for the same reason, but this time he was unable to survive his injuries. While he was dying in the hospital, a group of college students placed a Matthew Shepard scarecrow, with "I'm gay" and an obscene message written on its shirt, on their homecoming parade float; they thought it would be a good "joke." During his funeral, members of extremist Christian groups paraded nearby, carrying signs that said "AIDS cures fags" and "God hates fags"; after his funeral, people came to dance on his grave. Although an extreme case, the murder of Matthew Shepard illustrates the depth of stigmatization that homosexuals potentially face in society today. And their risk of criminal victimization is considerably higher than that of the general population not only in North America (Herek, Gillis, & Cogan, 1997; Bochenek & Brown, 2001), but also in the United Kingdom (Mason & Palmer, 1996), and Australia (Mason & Tomsen, 1997). For example, one California study found that 41% of homosexuals and bisexuals had been victims of a hate-related crime at some time since the age of 16 (Herek, Gillis, & Cogan, 1997). At the time of this writing, a large-scale national Canadian study involving police departments and other organizations across the country is underway, which will document the prevalence of hate crimes in Canada; part of the analysis will document the incidence of hate crimes based on sexual orientation.

Overall, Western cultures are characterized by considerably more freedom in the choice of sexual partners today than in the past. However, freedom is not unlimited. The choice of sexual partners is still regulated by the law and other formal means, as well as informal means such as social stigmatization. The nature of the sexual partner is an important criterion in our evaluations of people's sexuality as either deviant or normal (Goode, 1997; Wheeler, 1960). However, even if the sexual partner is considered acceptable and "normal," other criteria become involved in our evaluations as well, such as the nature of the sexual act.

TIME TO REVIEW:

- How does the earlier discussion on historical and cross-cultural variations in sexual cultures illustrate the nature of the sexual partner as a criterion for evaluating deviance?
- How is choice of sexual partners formally and informally regulated?
- In what ways have members of the same sex come to be seen as more acceptable sexual partners than in the past? In what ways do members of the same sex continue to be defined as unacceptable sexual partners?

Nature of the Sexual Act

Even if the nature of your sexual partner is defined as normal and acceptable, is what you are doing with that partner considered "kinky" (Goode, 1997, p. 208)? That is, are you engaging in "normal" or "deviant" acts? The answer to that question is both culturally and historically specific, and at times is tied in with the nature of the partner. In Sambian society, oral sex between males is considered acceptable, but only if the younger male is performing the act on the older male, and only if the older male has not yet become a father. In 5th century B.C. Athens, oral sex between males was perceived as appropriate, but only if the males were not of equal social status, and only if the younger male was not paid for the act. Following European colonization of the Americas, sexual intercourse between husbands and wives was the only acceptable sexual act, and only if in the "missionary" position.

Even over the last century there have been significant changes in which sexual acts are perceived as being "deviant" or "normal." For example, in Chapter 1 there was a discussion of the extreme measures taken in the early 20th century to prevent masturbation in children, based on medical discourses of the time, which claimed a wide range of physical, mental, and social harms as consequences of masturbation. Now, in the early 21st century, the same stigma is no longer attached to masturbation. The growing sexual freedom of the last century has allowed a range of sexual acts to be seen as more acceptable. Walk into any bookstore or public library, and you will find books that present information on various new sexual positions to try, and new techniques to use. Retail stores that sell a variety of "sex toys" to incorporate into sexual acts abound, both on the streets of any city as well as on the Internet. Sexologist Isadora Alman (cited in *First for Women*, 2001) suggests "the average couple has played a bondage game, shared a fantasy, and made love in the shower or pool. To restrict lovemaking to kissing, manual foreplay and intercourse in two basic positions and to do so only in bed is to live like your grandparents did" (p. 31).

Due to the rapid growth in sexual freedom during the 20th century, greater subjectivity has emerged in precisely which sexual acts are perceived as "kinky." In other words, what is considered a sexually deviant act is now more in the eye of the beholder than was true in the past. Our sexual culture has come to be infused with an ideology of privacy; as long as a particular sexual activity is performed by consenting adults outside the view of others, we define it as being nobody else's business. And although each of us, individually, might perceive particular sexual acts as "kinky," the ideology of privacy limits contemporary social controls on sexual behaviours, particularly at a formal level. In the late 1960s, Justice Minister Pierre Trudeau suggested that the government has no place in the bedrooms of adult Canadians, monitoring their sexual behaviors. Today, we not only continue to accept that perception, but also think that none of us as individuals has a place in the bedrooms of others, monitoring their sexual behaviours, either.

The issue of consent, the nature of the sexual partner, and the **nature of the sexual act** are three of the core criteria by which we evaluate sexuality and subsequently judge it as deviant or normal. In addition to these three core criteria, there are also a number of more peripheral criteria that are utilized for judgment in contemporary sexual culture (Goode, 1997). For example, sexual activities within certain locations are considered to be deviant. An episode of the popular TV show *Seinfeld* highlights the issue of location in determining deviance. In this episode, George Costanza has a sexual encounter with the cleaning lady in his office cubicle. The next day he is called into his boss's office and fired for that encounter, despite his protests that he had never been warned that the company frowned upon having sex in the office. This *Seinfeld* episode points out that the workplace is seen as an inappropriate setting for sexual activity in North American society. In Canada, the law defines certain locations (i.e., public places) as unacceptable for sexual activities. People who enjoy having sex in places where others might see them are labelled **exhibitionists**.

The **frequency of sex** is another one of the more peripheral criteria used to evaluate sexuality. Is someone having sex too often, not often enough, or just the right amount? This is a common question that is asked of advice columnists, sex therapists, and marriage counselors. Popular TV psychologist Dr. Phil McGraw deals with this issue in the "relationship" section of his Website, responding to the question of whether it is "normal" for a married couple to rarely or never have sex. One issue of the women's magazine *First for Women* (August 6, 2001) devotes an entire article to what constitutes "normal" sex, including a table that readers can refer to in order to determine the "normal" frequency of sex based on age at marriage and number of years married. In fact, this table is titled "How much sex is normal," implying that frequency outside of the numbers listed is "abnormal." This magazine article also addresses the previous criterion mentioned, that of the nature of the sexual act, explaining to the hundreds of thousands of monthly readers which particular acts are "normal." People who have sex infrequently may be perceived as "frigid" (Goode, 1997). Those who have sex too frequently may be labelled "nymphomaniacs," or may even be diagnosed with a sexual "addiction." Our collective interest in the question of frequency even results in its inclusion on the annual *Durex Global Sex Survey*. Durex surveys more than 50 000 people in countries around the world every year, providing data on which nation has the most sex (in 2002, France, at 167 times per person per year) and the least sex (in 2002, Singapore, at 110 times per person per year). Nation-specific data gathered for the survey indicates that, in Canada, people in Quebec have more frequent sex than Canadians in other provinces or territories.

Discussions of frequency, location, nature of the act, nature of the partner, and the issue of consent point to both the increasing freedom that has come to characterize our sexual culture, and the formal and informal limitations that continue to be placed on that freedom. As a society, we perceive a narrower range of behaviours as sexually deviant than we did in the past but, through the use of various criteria, sexual deviance continues to be defined, identified, and controlled. However, the processes of defining, identifying, and controlling sexual deviance are not uniform; they are part of the "deviance dance."

TIME TO REVIEW:

- How does the earlier discussion on historical and cross-cultural variations in sexual cultures illustrate the nature of the sexual act as a criterion for evaluating deviance?
- In what ways is a growth in sexual freedom evident regarding the nature of the sexual act in Canadian society? How is the ideology of privacy related to this?
- How do location and frequency serve as criteria by which we evaluate sexuality as being "deviant" or "normal"? Provide examples.

Sexuality and the "Deviance Dance"

In any given culture at any particular time in history, certain trends or characteristics can be identified within the sexual culture. However, a multiplicity of perceptions, reactions, and social controls are also intertwined with those broader trends. For example, Herdt's (1984, 1993) description of **ritualized homosexuality** among the Sambians includes some description of the mixed feelings about the practice, particularly as the boys were being separated from their mothers. Sexual relationships between aristocratic adult and adolescent males, although common in 5th century B.C. Athens, were not uniformly accepted. Segments of Athenian society were critical of such relationships, and often sought to initiate levels of control for the purposes of protecting these "exploited" adolescent males (Bloch, 2001). The discussion of the Canadian and American history presented earlier in the chapter captured some of the diversity entwined within sexual culture, wherein class, race, and gender variations were central to the ways that sexuality was constructed and controlled. For example, although relationships between black men and white women were considered deviant and made subject to considerable social control, such relationships sometimes resulted in marriages that were accepted within some communities. During the Victorian era, considerable restrictions on sexual behaviour (such as extensive controls on childhood masturbation) were countered with the expansion of the sex industry—photographs, books, and sexually oriented live performances (D'Emilio & Freedman, 1997; Ullman, 1997).

In contemporary North America, considerable debate exists over many aspects of sexual culture. The large numbers of retail shops selling sexual "toys" coexist with organizations that condemn TV programs that include references to "kinky practices" (Parents Television Council, 2001, para. 9) like masturbation, oral sex, and bondage. Gay, lesbian, and bisexual activist groups, and changing human rights legislation, coexist with segments of society that continue to stigmatize and condemn homosexual practices. Widespread efforts to eliminate the sexual abuse and exploitation of children even coexist with organizations trying to place limits on those controls, such as NAMBLA. Academic scholarship on variations in sexuality across cultures and time exist alongside scholarship that condemns the uncritical acceptance of cross-cultural sexual behaviours, such as the ritualized homosexuality involving children within Sambian society. College tours by sex educator Sue Johanson are countered by administrators' attempts to censor the publication of a student sex survey in a college newspaper (*Intercamp*, 2001). Rapidly changing technologies are raising additional questions and debates about "deviant" sexuality—popular psychologist Dr. Phil McGraw answers the question of whether using Internet pornography constitutes as "cheating" on one's spouse (he says it does), and others are asking the question of whether sexually explicit conversations with strangers in Internet chat rooms constitute adultery (Mulgrew, 2001).

The "deviance dance" is evident with many issues related to sexuality, but perhaps at no time is it more evident than when considering the issue of pornography. Anti-pornography activism exists alongside anti-censorship groups seeking to control the influences of such activism, and the question of whether pornography is "harmful" continues to be a nexus of passionate debate. Even the question of what pornography *is* remains subject to debate.

Pornography

What is **pornography**? Is it harmful? Should it be controlled, and if so, how? These questions represent continuing discrepancies of opinion when the topic of pornography arises. Many definitions of pornography incorporate some notion of *explicit sex*, which at the surface seems a common-sense assumption. However, even this common-sense assumption is more ambiguous than it may initially appear (Childress, 1991). A certain level of subjectivity is involved when trying to determine precisely what constitutes "explicit" sex—whether it can be found in mainstream media like *Dawson's Creek*, or only in those videotapes and magazines that only adults may purchase. The often-cited words of US Supreme Court Justice Potter Stewart (e.g., Childress, 1991) suggest that, despite the difficulties in defining pornography, we all know it when we see it. However, as Childress (1991, p. 178) points out, "Although everyone knows hard-core pornography when they see it, they see it in strikingly different places, and so no one really knows it at all."

Academics, politicians, and social activists have tried to define pornography, resulting in several different types of definitions. Some are **functional definitions** that suggest pornography is anything that is used by an individual for the purposes of sexual arousal (Goode, 1997)—pornography is "in the groin of the beholder" (*Edmonton Journal*, March 24, 2002, p. D6). The broad nature of this definition means that the women's undergarment section of the *Eaton's* catalogue of the early 20th century (which boys would sneak peeks at), the *Victoria's Secret* catalogue today (which many boys and men sneak peeks at), and women's romance novels (e.g., *Silhouette Desire*) could be considered "pornography" if they are used to become aroused.

Other definitions are **genre definitions** (Goode, 1997), which propose that products created for the purposes of arousing the consumer constitute "pornography." Even the definition of pornography offered in the Merriam-Webster dictionary (2002) adheres to this principal: pornography is "the depiction of erotic behavior (as in pictures and writing) intended to cause sexual excitement." Of course, this type of definition leads us to try to infer what the producer's intentions were in some cases. Are *Harlequin* romance novels trying to cause sexual excitement? How about the publishers of *Maxim* magazine or the *Sports Illustrated* swimsuit issue?

Labelling definitions of pornography focus on community standards—anything that community members deem obscene (Goode, 1997). The notions of obscenity and community standards are central to Canadian law. Section 163 of the Criminal Code defines an obscene publication as "any publication a dominant characteristic of which is the undue exploitation of sex, or of sex and any one or more of the following subjects, namely, crime, horror, [or] cruelty and violence...." Exceptions to this definition include publications that have artistic/literary merit, or that are for educational or medical purposes. The "community standards test" is one way of determining whether a publication can be considered obscene; the question here is what a majority of Canadians would not tolerate other people seeing (rather than what they might find personally distasteful). The Supreme Court of Canada (R. vs. Butler, 1992; R. vs. Sharpe, 2001) sets out criteria for determining the presence of "undue exploitation of sex," "educational or medical purposes," "artistic/literary merit," and other characteristics mentioned in debates over pornography. However, some level of subjectivity is involved with the descriptions of all of the criteria integrated into Canadian law. For instance, how does the court determine what a majority of Canadians would not tolerate other people seeing, unless research has been done to measure Canadian attitudes? Such subjectivities make even the legal definition of obscenity somewhat amorphous.

The legal definition of **child pornography** is considerably clearer. Section 163 of the Criminal Code defines child pornography as any representation of someone under the age of 18 engaged in explicit sexual activity, or any representation of someone under the age of 18, "the dominant characteristic of which is the depiction, for a sexual purpose, of a sexual organ or the anal region." Again, materials having artistic/literary merit or those that are for educational or medical purposes are excluded from this definition, as are personal writings that are kept private (such as a diary or a short story) and self-photographs that are kept private. However, even though the legal definition of child pornography has greater clarity than the legal definition of obscenity (not involving children), both have been subject to social and legal debate.

In 1992, the Supreme Court of Canada reviewed the Butler case, in which a storeowner had been convicted of selling obscene materials. The defence claimed that prohibiting the possession and/or selling of obscene materials was a violation of the freedom of expression, guaranteed in the Canadian Charter of Rights and Freedoms. The Supreme Court agreed that is was a violation of this right, but that the violation was reasonable in pursuit of the protection and greater good of society. Debate over this issue extended beyond the criminal justice system as well. In the ensuing years, some Canadian feminist groups protested that the Butler decision had resulted in the biased suppression of the sexual expression of minorities, such as materials portraying gay and lesbian sexuality. They argued that, because homophobia pervades society, those "community standards" that are used as a test for obscenity integrate homophobia and result in discrimination based on sexual orientation within the criminal justice system (Bell et. al, 1998). The question of whether obscenity laws violate basic human freedoms, and whether this is a reasonable violation, extend beyond Canada's borders as well, into the United States (e.g., Greco, 1995/1996) and Britain (e.g., Carol, 1994). Even the prohibition against possessing child pornography has been challenged. In 2001, the Supreme Court of Canada (R. vs. Sharpe) once again agreed that the law does violate freedom of expression, but that it is a reasonable violation of that freedom, in the name of the protection of children's rights.

The reasons why obscenity laws and child pornography laws are considered to be a reasonable violation of the freedom of expression are based on the concept of *harm*. That is, obscene materials and child pornography are deemed to be harmful. In the case of child pornography, the Supreme Court concluded that, although scientific research could not definitively prove that people who possess child pornography will subsequently sexually harm particular children, the possessors of child pornography create a demand that results in the production of child pornography, which does harm the children represented in that pornography. In the case of obscene materials not involving children, the harm referred to by the Supreme Court is a generalized harm based in part on the degradation of a particular social group protected in human rights legislation (women).

The question of whether pornography that does not include children is harmful has been a matter of considerable debate outside of the legal realm as well (Childress, 1991; Greco, 1995/1996; Stark, 1997; Davies, 1997). Some participants in this debate focus on the question of physical harm—whether male consumers of pornography will be driven to sexually victimize women. Other participants in this debate focus on the question of a broader harm to the functioning of society, that is, whether pornography is harmful to women in terms of attitudes toward them and perceptions of them in the larger society. And yet other participants direct their attention at questions of ontological harm; such questions may address religious issues or concerns about the moral fibre of society. Regardless of the particular type of harm being addressed, research results are similar in that they are contradictory and inconclusive (Davies, 1997), and are often confounded with the moral or social agendas of the specific researchers or sponsors of such research (Stebbins, 1996). As with other issues related to sexuality, the issue of pornography is one characterized by the "deviance dance"—disagreement, debate, resistance, and plurality.

Amidst the plurality that exists surrounding sexuality in our society and others, there have been attempts to create cross-cultural standards for evaluating sexuality, trying to strike a balance between sexual freedoms and sexual protections that can be applied universally (see Box 4.3).

Box 4.3 The Universal Declaration of Sexual Rights

The World Association for Sexology adopted the following declaration at the 14th World Congress of Sexology, August 26, 1999:

Sexuality is an integral part of the personality of every human being. Its full development depends upon the satisfaction of basic human needs such as the desire for contact, intimacy, emotional expression, pleasure, tenderness and love. Sexuality is constructed through the interaction between the individual and social structures. Full development of sexuality is essential for individual, interpersonal, and societal well-being. Sexual rights are universal human rights based on the inherent freedom, dignity, and equality of all human beings. Since health is a fundamental human right, so must sexual health be a basic human right. In order to assure that human beings and societies develop healthy sexuality, the following sexual rights must be recognized, promoted, respected, and defended by all societies through all means. Sexual health is the result of an environment that recognizes, respects and exercises these sexual rights.

1. *The right to sexual freedom. Sexual freedom encompasses the possibility for individuals to express their full sexual potential. However, this excludes all forms of sexual coercion, exploitation, and abuse at any time and situations in life.*
2. *The right to sexual autonomy, sexual integrity, and safety of the sexual body. This right involves the ability to make autonomous decisions about one's sexual life within a context of one's own personal and social ethics. It also encompasses control and enjoyment of our own bodies free from torture, mutilation and violence of any sort.*
3. *The right to sexual privacy. This involves the right for individual decisions and behaviors about intimacy as long as they do not intrude on the sexual rights of others.*
4. *The right to sexual equity. This refers to freedom from all forms of discrimination regardless of sex, gender, sexual orientation, age, race, social class, religion, or physical and emotional disability.*
5. *The right to sexual pleasure. Sexual pleasure, including autoeroticism, is a source of physical, psychological, intellectual and spiritual well-being.*

6. *The right to emotional sexual expression. Sexual expression is more than erotic pleasure or sexual acts. Individuals have a right to express their sexuality through communication, touch, emotional expression and love.*
7. *The right to sexually associate freely. This means the possibility to marry or not, to divorce, and to establish other types of responsible sexual associations.*
8. *The right to make free and responsible reproductive choices. This encompasses the right to decide whether or not to have children, the number and spacing of children, and the right to full access to the means of fertility regulation.*
9. *The right to sexual information based upon scientific inquiry. This right implies that sexual information should be generated through the process of unencumbered and yet scientifically ethical inquiry, and disseminated in appropriate ways at all societal levels.*
10. *The right to comprehensive sexuality education. This is a lifelong process from birth throughout the life cycle and should involve all social institutions.*
11. *The right to sexual health care. Sexual health care should be available for prevention and treatment of all sexual concerns, problems and disorders.*

Ask Yourself:

Go back to the various aspects of sexuality discussed in this chapter, such as the historical and cross-cultural analyses, and the criteria for judging "deviant" and "normal" sexuality. In the context of the Universal Declaration of Sexual Rights, how would these aspects of sexuality be perceived and evaluated? Are they "deviant" or "normal" according to the propositions of the declaration?

Sexual culture is of considerable complexity, integrating sexual, scientific, religious, political, family, and popular discourses. What is considered to be sexually deviant varies among cultures on the basis of these varying discourses; however, all cultures do differentiate between deviant and normal sexuality, and all cultures formally and informally regulate sexuality.

TIME TO REVIEW:

- How is sexuality involved in the "deviance dance"? Give cross-cultural, historical, and/or contemporary examples.
- What debates and issues surround the topic of pornography in society?
- How does the Universal Declaration of Sexual Rights fit into the "deviance dance"?

Chapter Summary

The issue of sexuality crosses the boundaries of the biological and the social. What is biologically possible is of a tremendous range; however, what is socially acceptable is of a much narrower range. Social acceptability, that is, perceptions of "deviant" and "normal" sexuality, vary cross-culturally and historically, but also vary among different social groups within a particular culture at a particular time in history. When exploring this variation, more objective deviance specialists talk about *variations in norms*, while more subjective researchers refer to the *social construction of sexuality*.

The practice of what Western anthropologists have called *ritualized homosexuality* in Sambian society illustrates cross-cultural variations in the very concepts used to discuss sexuality (such as *homosexuality*, *heterosexuality*, and *bisexuality*), as well as the fundamental meaning of sexuality within society.

An analysis of the sexual culture of 5th century B.C. Athens reveals the linkages of *power* to the sexual culture of the time, revolving around the interests of aristocratic males. Such males were permitted sexual activity with the greatest range of partners, including wives, slaves, foreigners, prostitutes, and aristocratic adolescent males.

Traditional Aboriginal societies had very different sexual cultures than those of the colonizing Europeans, particularly in terms of the relationship between sexuality and pleasure, as well as perceptions of people who were erotically attracted to members of the same sex. With European colonization, the sexual cultures of Aboriginal societies were made subject to significant measures of social control.

Tremendous changes in the sexual cultures of both Canadian and American society occurred from the 16th century to the 20th century. Meanings of sexuality shifted from focusing on *reproductive ideals*, to *intimacy within marriage*, to *personal fulfillment*; agents of social control changed during this time as well. During all eras, hierarchies of race, class, and gender influenced the complexities of sexual culture.

In North America today, although sexual freedom has increased considerably since previous eras, judgments of "deviant" and "normal" sexuality continue to be made. Criteria we use to make these judgments include *consent*, *nature of the sexual partner*, *nature of the sexual act*, *location*, and *frequency*.

Exploring sexual cultures across societies and over time enables us to identify certain trends and larger patterns that characterize a particular sexual culture. However, within any given culture at any given time, there is also a multiplicity of perceptions, reactions, and social control measures present. Whether we focus on Sambian society, ancient Athens, traditional Aboriginal cultures, or North American society of the past and the present, the *deviance dance* is evident—particular social groups with varying, and even contradictory, views of the same behaviours and perceptions of appropriate social control measures. This is particular clear when considering the debates over issues related to pornography.

Recommended Readings

Valverde, M. (1993). *The age of light, soap, and water: Moral reform in English Canada, 1885-1925.* Toronto: McClelland & Stewart.

* This book explores the sexual culture of the late 19th and early 20th centuries through the social purity movement. The entwining of sexual, racial, gender, and class discourses is explored in considerable detail.

D'Emilio, J., & Freedman, E. B. (1997). *Intimate matters: A history of sexuality in America* (2nd ed.). Chicago: University of Chicago Press.

* The changing sexual culture of American society from the Colonial era through the late 20th century is the focus of this book. Its particular strength is the way it captures the complex nature of sexual cultures as dynamic and varied, not only across time but even within a single historical era. The concept of the "deviance dance" comes through quite clearly in this historical analysis.

Herdt, G. (1999). Clinical ethnography and sexual culture. *Annual Review of Sex Research, 10,* 100-119.

* This paper raises important issues regarding the cross-cultural analysis of sexuality, both in terms of how such analyses have contributed to our current understandings of the construction of sexuality, as well as how such analyses are conducted.

Cossman, B., Bell, S., Gotell, L., & Ross, B. L. (1997). *Bad attitude/s on trial: Pornography, feminism, and the Butler decision.* Toronto, ON: University of Toronto Press.

* This book explores the development of Canada's current obscenity laws, and the debates surrounding those laws.

Childress, S. A. (1991). Reel "rape speech": Violent pornography and the politics of harm. *Law and Society Review, 25(1),* 177-214.

* This article contains an excellent review of the diverse and contradictory research done about the question of pornography and harm.

Endnotes

1 Alfred Kinsey. Retrieved June 15, 2002 from the World Wide Web: **www.quotationspage.com**

2 W. Somerset Maugham. Retrieved June 15, 2002 from the World Wide Web: **www.bartleby.com**

Key Terms

patriarchy, **p. 102**
misogyny, **p. 102**
ethnocentrism, **p. 104**
nadles, **p. 107**
alyha, **p. 108**
hwame, **p. 108**
les femmes du pays, **p. 108**
social purity/sex hygiene movements, **p. 114**
consent, **p. 120**
date rape drugs, **p. 120**
nature of the sexual partner, **p. 124**
nature of the sexual act, **p. 127**
exhibitionists, **p. 128**
frequency of sex, **p. 128**
ritualized homosexuality, **p. 129**
pornography, **p. 130**
functional definitions, **p. 131**
genre definitions, **p. 131**
labelling definitions, **p. 131**
child pornography, **p. 131**

CHAPTER 5

The Troubling and Troubled World of Youth[1]

Learning Objectives

After reading this chapter, you should be able to:

- Compare popular images of youth crime with statistics on the nature and prevalence of youth crime, and explain why a gap exists between the perceptions and realities.
- Describe theoretical and empirical research on (a) youth crime, and (b) gang involvement.
- Explain how gangs and youth crime are socially controlled.
- Describe the extent and patterns of use of tobacco, drugs, and alcohol among youth, as well as how their usage is socially controlled.

- Explain what the concept of "at risk" youth means, and what the "science of risk" does.
- Describe how *all* teenagers are perceived as deviant in society, and explain the nature of the generation gap in the past, present, and future.

"Our concern with the deviant nature of youth is most evident in headlines that warn us about escalating rates of juvenile crime and in political rhetoric that sees the solution to the problem of crime in the reform of the juvenile justice system. Public views of the troublesome character of youth, however, extend beyond any narrow conceptualization of criminal conduct. Many elements of contemporary youth culture, including hip-hop or heavy metal music, raves, video arcades, and spectacular styles of dress are widely seen as reflecting, stimulating, or resulting from the social problems that plague adolescents." (Tanner, 2001, preface)

As the opening quotation suggests, "youth" and "deviance" appear to go hand-in-hand in the public mind. More than any other age group, it is youth who are perceived as having lifestyles built around deviance. They are seen as being both "troubling" and "troubled"—and "troubling *because* they are troubled" (Tanner, 2001, p.2). **"Troubling" youth**, such as young offenders, gang members, and street youth, are seen as a threat to society. **"Troubled" youth** are perceived first and foremost as a threat to themselves, for example, through substance abuse; they are also seen as potential threats to society as well, likely to become "troubling" if their problems are not solved early enough. However, at some level *all* youth are viewed as potential threats to both themselves and the larger society. It is not just *some* youth who are seen as being deviant; rather, youth culture, and indeed this period in the lifecycle itself, are deemed to be deviant and in need of social control.

Deviant Youth: "Troubling" Youth

Youth Crime

As indicated by the opening quotation of the chapter, when we think of deviant youth, those who are criminals are likely to be the first to come to mind. Indeed, when the search terms "youth and deviance" are inserted into numerous academic and popular databases, the majority of articles retrieved are about youth crime in particular. A closer look at these articles brings forward a central theme—there are significant differences between the *perceptions* of youth

Ask Yourself:

When you think of "youth crime," what images and information come to mind? Is youth crime a problem in Canadian society? How big a problem is it? Where do those images and pieces of information come from?

crime and *patterns* of youth crime. Your responses to the questions asked above may reflect the images and information contained in popular discourse, which illustrate "the singular collective perception that kids are out of control, are more dangerous now than ever, and that youth crime is expanding at an alarming rate" (Schissel, 2001, p. 86). Calls for a "crackdown" on youth crime can be heard on the news, in politicians' comments to the press, and from victims of youth crime. But to what extent is this perception of youth crime accurate? Are kids out of control? Is youth crime expanding at an alarming rate?

Schissel (2001) points out that there is a vast "gulf between reality and perception" (p. 86). The extent and nature of youth crime is far from approximating the frightening picture painted in the popular mind. Official statistics gathered through the Uniform Crime Reporting System reveal that there was an increase in youth crime rates between 1962 and 1990 (Statistics Canada, 1992). However, analysts point out that some of this increase is due to factors *other than* actual increases in youth crime, such as changing policing and administrative practices, changes in legislation, and greater public pressure to control youth crime, all of which may have resulted in more youth being brought into the criminal justice system over that period of time (Schissel, 1997). Furthermore, adult crime rates, not just youth crime rates, also increased during this period of time (Statistics Canada, 1992).

Following this period of increasing crime rates, youth crime declined each year during the 1990s (Statistics Canada, 2002a), such that the rate of youths charged with crimes in 1999 was 21% lower than a decade earlier (Statistics Canada, 2001a). Youth crime rates increased slightly in 2000, and then again in 2001 (by 1%); this increase in youth crime rates reflects an overall increase in crime rates in Canada during that time, and includes an increase in adult crime rates. Youth crime rates in 2001 include a 2% growth in violent crime, predominantly minor assaults between acquaintances; this follows a period from 1995–1999 during which violent crime rates among youth steadily declined. Youth crime rates in 2001 also include a 3% *decline* in property crimes, continuing a downward trend beginning ten years earlier (Statistics Canada, 2002a). Although 12- to 17-year-olds are overrepresented in the criminal justice system, wherein they comprise 21% of those charged with criminal offences (but constitute only 8% of Canada's population), 18- to 24-year-olds are the most overrepresented age group in the criminal justice system, and adults are responsible for the majority of crimes in every criminal offence category, including 84% of violent crimes (Statistics Canada, 2001a; 2001b). There is no criminal offence category for which youth constitute the majority of offenders.

Looking at this data, the answer to the question of whether youth crime is a problem for society may be somewhat different than the answer you gave to that question earlier. Of course, any level of crime is a problem for society, and for those victimized by such crimes. But youth crime is no more of a problem, and indeed may be less of a problem, than adult crime—data shows us that the 18- to 24-year-olds are the age group to really be concerned about when it comes to crime (which is the age group that likely includes many of you reading this textbook)! One area in which issues of youth and crime are certainly more problematic than issues of adults and crime is that of victimization. Youth ages 12 to 17 are far more likely to be the *victims* of crime than adults are. For example, in 1999 researchers found that 40% of youth had been victims of crime during the previous year (Statistics Canada, 2001a)—likely a surprising statistic for those who rely primarily on popular or media images as their source of information about crime in Canada.

Where does this gap between the perceptions and patterns of youth crime come from? Many criminologists attribute this gap, in part, to the **moral panics** (Cohen, 1973) that are constructed by the media, wherein youth crime is overrepresented, is presented as a new problem for society, and is consistently linked to particular ethnic groups and classes (Tanner, 2001; Cohen, 1973; Bortner, 1988; Pearson, 1983). But as Pearson's (1983) analysis of the British media illustrates, this portrait of youth crime is one that has been repeatedly painted throughout the 20th century; public concerns about youth crime today are quite similar to public concerns about youth crime during the last one hundred years. Even a century ago, gaps between the perceptions and realities of youth crime were present and "moral panics" about youth crime were being conveyed in popular discourse, creating a distorted view of youth crime in the eyes of the public. Moral panics about youth crime are not limited to contemporary North American society, but have also been found in Austria, Germany, and other European societies as far back as the late 19th and early 20th centuries (Wegs, 1999).

TIME TO REVIEW:

- In what ways are youth perceived as both "troubling" and "troubled"?
- What are the broader patterns of youth crime, as revealed by the Uniform Crime Reporting System? Is youth crime increasing or decreasing? How does youth crime compare with adult crime?
- Is youth crime a problem in Canadian society? Is youth victimization a problem?
- What are the common perceptions of youth crime? Where does the gap between perceptions and realities of youth crime come from? Where and when has this gap existed?

Even though the nature and extent of youth crime diverges considerably from public perceptions and media portrayals, concerns about those youth who *are* involved in criminal activity have stimulated a significant body of research over the past several decades. Thus, research on the causes of youth crime abound. Many of the more objective theories of deviance that were addressed in Chapter 2 are theories that were initially created as explanations of the causes of juvenile delinquency, or were quickly appropriated for explaining youth crime—differential association theory, control theories, strain theories, and social learning theories. Differential association theory explains youth crime in terms of the preponderance of learning "deviant" techniques and motives over "conforming" techniques and motives within small intimate groups (such as families and peer groups) at early points in life (Sutherland, 1947). Social control theories suggest that criminal activity is inherently rewarding, and the reason that some people do not become criminals is because of social restraints (such as emotional attachments to others, investments in the conventional world, and the development of self-control) that prevent people from becoming involved in criminal activity (Hirschi, 1969). Strain theories point to the way that inequalities in the access to opportunities in society serve as the stimulus for criminal behaviour. Within strain theories are Merton's (1938; 1968) theory of the gap between culturally-exalted goals and access to the legitimate means of achieving those goals, Cloward and Ohlin's (1960) theory emphasizing differential access to illegitimate opportunities, and Cohen's (1955) status frustration theory, which addresses the formation of criminal subcultures, such as lower-class youth gangs. Social learning theories explain the development of criminal behaviour in terms of the behaviours that people (and especially children) are rewarded and punished for, or that they see others being rewarded or punished for.

In addition to theoretical formulations, empirical research has also tried to establish the causes of youth crime, and has investigated the roles of intelligence (Liska & Reid, 1985), family structure and processes (Baumrind, 1991; Thornberry et al., 1991), school performance (Davies, 1994), and peer influences (Regioli & Hewitt, 1994). Parent and peer influences have been the particular subject of many analyses of the causes of youth crime. Various aspects of family life have been studied, such as family structure (e.g., single-parent versus two-parent homes), parental supervision or control of child behaviour, and emotional ties between parent and child. Early research suggested a link between single motherhood and delinquent behaviour in children, but that link has subsequently been shown to be a relatively weak relationship, and likely due to the quality and effectiveness of parenting rather than the structure of the household itself (Milan, 2000; Wells & Rankin, 1991). The quality and effectiveness of parenting is often referred to as the **parenting style**, which incorporates several characteristics, including parental supervision, parental control, and emotional ties between parent and child. Although different researchers label parenting styles in various ways, their conclusions about the parenting characteristics that improve child outcomes are quite similar. Moderate control of the child's behaviour, combined with moderate levels of supervision and strong, positive emotional ties between parent and child, are effective means of influencing child behaviour in both the short and long term, as the children develop their own internal moral standards and higher levels of self-control. This parenting style involves having high expectations for children, knowledge of and interest in who the children are with and what they are doing, as well as clearly explained rules and consequences for breaking those rules. In addition to the high expectations, there is also some flexibility wherein parents are willing to listen to the children's point of view, and substantial levels of warmth and affection. This kind of parenting reduces the risk of negative out-

Parenting styles combining control, supervision, and high levels of affection are associated with a wide range of positive child outcomes, including a lower risk of criminal behaviour.

comes in children, including criminal activity, substance use, poor school performance, low self-esteem, and susceptibility to negative peer influence. In contrast, both lax and extremely strict parental controls, as well as weak or non-existent emotional ties, are associated with negative child outcomes (Baumrind, 1991; Thornberry et al., 1991; Jang & Smith, 1997; Brook et al., 1999).

Not only do family variables influence child outcomes in themselves, but they also affect peer influence. Effective parenting styles are associated with children who select higher quality peers as friends, who have stronger, more emotionally intimate and trusting relationships with those friends, and who are less susceptible to negative peer influences. These relationships have been found in a number of societies in the world, including Columbia, where, despite extremely high societal levels of drug use and violence, parenting variables improve child outcomes and mediate negative peer influences, such as criminal behaviour and marijuana use (Milan, 2000; Brook et al., 1999). The role that parenting plays in peer selection and influence is significant, because the single most effective predictor of criminal activity among youth is criminal activity among friends (Brownfield & Thompson, 1991). Parenting is central in reducing the likelihood of the initial association with criminally involved peers, and the likelihood of adopting criminal behaviour if a relationship with a criminally involved peer does form.

Exercise Your Mind:

Although the theoretical research on the causes of youth crime was discussed above separately from the empirical research, theory and empirical research are intertwined. That is, theories are frequently formed on the basis of empirical research results, and empirical research is frequently embedded within particular theories–sometimes explicitly (as when a researcher concludes that the empirical results either fit within, or contradict, a specific theory) and sometimes implicitly (when the link is not overtly made by the researcher, but a reader is able to see how specific empirical results correspond to particular theories). After reviewing the research described above, try to embed the empirical results within the theories. That is, in what way does the empirical research on parental and peer influences fit within some of the theories you have learned about?

Crime itself is, indeed, a social problem in need of control. Subsequently, a great deal of theoretical and empirical research has been conducted to determine the origins of criminality, particularly during childhood. However, the crime problem, and particularly the youth crime problem, are nowhere near the level that public images convey. Schissel (2001) suggests that the bulk of public images of, and worries about, youth crime today centre on the most "troubling" of youth subcultures, the gang.

TIME TO REVIEW:

- Briefly, how do the following theories explain youth crime: differential association; control theories; strain theories; social learning theories?
- What factors have predominated in empirical analyses of the causes of youth crime?
- What roles do family structure and parenting style play in the origins of youth crime?
- What role do peers play in youth criminality? How does parenting style affect peer influence?

Youth Gangs

Youth street gangs are a popular topic for newspaper articles, politicians' speeches, movies, and both fictional and non-fictional television. The portrayal of youth gangs in the American media is particularly influential in determining Canadian's perceptions of youth gangs, despite the differences that exist among youth gangs in the two countries. (Mathews, 2000). Youth gangs can be found throughout much of the world; however, the prevalence of youth gangs in the United States, combined with the emphasis placed on youth gangs in the American media, means that much of the research done on gangs is American research. In fact, Canadian research on youth gangs continues to be rather sparse (Mathews, 2000; Smandych, 2001). Although some more recent research on youth gangs in Canada has emerged, American research has dominated Canadian academic, public, and governmental policy discussions (Gordon, 2001).

Two broad streams of research can be identified. One of those streams focuses on causation or motivation—why gangs form, why youth join gangs, and why gangs engage in particular behaviours. The second stream of research focuses on various aspects of the social construction of the "gang problem," such as how and why moral panics about gangs emerge, and even the problems involved in the very definition of "gang" itself.

The "How" and "Why" of Gangs

Research that focuses on gang emergence, gang membership, and gang behaviour comes from both theoretical and empirical orientations. Some theorizing, both more objective and more subjective, has focused specifically on gangs (e.g., some strain theories and some symbolic interactionist theorizing). Other theories may not focus specifically on gangs; instead, inherent in their explanations of youth crime more generally is the possibility that youth crime may occur within gang settings (e.g., differential association theory, control theories, social learning theory). Empirical research seeks those variables that are associated with gang emergence and gang membership.

A number of the strain theories reviewed in Chapter 2 were developed specifically in reference to youth gangs. The underlying proposition of many of these strain theories is that gangs will emerge in socially and economically disadvantaged communities. In such communities, where legitimate opportunities to achieve social status and economic success are limited, gangs form as an alternative way of achieving status, social acceptance, and economic success. The status and economic success to be gained via gang activity is not to be underestimated, given the amount of money to be made in the drug trade; some researchers point out that, at least in the United States, youth gangs are now the primary suppliers of certain types of illegal drugs (Padilla, 1992). However, the pursuit of economic success is not central to the activities of all youth gangs. Strain theorists have pointed out that different types of gangs have different types of activities as their foundation. For instance, Albert Cohen (1955) suggested that lower-class boys, unable to live up to the middle-class measuring rod that pervades the education system, would join with other similar boys in forming gangs. The gang's behaviour is based on **reaction formation**, a set of oppositional standards that results in expressive, destructive, non-utilitarian behaviours (e.g., vandalism, violence) rather than economically driven activities. Cloward and Ohlin (1960) propose that the types of illegitimate opportunities that are present within the community determine the particular nature of gang behaviour; this results in the formation of gangs that may be economic enterprises, violent gangs, or drug-using retreatist gangs. Although the pursuit of economic success is not a component of all youth gangs, the pursuit of status is—the type of status that can be achieved through gang membership depends on the type of gang in question.

Research on gangs also comes from more subjective theoretical orientations. During the 1990s, **ethnographic research**—a true blend of theoretical and empirical work—on gangs grew. Ethnographic research, emerging from the symbolic interactionist perspective described in Chapter 3, involves the researchers embedding themselves within gangs for extended periods of time, interviewing gang members and observing their daily activities. For example, Jankowski (1991) conducted an ethnographic study, which led him to the conclusion that individuals join gangs for a variety of different reasons, rather than for any one reason (such as blocked opportunities). The various reasons for joining a gang are based on a rational calculation of what is in the best interests of the individual at a particular time. Echoing the work of some of the strain theorists, Jankowski suggests that one of the reasons for gang membership is **material incentives**. Some people join gangs based on the belief that the gang will provide an environment that increases the chances of making money—more regular money, and with less individual effort, than if pursuing economic success individually. Jankowski found that material incentives also include financial security for gang members and their families during difficult times, as well as networking for future economic endeavours. **Recreation** serves as another reason for gang membership. That is, gangs provide entertainment and a social life, and in some communities may serve as the primary social institution in the neighbourhood, promoting social events and supplying drugs and alcohol. The comments of one gang member illustrate the recreational aspect of gang membership: "Man, it [the gang] was a great source of dope and women. Hell, they were the kings of the community so I wanted to get in on some of the action" (p. 283). Gangs may serve as **a place of refuge and camouflage**, motivating some individuals to seek gang membership. Being just "one of the gang" provides a level of anonymity, removing a sense of personal responsibility for illegal activities—"the gang is going to provide me with some cover" (p. 283). Other people are drawn to gangs for the **physical protection** it provides from known dangers in the neighbourhood. As Cory points out, "Now that I got some business things going I can concentrate on them and not worry so much. I don't always have to be looking over my shoulder" (p. 284). For some people, joining a gang may serve as **a time to resist** living the kinds of lives their parents lived. In this vein, becoming a gang member is a statement of rejection to society, a rejection of the type of lives being offered. At the same time, the economic prospects of gang membership may be a way of avoiding just that type of life—"Hey, I just might make some money from our dealings.... If I don't [make it, at least] I told those fuckers in Beverly Hills what I think of the jobs they left for us" (p. 284). In some neighbourhoods, certain gangs have existed for generations, so that individuals whose fathers, uncles, and grandfathers have been members of the gang at some point in their lives feel a **commitment to the community**, and join the gang in order to continue a tradition. As Pepe states, "A lot of people from the community have been in [the gang].... I felt it's kind of my duty to join 'cause everybody expects it" (p. 285). Feeling a commitment to the community, along with the other possible motivations for gang membership, leads individuals to conclude that joining a gang is currently in their best interests. Both the more objective and the more subjective theorizing on gangs frequently points to gang formation and gang membership as a rational alternative for the individuals involved, given their current sociocultural surroundings and their networks of social interaction.

In addition to theoretical research, empirical research has also investigated numerous aspects of gang formation and membership. Research has identified a number of different variables, including the personal, family, community, and educational factors that increase the likelihood of gang involvement (e.g., Gordon, 1995; Flannery, Huff, & Manos, 2001; Edmonton Police Service, 2003). In Box 5.1, you will find a summary of these various types of factors.

Box 5.1 Factors Influencing Gang Involvement

Family Indicators

- excessive parental controls
- lax parental controls
- low parental nurturance
- abuse/neglect
- low parental educational level
- criminality among other family members

Personal Indicators

- low self-control
- low motivation
- truancy
- failing grades
- low aspirations or goals in life
- substance abuse

Community Indicators

- community disorganization
- high crime rate
- high population turnover
- lack of cultural resources
- lack of recreational resources
- gang presence

School Indicators

- negative school environment
- violence within the school
- low expectations for students
- inadequate funding for school resources (e.g., library books, extracurricular activities)
- lax controls over students

Exercise Your Mind:

In order to further explore the linkages between theory and empirical research, identify which of the above risk factors might fit within: (a) Merton's strain theory; (b) Cloward and Ohlin's theory of differential opportunities; (c) Sutherland's differential association theory; (d) social learning theory; (e) Hirschi's social bonds theory; and (f) Gottfredson and Hirschi's general theory of crime. You may find it useful to briefly return to Chapter 2 to review the content of these theories.

Although many of the theories that focus on gangs suggest that gang formation and gang membership are rational alternatives within particular social contexts, the existence of gangs is considered to be problematic for those communities in which they reside, and for society as a whole. A rational alternative is not necessarily a healthy alternative; the various factors influencing gang involvement that were identified in Box 5.1 demonstrate that gang involvement emerges, in part, from unhealthy personalities, unhealthy relationships, unhealthy families, and unhealthy communities.

The Construction of the "Gang Problem"

While the first stream of gang research explores the causes of or motivations for gang emergence, gang membership, and gang behaviour, the second stream of research concentrates on a different set of issues, those related to the nature of the construction of the "**gang problem**" in society. Discussions of media representations of gangs have been central to research coming from this perspective.

The way that youth gangs are represented within the media and other forms of public discourse is similar to the portrayal of youth crime more generally. Gangs are portrayed as a new and growing problem for society, one that is out of control (Fasiolo & Leckie, 1993; Tanner, 2001; Gordon, 1993; Gordon, 2001). Just as with youth crime at a broader level, public images of gangs far surpass their actual existence; gangs are not as prevalent as media coverage implies. Not only are stories about gangs easily found on television news and in newspapers, they can also be easily found in the fictional media—on television shows like *Law and Order* and *CSI*, and in movies. The involvement of particular ethnic and age groups is a significant component of the public images of gangs.

Canadian newspapers **racialize** the "gang problem" (Bell, 2002). In other words, stories about gangs frequently include references to specific racial or ethnic groups, especially "Asian" gangs (Fasiolo & Leckie, 1993; Young, 1993; Tanner, 2001; Gordon, 1993; Gordon, 2001). This is problematic on two fronts. First, a distorted picture of Canadian gangs is given to the audience, when the reality is that gangs are not associated with any single racial or ethnic group, but are ethnically diverse (Tanner, 2001; Gordon, 2001; Bell, 2002; Fasiolo & Leckie, 1993; Edmonton Police Service, 2003; Mathew, 2000). In fact, even those gangs that have been publicly labelled as "Asian gangs" are typically multicultural, and sometimes may have more non-Asian than Asian members. Second, race or ethnicity are only overtly linked within the media to gang activity when it is non-whites that are involved; when Caucasians are involved in gang activity, no references to their race or ethnicity are made. Thus, you are far more likely to see a news headline that says, "Asian gang member gunned down," than one that says, "White gang member of English descent gunned down"—and it is not because Asians are any more likely to be members of gangs than Caucasians of English descent. If it were a Caucasian gang member that is involved, the headline would likely read simply, "Gang member gunned down." Because of this differential inclusion of racial and ethnic references, "Asian" and "gang member" become linked in the public mind, subsequently reproducing existing stereotypes that perpetuate racism in Canadian society.

Media representations of the gang problem do vary in different parts of Canada, particularly in Quebec compared to the other provinces and territories. In Quebec, the racialization of gangs is less common and instead age is one of the areas of focus within the media; gangs are most commonly referred to as "youth gangs" (Fasiolo & Leckie, 1993). Just as with race and ethnicity, the linking of "youth" and "gangs" is inaccurate, in that most Canadian gangs have considerable age diversity. In one Canadian study, Gordon (1993) found the average age of convicted gang members to be 19, and the majority of gang members to be "young adults" rather than "teenagers" (ages 12–17). Thus, although calls from politicians and the general public to strengthen young offender legislation often follow publicized gang incidents, it is young adults who predominate in Canada's gang landscape. When combined, the media's overrepresentation of gangs, its racialization of gangs, and its distortion of the age composition of gangs, contribute to a view of Canada's gangs that is quite different from the reality—a "moral panic" has been created.

Certain groups may benefit from the creation of a moral panic about street gangs. Drawing upon the conflict and critical theoretical perspectives addressed in Chapter 3, a number of researchers suggest that not only do the media benefit from the creation of moral panics, so do some politicians, interest groups, and law enforcement (Bell, 2002; Tanner, 2001; Gordon, 2001; Schissel, 2001; Cohen, 1973). By presenting sensationalistic and fear-provoking stories, the media draws an audience, and thereby increases profit. Some politicians may similarly engage in fear-mongering, and then vow to toughen legislation and enforcement if elected; by contributing to a moral panic and then promising to reduce the social problem, they are able to obtain more votes. Interest groups and community agencies that want legislation strengthened or that provide social programs may receive more funding by exaggerating the nature of the problem. Law enforcement may benefit in some communities by also receiving more funding to hire more officers or to create specialized gang units, if they are able to convince municipal, provincial, and federal politicians that the "gang problem" is out of control. Some researchers suggest that even gangs themselves may benefit from this moral panic, which provides them with free publicity and may thereby increase their membership and their power in the community; youth who are currently not involved in gangs may form new gangs in order to protect themselves from the perceived threat (Tanner, 2001).

However, although the gang research done within this second stream suggests that the moral panic surrounding youth gangs surpasses what is actually going on, and that various groups benefit from that moral panic, it does not claim that gangs are a figment of social imagination, or that gangs are nothing to worry about. It shines a spotlight on a different aspect of gangs than does the first stream of research, where the causes of and motivations for gang emergence, membership, and behaviour are explained. Nevertheless, both types of gang research are contributing forces to the social control of gangs in North America.

TIME TO REVIEW:

- What are the two broad streams of gang research?
- What is the underlying proposition of those strain theories that focus on gangs? That is, where do gangs form, and why?
- Do all gangs revolved around the pursuit of economic success? In your answer, utilize Albert Cohen's status frustration theory as well as Cloward and Ohlin's differential opportunities theory.
- What is ethnographic research, and what are the reasons for joining a gang that Jankowski found in his ethnographic research?
- How does the media represent the "gang problem"? In what ways are age and the racialization of gangs involved?
- Who benefits from the moral panic about gangs in Canadian society?

Controlling Youth Gangs and Youth Crime

Throughout North America, street gangs are socially controlled at multiple levels—formal and informal, retroactive and preventative. These social control efforts occur within families, communities (i.e., schools, community agencies, community organizations, businesses, police, and religious institutions), and the criminal justice system (i.e., government, courts, and law enforcement).

At a formal level of regulation, many schools have integrated gang awareness programs to teach children about the dangers of gangs and the consequences of gang membership. These programs are intended to prevent children from joining gangs. Community agencies, particularly those operating in gang-ridden neighbourhoods, frequently have both retroactive and preventative programs. Retroactive programs are designed to try to get existing gang members to leave that lifestyle; they may be offered educational upgrading, job training, assistance in finding employment, free tattoo removal, and various types of counselling. Preventative programs in communities may operate in conjunction with schools, teaching young children basic life skills (e.g., nutrition, grooming) and social skills (e.g., problem solving, anger management), or providing organized community activities. Many police departments in North America have specialized gang units, to become familiar with and closely monitor known gang members, as well as deal with gang issues and events that arise. Governments provide gang-related legislation and social programs (e.g., job-training programs). Bill C-24, which was passed in 2002, defines **criminal organizations**, which includes gangs. A criminal organization is defined as "a group, however organized, that is composed of *three or more persons* and that has as one of its main purposes or *main activities* the facilitation or *commission of one or more serious offences*, that if committed, would likely result in the *direct or indirect receipt of material benefit*, including a financial benefit, by the group or by any one of the persons who constitute the group" [italics added].

Informal social controls occur at the level of everyday social interaction, typically focusing on preventative efforts. This includes parenting efforts (e.g., parenting style, talking to your children about gangs) and community involvement with neighbourhood children (e.g., becoming a soccer coach, helping the neighbourhood children organize a food drive). The lines between formal and informal social controls often become blurred. The behaviour of parents and other adults within the community may be influenced by their awareness of formal social control efforts. For instance, suggestions for parents regarding gang prevention are included in the Edmonton Police Service's resource guide on gangs. Within this resource guide, parents are given specific suggestions for facilitating the development of good social skills in their children, providing a balance between nurturance and discipline, and explaining the dangers of gangs to children.

Coordinated efforts at gang control, at multiple levels, are supposed to be the most effective means of prevention and response to the gang problem. However, the regulation of gangs is even more complex in that different types of specific controls may be required in cities with varying levels of gang activity. A community that currently has no signs of gang presence requires a basic foundation of control, such as community parenting programs, teaching children multicultural sensitivity, and reinforcing codes of conduct. In contrast, a community with the highest level of gang activity wherein gangs dominate the neigbourhood will require the assistance of anti-gang professionals, and intense efforts to reclaim the neighbourhood (Edmonton Police Service, 2003).

Measures to control youth gangs are intertwined with the regulation of youth crime in general. Many of the formal and informal social controls that were discussed in the context of gangs are also utilized in relation to youth crime—it is presumed that the prevention of gang involvement is also the prevention of crime at a broader level. For instance, effective parenting, community involvement in children's lives, and effective classrooms will not only reduce the likelihood of gang involvement, but also the likelihood of all types of criminal activity.

Over the past century there have been considerable changes in the way youth crime has been formally controlled or regulated. Public concerns about youth crime gained force during the late 19th century. This was a period of tremendous social and economic changes in Canadian society. The process of industrialization was well underway, cities were growing, and an identifiable working class was present. Due to the long hours that working-class parents had to spend at work simply to ensure the survival of the family (remember, this was a time when labour laws were rare, and there were few protections like minimum wages or maximum working hours), their children were left unsupervised more than the children of middle-class parents. Social reformers during that era were concerned with the lack of supervision these children faced, as well as the subsequent danger they presented to middle-class personhood and property (Leon, 1977; Sutherland, 1976). Various small pieces of legislation encompassed the control of youth crime, but also of neglected and abandoned children. Children under the age of 7 were presumed to not know the difference between right and wrong, and so could not be charged with criminal offences. Those ages 7 to 14, if proven to know the difference between right and wrong, were subject to the same sentences that adults were; thus, it was possible for a 7-year-old child who had committed a crime to be sentenced to death or to life in prison. Youth over the age of 14 were considered equal to adults within criminal law.

It was in 1908 that the Canadian juvenile justice system was created, with the implementation of the Juvenile Delinquents Act. Its foundation was the principle of **parens patriae** (i.e., "parent of the country"), meaning that the state would act in the best interests of children under the age of 16 when it became clear that their own parents were unwilling or unable to—both neglected and delinquent children were presumed to need such legislative attention. Although it controlled youth criminals, the Juvenile Delinquents Act was more a *child welfare* piece of legislation, since it was believed that, with the right assistance and correct teaching, young criminals could be set upon the right path in life. Separate detention facilities and jail facilities were created for youth, based on the belief that integrating juvenile delinquents with adult criminals would simply further juvenile delinquency (Reitsma-Street, 1989-90).

The Juvenile Delinquents Act was amended several times during the ensuing decades, and in 1984 was replaced by the Young Offenders Act. This new piece of legislation was based on *justice* principles rather than child welfare principles. It extended the legal rights that adult offenders had guaranteed for decades (e.g., due process, the right to an attorney) to youth as well, who were not guaranteed such protections under the Juvenile Delinquents Act. Youth who committed crimes were no longer perceived as juvenile delinquents, but **young offenders**; an offending youth was now seen as a *criminal* rather than a child gone astray (West, 1984, 1991). After a number of amendments throughout the 1990s, the Youth Criminal Justice Act replaced the Young Offenders Act on April 1, 2003. Under this new legislation, chronic and/or violent young offenders are treated more stringently, while first-time and non-violent young offenders are more likely to be treated via community and alternative measures. The Youth Criminal Justice Act is one component of the federal government's Youth Justice Renewal Initiative, a multi-faceted initiative involving the criminal justice system, schools, community agencies, and more; its underlying principles are prevention, meaningful consequences for youth crime, and intensified rehabilitation and reintegration.

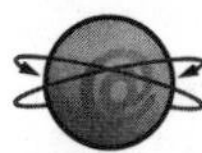

AN INTERNET MOMENT:

On the Website for the Department of Justice, http://www.canada.justice.gc.ca/, you will find "Programs & Services" listed along the top of the page; on the drop-down menu, select "Youth Justice." This extensive site reviews all of the components of the Youth Justice Renewal Initiative, including an overview of the differences between the old Young Offenders Act and the new Youth Criminal Justice Act.

The social control of youth crime has been modified in substantial ways over the past century, including more recent efforts to control gangs. The avid pursuit of more effective ways of dealing with young criminals will continue into the future as well. Although legislation, criminal justice programs, and social programs are continually changing, the desire to control "troubling" youth is as old as civilization itself. However, youth who are perceived as threats to society because of their criminal activities are not the only ones considered deviant and in need of social control; "troubled" youth are a focus of concern as well.

TIME TO REVIEW:

- At what levels does the social control of gangs occur? Provide some examples of control within families, schools, community agencies, and the criminal justice system.
- In what ways is the social control of gangs intertwined with the control of youth crime more generally?
- How has legislation governing youth crime changed over the past century?

Deviant Youth: "Troubled" Youth

Some youth are considered to be deviant and are made subject to measures of social control, not because they are "troubling" and therefore currently a danger to society, but because they are "troubled." "Troubled" youth are first and foremost a danger to themselves; their behaviour threatens their own well-being, physical or mental health, and their futures. But "troubled" youth are also perceived as potentially "troubling"—if they are uncontrolled, or if their problems are not effectively dealt with, they may become more than just a danger to themselves, but a danger to society as well. Youth who abuse drugs or alcohol, engage in premature sexual activity, become teenage parents, live on the streets, or have mental health problems are just some of those youth who are considered "troubled." When considering "troubled" youth, one of the areas of greatest public concern in contemporary Canada, as well as the United States, is substance abuse. The daily lives of substances abusers are affected, whether through ill health, the feeling of being unable to resist the draw of whatever substance they are abusing, missing work or school, falling grades, job loss, or the loss of social relationships. But substance abuse can also have a negative impact on society, such as through greater use of the health care system, physical and emotional harm caused to others because of the substance abuse, and potential criminal activity; in fact, the possession of some substances is criminal itself.

Substance Use Among Youth

We live in a culture in which substance use, in some form, is widely evident. Step outside the doorway of office buildings, shopping malls, and even hospitals, and you will see groups of people gathered, a haze of cigarette smoke hovering over their heads. Attend a wedding, retirement party, or dinner party, and alcohol will likely be served. Prior to New Year's Eve, liquor stores sell out of bottles of champagne. Some single people who are searching for Mr./Ms. Right (or Mr./Ms. Right-Now) carry out those searches in bars; those bars likely have "Happy Hour" (when drinks are less expensive), or even "Ladies Drink for $1.99 Night." Attend a Bob Dylan concert, and although cameras will be confiscated, marijuana will not, and even those members of the audience who are not drug users will find themselves getting high from second-hand marijuana smoke. On television and in movies, the characters may be smoking, drinking, or using drugs. For example, on *Friends*, when "Fun Bobby" became sober he was no longer fun, and despite everyone's best efforts to support his sobriety, they eventually found themselves trying to convince him to start drinking again.

Ask Yourself:

Estimate how many youth use the following substances: alcohol; tobacco; marijuana; other illegal drugs. Upon what did you base your estimates—youth whom you know personally, your own observations, media portrayals, or public information campaigns? How do your estimates compare to your own levels of usage of these substances?

Further evidence of substance use is the related social control that we see around us. Following her death, we saw Barb Tarbox on the front page of every newspaper in the country, due to her anti-smoking crusade in schools. Walk into your college's student resource center, and you will find pamphlets about alcohol abuse, smoking, and "club drugs". Prior to reading week (or spring break), active abuse prevention campaigns might be displayed throughout your campus. If you tell someone you are going to a rave, they may warn you about the dangers of Ecstasy and "date-rape" drugs. In school, you may have been exposed to educational programs about smoking, alcohol use, and drug use, beginning in early elementary school. Rarely does a day go by when each of us does not see someone using a substance (whether in person or in the media), or see some type of substance control efforts.

The most commonly used substances among Canadian adolescents and young adults are, in order of use, alcohol, tobacco, cannabis (i.e., marijuana and hashish), and hallucinogens (e.g., LSD). Substance use among youth peaked in 1979, and then steadily declined until the early 1990s; since that time, usage has increased, as has the use of multiple substances (Roberts et al., 2001). Contemporary patterns of substance use are somewhat of a contradiction. More youth are using substances, and their attitudes toward substance use have become more lenient, but their age at first use is later. For example, approximately 20 years ago, 17% of students in grade 7 said they had first used alcohol by the time they were in grade 4; in 1999, only 13% had done so (Roberts et al., 2001). Only 25% to 33% (depending on province/territory) of high school students today remain substance-free (Roberts et al., 2001).

Tobacco

The health risks associated with smoking, and with exposure to second-hand smoke, have now been well established by medical research. When those risks were first publicized during the 1970s, smoking rates among youth began a steady decline that lasted until 1990, despite the claims being made by tobacco companies that disputed these research results. However, beginning in 1990 youth smoking began to grow once again, especially among girls (Health Canada, 1999). By grade 10, 66% of girls and 61% of boys have tried smoking at least once; of those who have tried it, 21% of girls and 15% of boys smoke on a daily basis. The pattern of adolescent girls being more likely to smoke than adolescent boys occurs in most Western countries in the world, including Canada, Germany, France, England, Norway, Denmark, and Sweden (Health Canada, 1999). Of 11 countries, Canada ranks 5th in rate of teenage smoking, behind several Western European countries, but ahead of the United States (which ranks 11th).

The increase in youth smoking over the last decade has been one of the central stimuli for anti-smoking efforts. After a number of cigarette companies were widely criticized for their use of animated characters in their advertising (which was presumed to be attractive to children), laws governing cigarette advertising became more stringent.

Laws that prohibit those under the age of 18 from buying cigarettes have existed for many years, but the enforcement of those laws has been lax for many of those years. In the 1970s, it was not uncommon for children as young as six or seven to be sent to the corner store to buy cigarettes for a parent or an older sibling. But, in recent years, the enforcement of the laws has become more stringent, and penalties for selling cigarettes to minors have become more severe. Social control efforts at curtailing youth smoking specifically are part of broader forms of regulation for smoking more generally. We have come a long way from the days when cigarette commercials were shown on television, when people could smoke any-

The use of this animated character in cigarette advertising was highly criticized for its apparent attempts to attract the attention of children.

where they wished (including college classrooms and hospitals), and when doctors prescribed smoking as a weight loss tool. Today, cigarette commercials cannot be shown on television, and in fact cigarette advertising is widely restricted. The media is now a central source for public service campaigns to reduce smoking. In many communities, recent laws have banned smoking in many workplaces, shopping malls, hospitals, and restaurants; other communities have taken legislation a step further, prohibiting smoking in all public buildings, including bars (e.g., New York, Victoria, San Francisco). And, of course, instead of prescribing smoking as a weight loss tool, contemporary doctors try to convince their patients to stop smoking, and provide resources to help them quit (e.g., nicotine patches, support groups). All of these efforts to socially control tobacco use were integrated on a worldwide scale in May 2003, when the 192 countries that are members of the World Health Organization unanimously voted to implement the Framework Convention on

Tobacco Control. The Framework Convention will "require countries to impose restrictions on tobacco advertising, sponsorship and promotion, establish new labeling and clean indoor air controls and strengthen legislation to clamp down on tobacco smuggling" (World Health Organization Press Release, May 21, 2003, para. 2). This new initiative has considerable overlap with Canada's existing legislation, and Canada has been one of the first countries to sign this international pact. However, at the time of writing, the United States was indicating that it would not sign this international agreement.

The health dangers of smoking are well known, and have led to comprehensive anti-smoking efforts for people of all ages. However, smoking among youth is a public concern not only because of the health dangers, but also because of its association with other forms of substance use. Youth who smoke are also more likely to use other drugs, particularly marijuana (National Institute on Drug Abuse, 2002); for instance, in Quebec, 90% of youth who smoke have also used marijuana (Roberts et al., 2001).

TIME TO REVIEW:

- Who are "troubled" youth?
- Why are troubled youth perceived as being dangers to both themselves and to society? Use the example of substance use in your answer.
- In what ways can we see substance use everywhere around us?
- What are the most commonly used substances among Canadian youth?
- Why are patterns of youth substance use somewhat of a contradiction?
- What are the patterns of tobacco use among youth, and how have those patterns changed since the 1970s?
- How is youth smoking socially controlled?

Drug Use

Cannabis is the most widely used psychoactive drug among Canadian youth (excluding alcohol). Nationally, 40% of junior and senior high school students have tried cannabis (usually in the form of marijuana). Data from Ontario shows that 5% of adolescents have used marijuana by age 12, and by age 19 that number rises to 40% (Roberts et al., 2001). The proportion of youth who have tried marijuana has increased over the last decade. For example, in 1990 only 25% of Canadian students in grade 10 had used marijuana, compared to 42% in 1998 (Health Canada, 1999). However, although most youth have used marijuana, they do not use it regularly. Data from Nova Scotia shows only 13% of youth who have tried marijuana use it more than once a month (Roberts et al., 2001).

Other psychoactive drugs have lower rates of usage than cannabis, although usage rates did increase during the 1990s (Health Canada, 1999), as illustrated in Table 5.1:

Table 5.1 PERCENTAGES OF YOUTH WHO HAVE TRIED PSYCHOACTIVE DRUGS, 1990 AND 1998

DRUG	1990	1998
Solvents/inhalants	6%	8%
Cocaine	3%	6%
Amphetamines	7%	9%
LSD/Acid	8%	13%

Source: *Health of Canada's Children*, Health Canada, (1999). Reproduced with the permission of the Minister of Public Works and Government Services Canada, 2003.

Of those youth who have tried psychoactive drugs other than cannabis, fewer than 10% have used that drug within the previous 12 months (Roberts et al., 2001). More recent drugs, such as Ecstasy, also have fairly low rates of use among Canadian youth; for example, 10% of students in grade 11 have used Ecstasy or other "club drugs" in the past year (Roberts et al., 2001). However, Canadian youth are more likely to use psychoactive drugs, including marijuana, than European youth are, even those European youth who live in nations with more lenient marijuana laws than Canada currently has (Harkin, Anderson, & Goos, 1997; Health Canada, 1999).

Although the regular use of psychoactive drugs is fairly uncommon among Canadian youth, those who do regularly use psychoactive drugs often do so problematically, increasing their risk of negative life consequences. In Quebec, of those 14- to 17-year-olds who have used an illegal substance more than five times, more than half have gone to school high or stoned, used an illegal substance in the morning, or used an illegal substance while participating in a competitive sport (Roberts et al., 2001). Thus, even though most youth do not use illegal drugs, and those who have used them do not use them regularly, youth who are regular substance users typically show problematic usage.

The reasons for drug use vary among different groups of Canadian youth. Some may use drugs for reasons similar to adult drug users—to relieve stress, as a form of escapism, or as a social activity. However, youth may also have distinctive motivations for drug use as well, such as to satisfy their curiosity, show their independence, or become part of a peer group (Roberts et al., 2001). Whether drug use becomes problematic depends on a variety of factors, the same ones that influence youth crime or gang membership—individual, community, family, and school factors (Roberts et al., 2001). Individual factors that influence whether substance use becomes problematic include the following: genetic and environmental predispositions; degree of personal competence (e.g., extent to which the individual feels in control of life and optimistic about the future); connection with violent behaviour; and gang involvement. Community-level factors include the norms about substance use, prevalence of crime, price and availability of substances, economic conditions, and nature of peers. At the level of the family, parenting style, degree of parent-child emotional attachment, and family history in relation to substance use play significant roles. Finally, within the school, the youth's academic success, reading skills, problem-solving abilities, participation in extracurricular activities, and feelings of belonging influence the nature and extent of drug use (Brounstein & Zweig, 1999; Benard, 1991).

Due to the multiple factors operating at different levels that influence youth drug use, effective programs are comprehensive, targeting factors at all levels and thus involving families, communities, schools, and youth themselves (Roberts et al., 2001; Health Canada, 1999). Programs must be age appropriate, and occur *prior to* the child's likely exposure to particular types of drugs. Effective programs integrate youth's own perceptions of drugs and drug use, and realistically take their lifestyles into consideration. For example, the "Just Say No" campaign is seen by many adolescents as being unrealistic, not providing them with the tools they really need to deal with the situations they will encounter in their lives.

Much of the data on youth substance use and its effective control has been done on mainstream youth—regular teenagers and young adults who live at home, go to school, and live routine lives. However, different patterns of illegal drug use exist for youth who live outside of the mainstream, such as street youth. Street youth are more likely to use all illegal substances, use them more frequently, and at more problematic levels (Smart et al., 1992; Caputo, Weiler, & Anderson, 1996; Roberts et al., 2001). Research done with street kids in Montreal found that 80% of them had used cannabis within the previous month (compared to approximately 10% of mainstream youth), and research done with street youth in Toronto found that almost 60% had used LSD within the previous month (compared to less than 10% of mainstream youth). Their different patterns of drug use, and the distinctive environments within which drug use occurs, means that drug reduction programs must be located in those spaces where they spend their time—on the street, in local health clinics, and in shopping malls. These programs must deal with factors additional to those for mainstream youth, such as assistance in finding housing, food, safety of the person, and employment (National Institute on Drug Abuse, 1997; Roberts et al., 2001).

The problematic nature of drug use among regular users makes the reduction of drug use (i.e., preventing initial use and facilitating reduction in use) and the safer use of drugs (e.g., by preventing the spread of disease via shared needles) important goals for these comprehensive programs. However, it is important to keep in mind that only a small percentage of youth use drugs, and an even smaller percentage use them regularly. In contrast, the use of alcohol is far more prevalent among Canadian youth.

TIME TO REVIEW:

- What are the patterns of marijuana use among youth, and how have those patterns changed since 1990?
- How many youth use other forms of psychoactive drugs? How do usage rates compare in Canada and Europe?
- What problems do teenagers who are regular users of drugs experience?
- Why do youth use drugs, and what factors determine whether drug use becomes problematic?
- What are the characteristics of effective drug programs for youth?
- How do patterns of drug use and effective programming differ for street youth?

Alcohol Use

Alcohol use is a normative behaviour among contemporary youth in Canadian society. By age 12, 40% of adolescents have already tried alcohol, and by the end of high school, almost all teenagers have (Health Canada, 1999; Roberts et al., 2001). Two-thirds of junior and senior high school students have used alcohol in the previous year (Roberts et al., 2001). Not only have most adolescents used alcohol, but almost half have experienced a "**heavy-drinking episode**" (i.e., more than five drinks in one setting) within the previous month, and by grade 10 almost half admit to having been "really drunk" at least twice in their lives (Roberts et al., 2001; Health Canada, 1999).

Adolescent drunkenness is more common in Canada than in many other countries in the world. Out of 11 countries, Canada ranks 3rd in the prevalence of youth drunkenness, after Denmark and England (the United States ranks 8th). International research has found that youth drunkenness is less common in cultures that have more ritualized alcohol use (such as wine with dinner every evening) and more lenient alcohol policies—for example, France, Switzerland, and Greece. In contrast, youth drunkenness is more common in cultures that have more restrictive alcohol policies, such as Canada (Health Canada, 1999).

Problematic drinking among youth is made subject to many of the same programs that target drug use, as described in the previous section of this chapter. These programs are frequently broad programs that focus on all types of problematic substance use—alcohol, marijuana, "hard" drugs, and sometimes even tobacco. More recently, one particular aspect of problematic alcohol use has garnered public attention—binge drinking among college students.

Binge Drinking Among College Students. Research on binge drinking among college students has found it to be a rather unique pattern of behaviour, different from alcohol use among younger youth or even among youth the same age who are not college students. The unique nature and pattern of college binge drinking necessitates distinct social control measures.

> ***Ask Yourself:***
>
> How do you define "binge drinking"? What proportion of students at your college do you think engage in binge drinking?

In many people's minds, "colleges" and "parties" go hand in hand. Popular college rating guides often rate colleges not only on academic factors, but also social factors like the best "party colleges." Picture yourself at a college party, such as a fraternity party. The images that come to mind likely contain large numbers of people present and loud music playing. Some of you might picture a few party attendees smoking marijuana, or using other types of drugs, but in all likelihood it is images of alcohol that prevail—kegs of beer, drinking contests, and large punch bowls of brightly coloured and highly potent beverages. You might imagine people at these parties consuming five, six, or even more drinks in one evening, perhaps even passing out. These kinds of images are images of the "binge-drinking problem" on college campuses.

Binge drinking and the college lifestyle go hand in hand within the popular imagination.

Since 1993, Harvard University has conducted a recurring College Alcohol Study involving more than 14 000 students at more than 100 colleges across the United States.

This research provides us with the most in-depth information available about the nature and extent of the "binge-drinking problem" on college campuses. **Binge drinking** is commonly defined as five drinks in a row for males, and four drinks in a row for females. Based on this measure, approximately 40% of college students are binge drinkers; this proportion has remained fairly consistent in the 1993, 1997, 1999, and 2001 versions of the College Alcohol Study (Weschler, cited in Keeling, 2000; Keeling, 2002). Although the proportion of binge drinkers remained consistent throughout the 1990s, some important changes in binge-drinking patterns did emerge. Alcohol use among college students became more polarized during the 1990s: the proportion of abstainers (i.e., people who do not drink alcohol) grew to 19% of college students, but the proportion of "frequent" binge drinkers (i.e., 3 or more binge-drinking episodes within the past 2 weeks) grew to 23% of college students. Another change in binge drinking is that it has increasingly moved off campus. Between 1993 and 2001, there was a decline in attendance and heavy drinking at fraternity and sorority parties, but an increase in attendance and heavy drinking at off-campus parties (Keeling, 2000; Keeling, 2002).

It has been suggested that more stringent college alcohol policies that emerged during the 1990s may have created a more supportive environment for abstainers, contributing to the increase in the proportion of non-drinkers. However, for heavier drinkers and for student subcultures in which drinking is more common, the more stringent policies may have facilitated resistance and rebellion. As these subcultures isolate themselves within their more accepting social networks and move their drinking activities to less-supervised off-campus areas, their social contact with non-drinkers declines. Their environment becomes one of heavy drinkers reinforcing other heavy drinkers, subsequently increasing the proportion of college students who are "frequent" binge drinkers (Keeling, 2000; Keeling, 2002).

The typical college binge drinker is a white, middle-class male, with college-educated parents (Weschler, cited in Keeling, 2000). Individual binge drinking is correlated with the rate of binge drinking among the individual's peers, particularly close friends; that is, binge drinkers tend to associate with other binge drinkers, and non-binge drinkers tend to associate with other non-binge drinkers (Weschler & Kuo, 2000). Patterns of binge drinking change during the academic year. There is a significant amount of binge drinking at the beginning of the year, but then as class demands increase during the middle portion of the academic year and students become entrenched in their study routines, binge drinking declines; it increases once again following exams. Binge drinking is especially prevalent during students' first year at college, and then declines during subsequent years (Brower, 2002).

When college binge drinking first came to widespread public awareness, a common concern was that the current cohort of binge drinkers would turn into the alcoholics of the future. However, the research conducted over the last decade finds no evidence that binge drinking in college is associated with alcohol abuse or alcoholism in later life; in fact, binge drinking usually ceases following graduation (Brower, 2002). Even though college binge drinking is not associated with problem drinking in later life, there is no doubt that it can create problems—the destruction of property, self-injury, death, injury to others, and falling grades. Thus, a wide range of social control measures have been implemented on campuses throughout North America to curb the problematic consequences of binge drinking.

College alcohol policies vary, depending on the size of the college, whether it is urban or rural, whether it is public or private, and whether it is religious or secular (Weschler et al., 2000). Virtually all colleges provide general alcohol education to students, such as through awareness and safety campaigns prior to Spring Break. However, fewer colleges have alcohol education programs targeted at known higher-use groups, such as fraternities and athletes. Many colleges place restrictions on alcohol supply, such as prohibiting keg deliveries to buildings on campus. College sporting events are frequently alcohol-free, and alcohol advertising may be banned at those events. Most colleges provide services for students with serious alcohol abuse problems, and provide alcohol-free social events. Some colleges have gone as far as declaring themselves "dry," prohibiting any and all alcohol use on campus property. However, the effectiveness of these efforts at controlling binge drinking is suspect; as Keeling (2000, para. 9) points out, "We know more about what does not work than what does."

Brower (2002) proposes that the shortcoming of many traditional social control efforts is that they mirror approaches for controlling alcohol abuse in society at large, which is based on the presumption that college binge drinking is the same as any other type of "problem drinking." However, the fact that binge drinking usually stops following graduation suggests that it is a product of the college environment combined with a particular developmental stage in life, rather than being associated with alcoholism or other types of "problem drinking." Treating alcoholism (or other types of problem drinkers) effectively usually means individual treatments that are based on complete abstinence from alcohol. But if binge drinking is a product of the college environment, then control efforts must modify the role that alcohol plays in the college environment. Brower (2002) suggests that this is most effectively done through comprehensive efforts that decrease student anonymity, provide consistent expectations about what it means to be a "student" at a particular college, consistently enforce student behaviour policies, and more. College students are actually largely in favour of rigorous, but fair, alcohol policies and enforcement of those policies, but only when the students themselves are involved in their creation (Keeling, 2002). Strict prohibition, such as declaring campuses "dry," are met with resistance; "students—like most of us—will react defensively and angrily to actions taken 'against' them" (Keeling, 2002, para. 29).

Whether traditional or non-traditional approaches at controlling binge drinking among college students have been utilized, the proportion of binge drinkers has remained virtually unchanged over the last decade. And although there are more abstainers than in the past, there are also more "frequent" binge drinkers than in the past. It appears that regardless of the efforts, a dent has not been made in this drinking pattern.

"Whatever we have done (and we have done a great deal), we have not yet significantly changed the dominant patterns of dangerous drinking—not with peer educators; not with social marketing; not with 'social norming'; not with 'dorm talks'; not with student assistance programs; and not with the arrayed forces of grants, campus-community coalitions, and concerned leaders." (Keeling, 2002, para. 13)

Ask Yourself:

What is your college doing to curb binge drinking? Your Student Resource Centre may have information on the various aspects of your college's social control efforts—education programs, peer support, services for students with serious drinking problems, and college policies.

Binge drinking among college students, teenage alcohol use, drug use, and teen smoking are harmful to the individuals consuming those substances, but are also perceived as dangers to society. Youth who engage in these behaviours are therefore seen as both "troubled" and "troubling." Young offenders, youth gang members, and young people who engage in substance use are just some of those youth who are considered deviant in our society, and made subject to various measures of social control. However, other youth are also considered "troubled," "troubling," or both—street kids, runaways, those with mental disorders, and those who are prematurely sexually active. More recently, the concept of *at-risk youth* has emerged, able to encompass all of these groups of deviant youth, and even more.

TIME TO REVIEW:

- What are the patterns of alcohol use and "heavy drinking" among youth?
- How does the prevalence of adolescent "drunkenness" compare in Canada and other cultures?
- What is "binge drinking"?
- What proportion of college students engages in binge drinking, and how do patterns of use change during the duration of the students' time in college?
- How have patterns of binge drinking changed since the early 1990s? Why?
- How is college binge drinking controlled, and how does controlling college binge drinking differ from controlling "problem drinking" in other parts of society?

Youth "At Risk"

The concept of "**at-risk youth**" has come to permeate many sectors, including health, social services, education, policing, and even industry (Bessant, 2001; Ericson & Haggerty, 2001). This concept emerges from the broader notion of a **risk society**, which Beck (1992; 1999) suggests has emerged over the last several decades—a society in which knowledge experts warn us that risks are everywhere around us. It is the job of professionals to then identify those populations that are "at risk" of various negative outcomes, and implement programming that will manage those risks. The precise nature of those risks and their potential negative consequences depends upon the particular social group in question. For youth, the risks and consequences are seen as many. "It has become part of the contemporary common sense that leaving school 'early,' living in certain family arrangements and having a particular socio-economic or ethnic background put a young person 'at risk' of various other social ills like unemployment, crime, suicide, homelessness, substance abuse and pregnancy" (Bessant, 2001, p. 31).

Particular groups of youth are perceived as "at risk" because of numerous personal, family, community, and educational factors, similar to those we addressed in looking at youth crime, gang involvement, and substance use. Those outcomes are just some of the possible consequences when risks remain unmanaged; thus "at-risk youth" has become a label that replaces "troubling," "troubled," "delinquent," and "maladjusted." It is an encompassing category into which those youth who are threats to the social order or threats to themselves can be placed, and then subsequently controlled through the **science of risk** (Bessant, 2001; Ericson & Haggerty, 2001). The science of risk, constructed by those experts and professionals who are presumed to have the necessary knowledge in the area, enables management of young criminals, gang members, substance users, street kids, teenagers who are prematurely sexually active, runaways, and even those youth whom the science of risk identifies as having a higher probability of any of those outcomes *in the future*.

Via the social typing process, "high-risk" youth are identified in schools, in community agencies, or by the police, and they are then subjected to particular risk management strategies in order to reduce their risks of negative outcomes. For example, schools in "high-risk" neighbourhoods frequently have their own police officers to provide drug education, interact with students to create more favourable perceptions of the police, help resolve conflicts so that they do not escalate, and liaise with other individuals or agencies that can help individual youth whom the police have identified as facing more "risks" than others (Ericson & Haggerty, 2001). High-risk youth will find themselves on the receiving end of an array of risk management strategies. They may be entered into special educational programs within the school to increase their commitment to education and their grades, they may be provided with necessary types of counselling or personal programs (e.g., anger management), or their families may be provided with needed resources or counselling.

The intention is to divide "at-risk youth" from those who are not "at risk." However, as Ericson and Haggerty (2001) illustrate in their analysis of policing, in practice *all* youth end up being targeted for risk management. For example, youth are more likely to be stopped by the police than older people are. And even schools that are not in "high-risk" communities may have on-site police officers and social workers to provide drug education, conflict resolution, and liaison with additional risk management agencies. Professionals within the numerous sectors that the science of risk permeates frequently implement risk management strategies with all youth, rather than distinguishing between those who are and are not "at risk"; the implication is that all youth are "at risk" (Bessant, 2001; Ericson & Haggerty, 2001). Bessant (2001) suggests that although the label "at risk" has replaced older categories of troubled and troubling youth, "…the youth-at-risk categories are different from the older categories in terms of their capacity to incorporate the entire population of young people" (p. 32). All youth are perceived as being potential threats to the social order, or threats to themselves and their own futures. The very nature of youth itself is seen as being deviant and in need of social control. "The wider culture constitutes youth as a symbolic threat. Disorderly youth are an expression of 'respectable fears'…about disorder and decline in general" (Ericson & Haggerty, 2001, p. 107).

TIME TO REVIEW:

- Where is the concept of "at-risk youth" used?
- What leads groups of youth to be considered "at risk," and what are the potential consequences of such risks?
- What does the "science of risk" do?
- How has the application of risk management strategies expanded in recent years?

Aren't All Youth Deviant?

"It was about the fourth time my daughter Katie had made cookies on her own. She was 12, which is precariously close to 13, which in humans is not an age but a serious mental disorder" (Beck, 2001, p. 69).

The above statement, although merely intended to be a humourous comment in a magazine article, reflects the cultural perception that youth are problematic—not just *some* youth, but *all* youth. The popular image of the teenager is imbued with both "troubled" and "troubling" facets. Most of us have heard (or even participated in) conversations espousing the problems of adolescents. Themes in these conversations typically include phrases like the following: "They have no respect for authority anymore!" "Back in my day, things were different!" "Society is in trouble if they're the ones who will be running things in a few years!" These kinds of laments construct adolescents as a very distinct and separate group, a group that is at the very least an annoyance, and that may even pose a danger to themselves, to society, and to the future of civilization. As the title of Patricia Hersch's (1998) book suggests, they are "a tribe apart."

As we look around ourselves as we go about our daily lives, it does appear that teenagers might be "a tribe apart." We do often see a separation of the world of adults and the world of adolescents, suggesting that there may be a separate youth subculture, one that many members of the adult world perceive as breaking all of the rules—a subculture that is deviant and in need of intense control. We see them congregating in groups in which all are roughly the same age; 12- and 13-year-olds are usually with others of the same age, not with 20-year-olds and not with 9-year-olds. In fact, 14-year-olds are likely to refuse to take younger siblings with them when going out with friends, even when parents plead with them to do so. These age-based groupings are even evident in schools, where teenagers of similar age are usually in the same grades. We see teenagers attending concerts that few adults are attending (e.g., Britney Spears) and listening to CDs that their parents often describe as "noise." At the movie theatre, those seeing certain movies (e.g., *Scream 3*) are predominantly high school students; in the 1980s, movies with a similar audience included *Porky's* and *Ski School*. Particular sub-groups of teenagers are often seen wearing similar clothes, like flared pants and platform shoes (although the teenage "uniform" will have most certainly changed by the time you are reading this). If we go into a shopping mall—*the* hangout for contemporary adolescents—teenagers are shopping at particular clothing stores that carry the "uniform," and that have certain types of music playing in the background. Within these stores, parents and their teenage children can frequently be heard arguing over the clothes being too revealing, too expensive, or too sloppy. Continuing a journey through the mall, if we enter a bookstore we can see that family conflicts are becoming too much for some parents, who are in the "Parenting" section of the bookstore, perusing titles like *How to Talk So Your Teen Will Listen*, or *How to Survive Your Child's Adolescence*.

The problematic nature of adolescence began receiving widespread public attention not long after the "teenager" was labelled in the 1950s. At that time, articles about how to parent teenagers could be found in women's magazines such as *Ladies' Home Journal* and *Good Housekeeping*, and parenting manuals that focused specifically on teenagers began to be written, similar to those we can see today in our local bookstores. However, since the 1950s the problem of teenagers has been seen as a problem not only for the parents raising them, but also a problem for society as a whole. That is, those problems that result in conflicts between parents and teenage children within individual families are perceived as indicative of problems between the adult and adolescent generations within the broader society. A euphemism that many of us are familiar with—"**the generation gap**"—

captures this cultural perception. Why does a generation gap exist between adults and teenagers? According to this widespread cultural perception, the generation gap is certainly not because of the adults. It is because of the teenagers; they are the problem that needs to be controlled. Adolescence itself has come to be defined as a time in the life cycle that is inherently deviant, and of all the different stages in the life cycle, arguments are that it is adolescence that requires the greatest degree of regulation. Several large-scale surveys of adults (including parents and teachers), and even college students, reveal that teenagers are stereotypically perceived as embodying a range of negative characteristics—sexually active, substance using, materialistic, emotional, awkward, anxious, confused, easily influenced by friends, rebellious, rude, and difficult to get along with (Buchanan, cited in Arnett, 1999; Buchanan & Holmbeck, 1998). Because cultural perceptions of adolescents are based on these types of characteristics, considerable social control or regulation is seen as necessary.

We can see the formal regulation of adolescents in debates over the value of school uniforms in high schools, in community curfews for those under the age of 18, special laws for teenagers (e.g., in Canada, the *Youth Criminal Justice Act*), special risk management programs in many junior high and high schools, and more. In all of these instances, the intent is to regulate, monitor, and control what is perceived as the inherently problematic nature of adolescence. We can see informal regulation within the changed approaches to parenting once adolescence arrives, the greater monitoring of teenagers in retail stores, the desire to sit as far away from a group of teenagers on the subway as possible, and the informal conversations we hear about "those kids today." Such forms of formal and informal social control are intended to manage the deviant nature of adolescence, and the subsequent "generation gap."

The Generation Gap: The Past

The perception of youth as a problem in need of control is nothing new, extending back thousands of years. Socrates complained that youth "contradict their parents" and "tyrannize their teachers" (cited in Arnett, 1999, p. 317). Aristotle described youth as having an absence of self-control (especially sexual self-control), prone to emotional angry outbursts, spending too much time with friends, and thinking they know everything (*Rhetoric, Book II*). At the turn of the 20th century, psychologist G. Stanley Hall (1904) spoke of the **sturm und drang** (i.e., storm and stress) of adolescence, suggesting that individual development mirrored the evolution of the human species. According to Hall, the process of growing up is a transition from "beast-like" to "human-like"; the period of adolescence mirrored the evolutionary stage of primitive man, prior to human civilizations evolving. The problems of adolescence could not be avoided, but with the appropriate controls to deal with that stage of psychological development and to minimize the damage adolescents might do, adolescents would eventually "grow out of it" as they reached the civilized stage of adulthood. People born during and immediately after World War II became the "original" teenagers of the 1950s (Doherty, 1988, p. 45). They differed from previous generations in terms of sheer number, economic prosperity, and generational cohesion; they had an "awareness of themselves as teenagers" (Doherty, 1988, p. 45). Society accorded them a particular social status—"teenager"—and this group became part of a recognized youth culture. There was some dismay at the recognition of the teenager and the associated youth culture, which "cultural guardians…likened to barbaric hordes descending upon a city under siege" (Doherty, 1988, p. 51).

Empirical research in the mid-20th century frequently concluded that teenagers were a distinct and oppositional subculture, and that the future of society was at risk. For example, research found that, for teenage boys, being a star athlete was of ultimate importance; for teenage girls, being popular was the most important. These kinds of empirical results reinforced the perception that teenagers were as different from adults as was possible, and that all adolescents were "troubling," a threat to the social order (Tanner, 1992). Other researchers (e.g., Berger, cited in Tanner, 1992), who suggested otherwise, were largely ignored within popular discourse. They claimed that the generations are far more similar than they are different, that most parents and their teenage children get along fairly well, and that there are many things they agree upon. Berger suggested that it is parents who bring the emphasis on sports to their sons' lives, and the emphasis on popularity to their daughters' lives. Furthermore, interests in sports and peer acceptance and not just limited to the lives of teenagers, but to adult lives as well (Tanner, 1992). Moving into the present day, we can still see the reality of Berger's claims.

The Generation Gap: The Present

Why do children get involved in organized sports? Because their parents get them involved, and at increasingly younger ages. How many 3 or 4 year olds are actually the ones insisting to their parents that they want to play T-Ball? Parents enroll these young children in sports because they are quite adorable to watch. Where do children learn that sports are important? Again, from the adults in their lives—parents, teachers, coaches, and the media. Children's sporting leagues have had to institute regulations governing parental behaviour, simply because of the preponderance of cursing at the officials, name-calling of the children on other teams, and even physical violence. In the United States in 2002, a father was convicted for murdering another boy's father during a disagreement at a children's hockey game. The extreme behaviour of parents at children's sporting events demonstrates to children from an early age how important sports are. The importance of sports is also demonstrated to children by the fact that some of the most highly paid people in North America are professional athletes, who frequently make millions of dollars in salary and bonuses every single season. Entire channels are devoted to sports, as are entire sections in the daily newspaper. If sports are so important to teenagers, it is only because their parents, and other adults, put so much stress on them. Berger (1963) made these claims 40 years ago, but in contemporary society this pattern is even more evident than it was then.

Why is popularity important to teenagers? Again, it is because adults have made it so. Parents, teachers, and other adults encourage children to "make friends," and express concern if their children have too few friends. At a very young age, how many of us have heard adults say, "You must share your toys *or the other kids won't like you*," or "You have to be nice, *or the other kids won't want to play with you anymore*"? The importance of having all the other kids like you and want to play with you is made clear before a child even enters first grade. Popularity is also important in the adult world, although we are unlikely to use the word "popularity" to describe it. The phrase "keeping up with the Joneses" refers to adults who want the same status of car, house, boat, or vacation as their neighbours or co-workers. One student recently described to me how when one family on the block re-landscaped their yard in a certain way, almost every other family on the block did the same thing. This begs the question of whether this is really any different than teenagers who want the same kind of clothes or shoes as their peers. Many of us have felt obligated to go along with a group of co-workers for drinks or coffee after work, even when we would have rather gone straight home. As adults, when we move to a new city, or some traumatic life change occurs (e.g., divorce), the advice we are given is to join clubs or community organizations so we can make new friends—finding more friends is the solution to our problems. And recent research being widely reported in the media (e.g., *Chatelaine, Ladies' Home Journal, Health* magazines) points out the link between physical health and the extent of one's social network; these popular magazine articles are telling us we have to "make friends" because our lives really do depend on it!

Adults and youth are more similar than early research claimed. Most teenagers do conform to the larger society. Most get good grades in school. Most go on to postsecondary education. Most never get into trouble with the law, use drugs, or get pregnant (or, alternatively, get someone pregnant). In fact, even by taking a closer look at families, we see that parent-teen conflict is not as large a problem as popular images suggest. Disagreements are quite common, with 40% of teenagers saying they have disagreements with parents at least once per week (Bibby, 2001). However, conflicts are usually over smaller daily issues rather than large life-altering issues (Smetana, 1988). When conflicts do occur, it is frequently over social life, peer group social customs, and household responsibilities rather than educational/career goals or moral issues (e.g., Laursen, 1995). A survey of teenagers in 2000 (Bibby, 2001) finds the most common source of parent-teen conflicts to be jobs around the house, but even then only slightly more than half of teens say they argue about this issue "fairly often" or "very often." Even though conflicts do increase during adolescence (Arnett, 1999), 59% of teenagers say family life is "very important" to them, 71% say they get a "high level" of enjoyment from interactions with their mothers, 91% say the way they were brought up has a significant influence on their lives and their decision-making, and 71% "want a home like the one I grew up in" (Bibby, 2001). In the end, the vast majority of teenagers turn out all right.

Thus, some scholars say that the concept of the "generation gap" is somewhat of an exaggeration, facilitated by stereotypes of teenagers, sensationalistic media portrayals that will attract an audience, and moral panics stimulated by interest groups that want to advance a political or economic agenda. Even research itself tends to focus on problems with teenagers rather than on the rather mundane everyday lives of mainstream teenagers. Our cultural focus on problems leads us to lose sight of the fact that most families and most teenagers are doing just fine.

The Generation Gap: The Question of the Future

Although a considerable amount of research has claimed that the concept of the "generation gap" and the notion that adolescence is an inherently deviant time in the life cycle are exaggerations, the teenage years are accompanied by increases in "storm and stress," such as conflicts with parents (Laursen, Coy, & Collins, 1998), extremes of emotion (Larson & Richards, 1994), and risk-taking behaviour (Arnett, 1992). And some social analysts are now expressing the concern that, given contemporary social patterns and particularly family trends, the possibility of a significant generation gap may arise in the near future.

Contemporary family life is frequently characterized by a culture of busy-ness, where scattered work, education, and extracurricular schedules of family members often means that they spend little time with each other. This is especially the case once children become adolescents, when even as far back as 1984 (early in the development of the culture of busy-ness), teenagers were found to spend only 4.8% of their time with parents and only 2% of their time with other adults (Csikszentmihalyi & Larson, 1984). Hersch (1998) says the following of the lives of contemporary teenagers: "[They are] a vague mass of kids growing up in a world that rushes past them until one of them steps out of the shadows and demands attention by doing something extraordinarily wonderful or troublesome, outrageous or awful. The rest of the time, especially for the average, everyday kid who goes along not making any waves, the grown-up world doesn't pay much attention. Adults, burned out by the years of day care arrangements, are happy the kids are old enough to be on their own. Besides, most believe adolescents prefer being left along…" (p. 11).

It is in this aloneness that the potential for a new and significant generation gap emerges. In living what are increasingly separate lives, the possibility of similar values, similar interests, and an enjoyment of time spent together declines. Furthermore, considering the central roles that parenting factors (like the quality of parent-teen relationships) and community structures that support and integrate youth play in the emergence of youth crime, gang involvement, and substance use, adolescents' aloneness may set the stage for such "troubling" and "troubled" behaviours to emerge in the future.

"The new generation gap has nothing to do with social change, with intellectual questioning or opposition to causes. Instead it arises from a new social reality. Today's kids have an abundance of that 'space' that sixties kids coveted, enough to do their 'own thing' with great regularity. Their dramatic separation from the adult world is rarely considered a phenomenon in its own right, yet it may be the key to that life in the shadows. It creates a milieu for growing up that adults categorically cannot understand, because [it is] their absence that causes it" (Hersch, 1998, p. 23).

The exaggerated generation gap of the past may become a reality in the future. But is it because of the inherently deviant and problematic nature of adolescent itself? It may be that, just as in the past, today's teenagers are simply living the lives that adults are creating for them. Youth who end up being "troubled" or "troubling," and those who are identified as being "at risk" then require social control. But even more significant is that the perceived "deviant" nature of adolescence and youth culture may be reinforced by the resulting realities of their lives.

TIME TO REVIEW:

- What does the "generation gap" refer to, and what has traditionally been considered the cause of the generation gap?
- How are teenagers perceived in society?
- How is formal and informal social control of teenagers, as an age group, evident?
- How were youth perceived in ancient Greece, at the turn of the 20th century, and in the 1950s?
- What led some mid-20th centuries researchers to conclude that teenagers formed a distinct and oppositional subculture? How was that research disputed at the time?
- In what ways do adults emphasize to youth how important sports and popularity are?
- What is the nature of parent-teen conflict, and what do teenagers think of their own families?
- Why might a new and significant generation gap emerge in the future?

CHAPTER SUMMARY

Youth and deviance seem to go hand-in-hand in Canadian culture. Of particular concern are "troubling" youth, "troubled" youth, and "at-risk" youth; however, to some extent, all youth are perceived as deviant.

The "troubling" youth that receive the greatest attention are those involved in crime, and those who are members of gangs. A substantial gap exists between popular images of youth crime (which suggest that youth crime is out of control), and the actual prevalence and nature of youth crime. The media, politicians, and various interest groups contribute to this *moral panic* about youth crime in Canadian society.

Although youth are not as involved in crime as popular images suggest, concerns over those youth who *are* involved in crime have stimulated a wealth of research on the causes of youth crime. Research has explored the roles of differential opportunities, peer groups, and more, but has particularly highlighted the role of family factors such as parenting style and emotional attachment between parent and child.

Two broad streams of research about youth gangs have emerged. The first stream of research focuses on the factors influencing gang emergence, involvement in gangs, and specific gang activities. This research has concluded that a complex set of individual, family, educational, and community factors influence the emergence of and involvement with gangs. The second stream of research focuses on the construction of the "gang problem" inside and outside of the media. Gangs are frequently portrayed as a serious threat that is out of control in society; the "gang problem" is also typically racialized and contains age distortions.

Because gang emergence and individual involvement in gangs arise from a complex set of factors that exist at multiple levels, the effective control of gangs requires comprehensive, multifaceted efforts at all of those levels. The social control of gangs is intertwined with the control of youth crime more generally, which has shown considerable variation over the past century.

"Troubled" youth includes those who are prematurely sexually active, street kids, those with mental disorders, and more, but of particular concern in contemporary society are youth who use various substances—tobacco, drugs, and alcohol. The most commonly used substances are alcohol, tobacco, marijuana, and hallucinogens. Although almost all youth have used alcohol by the time they graduate from high school, less than 25% of teenagers (more girls than boys) regularly use tobacco, approximately 10% regularly use marijuana, and even less than that have ever even tried other drugs. Over the last decade, binge drinking on college campuses has drawn widespread attention, resulting in a wide range of social control efforts; questions about the effectiveness of these efforts remain.

The concept of *at-risk* youth is a recent formulation that integrates various types of "troubling" and "troubled" youth. The *science of risk* attempts to identify those youth who are at greater risk of negative outcomes in their lives, and then target risk management efforts at those youth. In practice, all youth have come to be seen as "at risk," and made subject to risk management techniques.

To some degree, *all* youth are perceived as being deviant and in need of social control—adolescence is seen as an inherently deviant time in the life cycle. This view is not limited to modern society, but existed as far back as ancient Greece. In the 20th century, the concept of the "generation gap" reflects the conflicts that emerge between the teenage and adult generations. Traditionally, the generation gap has been seen as resulting from the deviant nature of adolescence rather than from anything that adults may be doing. However, many researchers suggest that the generation gap has been more of an exaggeration than a reality. More recently, the extent to which recent cohorts of teenagers are left alone and unsupervised (more than any prior cohorts of adolescents) has led some people to conclude that a new and significant generation gap may actually emerge—not because of the deviant nature of youth themselves, but because of the consequences of the kinds of lives adults are creating for them.

Recommended Readings

Bibby, R. W. (2001). *Canada's teens: Today, yesterday, and tomorrow.* Toronto, ON: Stoddart Publishing.

* Bibby has conducted large-scale surveys of more than 3000 Canadian teenagers in 1984, 1992, and 2000. This book integrates the results of these three separate surveys, as well as national surveys of adults (reflecting on their teenage years) as far back as 1975. The surveys address a wealth of topics—family, friends, drugs, sex, religion, values, concerns, and more. This is an excellent source of information about how teenagers have changed since the 1960s, and how they have remained the same.

Hersch, P. (1998). *A tribe apart: A journey into the heart of American adolescence.* New York: Ballantine Books.

* Hersch is one of the social analysts who suggest that a new generation gap is emerging because of the absence of adults in the lives of adolescents. She illustrates the components of her argument via intensive interviews with adolescents, as well as several in-depth case studies, using the words of teenagers themselves. This is a close look at the world of teenagers, from the perspective of teenagers.

Tanner, J. (2001). *Teenage troubles: Youth and deviance in Canada* (2nd ed.). Scarborough, ON: Nelson Thomson Learning.

* Tanner's book explores youth crime, youth subcultures, moral panics, and theoretical developments in the study of deviant youth.

Endnotes

1 The notion of "troubling" and "troubled" youth is drawn from Tanner (2001).

Key Terms

troubling youth, **p. 139**
troubled youth, **p. 139**
moral panics, **p. 141**
parenting style, **p. 142**
reaction formation, **p. 146**
ethnographic research, **p. 146**
material incentives, **p. 146**
recreation, **p. 146**
a place of refuge and camouflage, **p. 146**
physical protection, **p. 146**
a time to resist, **p. 146**
commitment to the community, **p. 147**
the "gang problem", **p. 148**
racialize, **p. 148**
criminal organizations, **p. 151**
parens patriae, **p. 152**
young offenders, **p. 152**
heavy-drinking episode, **p. 160**
binge drinking, **pp. 160, 162**
at-risk youth, **p. 165**
risk society, **p. 165**
science of risk, **p. 165**
generation gap, **p. 167**
sturm und drang, **p. 168**

C H A P T E R 6

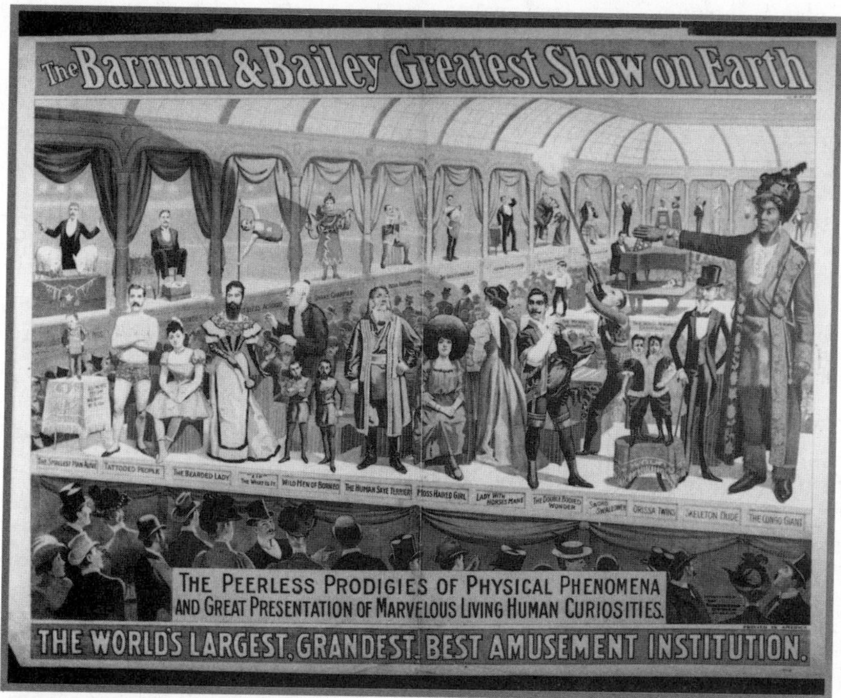

Looking Deviant: Physical Appearance

Learning Objectives

After reading this chapter, you should be able to:

- Describe the importance of physical appearance in our society, and explain the various types of physical appearance that can be socially typed as deviant.
- Define the "ideal" body weight according to scientific standards and social standards, and describe how many people are "too fat" and "too thin" according to these standards.
- Explain how people who are overweight are perceived and treated, and describe the range of social control measures targeted at "too fat."
- Explain how people who are underweight are perceived and treated, and describe the range of social control measures targeted at "too thin."
- Describe the various ways that the social typing of "too fat" and "too thin" as deviant are resisted.

"Talent counts thirty percent; appearance counts seventy." (Chinese proverb)[1]

If you had not been told where the above quotation was from, you might have thought it was a contemporary Canadian or American quotation. Indeed, we do live in a culture where physical appearance is important. In fact, some people would say that looks are everything. Think of your own physical appearance, and how you maintain it. You have chosen a particular hairstyle, and perhaps even hair colour. Every morning, you might blow dry, straighten, curl, gel, or spray your hair in order to achieve a specific look. Perhaps you put on makeup. Then you choose certain clothes, depending on what your plans are for the day. Are you going to work, school, a job interview, a date, dinner with your grandparents, a rave, or to write a final exam? For all but the last item on that list, you probably choose your clothes carefully. Maybe you have a tattoo, piercings, or some other type of body art. Perhaps you are dieting to lose weight, working out to become more sculpted, or taking supplements to increase muscle mass. As part of a select few, you may be gulping milkshakes in order to gain weight. You may even be contemplating plastic surgery to fix your nose, lift your eyes, suck the fat out of your love handles, or increase the size of your breasts. The time, effort, and money we spend on our physical appearance illustrate how important it is to us.

Our appearance is important to us, in part, because we wish to express ourselves, paint a picture of who we are. But our appearance is also important to us because we know *people judge us by how we look*. Our employers, grandparents, colleagues, classmates, and even people we merely pass by evaluate our appearance in some way. The way we look can affect whether we get hired for a job, what our grandparents think of us, who will and will not want to start a conversation with us or become our friends, whether we are asked on a date by the person we are interested in, and whether people stare at us as we walk down the street. Physical appearance is the stimulus for social typing that we do every day, and that we are subject to every day. But social typing based on physical appearance goes beyond our own individual likes and dislikes. You might think brunettes look more professional than blondes, but I might think the reverse; you might be attracted to people who are bald, I might not. However, regardless of our own personal preferences, there are larger patterns of social typing that occur in our society. For instance, we all know that our chances of being hired are small if we appear at a job interview wearing sweatpants. Similarly, we know that someone dressed in a Gothic style is far more likely to be stared at or teased while walking down the street than someone who is wearing Dockers and a button-down shirt; and yet, that person chooses to dress in a Gothic style anyway, despite (or perhaps because of) that social reaction.

Voluntary and Involuntary Physical Appearance

Some forms of physical appearance that are socially typed as deviant and subsequently made subject to measures of social control are voluntarily adopted—hairstyles, clothing, makeup, and body art. Precisely which forms of voluntary physical appearance are considered deviant depends upon the sociohistorical context. Slicked-back hair, "dungarees" (i.e., jeans), and leather jackets were perceived so negatively in the 1950s that they were prohibited in many high schools. Men with long hair who wore beads were considered deviant in the 1960s and 1970s; some store windows contained signs saying "No Hippies Allowed." During most of the 20th century, people with tattoos were viewed negatively, and presumed to have other negative characteristics as well (Sanders, 1989). However, by the end of the 20th century and the early 21st century, tattoos and other forms of body art (e.g., body piercing) were less stigmatized and more widely adopted. In many other cultures in the world, body art has been commonplace for centuries. Voluntary aspects of physical appearance that may be deviantized also include that which is associated with certain lifestyle groups, such as goths (Tait, 1999), ravers (Wilson, 2002; Weber, 1999), and punk rockers (Baron, 1989; Davies, 1996; Mattson, 2001). In these cases, appearance is only one aspect of the overall lifestyle.

Political, philosophical, and/or social foundations underlie the emergence of Gothic, rave, and punk rock cultures. All of these lifestyle groups embody a rejection of the status quo and traditional forms of authority; however, each embraces different alternatives. For example, rave culture emphasizes love and freedom, while punk rock focuses on being antiestablishment and anarchist. Within each of these lifestyle groups are numerous sub-groups, which differentially emphasize the political, ideological, and stylistic aspects of the broader lifestyle.

Other forms of physical appearance are involuntary in nature, such as extremes in height, disfigurements, and visible disabilities. Although individuals have little or no choice regarding these aspects of their physical appearance, they are frequently stigmatized in our society—stared at, laughed at, teased, and in many ways excluded from opportunities, activities, and relationships (Westbrook, Legge, & Pennay, 1993; Gardner, 1991). In Nazi Germany, people with visible disabilities were even targets for genocidal efforts (Mostert, 2002). Some forms of physical appearance combine voluntary and involuntary aspects; a good example of this is body weight. People choose how much to eat and how much physical activity to participate in (voluntary); however, psychological factors, social factors, and biological factors may influence those outcomes (involuntary). The social typing of body weight saturates the everyday lives of all of us living in Canadian society today. The social control of body size permeates the field of medicine, the media, commercial industry, education, and daily interactions. Because the social typing of body weight is so pervasive, and affects so many people's lives, that will be the focus of this chapter.

With all forms of physical appearance that are socially typed as deviant, it is not necessarily the appearance itself that generates a negative reaction, but rather the meanings, stereotypes, and interpretations that are attached to that appearance. Physical appearance constitutes what Howard Becker (discussed in Chapter 3) called a **master status**, one of those categories we immediately place people in upon first seeing them, which subsequently defines who the person is. The auxiliary traits we attach to master statuses are what makes them significant. Thus, people with disabilities were systematically killed by the Nazis not simply because of their appearance, but because they were perceived as useless and a drain on society. Similarly, people who are obese are not stigmatized because of their appearance per se, but because that appearance is presumed to be indicative of laziness, a lack of self-control, and psychological problems.

TIME TO REVIEW:

- Why is physical appearance important to us?
- What is the difference between voluntary and involuntary physical appearance? Give examples of each, and explain how appearance can be related to lifestyle groups.
- Why are certain physical appearances socially typed as deviant?

Weight: "Too Fat," "Too Thin," and "Ideal"

"You can never be too rich or too thin." (Dorothy Parker, 1893–1967)[2]

Poet and screenwriter Dorothy Parker was the first to utter the above phrase, which was subsequently repeated by actress and wealthy socialite Zsa Zsa Gabor in the mid-20th century. Does that phrase still hold true? Is thinner better? Is it possible to be *too* thin? In any culture at any specific time in history, only a certain range of body sizes are perceived as normal, conforming, or ideal. Anything outside of that ideal is considered unacceptable, deviant, and requiring modification—overweight or underweight, or using more popular terminology, "too fat" or "too thin."

If the "ideal" body you initially pictured was a female body, you should not be surprised. Weight is more likely to be used as an evaluative criterion for women than men; for the latter, a wider range of body types are seen as acceptable (Rabak-Wagener, Eickhoff-Shemek, & Kelly-Vance, 1998). But even though men tend to have more freedom in what is considered an acceptable body, at some point they are subject to the judgments of others based on their weight, just as women are.

Ask Yourself:

Take a moment to picture the "ideal" body. Notice the details. What does the "ideal" body look like? Is it a female body? If so, whom does that body type most closely approximate–a runway model like Kate Moss, an actress like Halle Berry, a "plus-size" model like Emme, a competitive athlete like a member of the Canadian women's hockey team, or the average woman you see on the street? If it is a male body, whom does that body most closely approximate–actor Sylvester Stallone ("Rambo"), a competitive bodybuilder, heartthrob Brad Pitt, a male figure skater, or the average man you see on the street?

What is the "ideal" body weight according to our current cultural standards? To some extent, the answer to that question depends upon whose criteria we are using—the criteria used by physicians in their evaluations of health, or the criteria used by average people in their judgments of people's physical appearance.

The "Ideal" Body According to Science

Within the field of medicine, acceptable and deviant body weights are determined on the basis of "risks" for negative health consequences. Relative risk can be measured in a number of ways, such as Waist-Hip Ratio, and simple height/weight tables. However, the most common measurement tool used by physicians and scientists today is the **Body-Mass Index (BMI)**. An individual's BMI is determined through a comparison of height and weight, as illustrated in the chart on the following page.

The standards of the World Health Organization (2002a), which have been adopted by many countries in the world, categorize a BMI between 18.5 and 24.9 as "acceptable," because it is associated with the lowest health risks. A BMI between 25.0 and 29.9 is considered "**overweight**" due to increased risks of high cholesterol, Type 2 diabetes, heart disease, high blood pressure, arthritis, and more. A BMI of 30.0 and higher is categorized as "**obese**," with considerable risks for these illnesses. A BMI of 18.4 and lower is considered "**underweight**" due to greater risks of heart problems, lowered immunity, anemia, depression, and death.

Although governments and health organizations in many countries have adopted the World Health Organization standards, there are some variations. For example, Asia-Pacific standards define a BMI of 25.5 as the cutoff point for "obesity," due to some research that suggests being overweight has more significant consequences at earlier stages for Asia-Pacific populations (Health Canada, 2002a).

According to the World Health Organization standards, being overweight is a significant problem throughout much of the world, and obesity is defined as an "epidemic" (World Health Organization, 2002a; International Task Force on Obesity, 2003). Approximately 1.7 billion people in the world are overweight, and 300 million of those are obese; 2 million people in the world die each year due to complications arising from being overweight and/or sedentary (Obesity

Figure 6.1 BODY MASS INDEX (BMI) NOMOGRAM

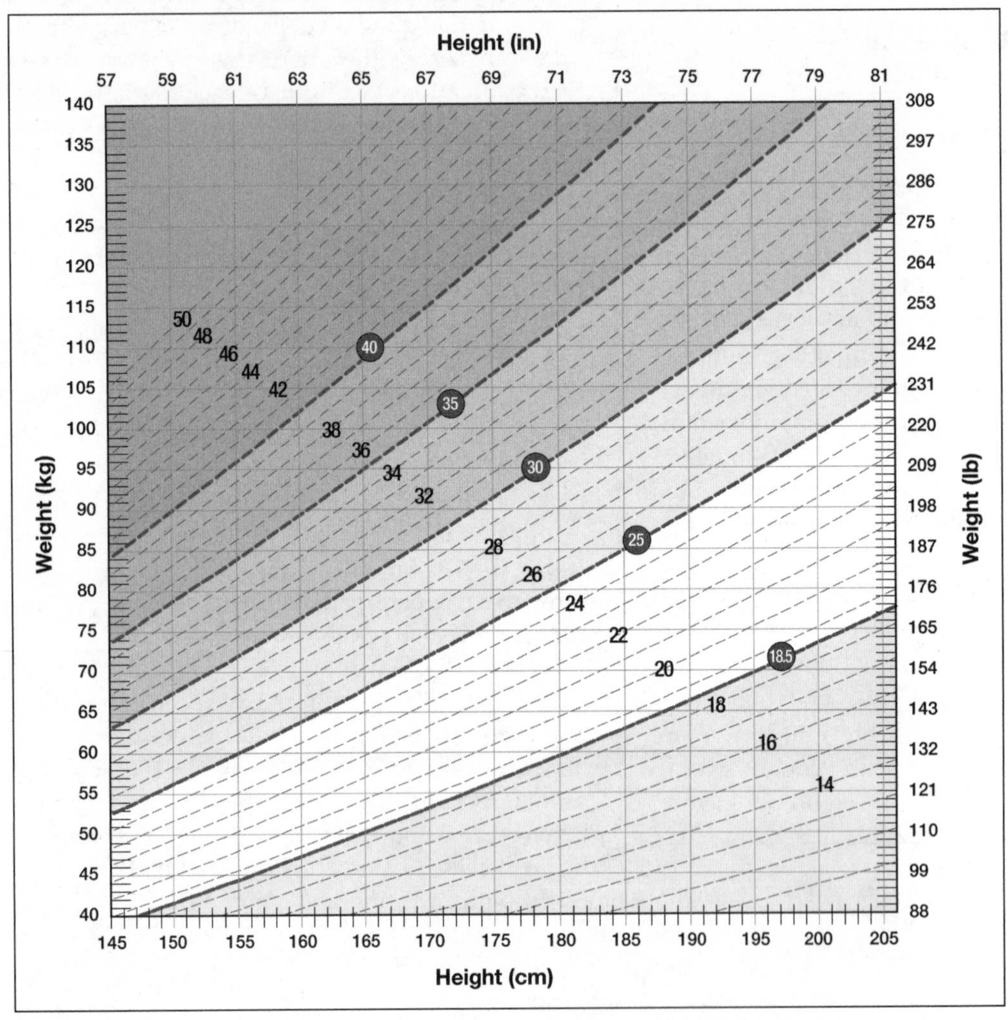

Source: *Body Mass Index Nomogram*, Health Canada, (2003).

Reproduced with the permission of the Minister of Public Works and Government Services Canada, 2003.

Association, 2003). In Canada, 35% of adults are overweight, and another 15% are obese (Statistics Canada, 2002b); the prevalence of obesity is even greater in the United States, where more than 60% of adults are either overweight or obese (International Obesity Task Force, 2003). Even among children, obesity has been defined as a serious problem. In countries like Egypt, Mexico, Peru, Chile, Italy, and the United States, more than 25% of children are obese (Bellizzi, cited in International Obesity Task Force, 2003). In Canada, 37% of children ages 2 through

11 are overweight, and 18% of those overweight children are obese (Statistics Canada, 2002b). In the United States, childhood obesity increased between 1986 and 1998, from 20% to 25%; for Hispanic-American and African-American children, the increase was even greater, from 20% to 40% (Bellizzi, cited in International Obesity Task Force, 2003). Throughout much of the world, children are developing diseases related to being overweight (e.g., Type 2 diabetes; high cholesterol; cardiovascular disease), diseases that used to be limited to adults (World Health Organization, 2002a; Health Canada, 2002a; DeMont, 2002; International Obesity Task Force, 2002).

The prevalence of people worldwide who are underweight is not as widely known. Although the World Health Organization has been mapping the number and geographic regions of people who are overweight and obese, they are only beginning to map the number of people who are underweight; their first report is expected in 2004. In Canada, only 2% of adults are considered underweight, based on BMI standards. However, the problem of being underweight is greater when we look at adolescents, and the presence of anorexia, which is included as a mental disorder by the American Psychiatric Association (1994). The diagnostic criteria for anorexia can be seen in Box 6.1.

Box 6.1 Diagnostic Criteria for Anorexia Nervosa

The DSM-IV (Diagnostic & Statistical Manual) defines **anorexia nervosa** in the following way:

- At least 15% below normal body weight
- Extreme fear of becoming fat
- Abnormal self-perception of body, consisting of at least one of the following:
  - undue emphasis on weight or shape in self-evaluation
  - denial of seriousness of weight loss
  - distorted perception of body shape or weight
- For females, must have missed at least three consecutive periods

International definitions go a step further than the DSM by pointing out that the weight loss must be self-induced, through extreme calorie restrictions and/or intense exercise. International definitions also refer to **atypical anorexia,** in which many, but not all, of the above symptoms are present; for example, some females may have not yet missed any periods, or their weight may not yet have fallen to 15% below normal body weight (Shuriquie, 1999).

Based on these diagnostic criteria, 5% of young women in Canada have anorexia, and another 10–20% have many of the symptoms (Marble, 1995). The majority of people with anorexia are female (estimates are approximately 9 out of 10), although the incidence among males is increasing. Eating disorders include more than just anorexia; however, it is primarily anorexia that results in being underweight. The emaciated appearance of people with anorexia represents what Goffman (1963) calls a **discredited (visible) stigma**, a characteristic easily observed by others (McLorg & Taub, 1987). It is estimated that approximately 10% of individuals with anorexia will die as a result of the physical complications that arise.

The negative health consequences of having anorexia, being overweight, or being obese have stimulated an abundance of research on how people come to have these experiences. Genetic, psychological, family, and larger sociocultural factors have all been areas of focus for those researchers who take a more objective approach to these conditions by searching for causes (e.g., Sandbek, 1993; Gordon, 2000; Caldwell, 2001; Levy, 2000). The research on being overweight consistently identifies the central cause as consuming more calories than are being expended, but the factors underlying that characteristic are multifaceted—the inability to deal with negative emotions in an effective way, the way that unhealthy food saturates our culture, and the simple formation of bad habits are just some of the factors that have been identified. The research on being underweight, and particularly anorexic, is far more tenuous. Four general categories of causal theories continue to be explored by researchers (McLorg & Taub, 1987). First are **ego-psychological theories**, which emphasize impaired psychological functioning emerging from the child-mother relationship. Second are **family systems theories**. These theories suggest that anorexia is facilitated by emotionally enmeshed, rigid, overly controlling families. The third type of explanation is **endocrinological** in nature, exploring various hormonal defects. The last category of explanations is **sociocultural**, looking at social norms emphasizing thinness, media images, and social learning/modelling.

In addition to research into causation, other areas of interest in research on body size, ones that are of particular interest to more subjectively oriented social analysts, are the social definitions of the "ideal" body, the social control of body weight, and the implications of those social messages. While scientific definitions of anorexia, obesity, and the more general conditions of being underweight or overweight are based on their medical implications, social definitions have a very different foundation. Social judgments of people's physical appearance based on body weight more typically emerge from tacit definitions of the ideal body rather than scientific definitions; that is, when we react to our own weight or the weight of people we see, health risks are rarely the stimulus for our responses.

TIME TO REVIEW:

- What is the "ideal" body weight, according to scientific standards?
- How does science define "too fat" and "too thin," and why are scientists concerned about these characteristics?
- How many people are overweight and underweight, based on scientific standards?
- What areas do scientists emphasize as causes of being overweight, and being anorexic?

The "Ideal" Body According to Social Standards

As we judge the physical appearance of others, or as our own physical appearance is judged, medical standards such as BMI or DSM criteria rarely come into the picture. Instead, social standards determine the nature of the social typing process. These standards vary across cultures and over time, but at any given cultural moment we can identify what standards constitute the "ideal" body (see Figures 6.2 & 6.3).

Figure 6.2 THE "IDEAL" FEMALE BODY: CURRENT CULTURAL STANDARDS

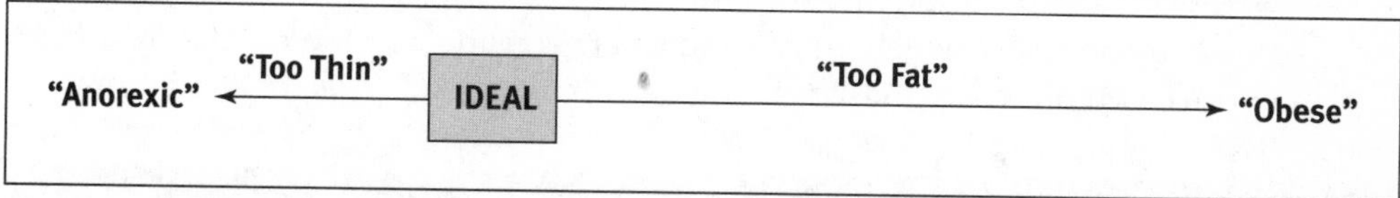

Figure 6.2 THE "IDEAL" MALE BODY: CURRENT CULTURAL STANDARDS

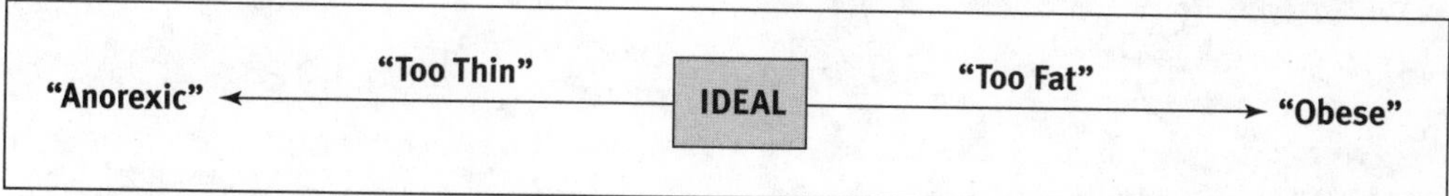

Looking at our current cultural standards, you can see that only a small range of bodies are considered "ideal." Note that the "ideal" body leans toward the "thin" side of the continuum; our current cultural standards define a greater degree of "thinness" than "fatness" as being acceptable. You will also note that the "ideal" range is thinner for females than for males. While the "ideal" female is tall, very thin, and toned, the ideal male is medium-sized and muscular (Rabak-Wagener, Eickhoff-Shemek, & Kelly-Vance, 1998; Salusso-Deonier, Markee, & Pedersen, 1993). Anything outside of this "ideal" range is judged as deviant, and in need of fixing—popular discourse labels it as either "too thin" or "too fat." At the extreme ends of the continuum are "anorexic" and "obese"; however, the popular usage of these terms does not necessarily correspond to the medical criteria for those conditions. This thin ideal is the one reflected in magazines, on television, and in movies. A recent study of male and female college students found strong support for the notions that "adult models in advertisements have an ideal body size and shape," and that women or men "would look more attractive if their body size or shape looked like most of the models in advertising." They consider media images to represent the ideal even though they acknowledge that looking like those media images would not necessarily be good for one's health (Rabak-Wagener, Eickhoff-Shemek, & Kelly-Vance, 1998). Even children consider the adult body images portrayed in the media as the desirable ideal. The Kaiser Family Foundation (1997) found that

70% of girls want to look like a female on television, even though 61% realize that women on television are much thinner than women in the "real world."

In other cultures, the "ideal" body weight can be substantially different than in our own. The slender ideal tends to be characteristic of industrialized countries where food is plentiful. In contrast, in developing countries where food availability is less consistent, plumpness is idealized, especially in women (see below). Once those cultures that have traditionally valued plumpness become more permeated with American media influences, the standards for the "ideal" body weight (especially for women) become considerably thinner (Shuriquie, 1999). Most cultures around the world define a only a specific range of body weights as "ideal," and subsequently socially type individuals as "too fat" or "too thin;" however, precisely which body weights are considered "too fat" or "too thin" varies based on where the "ideal" range falls along body weight continuum.

The "ideal" body weight according to current North American standards is very different than in many other parts of the world.

"Too Fat": Commercialization, Societal Reaction, and Social Control

Perceptions of People Who are Overweight

Although half of Canadian adults and more than 60% of American adults are either overweight or obese, people who are overweight face considerable stigmatization. Overweight people are stereotyped as emotionally handicapped, socially handicapped, lazy, sad, and lacking in self-control by children, teenagers, parents, doctors, nurses, and teachers (Roehling, 1999; Price et al., 1987). Approximately one-quarter of schoolteachers say that "the worst thing that can happen to a person" is obesity, and a similar proportion of nurses say they are "repulsed" by obese people (Puhl & Brownell, 2001). This certainly raises important questions about the messages those schoolteachers pass on to the children in their classrooms, the way teachers treat overweight children, and the kind of care and treatment that those nurses provide their overweight patients. The stigma that we attach to people who are overweight is overwhelmingly clear when looking at the perceptions of children. Children in grades 3 and 4 say they would rather lose a parent, get cancer, or live through a nuclear war than be fat (National Eating Disorder Centre, 2003). Of course, most children in this age group do not have detailed knowledge about the true nature of many of these negative life events (such as what having cancer would actually be like); however, their responses clearly indicate an awareness of the importance of weight in our society. Latner & Stunkard (2003) presented children in grades 5 and 6 with photographs of various types of disabled children (i.e., on crutches, in a wheelchair, with an amputated hand, and with a facial disfigurement) and overweight children; the overweight children were rated as the least desirable as friends.

The negative way that "too fat" is perceived in our society is also widely evident with media portrayals of body weight. The average fashion model is 20% thinner than is healthy, and is significantly thinner than 50 years ago (International Size Acceptance Association, 2003). Portrayals of women in all forms of media have become much thinner over the last several decades (Wiseman et al., 1992; Spitzer, Henderson, & Zivian, 1999; Owen & Laurel-Seller, 2000). Since the 1950s, *Playboy* centerfolds have become thinner (Owen & Laurel-Seller, 2000; Wiseman et al., 1992), such that they are currently at their lowest weight ever. Almost all centerfolds are underweight according to health standards, and approximately 30% meet the weight criteria for anorexia (Spitzer, Henderson, & Zivian, 1999). Miss American pageant winners have also become much thinner since the 1950s, with 17% currently meeting the weight criteria for anorexia (Spitzer, Henderson, & Zivian, 1999). During this period of time, the gap between the body size of media women and the average woman in society has grown, and is continuing to grow (Spitzer, Henderson, & Zivian, 1999). Almost 70% of female television characters are thin, and only 5% are overweight (Silverstein et al., 1986). Even media icon Jennifer Aniston was told by her agent to lose weight in the early 1990s, when she was approximately 5 feet 5 inches and 140 pounds; after losing that weight, she attained the role of Rachel on *Friends* (Cohen, 1996; Fink, 1999). Even some actresses being lauded within the media as "real-sized" women who are accepting of their size (Tauber et al., 2001) are actually thinner than normal—Charlize Theron (6 feet tall and a size 8), Christina Ricci (size 2-4), and Drew Barrymore (size 2-4). In contrast, the average clothing size for women in North America is size 14.

Media portrayals of male bodies focus less on weight, and more on muscularity. In various forms of media, media portrayals of men have become larger and more muscular (but not "fatter") since the 1950s (Wroblewska, 1997). Over the last two decades, male centerfolds in *Playgirl* magazine have actually increased in body size, largely due to greater muscularity; no male centerfolds are underweight (Spitzer, Henderson, & Zivian, 1999). In popular men's magazines from 1960 to 1992, men's bodies did not change significantly (Petrie et al., 1996); however, Erwin (1998) suggests that, more recently, the number of very thin male models has been growing. These media portrayals reinforce the notion that a wider range of body sizes are seen as acceptable for men compared to women, but there are social consequences of being overweight for both women and men.

The behaviours that accompany these negative perceptions for people who are overweight are significant. Among children and adolescents, the most frequent stigmatizing experiences are the direct and intentional teasing or name-calling by classmates (and even strangers). Less intentional negative comments by family members are also common (Neumark-Sztainer, Story, & Faibisch, 1998). In fact, Puhl and Brownell (2001) found that overweight youth receive less financial support for college from their parents than normal weight youth do (controlling for grades and family income). Critical comments and name-calling have a significant impact on adolescents who are on the receiving end. They rate messages from peers and family members as second and third (respectively) only to media messages as influences on their own perceptions of weight and their feelings about their own bodies (Wertheim et al., 1997). In adulthood, teasing and name-calling may become less frequent, replaced by subtler messages from peers and strangers. An episode of the television show *Oprah* provided an obese woman with a hidden camera to document people's reactions as she went about her day. The camera recorded other adults staring as she walked by, quietly snickering, whispering comments to companions, and straining to see what she was ordering in a restaurant and what foods she had put in her shopping cart at the supermarket. In a cafeteria, a fellow patron openly criticized her food choices and told her she wouldn't be so "fat" if she ate better.

Behaviours extend beyond the casual comments of peers, family members, and strangers as well. Research has consistently found that people who are overweight face discrimination within the institutions of society—education, health care, and employment (Puhl & Brownell, 2001). For example, discrimination in employment decisions is common. Potential employees who are overweight are perceived more negatively than those who are former mental patients, or even ex-cons (Kennedy & Homant, 1984). Within lab settings, several studies (e.g., Pingitore et al., 1994) have asked participants to pretend to be employers making hiring decisions. They were provided with hypothetical resumes and photographs of job applicants. The results of these studies conclude that people who are overweight are significantly less likely to be hired for jobs, even given equivalent qualifications as normal weight applicants. For example, Pingitore and colleagues (1994) found that body weight accounted for more than one-third of the variance in hiring decisions, while sex accounted for only one-tenth. As a result of discrimination in hiring and promotion, wages are affected. Mildly obese women have an average wage that is 6% lower, and significantly obese women have an average wage 24% lower, than that of normal weight women (Roehling, 1999). The implications for men's wages are not as significant. Obesity lowers men's wages only at extreme levels; in fact, the average wage of mildly obese men is actually higher than that of normal weight men.

The popular perceptions of people who are overweight, media portrayals of "ideal" body sizes, the reactions that permeate the everyday interactions of children and adults who are overweight, and institutionalized discrimination against people who are overweight (e.g., in employment) do not merely tell us how society *sees* "too fat." As significant aspects of social control, they also tell us how "too fat" is *treated*. As we delve more deeply into informal, formal, and self-regulation, the extent to which "too fat" is made subject to social control efforts in society may surprise you.

TIME TO REVIEW:

- What is the relationship between scientific definitions and social definitions of the "ideal" body?
- What are the "ideal" male and female body weights, according to social definitions?
- In what way is the "ideal" body reflected in the media?
- How do standards for the "ideal" body vary across cultures?
- How are overweight people perceived in our society? Refer to common perceptions and media portrayals in your answer.
- How are overweight people treated in our society?

Social Control

Being overweight is clearly considered to be a negative quality throughout North America, a characteristic that individuals are told they should try to prevent or remedy. A wide range of efforts is directed at people in this regard. Some forms of social control revolve around reducing the health risks associated with the scientifically defined categories of overweight and obesity, while other forms of social control are based on reinforcing the overly thin social standards that define the "ideal" body. Some forms of social control are directed at all of us—to motivate weight loss or prevent weight gain. Other forms of control are restricted to people who are considered (by the medical community or by social norms) to be in need of losing weight. All of these control efforts that are directed *at* people ultimately are related to *self*-regulation; in the end, we are supposed to monitor and control our own body weights. Hurtful comments by others, the portrayals of male and female bodies in the media, and the differential treatment of overweight people in employment, all act as stimuli for weight loss in many people's lives. So do other aspects of the media, commercial industry, medicine, government, and community programs.

Media. The mass media permeates our lives. Television, movies, music, radio programs, magazines, and popular books surround us every day. Much of that media not only contains images about the "ideal" body, but also includes messages about controlling our own bodies. Daytime talk shows frequently present information about new weight loss plans, such as the high-protein, low-carbohydrate diets. Millions of people around the world have followed Oprah Winfrey's repeated weight losses over the years on her show; her show has featured authors of high-protein diet books, yoga instructors, chefs who specialize in low-fat cooking, and her own personal trainer Bob Greene. After musician Carnie Wilson recovered from weight-loss surgery and lost more than 100 pounds, she was interviewed on numerous daytime talk shows and nighttime news programs, as well as in a number of popular magazines. In these interviews she typically spoke of how happy she felt to now be attractive. Actor John Travolta's weight gains and losses have been the subject of media coverage for many years; when he recently lost weight and re-attained a high level of fitness for a movie role, television and magazine interviews were sure to ask him for his secret.

Magazines, particularly women's magazines, are one of the principal media sources of social control efforts regarding body size and other aspects of physical appearance. An analysis of *Seventeen* magazine for girls from 1945 to 1995 found that articles about physical appearance were the most common type of article in every issue (Schlenker, Caron, & Halteman, 1998). In women's magazines, morality is frequently linked to body weight, fitness, and food choices (Pongonis & Snyder, 1998). The "right" body, fitness level, and eating habits are represented as indicators of strong morality, while the "wrong" physical characteristics are indicative of a lack of morality in the individual. Those of you who read women's magazines may have noticed a set of common advertisements over the last few years, for a certain type of low-fat breakfast bar. The photograph shows a woman with a giant pastry around her waist, or cinnamon buns protruding from her hips. The tag line reads, "Respect yourself in the morning," suggesting that only by eating this low-fat breakfast bar can a women respect herself—eating a pastry means a woman is undeserving of respect. Even looking at the headline stories on the covers of women's magazines illustrates the extent to which body size is regulated.

Exercise Your Mind:

Take a trip to your nearest magazine stand (there is probably one right on your campus or in your local convenience store) and look at the covers of the dozens of women's magazines you will likely see. First, take note of the women featured on the covers of the magazines, and what they look like. Then look at the headlines for the main stories in each magazine. How many headlines regarding body size and shape do you see? What messages do you think these magazines give?

The covers of these magazines tell us a great deal about their content, and the emphasis on controlling body weight within that content. The cover models usually portray the "ideal" body weight, although even their bodies are not sufficient in themselves and frequently must be computer-altered to make their waists smaller, hips narrower, and thighs thinner. The magazines you saw likely have headlines similar to the following: "How I dropped two dress sizes" (*Chatelaine*, July 2003); "Walk it off: 35 pounds—gone" (*Good Housekeeping*, June 2003); "Renée Zellweger: Love, loneliness and losing weight" (*Good Housekeeping*, June 2003); "Slimmer arms and legs (no diets, we swear)" (*Redbook*, June 2003); "Toned arms, tight abs" (*Self*, June 2003); "5 easy ways to burn 1000 calories" (*Self*, June 2003); "Get a bikini body in 28 days!" (*Fitness: Mind, Body & Spirit*, May 2003). The articles usually focus on becoming slimmer, thinner, and looking sexier, rather than on issues of health related to being overweight. Even *Health* magazine (April 2001) has as its largest headline, "Change your shape," referring to physical appearance rather than health.

Women's magazines typically focus more on weight loss, while men's magazines focus more on fitness and muscularity. In an analysis of the ten most popular women's and men's magazines, Andersen and Didomenico (1992) found that women's magazines had 10.5 times as many articles about dieting and weight loss as men's magazines. Since the mid-20th century, while the proportion of articles about weight loss has increased in women's magazines, they have declined in men's magazines. Instead, men's magazines have been characterized by a growth in the number of health and fitness articles, reflecting the increasing emphasis on muscularity (Petrie et al., 1996).

An important aspect of the media's control of body size lies in its integration of advertisements and commercials for weight-loss and fitness products. The commercialization of weight loss exists not only in the media, but outside of the media as well.

Commercialization. Commercial industry provides a massive range of products for controlling body size—books, videos and DVDs, packaged foods, weight loss programs, gym memberships, fitness equipment, pills, powders, patches, and more. In the United States alone, the diet industry made $33 billion dollars in 1996, a substantial increase from the $10 billion dollars it made in 1970 (Schneider et al., 1996). Not only is weight loss highly commercialized, especially for females, so is muscle growth commercialized, especially for males. Gym memberships, protein shakes, anabolic steroids, and pills purported to increase muscle mass are all aspects of controlling the muscular aspect of body size. It is in the best interests of commercial industry to attract as many consumers as possible; thus, the more of us that can be convinced that our bodies are lacking, the more money the diet and fitness industry makes.

Medicalization. Despite the profit-driven motives of the diet and fitness industry that may distort their efforts to convince people that they are overweight, there is no doubt that being overweight is a health risk. The World Health Organization, along with many governments of the world (including Canada), emphasizes these health risks. Heart disease is the number one cause of death in adults in North America, and being overweight is one of the central risk factors for heart disease. In the United States alone, more than 300 000 people die each year due to obesity (Obesity Association, 2003). Consequently, the medical community is heavily involved in the social control of people who are "too fat."

You arrive at your doctor's office for your annual checkup, and the first thing your doctor does is ask you to step on the scale. If you are like approximately half of Canadians, you may be dreading this moment because you know that you are overweight or obese. After recording your weight, your doctor may make a number of suggestions. "Perhaps you should take up walking," your doctor may politely suggest. Maybe the doctor hands you a pamphlet on nutrition and physical fitness, or gives you information about a medically-supervised weight loss program in your community, or writes you a prescription for a medication that will reduce your appetite, or refers you to a specialist who does weight-loss surgery (e.g., gastric bypass surgery). Perhaps the doctor will matter-of-factly tell you your health is in danger and you must lose weight. In their daily interactions with overweight patients, physicians engage in a number of social control measures. The most common forms of regulation by personal physicians are instructions to decrease calories (92%), suggestions to join a commercial weight-loss program (84%), referrals to a dietician or nutritionist (76%), and suggestions to engage in regular aerobic exercise (75%) (Price et al., 1987). Most of these forms of medicalization are based on the goal of reducing the health risks associated with being overweight.

However, the medical control of people who are "too fat" sometimes steps outside of the realm of health, and into the realm of physical appearance. For many decades in the 20th century, it was quite simple for anyone who wanted to lose weight (regardless of whether they needed to) to obtain prescriptions for diet pills. From the 1950s through the 1970s, amphetamines (i.e., "speed") were prescribed for weight loss; beginning in the 1980s, other medications that decrease appetite were developed. In the 1990s, some of these medications were taken off the market due to health complications (and deaths), but were replaced by new drugs. A recent commercial for one of these weight-loss drugs pointed out the side effects—nausea, vomiting, headaches, and uncontrollable bowel movements. The complications from weight loss surgery are even more frightening. Even the *normal* consequences of the surgery sound unappealing, to say the least; only a few tablespoons of food can be eaten as one time, and "one bite of the wrong thing, or even a morsel too much of the right thing, can cause vomiting, explosive diarrhea or a frightening attack of cramping and faintness known as dumping" (Dunleavey, 2001, p. 174).

Less common complications include chronic malnutrition, intestinal leaks, infections, and even death due to heart and lung failure. As a result of these routine complications and less frequent complications, Dr. Edward Livingstone (cited in Dunleavey, 2001) says, "By doing this operation, you're creating a medical disease in the body.... Before you expose someone to that risk, you have to be absolutely sure that you are treating a disease equal to or greater than the one you're creating" (p. 175). Yet despite the dangers of this surgery, people who do not meet the obesity criteria for the surgery (i.e., a BMI of at least 40) routinely have this surgery available to them (Dunleavey, 2001).

Liposuction, surgery that uses a vacuum-like instrument to suck fat cells out of specific parts of the body, has nothing to do with health and is based solely on physical appearance. In fact, the medical criteria say that liposuction should not be done on someone who is medically overweight. In past decades, doctors even told women who wanted to lose weight to take up smoking (Personal Communication, 2002).

Medicalization tries to help people who are overweight and in danger of health problems to reduce those risks and develop healthier lifestyles. However, the medical community can also be involved in controlling the appearance of people who are "too fat" (or who think they are "too fat"). Even when physicians are trying to help individuals whose weight puts them at risk, the treatments are sometimes just as dangerous, or even more dangerous, than being overweight.

Governments. The health risks associated with obesity and with being overweight more generally have a significant impact on the health of the world's population. By negatively impacting the health of large numbers of people, nations experience economic drains due to consequences like health care costs, absenteeism from work due to illness, and lost tax revenue. As a result, governments of the world have recently initiated considerable efforts to reduce the proportion of overweight people in their countries. Federal and provincial governments in Canada are trying to reduce physical inactivity by 10% by the end of 2003, which they say could save $5 billion dollars in lifetime costs for health care, sick leave, and lost tax revenue (Health Canada, 2003). In the United States, eliminating inactivity would save $76 billion dollars per year in medical costs (Krucoff, 2003).

At an international level, the World Health Organization has declared obesity to be a worldwide health epidemic. At their annual meeting in 2002, they were given a mandate to develop a Global Strategy on Diet, Physical Activity and Health. This strategy, to be presented to the World Health Assembly in 2004, will (a) synthesize existing research knowledge on weight, diet, physical fitness, and health; (b) advocate for policy change; and (c) develop a strategic framework for action that national governments can then try to implement (World Health Organization, 2003). As a precursor to this global strategy, the first annual Global Move for Health Day was promoted on May 10, 2003 in Canada, Britain, and dozens of other countries. The International Obesity Task Force is another international body, comprised primarily of scientists who are engaging in research about obesity and its solution; another part of their mandate is to advise other health bodies (e.g., the World Health Organization) and governmental health divisions.

Countries around the world are trying to create effective measures for improving the body weight and physical fitness of their citizens. For example, in the United States people who are diagnosed by their doctors as obese and needing weight loss for medical reasons are able to claim their weight-loss expenses (excluding food and gym memberships) as tax deductions. In Canada, there are debates over the possibility of mandatory daily physical education classes in schools, a "fat tax" on junk food, and tax deductions for sports activities (Demont, 2002). In Britain, government officials are discussing the possibility of making overweight patients sign lifestyle contracts with their doctors, perhaps as a condition of medical treatment (*Maclean's*, June 16, 2003). Not only are federal, provincial, and territorial governments trying to create effective programs and policies for weight loss, so are individual communities.

Communities. Individual communities are developing a wide range of measures to reduce the proportion of people who are overweight. In the Aboriginal communities in the Interlake region of Manitoba, an integrated program run by the Anishinaabe Mino-Ayaawin is well under way. The Aboriginal people of these communities are at a much higher-than-average risk of weight-related health complications, such as heart disease and diabetes. As a result, a comprehensive program was initiated to (a) educate children and adults in a variety of settings about nutrition and physical fitness, (b) provide healthy breakfast and lunch programs in schools, and (c) build new recreational facilities for people of all ages (Demont, 2002). New recreational facilities have also been built in Surrey, British Columbia, to reduce the rate of obesity and improve the health of its citizens; $15 million dollars were spent on a new indoor pool, and $12 million dollars were spent on a new recreation center. Efforts to reduce the proportion of overweight children (who then frequently become overweight adults) have been integrated into a number of school programs. For example, at Evangeline Middle School in New Minas, Nova Scotia, all children are required to play intramural sports; however, this school program goes one step further by having intramural games played during regular classroom hours rather than at lunchtime or after school. The gymnasium remains open every evening, every weekend, and throughout the summer for those students and parents who want to use the facilities (Demont, 2002).

Community programs, government programs and policies, members of the medical community, commercial industry, and the media interact, creating a complex web of social control for body size and shape. Some of these control measures emerge from concerns over the health consequences of being overweight. However, the regulation of body size extends beyond health to concerns over physical appearance for those who are perceived as "too fat" (by others or by themselves), regardless of whether they actually are so. These perceptions are created, in part, by unrealistic and unhealthy body images represented in the media. Efforts to control "too fat" are not necessarily efforts to improve health, and in fact may even endanger health.

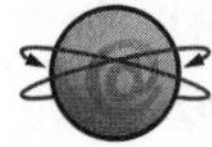

AN INTERNET MOMENT:

The Website for Health Canada can be found at www.healthcanada.ca. Along the left-hand side, select "Healthy Living." On this page you can choose to look at "Food & Nutrition" and "Physical Activity." This will provide you with an overview of, and links to, several federal government programs designed to improve the health of Canadians who are overweight and/or physically inactive. Once you have looked at a number of these health-based social control measures, go to the Internet search engine of your choice and search for "weight loss." This will bring up a number of weight loss sites, some of which represent health-based social control measures and some of which represent appearance-based measures. Contrast the health-based and appearance-based control measures. What types of information do they provide? What types of images are contained on the sites? How hard is it to distinguish between those measures that focus on health and those that focus on appearance?

TIME TO REVIEW:

- How does the media act as a social control agent for "too fat"?
- What differences exist between women's and men's media?
- To what extent is controlling "too fat" commercialized?
- How do doctors control body weight in their patients, why do they do so, and what are some of the side effects of medical advice or treatments?
- How do governments try to encourage weight loss in citizens, and why do they want to do so?
- What are some examples of community efforts to reduce the proportion of people who are overweight?

Consequences of Social Control

We are surrounded by a multitude of measures controlling body size. The consequences of these diverse social control measures are varied, for children and adults, for men and women. People's perceptions of their own bodies, psychological health, dieting patterns, and people's health are all affected. The media is particularly influential. Girls and women feel much worse about their own bodies, experience declines in their self-esteem, and show increases in depression and sadness after seeing images of models (Stice & Shaw, 1994; Crouch & Degelman, 1998). The extent of television watching in grade school boys and girls is correlated with the degree of stereotyping of overweight females, body shape standards, and symptoms of eating disorders (McCabe & Ricciardelli, 2003). Dissatisfaction with one's own body is increasing at a faster rate than ever, for both males and females, although more so for females (Garner, 1997; Paxton et al., 1991). More than 90% of Canadian women are dissatisfied with their bodies (Milne, 1998), and 89% of women in North America want to lose weight (Garner, 1997). Men are less concerned about their weight than women are; women feel "thin" at 90% of a healthy body weight (keep in mind that 85% of a healthy body weight is one of the criteria for a diagnosis of anorexia), while men feel "thin" at 105% of a healthy body weight (Andersen, 1995).

The proportion of people who are dieting, in either a healthy or unhealthy way, has shown a massive increase over the last two decades. The National Eating Disorder Information Centre in Toronto (2003) reports that at any given time 70% of women and 35% of men are dieting. Almost half of adults regularly watch their weight (Paxton et al., 1991). In children, the prevalence of dieting is particularly disconcerting. Among adolescents, 58% of girls and 25% of boys are dieting to lose weight; 6% of girls and 2% of boys say they use diet pills and vomiting in pursuit of weight loss (Neumark-Sztainer & Sherwood, 1998). By the age of 10, more than 80% of children have dieted at least once (Mellin, Scully, & Irwin, 1986). Many of these children are not in need of losing weight for health reasons; Green and colleagues (1997) found that many young women, whose body weights are healthy or even underweight, are currently trying to lose weight. Although males of all ages are less likely to be concerned about body weight and are less likely to be trying to lose weight, popular images of the "ideal" muscular body are influencing their health. For example, steroid use is increasing in adolescent boys and in male body builders; approximately 7% of junior-high boys are using anabolic steroids (Wroblewska, 1997). The long-term health consequences as these boys grow into adulthood remains to be seen.

The pressure placed on youth by the media is particularly intense, and influences body image and dieting practices (Wertheim et al., 1997). However, after media, comments or pressures by peers and family members rank second and third in their influence on youth body image and dieting. Overweight youth report that comments made by family members are hurtful (Neumark-Sztainer, Story, & Faibisch, 1998). Girls whose parents encourage them to lose weight are more dissatisfied with their bodies, are more likely to want to lose weight, and are more likely to be dieting (in healthy and unhealthy ways) (Thelen, & Cormier, 1995). Comments made by others trigger the adoption of a "fat" identity in individuals. Even people who may have been overweight since early childhood do not come to see themselves as "fat" until external cues give them that indication (Degher & Hughes, 1991). External cues may be of an active type (e.g., comments from others) or a passive type (e.g., seeing one's own reflection in a store window), but it is the active type of cues that have the greatest influence. Comments from others lead to the personal recognition that one does not have a "normal" body, but rather a "fat" body. Subsequently, a deviant definition of the self is internalized, and a "fat" identity emerges.

The social controls placed on body size, especially the controls exerted by media, peers, and family members, have considerable influence on the way people feel about themselves, their self-esteem, and their self-regulation practices (like dieting or using anabolic steroids). However, over the past two decades, as public control measures for body size have burst onto the scene in a magnitude never before seen, the proportion of both adults and children who are overweight

Ask Yourself:

What are some possible reasons for the increase in the number of people who are overweight, despite the way we are all bombarded with images and information about losing weight? Does the way body size is socially controlled in society backfire, and lead to an increase in weight rather than a decrease in weight? Are the social control measures for "too fat" contradicted by actions within other arenas of society (e.g., fast food advertising)?

or obese has actually grown rather than declined. Despite the fact that the vast majority of females, and a significant number of males, are trying to lose weight (and frequently in extremely unhealthy ways), more people than ever are overweight, and more people than ever are seen as "too fat."

"Too Fat": Resistance to Social Typing

The fact that the state of being overweight or obese has become so stigmatized in society, and that the popular definition of what constitutes "too fat" has reached absurdly thin standards, has done more than simply raise a few eyebrows. Many individuals and various organizations are taking active steps to curb this social typing process. A number of "fat acceptance" groups have formed in Canada, the United States, and Western Europe. For example, the National Association to Advance Fat Acceptance (NAAFA) has 26 local chapters in the United States, 1 chapter in Eastern Canada, and 1 in Western Europe. It provides information on current obesity research, facts about and dangers of weight-loss drugs and surgeries, and litigation updates. It also facilitates advocacy, such as providing instructions on writing effective complaint letters and on leading activism efforts. Other organizations have created beauty magazines, Websites, and clothing lines for people who are overweight.

Although the media is one of the primary social control agents for "too fat," and the central reproducer of overly thin body images, at times it also integrates aspects of resistance to the social typing process. For example, when overweight actress Camryn Mannheim won an Emmy award for her role in the television show *The Practice*, in her acceptance speech she dedicated it to "all the fat chicks." As many of us have followed Oprah Winfrey's weight losses and weight gains over the years, there has been a distinct shift in emphasis from losing weight in pursuit of physical appearance, to becoming healthy and fit. Some women's magazines have profiled women who have suffered weight loss surgery disasters (Dunleavey, 2001), provided information on "wacky weight loss products" and their ineffectiveness (*Good Housekeeping*, 2001), and pointed out that women who lose weight are not necessarily happier (*First for Women*, 2001). However, these types of articles do constitute the minority in women's magazines, and are contradicted by other elements within the magazines. For instance, after pointing out that women who lose weight are not necessarily happier (*First for Women*, 2001), the magazine contains an advertisement for a weight loss pill on the very next page.

Fat acceptance organizations, Websites, television personalities, and magazine articles are all participants in the resistance to social typing. The areas of emphasis for these resistance activities are twofold—first, to promote sound nutrition and physical fitness in pursuit of good health, and second, to remove the social stigma from people who are overweight and broaden the standards of physical attractiveness in our culture. Health and physical appearance are the two foundations (albeit sometimes contradictory ones) in the stigmatization and social control of "too fat," as well as resistance to these processes. Health and physical appearance are also foundations to discussions of the other deviant body size in our society, "too thin."

TIME TO REVIEW:

- What are the consequences of social control for people's perceptions of their own bodies, and their dieting behaviours?
- How do external cues trigger the internalization of a "fat identity"?
- What are some examples of resistance to the deviantizing of "too fat"? Refer to social organizations and the media in your answer.
- What are the two areas of emphasis for resistance activities?

"Too Thin": Commercialization, Societal Reaction, and Social Control

Perceptions of People Who Are Underweight

The "ideal" body size in a particular society is the one that is perceived as normal or conforming. Falling outside of that body size represents deviance, and a label of either "too fat" or "too thin" is attached; both are seen as requiring social control and, ultimately, self-regulation. In many Western industrialized societies today, such as Canada, the United States, and Great Britain, the range of body weights that represent the "ideal" leans strongly to the "thin" side of the fat/thin continuum. Thus, it takes a significantly greater degree of "thinness" to be considered "too thin," compared to the degree of "fatness" to be considered "too fat." In fact, widespread cultural perceptions support an extremely thin ideal, as was demonstrated earlier in the chapter in the review of people's perceptions of the overweight, and trends in media images. Consequently, considerable thinness is necessary before a "too thin" label is attached and the social typing process is initiated. This is especially the case when considering social definitions rather than scientific definitions.

Based on scientific definitions, a relatively small proportion of the population is underweight—2% of adults and slightly more adolescents (Statistics Canada, 2003; National Eating Disorder Information Centre, 2003). Social definitions likely put those numbers even lower, considering the value placed on underweight females as images of beauty (e.g., nude magazines, beauty pageants, modeling, television), and the frequency of dieting among females who are at a healthy weight or even underweight. However, at some point a "too thin" label does emerge. McLorg and Taub (1987) found that among people belonging to an eating disorders support group, family members and friends did not perceive them as "too thin" or "anorexic" until they had reached the point of being emaciated; prior to that point, family members and friends actually encouraged them in their pursuit of weight loss, and congratulated them on their successes. Once that label *is* finally attached, social control measures kick in.

Social Control

Medicalization, Education, and Formal Intervention. "Too thin" is socially controlled at various formal levels. The medical community, frequently in conjunction with social agencies and programs, makes people who are at the most extreme end of thinness (i.e., anorexic) subject to social control efforts. In immediate danger of sudden death, the medical community pursues immediate intervention. Various types of therapeutic, counselling, self-help, and psychiatric programs are being utilized throughout the world (Striegel-Moore, 2001; American Psychiatric Association, 2000). The difficulty in preventing and treating anorexia, and other eating disorders, has resulted in an extensive range of approaches that are employed at different points in the progression of this condition (British Columbia Eating Disorders Association, 2003; Lock, 2001; Matthews, 2001; Levenkron, 2000; Vendereycken, 1998; Levine & Maine, 2003). A summary of the range of treatments can be found in Box 6.2:

Box 6.2 Preventing and Treating Anorexia

1. *Prevention*

You know the old saying: "An ounce of prevention is worth a pound of cure." Preventing eating disorders is emphasized by many different social organizations (British Columbia Eating Disorders Association, 2003; Costin, 1999; Levine & Maine, 2003). **Primary prevention** involves efforts to prevent eating disorders from occurring in the first place. It entails school and community programs to raise awareness of eating disorders and their associated dangers, as well as the unrealistic body ideals portrayed in popular culture (British Columbia Eating Disorders Association, 2003; Matthews, 2001). However, primary prevention also must go much farther than this. At a societal level, the culture's obsession with thinness must be chipped away, the gendered norms that constrain both men and women must be changed, and institutions (e.g., schools) must adopt processes that facilitate the development of self-esteem and efficacy in a wide range of areas (Levine & Maine, 2003; Lock, 2001; Levenkron, 2000). **Secondary prevention** involves identifying those young men and women who may be in the very early stages of an eating disorder. It entails educating parents, teachers, and coaches about the warning signs of eating disorders and effective means of intervention (e.g., National Eating Disorder Association, 2003).

2. *Treatment*

An extensive range of treatments is available; which treatments are most effective depends entirely on the individual. People with eating disorders may choose from diverse forms of therapy and counselling—psychotherapy, group therapy, family counselling, and cognitive behavioural therapy (Lock, 2001; Levenkron, 2000; Costin, 1999; Levine & Maine, 1999; British Columbia Eating Disorders Association, 2003). For therapy to be effective, it must not only deal with the eating disorder itself, but also with the psychological, familial, and cultural factors that contributed to the eating disorder in the first place (Levine & Maine, 2003). There are medications that can help some individuals with eating disorders, such as anti-anxiety drugs or anti-depressants. Support groups are useful tools; the nature of support groups is quite varied, with some following a program pattern similar to Alcoholics Anonymous (e.g., Anorexia and Bulimics Anonymous). When severe health dangers are imminent, hospitalization or residential programs may be necessary so that medical monitoring and health supports are available around the clock (British Columbia Eating Disorders Association, 2003; Levine & Maine, 2003; Levenkron, 2000).

Physicians, psychiatrists, psychologists, and nurses carry out some of the formal social control measures described in Box 6.2, while social agencies and programs (e.g., educators) carry out others. For example, at Eastwood Collegiate Institute in Kitchener, Ontario, guest speakers are brought into the school to talk to girls about eating disorders and body image. Eating disorder associations frequently sponsor group meetings and peer support for people who have eating disorders like anorexia. People who work with adolescents in a variety of arenas—schoolteachers, coaches, school counsellors, and youth care workers—are educated about the signs of anorexia and other eating disorders. Even governments are becoming involved in the control of extreme thinness; for example, politicians in Spain and Great Britain are suggesting a ban on underweight models, acknowledging the influence fashion models have on female body images and dieting behaviours (*Women's Sports & Fitness*, 2000).

Media. The social control of "too thin" is evident in the media as well, although to nowhere near the extent that the social control of "too fat" is. After appearing at the 1998 Emmy Awards, actress Calista Flockhart was subjected to rumours of anorexia, jokes being made by Jay Leno in his *Tonight Show* monologue, and a Los Angeles radio station's "Meals-for-McBeal Drive" (collecting Twinkies and Ring Dings to be delivered to the set of *Ally McBeal*). Calista Flockhart's co-star, Courtney Thorne-Smith, told the media that one of the reasons she left the show was because of the unhealthy environment it provided, and the high level of pressure toward extreme thinness that was present (*People*, 2001). A recent article in *Us Weekly* (2003) magazine told the story of "The Incredible Shrinking Lara Flyn Boyle," asking whether her extreme weight loss was indicative of anorexia. Drew Barrymore, one of the producers of the movie *Charlie's Angels*, insisted the movie depict the female characters eating burgers and fries, in order to show adolescent girls that it is acceptable for women to eat what they want (*People*, 2001). Jennifer Lopez's ample bottom, initially the subject of media jokes, is now described as a "sexy" alternative to the waif-like look of many other female celebrities. Extremely thin celebrities are now having negative labels attached to them—"Rwandan chic" (in reference to the appearance of people living through the famine in the African country of Rwanda), and "Lollipop heads" or "Lollipop girls" (referring to stick-like bodies topped by comparatively large-looking heads).

Changing Ideals, Interactions with Family and Friends, and Informal Controls. Although common media representations of thin "ideal" bodies influence the stigma and stereotyping of the overweight in society, there are indications that some people's perceptions of the "ideal" body may be changing. In a popular survey of adult men and women, participants were shown four different female body types: curvy and fit (e.g., Yasmine Bleeth); a toned athlete (e.g., professional volleyball players); "skinny" (e.g., runway model Esther Cañadas); and muscular (e.g., 1997 Ms. Fitness America). Participants were asked which of those body types they found the most and the least attractive. The most attractive body type, according to more than half of the men and women, is curvy and fit; the toned athlete was ranked second. The least attractive body type is the muscular woman, according to approximately half of female and male participants. The attractiveness of the "skinny" runway model was ranked between the toned athlete and the muscular woman, although more men than women considered that body type to be attractive (Fleming, 1999). Although the "skinny" body type was not considered the most attractive in this survey, the fact that this body type was considered more attractive than the muscular body type illustrates that, to some degree, the value placed on a thin female body continues to be high. The message is that it is better for a woman to be extremely thin than to be muscular. It should also be noted that one of the exemplars of the curvy, fit body type, actress Yasmine Bleeth, has admitted to the media that she experienced eating disorders while on the television show *Baywatch*, in her pursuit of that body type.

Everyday interactions with family members and friends exert measures of control over people who are "too thin" (McLorg & Taub, 1987). Their eating habits are closely watched, and then openly identified as the cause of everything bad that happens in their lives, such as falling grades and the loss of friendships. People with more moderate degrees of "too thin" may have food pushed on them—"Come on, eat a piece of cake, you skinny thing! You need to put some meat on your bones." However, once others identify them as "anorexic," people may not offer them anything to eat or drink, even at social gatherings. Friends and family members withdraw from interactions with them, making them feel increasingly isolated and stigmatized. Even so, in the eyes of many people who have anorexia, the stigma attached to their emaciated appearances and strange eating patterns is frequently seen as preferable to the stigma of being overweight. It is through these everyday social interactions that people with anorexia eventually develop an "anorexic" identity. McLorg and Taub (1987) apply Lemert's labelling theory (discussed in Chapter 3) to this process. Identifying friends or family members as "anorexic" leads to the distinct types of treatment described above. People labelled in this way are isolated from "normal" relationships in their lives, and even say that others come to expect them to act anorexic. An "anorexic" identity forms, and a lifestyle becomes entrenched, the hallmarks of the transition from primary to secondary deviance.

"Too Thin": Resistance to Social Typing

Although "too thin" is considered deviant and made subject to measures of social control, largely because of severe and immediate health dangers, there is still resistance to this process of social typing. While resistance to the social typing of overweight people includes efforts to increase "fat acceptance," measures that promote extreme thinness (and even anorexia) constitute the bulk of resistance to the social typing of "too thin."

The idea that you can never be too rich or too thin, expressed in the quotation cited earlier in this chapter, resists the social typing of any degree of thinness as deviant and in need of social control. The extent to which weight loss products and messages permeate our media and commercial industry seems to reinforce this notion. The fact that magazine articles about the dangers of diet pills are frequently followed by advertisements for those very same diet pills maintains this idea as well. When young women hear model Cindy Crawford saying there are times when she envies Kate Moss's emaciated body (the model whose appearance popularized the term "heroin chic," referring to the physical emaciation of people who become addicted to heroin), many of them also may be left thinking that there is no such thing as "too thin." And although most of us would agree that the extreme thinness of anorexia *is* in need of both preventative and retroactive measures of control, there is less consensus on whether anything short of that degree of thinness is deviant. In fact, the social typing and social control of anorexia is even being resisted in some arenas.

In the last few years, popular discourse has come to include "Ana." Dozens of Websites are devoted to "Ana." When this term was first mentioned, people thought it referred to a young woman. In fact it is referring to anorexia, and the Websites are Ana's Websites. These Websites do not provide help with and support for ending anorexia, but rather for maintaining anorexia. They include photographs of certain models and actresses as motivation for continuing the pursuit of weight loss. There are tips for losing weight faster, charts listing the calorie count of different foods and the calories burned by different activities, and advice for maintaining motivation. Additional advice tells people how to dress so that others will not detect their extreme weight loss, and how to fool others into thinking that they are eating normally. Avoiding a deviant label is acknowledged as important, because detection results in social control measures, which interfere with weight loss. There are even tips on how to resist active control efforts, such as avoiding weight gain if hospitalized for treatment. Chat rooms and discussion groups provide an arena for support in resisting the deviantization of anorexia. "Ana" Websites themselves have now been identified as dangerous, and efforts are underway to control them; several Internet providers are investigating and removing suspected pro-anorexia sites.

TIME TO REVIEW:

- How is thinness perceived in our society, and at what point is someone labelled "too thin"?
- How is "too thin" controlled at formal levels?
- In what way does the media control "too thin"?
- What is the evidence suggesting that the "ideal" body may be changing?
- How do family members and friends treat someone who has been labelled "anorexic"? In what way can labelling theory be used in this discussion?
- How do the media and media figures act to resist the deviantizing of "too thin"?
- How are "Ana" Websites forms of resistance to the social typing of anorexia as deviant?

Look in the mirror. Is your body "too fat," "too thin," or "just right"? The process of answering that question has our cultural standards of the "ideal" body as a foundation. The bodies we see in the media and elsewhere around us, as well as people's responses to those bodies, tell us what "too fat," "too thin," and "just right" entail. The medical community, commercial industry, social agencies and organizations, and the individual people we encounter in our lives let us know the status of our own bodies, and exert means of control if our bodies need to be "fixed" in some way. If we are overweight, we are stigmatized by others, and provided with countless ways (both healthy and unhealthy) of losing weight. If we are underweight, others also stigmatize us, although to a lesser degree. We may have to become almost emaciated before people consider us to be "too thin," but once we are labelled in that way, attempts will be made to have us gain weight. In the end, we are expected to self-regulate our bodies—realize when we are "too fat," and take steps to lose weight, or when we are "too thin," and take steps to gain weight. Body weight is only one of many aspects of physical appearance that can potentially be socially typed as deviant by others. But it is an aspect of physical appearance that is judged within almost every arena in our society today, on a daily basis. Tomorrow, take note of how many times you judge other people's bodies as "too fat" or "too thin"; the extent to which you participate in this social typing process may surprise you.

Chapter Summary

Physical appearance is extremely important to us. Our appearance is an expression of identity, telling observers a little bit about who we are. Our physical appearance is also used in other people's judgments of us. Some forms of physical appearance are voluntarily chosen, such as hair colour, body art, or characteristics associated with certain lifestyle groups (e.g., goths). Other forms of physical appearance are involuntary, such as height or visible disabilities; even though we are unable to do anything about these aspects of our appearance, people may socially type these characteristics as deviant anyway.

Body weight is a form of physical appearance that blurs the boundaries between voluntary and involuntary; it is a nexus for social typing that occurs everywhere around us on a daily basis. The "ideal" body weight can be defined scientifically, on the basis of health risks, or socially, on the basis of social standards. Falling outside of this "ideal" range results in a label of "too fat" or "too thin," and triggers social control efforts.

People who are considered "too fat" are perceived negatively in our society. Stereotypes associate negative characteristics with being overweight (e.g., lazy), and many people perceive being overweight as "repulsive" and "the worst thing that can happen to a person." A wide range of behaviours accompany these negative perceptions, including discrimination within society's institutions, rude comments or name-calling, and even differential treatment by family members.

The images of the extremely thin "ideal" body that permeate the media (e.g., television, beauty pageants, magazines) tell us what our own bodies are supposed to look like. Although being overweight is portrayed as a negative quality for both women and men, women's media emphasizes body weight considerably more, and men's media emphasizes fitness and muscularity. If our bodies do not meet the "ideal," a wide range of opportunities to lose weight are made available to us—commercial products (e.g., videos, patches), medical services (e.g., supervised weight loss programs, drugs, surgery), government programs, and community services. The extensive nature of social controls for "too fat" have a significant influence on people's self-esteem, identity, and dieting behaviour. In recent years, resistance has formed in response to these social control efforts. They include efforts to broaden the range of body sizes that are considered attractive, and activities to improve the health and fitness of people in society.

A label of "too thin" is usually not attached to people until they reach an extreme level of thinness. Even family members encourage the early weight loss successes of people who develop anorexia, and do not identify them as "too thin" until they become physically emaciated. Once that label is attached, social control efforts are initiated. These include formal prevention and intervention measures, such as through medical treatment, counselling, and nutrition/health information services. The media, although it is a primary source of controlling "too fat," also makes some efforts to regulate extreme thinness; for example, magazines may include articles about the dangers of diet pills or critiques of the "Lollipop girls" on television. Social control efforts also emerge at the level of personal interaction, as friends and family members criticize and eventually distance themselves from those who are anorexic. The differential treatment that emerges, combined with the growing isolation, triggers the internalization of an "anorexic" identity.

Just as resistance has emerged to the social typing of "too fat" as deviant, it has also arisen to the deviantizing of "too thin." The "Rwandan chic" that permeates Hollywood is a key source of this resistance, suggesting that there is no such thing as "too thin." Pro-anorexia sites have even emerged on the Internet, providing support for people to *maintain* anorexia, and avoid detection by others.

Recommended Readings

Gay, K. (2002). *Body marks: Tattooing, piercing, and scarification*. Brookfield, CT: Millbrook Press.

* Although intended for a high school audience, this book provides a fascinating overview of body adornment. It addresses the history of body markings, both voluntary (e.g., choosing a tattoo) and involuntary (e.g., markings put on prisoners and slaves). The social control of physical appearance is also demonstrated in this book, through the safety precautions it provides for readers who may be considering body art, and the social implications of getting body art.

Goodman, W. C. (1995). *The invisible woman: Confronting weight prejudice in America*. Carlsbad, CA: Gurze Books.

* As the title suggests, this book elaborates upon the "ideal" body in contemporary Western cultures, perceptions of people who are overweight, behaviours directed at people who are overweight, and consequences.

Pope, H., Phillips, K. A., & Olivardia, R. (2000). *The Adonis Complex: The secret crisis of male body obsession*. New York: Free Press.

* This is one of the few books that analyzes body weight/size in men. The pressure on men to achieve a muscular but fat-free body is discussed, and the measures men take in pursuit of this ideal (e.g., eating disorders, steroid use) are explored.

Endnotes

1 Chinese Proverb. Retrieved February 3, 2003 from World Wide Web: **http://www.bartleby.com**

2 Dorothy Parker. Retrieved February 3, 2003 from World Wide Web: **http://www.bartleby.com**

Key Terms

master status, **p. 178**
Body Mass Index (BMI), **p. 179**
overweight, **p. 179**
obese, **p. 179**
underweight, **p. 179**
anorexia nervosa, **p. 181**
atypical anorexia, **p. 181**
discredited (visible) stigma, **p. 181**
ego-psychological theories, **p. 182**
family systems theories, **p. 182**
endocrinological theories, **p. 182**
sociocultural theories, **p. 182**
primary prevention, **p. 197**
secondary prevention, **p. 197**

C H A P T E R 7

Mental Disorders

Learning Objectives

After reading this chapter, you should be able to:

- Describe the prevalence of mental disorders in Canada and worldwide, as well as the patterns of mental disorders across various social groups.
- Describe the costs of mental illness for individuals, their families, and the larger society.
- Explain how mental disorders are subject to social control through (a) the stigmatization of mental illness, and (b) the medicalization of mental disorder.
- Describe the efforts to reduce the stigmatization of mental illness, and to improve the resources that are available to people with mental disorders.
- Explain why the diagnostic handbook used by mental health professionals is criticized.
- Describe Rosenhan's classic study on mental illness, and explain the consequences of his research.

"When terms like abnormal or mentally ill are spoken, what kinds of images come to mind? Usually, images of difference and alienation, suggesting that 'they' are not as competent, human, or safe to be around as the rest of 'us.' And often, 'abnormal' and 'mentally ill' are equated with 'crazy,' a label that calls forth images of someone who is out of control, out of touch with 'reality', incapable of forming a good relationship, untrustworthy, quite possibly dangerous, and probably not worth one's attention, time, or energy." (Caplan, 1995, p. 11)

The concept of mental disorder consists of two different dimensions. First is the experience of the disorder itself, the ways that the illness affects people's thoughts, feelings, or behaviours. But, as the above quotation illustrates, mental disorder also consists of a social dimension, the ways that others perceive and treat those with mental illnesses. Via both of these dimensions, mental disorder enters the realm of deviance.

Mental disorder, by definition, is a psychological, biological, or behavioural dysfunction that interferes with the kinds of lives most of us take for granted—"alterations in thinking, mood or behaviour...associated with significant distress and impaired functioning" (Health Canada, 2002b, p. 7), such as "impaired judgment, behaviour, capacity to recognize reality, or ability to meet the ordinary demands of life" (*Alberta Mental Health Act*, p. 7). Mental disorder can cause hallucinations, delusional thoughts, levels of depression that make getting out of bed too much of a challenge on some days, paralyzing levels of anxiety, and more. The "bad day" (or "bad week") that all of us have at times is not sufficient to be considered mental illness; the distorted thoughts, moods, and behaviours must be of a magnitude and duration substantial enough to interfere with our daily functioning. The *Diagnostic and Statistical Manual of Mental Disorders*, the diagnostic

Exercise Your Mind:

Obtain a copy of the DSM-IV from your library (a complete version of the DSM is not currently available on the Internet; however, some limited sites are available, such as **http://www.psychologynet.org/dsm.html**). Browse through the diagnostic categories to see what types of thoughts, moods, or behaviours are defined as constituting mental illness. Select three different diagnostic categories–a psychotic disorder, a mood disorder, and an anxiety disorder–and look at their descriptions and lists of symptoms. How do these three different disorders encapsulate the "distress" and "impaired functioning" that definitions of mental illness focus on? How do you think the daily lives of people with these symptoms would compare to your own daily life, in terms of differences and similarities?

handbook created by the American Psychiatric Association, clearly outlines precisely what types of thoughts, moods, and behaviours constitute mental illness, and under what circumstances. Mental health professionals utilize the *DSM*'s checklist of symptoms to determine which (if any) mental disorder a given individual may have (e.g., schizophrenia; generalized anxiety disorder; gender identity dysphoria; major depressive disorder).

Who Has Mental Disorders?

"If you have a brain, you can have a mental illness." (Canadian Mental Health Association, 2003)[1]

Mental disorders can strike anyone, and affect the majority of Canadians either directly (through experiencing mental disorder themselves) or indirectly (by having a friend, family member, or co-worker with a mental disorder). Health Canada (2002b) has found that approximately 20% of adult Canadians have experienced a mental illness, and 80% of Canadians know someone with a mental illness. The prevalence of a number of specific mental disorders can be found in Table 7.1

Table 7.1 PROPORTION OF CANADA'S POPULATION AFFECTED BY MENTAL DISORDERS (HEALTH CANADA, 2002B)

TYPE OF MENTAL DISORDER	PROPORTION OF THE ADULT POPULATION
Anxiety Disorders	12%
Major Depression	8%
Personality Disorders	6-9%
Bipolar Disorder	1%
Schizophrenia	1%

Source: *A Report on Mental Illness in Canada*, Health Canada, (2002b), Reproduced with the permission of the Minister of Public Works and Government Services Canada, 2003.

Although most national data on mental illness is drawn from medical treatment records (e.g., hospitalization records), some smaller-scale general population surveys have also addressed the topic of mental disorders, enabling researchers to identify that proportion of the population that has not sought medical assistance for their psychological problems. For example, one survey found that more than one-third of Canadians say they have experienced depression or anxiety (Health

Canada, 2002b). In the United States, a larger survey found that 30% of the general population is affected by mental disorders in any given year, and approximately 50% experience mental illness during their lifetimes (Kessler et al., 1994). Worldwide, the extent of the problem of mental illness is staggering. The World Health Organization (2001) finds that mental disorders affect 25% of the world population, more than 450 million people. The most common mental disorders—depressive disorders, anxiety disorders, and somatic complaints—strike 1 in 3 individuals. In 2001, more than 120 million people in the world suffered from depression, and 24 million were living with schizophrenia. In total, mental disorders constitute more than one-third of the disabilities seen throughout the world (World Health Organization, 2001).

Although mental illness can strike anyone, some social groups are more susceptible than others. Early research done in the United States and Britain claimed that more women than men experienced mental disorders. However, later research found that the surveys underlying these conclusions were methodologically flawed. By focusing their questions on the types of psychological distress that are more common in women and excluding questions on the types of distress that are more common in men, these surveys overestimated women's mental health problems, and underestimated men's (Simon, 2002). Today researchers agree that the overall rates of mental disorder are virtually identical in men and women, but there are distinct differences in the patterns and types of mental illness (Simon, 2002; World Health Organization, 2001). Antisocial personality disorder, substance abuse dependency disorders, and conduct disorders are much more common in men; for example, antisocial personality disorder is three times more common in men than women (Simon, 2002; Health Canada, 2002b; World Health Organization, 2001). Those disorders that are classified as the "common mental disorders" (or CMDs)—depression and anxiety—are much more common in women (Piccinelli & Homen, 1997; Health Canada, 2002b). The reasons why women in countries throughout the world are more likely to experience depression and anxiety are largely sociocultural in nature. Although there are strong arguments for biological predeterminants of many, if not most, mental illnesses, including depression and anxiety, CMDs have been consistently linked to particular life stressors and negative life events, ones that, on average, are more prevalent in the lives of women than men—low income or income inequality, low or subordinate social status, extensive responsibility for the daily care of others (spouses, children, elderly parents), and victimization by violence (World Health Organization, 2001; Roberts et al. 1998; Patel et al., 1999).

Although socioeconomic status interacts with gender (as well as with race, ethnicity, and other factors), both women and men of low socioeconomic status have higher rates of most types of mental illness, and especially depression and anxiety (World Health Organization, 2001; Dohrenwend et al., 1992; Miech et al., 1999;

Patel et al., 1999; Williams & Takeuchi, 1992). A longstanding question about the relationship between socioeconomic status and mental illness has been about the direction of causation. The **social causation hypothesis** suggests that more life stresses and fewer resources characterize the lives of the lower class, contributing to the emergence of mental disorders. This, in fact, was mentioned in Robert Merton's strain theory (discussed in Chapter 2). Although his theory and its later applications largely focus on crime, he did suggest that mental illness can emerge in response to the gap between institutionalized goals and the legitimate means for attaining those goals. The mode of adaptation that he labelled **retreatism**, wherein people give up on pursuing the goals as well as the legitimate means of attaining those goals, can include alcoholism, drug use, or mental illness. In contrast, the **social selection hypothesis** proposes the reverse—that people with mental disorders fall into lower economic strata because of their difficulties in daily functioning (Eaton, 1985). Although some debate continues among mental health experts, recent research finds that the direction of causation depends upon the specific mental disorder in question. Individuals with schizophrenia, conduct disorders, and attention deficit disorder are more likely to fall into the lower socioeconomic strata, and are less likely to be able to rise out of the lower strata, supporting the social selection hypothesis. Conversely, social causation appears to underlie depression, anxiety, substance use disorders, and antisocial personality disorder; the life stresses associated with economic difficulties contribute to the emergence of these disorders (Kessler et al., 1994; Dohrenwend et al., 1992; Turner, Wheaton, & Lloyd, 1995).

Independent of socioeconomic status and gender, age is correlated with mental illness as well. Mental illness is more prevalent among adolescents and young adults, and most mental disorders first emerge during this time in life (Health Canada, 2002b). Biological factors play a role in this pattern, as do psychological and social factors, such as the struggles involved in identity formation during this time, the dramatic nature of the transitions that occur after graduating from high school, and the stresses associated with developing the "adult" role (e.g., deciding what type of education and career to pursue, becoming financially independent, participating in the mate-selection process). The demands of university are particularly stressful, resulting in a higher prevalence of psychological distress among university students; for example, a survey of almost 8000 Canadian university students recently found that more than 30% reported significant levels of psychological distress (Adlaf et al., 2001).

Age, socioeconomic status, and gender are significant factors related to the prevalence and/or patterns of mental illness. But although certain types of mental illness are more prevalent in particular social groups, mental disorder can affect anyone, as illustrated by the conclusion that half of people in the United States will experience a psychological disorder at some point in their lives (Kessler et al., 1994). The resulting costs of mental illness are substantial.

TIME TO REVIEW:

- What is "mental illness"?
- How many people in Canada, the United States, and the world have mental disorders?
- What similarities and differences are there between men and women in the prevalence and patterns of mental illness?
- How does mental illness vary across socioeconomic groups, and why?
- What role does age play in the prevalence of mental disorder?

The Costs of Mental Illness

Mental disorders have a considerable impact on both people's lives and the larger society. Having a mental disorder contributes to a wide range of negative life outcomes. For example, having a mental disorder is associated with higher rates of teen pregnancy and early marriage, and a greater risk of marital instability, all of which contribute to difficulties for the children being raised in those environments (Kessler, cited in Ettner, Frank, & Kessler, 1998). Children being raised by parents with mental illnesses are more likely to have problems in cognitive development as well (World Health Organization, 2001). In quantitative terms, research suggests that mental illness results in lower levels of educational attainment, lower employment rates, and lower incomes. For example, women with mental disorders earn $3465 less each year, and men with mental disorders earn $4521 less each year, than men and women without mental disorders (Ettner, Frank, & Kessler, 1998). Individuals with mental illnesses, along with their families, must bear direct and indirect financial costs (e.g., the costs of health care or the costs associated with unemployment) (World Health Organization, 2001). Some mental illnesses are correlated with other physical ailments; for example, depression is related to a higher risk of heart disease. Furthermore, people with mental disorders are less likely to comply with medical instructions for other physical ailments, such as high blood pressure, diabetes, and cancer, resulting in poorer health overall and a greater likelihood of complications (World Health Organization, 2001). Finally, the emotional burden of living with a mental disorder creates a considerable challenge to all aspects of daily living, and influences the quality of life overall.

Beyond the level of individuals and their families, mental disorders also have a considerable impact on society. Five of the ten leading causes of disabilities in Canada are mental illnesses (Alberta Alliance on Mental Illness & Mental Health, 2003). Depression alone is the fourth leading global disease burden, and by 2020 it is projected to be the second leading global disease burden, behind only heart disease (Murray & Lopez, 1996; World Health Organization, 2001). Health care expenses, absences from work, and lost tax revenues due to mental illness cost the Canadian economy more than $14 billion each year (Stephans &

Jorbert, 2001). This substantial impact is not limited to Canada alone. The cost in the United States is $148 billion per year, 2.5% of their gross national product (World Health Organization, 2001). In Great Britain, it is estimated that 15-30% of illness-related absences from work are due to mental disorders (Lewis & Bebbington, 1998). Economies experience lost productivity due to the following: (a) premature deaths from suicide (which outnumber traffic deaths in some countries); (b) absenteeism from work due to illness; (c) inability to be employed; (d) decreased productivity while on the job during manifestations of the illness; and (e) family members' absence from work or withdrawal from the labour force in order to provide full-time care (World Health Organization, 2001; Lewis & Bebbington, 1998). Untreated mental disorders may also result in the costs associated with criminal and/or violent behaviour.

The magnitude of these various impacts means that effective treatment of mental illness would benefit the individuals who have mental illnesses, their families, and society as a whole. However, in North America estimates are that only half the people with mental disorders ever see health professionals (Mosher, 2002; Health Canada, 2002b). Worldwide, two-thirds of people who have mental disorders are never treated (World Health Organization, 2001), because they are uncomfortable with the level of self-disclosure that accompanies diagnosis and treatment, they are aware of the social stigma associated with seeing a psychiatrist or psychologist, or they are victims of neglect within their own families and communities (Mosher, 2002; World Health Organization, 2001).

TIME TO REVIEW:

- What are the costs associated with mental illness, for individuals, their families, and society?
- How many people with mental disorders seek professional help?
- Why do some people with mental disorders not seek professional help?

Controlling Mental Disorder: Perceptions, Stigmatization, and Treatment

The reactions of other people are an integral part of the experience of having a mental disorder. As we have already seen, one of the main reasons that people with mental disorders do not seek assistance from health professionals is because of the presumed reactions of other people, as well as the general stigma that is associated with mental illness in our society. The stigmatization of mental illness constitutes one of the major dimensions of social control; this will be the first aspect of social control that we will explore. The second major dimension of control, which we will explore later in the chapter, is embodied by the medicalization of mental disorder.

Ask Yourself:

Try to imagine that you have a mental disorder. How would your life be different? How do you think people would see you? Would your family treat you any differently? Would you have the same friends? How would your co-workers treat you? Perhaps you have experienced a mental disorder yourself, or are close to someone who has. If so, how have other people reacted to that situation?

Stigmatization and Perceptions of Mental Illness

"...[I]t's sort of like having 'crazy bitch' stamped across my forehead and everybody treats you differently because you have been a patient in a psychiatric unit." (cited in Bassett & Lampe, 1999)

More than 60 years ago, researchers were already identifying the prejudice and discrimination that people with mental disorders faced (Scheff, 1966). Since that time, attitudes have not significantly improved, and some researchers suggest they may have even worsened (Sayce, 2000; Crisp, 1999). We have only to look at the media to see the way mental illness continues to be stigmatized. When mental illness is addressed in the media, it is portrayed in an exceedingly negative light, and is typically associated with violent behaviour (Hannigan, 1999; Wahl, 1992; March, 1999). For example, one study found that 72% of those dramatic characters on prime time television who were portrayed as having a mental illness were associated with violence or evil (Signorielli, cited in March, 1999). This type of media imagery has a noteworthy impact on people's own perceptions of mental illness. Granello, Pauley, and Carmichael (cited in March, 1999) found that one-third of the undergraduate students they surveyed said the media is their primary source of information about mental illness, and the number-one influence on their own attitudes toward people with mental disorders. Given the biased portrayals of mental illness within the media and their impact, it is not surprising that public attitudes toward mental illness are negative as well.

Studies conducted in countries around the world have consistently found extreme prejudice against people with mental disorders; this prejudice manifests itself in the forms of social rejection and discrimination (Sayce, 2000; Wahl, 1999; Read & Harre, 2001). A recent Health Canada (2002b) survey found that more than one-third of adult Canadians believe that others would think less of them if they had a mental disorder, such as depression or anxiety—and, unfortunately, they are right! People with mental disorders are perceived as being unpredictable, violent, dangerous, and uncontrollable (Dobson, 1996; Stip, Caron, & Lane, 2001). As a consequence of these stereotypes, more than two-thirds of people surveyed express reservations about dating someone with a mental disorder, or even living next door (Read & Harre, 2001). In Great Britain, 34% of people with mental illnesses say they have been fired or forced to resign. Almost half have been abused or harassed by strangers in public, and 14% have been physically attacked (Dobson, 1996).

These attitudes are not limited to uneducated or uninformed laypersons, but are also found within the medical community itself (Lawrie et al., 1998; Monahan, 1992). Approximately half of people with mental disorders say health professionals have treated them unfairly, particularly in dealing with the individual's physical complaints. When their own doctors fail to lend credence to their physical complaints, instead blaming those symptoms on the mental disorder, actual physical illnesses remain untreated, only to worsen and potentially threaten patients' lives. Mental illness is even stigmatized by mental health professionals themselves, who frequently admit that they try to avoid having to treat patients with the more severe mental illnesses (Dobson, 1996; Read & Harre, 2001).

At a personal level, this kind of stigmatization has a negative impact on the quality of life for people with mental disorders. The sense of loneliness and isolation that accompanies social rejection can amplify psychological symptoms, actually making mental illnesses worse. Negative social perceptions are the key factor in people not seeking medical help for their disorders, and even if they do seek help, stigmatization hinders the effectiveness of community-based treatments and impedes recovery (Hannigan, 1999; World Psychiatric Association, 2003; World Health Organization, 2002b).

These exceedingly negative perceptions contribute to discrimination in employment, health care, and housing (World Health Organization, 2001; Wahl, 1999; Sayce, 1998, 2000). For those individuals residing in psychiatric institutions, their experience in many countries includes poor living conditions, inadequate care, and harmful treatment. The stigmatization of mental illness in this way affects program and policy development as well; societies that are characterized by extremely negative attitudes of mental disorder also tend to not rate mental illness as a policy or programming priority (World Health Organization, 2001, 2002b; March, 1999). Unfortunately, this is characteristic of most countries in the world (World Health Organization, 2002b) (see Box 7.1):

Box 7.1 The Status Of Mental Health Programming

Despite the fact that mental illness is a leading cause of disability in the world, and hundreds of billions of dollars are lost each year as a result, mental health policies and programs are not perceived as priorities:

- 40% of countries have no mental health policy.
- 30% of countries have no mental health program.
- More than 33% of countries allocate less than 1% of their budgets to mental health.
- Another 33% of countries allocate 1% of their budgets to mental health.
- More than half of the countries in the world have only 1 psychiatrist for every 100 000 people.
- 40% of countries have less than 1 hospital bed reserved for mental health issues for every 10 000 people.

The mental health policies and programs that do exist are embedded with the two different paradigms of mental disorder—the *disease paradigm* and the *discrimination paradigm*. The **discrimination paradigm** proposes that the experience of mental illness is primarily one of prejudice, discrimination, and stigmatization. Policies and programs within this paradigm constitute forms of resistance to the stigmatization of mental illness, and will be presented within that context later in the chapter. The **disease paradigm** proposes that the experience of mental illness is primarily one of experiencing *illness*—the signs and symptoms of the disorder, which subsequently hinder the individual's effective functioning and quality of life. Policies and programs within this paradigm revolve around the medicalization of mental disorder.

TIME TO REVIEW:

- How is mental illness portrayed in the media, and what impact do media portrayals have?
- What are the perceptions of mental illness among the members of the medical community?
- How does the stigmatization of mental disorders influence quality of life, discrimination, and mental health policies/programming?
- What are the two paradigms within which mental health policies and programming are embedded?

The Medicalization of Mental Disorder

The medicalization of deviance has been addressed in previous chapters. For example, in the chapter on body size, we saw how medical science defines what deviant body size is (i.e., "overweight," "underweight," "obese," and "anorexic"), explains why those body sizes are deviant (i.e., they are associated with a much greater risk of health problems), and then provides social control measures to ameliorate those problems (e.g., prescriptions for diet pills, references to a nutritionist, information about physical fitness). Similarly, mental disorders are also medicalized. Psychiatrists determine which thoughts or behaviours constitute mental illness, and then incorporate that into the DSM. They explain that these particular thoughts and behaviours are deviant because they cause significant distress and impairments in daily functioning. Finally, they provide measures of social control, that is, treatments for mental disorders to improve quality of life and level of functioning. However, an historical analysis reveals that medical treatment to improve functioning has not always been the focus of social control measures.

The History of the Social Control of Mental Illness

Through much of Western history, the thoughts and behaviours that we now define as mental illness were instead seen as demonic possession; the "treat-

During the Middle Ages, people with mental illnesses were some of those convicted of witchcraft and burned at the stake.

ment" was physical torture in order to drive out the demons. During the Middle Ages and early Renaissance, a refusal to conform to society's norms (even by those people who would now be considered to have mental disorders) was considered a sign of allegiance with the devil. As a result, people were labelled "witch" or "heretic," put on trial, virtually always convicted, and put to death (e.g., by burning at the stake).

As religious explanations were replaced by scientific explanations, authorities no longer saw these non-normative behaviours as signs of possession or allegiance with the devil. Families and communities took care of those individuals who exhibited "strange" thoughts and behaviours. As the size of communities grew, prisons were built to house not only criminals, but also the poor and the mentally ill (Grob, 1994). In the 18th century, "madhouses" were created specifically for those with mental illnesses. The purpose of these madhouses was not treatment or rehabilitation, but simply warehousing the disordered so that society's "normal" citizens could feel safe and secure (Rothman, 1971; McGovern, 1985). Over time, madhouses were replaced by "asylums" as some doctors proposed that, with appropriate treatment, people with mental illnesses could be trained to conform to society's norms; this is the era when the medicalization of mental illness came to predominate in Western cultures (Grob, 1994). These "asylums," later to be known as "mental hospitals" or "psychiatric institutions," continued to grow, well into the 1950s.

The treatments for mental illnesses provided in psychiatric institutions included practices that many people now see as almost barbaric—lobotomies and fever therapies, for example (McGovern, 1985). The failure of these types of therapies to "cure" mental illness, combined with social concerns about their harshness, eventually resulted in their large-scale abandonment. Broader concerns about the effectiveness of hospitalization itself began to take hold in the late 1950s as well. People began to wonder how removing individuals from their homes, the support of their families, and the semblance of normality that existed within their communities, and instead placing them within institutions where they were dehumanized and isolated, could possibly help in recovery from mental illness. These questions, along with new drug therapies that effectively controlled many forms of mental disorder, eventually led to **deinstitutionalization**—the social control of mental illness within community-based programs rather than within institutions.

Exercise Your Mind:

Rent the movie One Flew Over the Cuckoo's Nest. *Not only will you see a very young Jack Nicholson, you will also see representations of mental illness and a Hollywood portrayal of the dehumanizing treatment psychiatric hospital patients were perceived as facing. This movie was made in the very early stages of the deinstitutionalization movement, and although we cannot presume that movie portrayals are accurate representations of reality, this movie does capture the underlying mood that contributed to deinstitutionalization.*

Treating Mental Illness Today

The medicalization of mental disorders in contemporary society involves an extensive range of treatment options—psychotherapy, cognitive-behavioural therapy, medication, occupational therapy, and social supports. Treatment options today have become quite effective in improving functioning and the quality of life for individuals with mental disorders. Effective treatment helps 60% of people with depression fully recover, and prevents relapses in 80% of people with schizophrenia (World Health Organization, 2001). The combination of medical support (e.g., medications) and psychosocial support (e.g., therapy, community resources) is particularly effective for even the most severe mental illnesses (World Health Organization, 2002b). For example, without any treatment, 55% of people whose schizophrenia goes into remission will have a relapse within one year. Among those who receive psychopharmaceutical treatment alone, 20–25% will relapse within one year. Among those who receive both psychopharmaceutical treatment and psychosocial supports for the family, only 2–23% will relapse within one year (World Health Organization, 2002b). As a result of the deinstitutionalization movement, hospitalization is reserved for only the most severe cases of mental illness, and even then is perceived as a short-term intervention that will form only one small part of the overall program of treatment. Hospitalization today is primarily voluntary in nature, with the individuals themselves formally consenting to be hospitalized. Involuntary admissions to hospitals for psychiatric reasons are governed by the "**least restrictive alternative**"—legislation stating that involuntary admission can only occur if there are no reasonable non-institutional alternatives (Krieg, 2001).

The Legacy of Deinstitutionalization. When the deinsitutionalization movement began in the early 1960s, it was perceived as an evolution in treatment that would bring nothing but benefits—benefits to the individuals who would receive treatment in their own homes and communities, benefits to society in terms of the higher rate of recovery, and cost-savings benefits to the government and taxpayers. Indeed, many of these benefits have been realized to some extent. Treatment within the community is generally more effective in the long-term than treatment within institutions, and is considerably less expensive (World Health Organization, 2002b). There is also no doubt that many people consider it to be more respectful, more humane, and less emotionally disturbing. In fact, most people with mental illnesses *want* to live within the community while receiving treatment, keeping their daily lives as "normal" as possible (Tanzman, 1993). However, deinstitutionalization has had its drawbacks as well.

Ask Yourself:

In order for people with mental illnesses to be successfully treated within the community rather than in institutions, what kinds of resources are necessary? That is, what might people with mental illnesses need if they are to successfully recover in their own homes and neighbourhoods?

Your answers to the "Ask Yourself" questions at left may point to some of the assumptions that underlie deinstitutionalization. Perhaps you mentioned close families or friendship networks that can help provide necessary support or care. Deinstitutionalization emerged during an era when the image of the "ideal" family was everywhere. Popular television series such as *Leave It To Beaver, Father Knows Best,* and *Ozzie and Harriet* portrayed family life in a way that few people in reality ever experienced (Coontz, 1992). This type of popular imagery helped create the assumption that families were always caring, supportive, united, and happily willing to work together to overcome any difficulties. This was one of the key underlying assumptions of deinstitutionalization; that is, shifting the care of people with mental illnesses into the community was perceived as non-problematic because it was assumed that they would have loving families to help them (Accordino, Porter, & Morse, 2001). Of course, many of us do not have that type of network of family relationships. Some of us are closer to our families than others are. Some of us are able to depend on our families more than others are. Even though some of us are close to our families of origin, having to live with those family members in adulthood may be extremely trying, and the related stresses might actually be harmful to psychological health. Some of us may have close marital relationships that are a source of support, but others do not; furthermore, the experience of any type of serious illness can contribute to the dissolution of many marriages. With all of these variations in family form and quality of family relationships, the assumption of a social support network for people with mental illnesses is precarious. People who have close support networks may do very well with community-based treatment, but people who are lacking these networks may not do as well.

In your response to the last *Ask Yourself* question, you may have said that an accepting community that is free from stigmatization is necessary for successful community-based treatment. The prejudice and negative attitudes that pervade public perceptions of people with mental disorders have been addressed earlier in the chapter; stigmatization is a central obstacle to successful recovery and integration into the community (Accordino, Porter, & Morse, 2001). Although institutionalization was perceived as degrading to people with mental disorders, living within communities that are permeated with negative perceptions of mental illness, and the resulting discrimination that results, may be just as degrading to some individuals (Krieg, 2001).

Perhaps you listed adequately funded community resources as necessary for successful non-institutional treatment for people with mental disorders. In fact, this is one of the biggest problems worldwide that has plagued the deinstitutionalization movement (World Health Organization, 2002b). Although the intent was quite different, the reduction in hospital-based services was not accompanied by sufficient increases in community-based resources. This is because of the negative social perceptions of mental illness that make related programs and policies difficult for politicians to "sell" to voters, a lack of adequate health care funding overall, and the prioritizing of other areas of government spending (World Health Organization, 2002b; Krieg, 2001). The nature of available resources is also dependent upon community size. Individuals living in large urban centers have more community mental health resources available to them than do those living in rural areas. People with mental disorders who live in rural areas have a particularly difficult time with recovery, and are more likely to experience negative outcomes, including participation in and victimization by criminal behaviour (Sullivan, Jackson, & Spritzer, 1996).

You may have mentioned that in order for people to have a successful recovery within their own homes, they actually need their own homes—somewhere to live. This, in fact, can be a considerable challenge for some people with mental disorders, especially when we consider insufficient community resources, the stigmatization that inhibits integration within communities, and the lack of family or friendship networks for some individuals. People who, as a result of discrimination or the symptoms of their disorders, are unable to find employment or housing may become dependent upon family or friendship support networks. If those networks are lacking, and the resulting stresses exacerbate the illness, possible outcomes include alcohol or drug abuse (Davidson et al., 1996) and a failure to take medication that has been prescribed for the illness. The end result can be homelessness. It is estimated that, in North America, between 30% and 50% of the homeless are mentally ill (Krieg, 2001; Belcher, 1989; Grob, 1995). Research done by various organizations in Toronto finds that between 11% and 30% of the homeless there have serious psychotic disorders, such as schizophrenia (Valpy, 1998). Homelessness adds one more dimension to the social typing process that individuals must experience; not only do they face the consequences of being socially typed as mentally ill, but they also must face the consequences of being socially typed as homeless. Homeless people with mental disorders who also have substance abuse problems face the additional predicament that some community resources are designed to only deal with either substance abuse or mental illness, not both. That is, some organizations help only the mentally ill homeless who do not have substance abuse problems, while other organizations that help homeless people with substance abuse problems are not equipped to deal with those with mental illnesses.

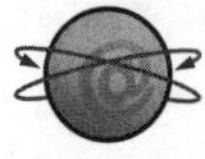

AN INTERNET MOMENT:

You can find the Government of Canada's National Homelessness Initiative at http://www21.hrdc-drhc.gc.ca/. On this site you can go to "Community Projects" and search for the specific projects that are underway in your own city. You may be interested in looking at the various projects to see if there are any projects that specifically target homeless people with mental illnesses.

The costs of community-based treatment are usually described as being lower than the costs of hospital-based treatments. However, when a significant number of people fall through the cracks of the community mental health system, other costs accompany deinstitutionalization. The costs associated with reducing homelessness are compounded by the social and economic losses emerging from higher suicide rates among individuals with untreated mental illnesses, more accidents, and a greater number of untreated physical illnesses (Krieg, 2001). The symptoms of some mental disorders, difficulties in finding employment or housing, and the emotional consequences of stigmatization lead some individuals into crime (Krieg, 2001; Sullivan, Jackson, & Spritzer, 1996; Accordino, Porter, & Morse, 2001), adding another layer of costs to society. The rate of criminal activity among people with major mental disorders is considerably higher than among those without mental disorders (Hodgins, 1995). A study at Toronto's Don Jail found that, during an 18-month period, 469 of the admissions (i.e., 1 in 12) involved individuals with major mental disorders; approximately 70% of criminals with major mental illnesses had multiple jail admissions (Valpy, 1998). As with homelessness, criminality adds a second dimension to the social typing process for some individuals with mental disorders. They face the consequences of being socially typed as mentally ill, but also of being socially typed as criminals. Problems with mental health programming emerge in some communities, in that community resources that help people with mental illnesses may not help those with criminal records, and resources that help former criminals may not be equipped to deal with the mentally ill.

The emphasis placed on deinstitutionalization by governments in North America and Western Europe over the past few decades has resulted in another problem—the reduction in hospital services for those people who may benefit from such services. For example, in the 1950s Ontario had 40 beds for the mentally ill for every 10 000 people; by 1995 that had been reduced to 5. In comparison, in 1995 Britain had 7.4 beds for the mentally ill for every 10 000 people, Spain had 1.7, and the Middle East had 1.4 (Valpy, 1998). The World Health Organization (2002b) reports that 40% of countries in the world have less than 1 hospital bed for the mentally ill for every 10 000 people. Despite the best of intentions on the part of its exponents and the positive outcomes for millions of people with mental disorders, deinstitutionalization has also had unintended negative consequences for millions of people worldwide.

TIME TO REVIEW:

- In what ways is mental illness medicalized?
- How has the social control of mental disorder changed through Western history?
- What types of treatments are available for people with mental disorders, and are they effective?
- What are the unintended negative consequences of deinstitutionalization?
- What role does mental illness play in (a) homelessness, and (b) crime?

The Deviance Dance: Resisting Stigmatization, Inadequate Care, and Psychiatry Itself

Mental disorders are socially typed as deviant at many different levels. Seen as "crazy" and "dangerous" by the general public, people with mental illnesses face stigmatization in everyday interactions (e.g., being teased or stared at, being called names, being perceived as "dangerous" and "weird," etc.) and discrimination in employment, housing, and medical care. To add to this burden, sometimes the treatments offered for these conditions fail to give back to the mentally ill control over their own lives. It is true that, once diagnosed with particular mental disorders according to the *DSM*, individuals with mental illnesses have a wide range of treatments available to them. The nature of these treatments has changed and expanded over time, making possible the deinstitutionalization movement that began in the 1960s. The move towards community-based treatment has benefitted many, and is the preferred form of treatment among people with mental disorders.

However, it has also had a number of unintended negative consequences for people who happen to fall through the cracks of the community mental health system—homelessness, criminality, suicide, substance abuse, and a lower quality of life. Individuals and groups in society are engaging in resistance against both stigmatization and inadequate treatment, trying to change the nature of the social typing process.

"The United Nations Principles for the Protection of Persons with Mental Illness and the Improvement of Mental Health Care state that there shall be no discrimination on the grounds of mental illness, that every patient has the right to be treated in his/her own community and to receive the least restrictive and intrusive treatment." (World Health Organization, 2002b, p. 4)

Resisting Stigmatization

The policies and programs that address the nature of treatment and support available to people with mental disorders arise from the *disease paradigm* of mental illness; within this paradigm, the emphasis is on ameliorating the symptoms of mental disorder, which distress and impair the functioning of people with those symptoms. Other policies and programs emerge out of the *discrimination paradigm* of mental illness, which emphasizes the role that stigmatization plays in the daily experiences of people with mental illnesses. These programs and policies constitute part of the "deviance dance," resisting and fighting back against the stigmatization of mental illness, and the social rejection or discrimination faced by individuals with mental disorders.

At the government level, many nations in the world have instituted legislation and policies prohibiting discrimination against people with mental disorders in housing, employment, health care, and more. Some policies target persons with mental illnesses specifically. In other cases people with mental illnesses are included under broader human rights legislation. For example, the *Canadian Charter of Rights and Freedoms* guarantees equality and prohibits discrimination, in part, on the basis of "mental and physical disability." At an international level, the *Universal Declaration of Human Rights* has a similar declaration. Provincial human rights codes integrate similar policies as well.

The medical community is also involved in trying to reduce negative attitudes toward mental illness. For example, the World Psychiatric Association coordinates an international program ("Open the Doors") to reduce the stigma of schizophrenia in countries including China, Egypt, Greece, and India. The World Health Organization devoted 2001's World Health Day to mental health, emphasizing issues of prejudice and discrimination. Reducing the stigma associated with mental illness is one of the dimensions of their Mental Health Global Action Programme (mhGAP), whereby they will coordinate advocacy efforts in member states to educate the public about mental illness, and protect or promote patient rights (World Health Organization, 2002b).

Self-help groups for people with mental illnesses can be found in many countries in the world. One of their mandates is acting to reduce the stigmatization of mental disorders through education, communication, and media information. For example, the Canadian Mental Health Association sponsors an annual Mental Health Week that is intended to dispel myths and reduce stereotypes; the tagline for Mental Health Week 2003 was "Respect, don't reject!" These types of groups also provide information about legislation, updates of mental health-related court cases, and materials to assist persons with mental illnesses in employment, housing, parenting, and more. Although the media is a key source of the stigmatization of mental illness, advocacy and self-help groups also use the media to spread their messages and raise public awareness about mental disorders.

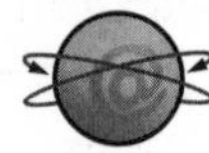

AN INTERNET MOMENT:

On the Website for the Canadian Mental Health Association (http://www.cmha.ca), you can usually view their current Public Awareness Campaign, such as magazine/newspaper ads and television commercials. You can also link to a site describing that year's Mental Health Week emphasis, obtain information that dispels the myths of mental illness, and download educational literature (e.g., educating employers about mental illness).

Not only do governments, the medical community, and self-help or advocacy groups act to reduce the stigma associated with mental illness and discrimination against people with mental disorders, they are also involved in the resistance to inadequate care for individuals with mental illnesses.

Resisting Inadequate and Insufficient Care

In addition to providing public awareness to reduce stigmatization, self-help groups are also involved in lobbying governments for better funding and improved services for people with mental disorders, as well as providing information to mental health consumers about the nature and appropriateness of the resources that are available to them. Support groups for specific mental disorders (e.g., depression; schizophrenia) provide detailed information about new medications that are available, the effectiveness of specific types of treatments, and research about potential negative side effects of different medications and treatments.

The medical community, of course, is continually engaged in research on new and improved treatments for different disorders. They also monitor the professional behaviours of their members, and negatively sanction those who do not provide appropriate care to patients. For example, professional associations of psychiatrists or psychologists provide ethical guidelines to their members, governing appropriate and inappropriate behaviours when counselling patients. On an international level, groups like the World Health Organization integrate their anti-stigmatization efforts with efforts to increase government funding for mental health, improve the training of mental health professionals, and more. Their Mental Health Global Action Programme's mission is to "support Member States to enhance their capacity to reduce risk, stigma, and burden of mental disorders and to promote the mental health of the population" (2002b, p. 11). To this end, their approach includes four core strategies. The first strategy is *information*, which includes coordinating an international observatory of the mental health situation in the world, providing evidence-based information to mental health workers, creating an Internet-based database of mental health information, and assisting with member state information systems. The second strategy is *policy and service development*. This includes providing guidance on effective policy development, coordinating international training networks for mental health professionals, and providing technical assistance to member states. The third core strategy is *advocacy* against stigma and discrimination, which was described above. The final strategy is *research*, and includes providing training to mental health researchers, assisting in finding sponsorship for research, and providing a forum for networking among researchers.

Individuals and groups who are involved in reducing the stigmatization of mental illness and ameliorating the problems of insufficient and inadequate care are trying to change aspects of the social typing process. Groups involved in the former efforts are working toward removing the label of "crazy," the evaluation of persons with mental illnesses as "dangerous" and "unlikable," and reducing the social rejection and discrimination that result. Groups involved in the latter efforts are trying to improve the ways that persons with mental disorders are treated within the mental health system—ensuring that enough of a priority is placed on mental health that there are enough resources available, that harmful or ineffective treatments are stopped, and that more effective treatments are instituted. However, resistance to stigmatization and to inadequate treatment are not the only ways in which the "deviance dance" is evident in the realm of mental illness. Some people resist the medicalization of mental disorder overall, and even question the notion of "mental illness" itself.

Resisting Medicalization

Resistance to the medicalization of mental disorder can occur at a number of levels, from criticisms of the *DSM*, to criticisms of the daily practices of mental health professionals, to questions about whether "mental illness" even exists.

Criticizing the *DSM*

Since its first edition, the *DSM* (the handbook used in the diagnosis of mental disorders) has been subject to considerable criticisms. Many of these criticisms have been based on the inclusion of particular disorders within the *DSM*. For example, homosexuality was included in the *DSM* from 1952 until its removal in 1973; it was first classified as a "sociopathic personality disorder," and then as a form of "non-psychotic sexual deviance." Factors contributing to its removal from the *DSM* included research demonstrating that homosexuality was not pathological and was not related to pathological outcomes, as well as the activism of gay and lesbian rights groups. More recently, controversy has emerged over the diagnostic category "Attention-Deficit Hyperactivity Disorder." Most experts agree that this is a disorder that affects people's lives by interfering with their abilities to concentrate on tasks, follow instructions, and sit still in situations that require it. However, critics argue that, in North America, far too many children are being diagnosed; in Britain, where different diagnostic criteria are used and different attitudes prevail, a significantly smaller proportion of children are diagnosed with this disorder (McConnell, 1997). One concern is that normal childhood restlessness and inattention is being diagnosed as a mental disorder. Another concern is that behavioural or attention problems that are actually being caused by social forces (e.g., family conflicts) are being diagnosed as a mental disorder, while the true cause of the children's problems remain untreated (McConnell, 1997; Shute, 2000). Furthermore, some social analysts suggest that the inability to focus or pay attention is the logical outcome for children growing up in a society in which the adults pride themselves on "busy-ness" and multitasking, and where being "stressed out" is seen by many as a sign of how important you are (see Box 7.2). All of these concerns reached a climax in 2000, when a class action lawsuit was launched against the American Psychiatric Association and the pharmaceutical company that manufactured the first drug for ADHD (Ritalin) for constructing a non-existent mental illness; the lawsuit has since been dismissed (Shute, 2000; Peck, 2001).

Box 7.2 Hurried Parents, Harried Kids[1]

It's not easy being a frog, particularly when you have to entertain 300 noisy, squirming children. But years of performance experience have taught me how to control my audience, and things were going my way last spring at a public elementary school in New York City when, dressed as a giant toad, I danced and rapped my way toward environmental awareness.

"Ribbut-Ribbut-Ribbut-Ugh. Oh Yeah, Ugh Ugh," I called out as the kids clapped and sang along with me.

Suddenly, out of the corner of my Styrofoam eyehole, I saw the vice principal marching down the aisle toward the front of the auditorium. "Miss!" she screamed at me. "Miss!" I stopped singing. The rap beat played on without me.

"Could I have the keys to your car?" she asked. "You're blocking the dumpster and the janitor can't get to it."

What could I do? I danced over to my bag, hidden behind the giant cardboard tree that served as my scenery, excavated my car keys and handed them to the vice principal. Satisfied, she marched away, leaving an audience of perplexed children, mouths hanging open in confusion, for me to draw back into fantasy once again.

An unlikely scenario? Unfortunately, it's not. I can barely remember the 1st time a performance of mine wasn't interrupted by an impatient adult. And yet, these very adults complain about the ailing attention spans of our children. Teachers complain they can't get our children to focus. Parents complain they can't get their children to listen. The government blames Hollywood; the rest of us blame television, overcrowded classrooms, video games, whatever.

I wonder if it ever occurs to the adult world that maybe we're the ones with the short attention spans. If we would focus on the real culprit—our own inability to direct our attention to one thing for more than a sound byte—we might begin to address the fault in our children.

As a professional storyteller, I've watched the slow and methodical process by which parents destroy their children's attention spans. I've seen it happen when fathers pull their children out of a storytelling performance after 10 minutes—even though their kids are completely enthralled—because they are due somewhere else. Or when mothers interrupt their kids' concentration by whispering instructive comments to them throughout a performance, things like, "That story takes place in Florida!"

In our desperate attempt to maximize our children's learning and manage their free play, we fill their days with constant distractions. I've performed in hundreds of classrooms throughout North America, and I've yet to experience fewer than two interruptions per 45-minute period. The most memorable was at a grammar school in Queens, New York, where my session was interrupted three times by announcements over the loudspeaker, the final one being the booming voice of the principal saying, "The word for the day is *octagon*!"

It would be nice if we could blame these interruptions on bad school policy. But the truth is, the fragmented behavior I witness in my work is only a microcosm of what all of us experience every day in small and subtle ways. We experience it when we encounter cashiers who haven't finished serving us before they go on to the next customer; when we try to talk to people who prefer looking everywhere but at the person who's speaking to them; when we deal with telephone operators who put us on hold and then come back on the line and confuse us with another caller.

What does this kind of behavior say about us? More important, what does it say to our children? Aren't we inadvertently sending them the cynical message that nothing is worth our full and undivided attention? Aren't we, in effect, telling them that the moment is no longer worth savoring, unless it leads to some newer, brighter, different moment?

I have a friend who intentionally lets her child sit quietly in the car while they drive—no radio, no toys, no audiocassettes. "And you know what?" she told me. "He becomes totally immersed in the roadside show—the trees whizzing by, the yellow lines on the endless road, the telephone poles dotting the sky. He's learned how to become completely absorbed in the moment."

Now, if only we adults could do the same.

1 Lipkin, L. (2001). Hurried Parents, Harried Kids. *Family Circle Magazine*, 4/3/2001, p. 112.

While some critics of the medicalization of mental disorder focus their disapproval on the inclusion of specific categories of disorder within the *DSM*, other critics express concerns over the *DSM* itself, and the power it holds. Caplan (1995) claims that the fact that research claims half of Americans experience a mental disorder at least once in their lives suggests that what is considered to be a "mental disorder" has escalated to ridiculous proportions. Critics of the *DSM* not only point to methodological shortcomings in its creation, but also the role played by power in determining what is and is not included in the list of mental disorders. For instance, the decision-making process can ultimately come down to a vote—majority rules. This is precisely what occurred when homosexuality was removed from the *DSM*; after lengthy presentations, debates, and passionate arguments, a *slight* majority of members voted to remove homosexuality as a mental disorder. Had even a few members of the committee felt differently, homosexuality would still be considered a form of mental illness—not because of "objective" scientific evidence, but because of "subjective" viewpoints influenced by a variety of sources. The frequency with which these kinds of decision-making process occur has led some critics to suggest that the *DSM* is just as much a political document as a medical document (e.g., Armstrong, 1993). Given the role that subjectivity plays in what is considered a "mental disorder" according to the *DSM*, the power that this handbook holds is disconcerting to some. The credibility and legitimacy that the public lends to science means that people are unlikely to question the diagnostic categories of mental illness—if the "experts" say something is a mental illness, most of us will believe them.

"The point is not that decisions about who is normal are riddled with personal biases and political considerations but rather that, by dint of a handful of influential professionals' efforts, those subjective determinants of diagnoses masquerade as solid science and truth." (Caplan, 1995, p. xvi)

Despite its shortcomings, there is considerable agreement that the *DSM* does capture many diagnostically useful sets of symptoms that *are* distressful to the people that experience them and *do* impair effective daily functioning. Furthermore, there is a sizable overlap in the psychiatric diagnostic categories contained in the *DSM* and in the *International Classification of Diseases* (ICD), used by the World Health Organization. However, even those social analysts and health professionals who acknowledge the validity of the *DSM* recognize that problematic patterns in its usage, and in other practices of mental health professionals, are all too common. Research consistently finds variables other than medical ones influence the diagnoses and treatments for mental disorders.

TIME TO REVIEW:

- What kinds of mental health policies and programs emerge from the discrimination paradigm of mental illness?
- What types of policies and programs that resist the stigmatization of mental illness exist at the levels of the government, the medical community, and self-help/advocacy groups?
- What roles do self-help/advocacy groups and medical communities play in resisting insufficient or inadequate care?
- Which disorders have critics said should be eliminated from the DSM, and why?
- What broader criticisms have been directed at the DSM?

Being Sane in Insane Places: Criticizing Mental Health Professions

Rosenhan (1973) was one of the early mental health professionals who documented the influence of social factors and other biases on psychiatric diagnoses. His influential study stirred tremendous controversy within the mental health community, but also motivated considerable changes in the mental health system. Rosenhan began with the question, "If sanity and insanity exist, how shall we know them?" That is, his fundamental question was whether the "sane" can be distinguished from the "insane"—whether the salient characteristics leading to diagnosis lie within the individual or within the environment. The medical view is that people present themselves with symptoms, which are then recognized by professionals as constituting a diagnosis, leading to treatment; as a parallel, people who present themselves with certain "symptoms" may also be told by professionals that those are not symptoms of any mental disorder.

D. L. Rosenhan's study, "Being Sane in Insane Places" has a resounding effect on the mental health system throughout the Western world.

Rosenhan had 8 research associates (including students, homemakers, and a psychiatrist) attempt to get themselves admitted to psychiatric hospitals. These "pseudo-patients" presented themselves to the mental health admissions people at 12 different hospitals, claiming that they had been hearing voices for the past few weeks, which were saying "empty," "hollow," and "thud." Rosenhan's underlying assumption was that if their sanity was not detected, it would indicate that the salient characteristics involved in psychiatric diagnosis reside more within the environment than within the individual. All of these research associates were admitted to the hospitals, with diagnoses of "schizophrenia." Once they were admitted, they were to begin acting normally, report that the voices had stopped, and try to get discharged from the hospitals. In interactions with the mental health professionals, they were to be truthful about the characteristics of their lives (with the exception that those in mental health professions would allege another occupation in order to avoid special treatment)—their relationships with family members, their life histories, their frustrations and joys in life. As patients, they were completely cooperative with staff, doing everything they were told to do (although they did surreptitiously flush their medication down the toilets). In the end, the pseudo-patients spent between 7 and 52 days hospitalized prior to being discharged, with the average stay being 19 days. The psychiatrists at the hospitals never detected the pseudo-patients' sanity; they were discharged with diagnoses of "schizophrenia in remission," suggesting that their mental illness was still there, but simply dormant for the present moment.

The lack of detection was not because they were not acting "sane" enough. They received daily visitors, who were to look for any potential abnormal behavioural consequences resulting from hospitalization; the visitors detected no abnormal behaviours. Furthermore, in many cases *other patients* detected the sanity of the pseudo-patients, saying things like, "You're not crazy" or "You must be a journalist or professor checking up on the hospital." Within the hospitals, the mentally ill label that they had received affected the nature of all of their interactions with staff. Normal behaviours were overlooked or misinterpreted through the lens of the diagnosis of mental illness. For example, although the pseudo-patients initially tried to hide their note-taking (for fear of being detected), it quickly became apparent that note-taking was seen as a *sign* of their mental disorder. As boredom set in and mealtime became a highlight of the day, waiting in the hallway for the cafeteria doors to be opened was described as indicative of the "oral-acquisitive nature" of schizophrenia. In a session with a psychiatrist, one male pseudo-patient spoke of how, as a little boy, he was closer to his mother, but as he progressed through adolescence he became closer to his father and more distant from his mother—psychiatric notes described this as "considerable ambivalence in relationships." When he described his marriage as generally positive, with just occasional arguments, the case notes identified those occasional conflicts as "angry outbursts."

Of course, one factor that might contribute to the misdiagnosis is the desire of mental health professionals to err on the side of caution; it may be safer to mistakenly label a healthy person as ill than to mistakenly label an ill person as healthy, and not provide them with the treatment they need. Rosenhan suggested that this desire to err on the side of caution can explain misdiagnosis at the initial time of admission, but is less able to account for continued misdiagnosis after a lengthy period of observation and analysis. So why did the misdiagnosis continue all the way until the time of discharge? One reason could be the lack of interaction between the mental health professionals and the patients. Nursing attendants, nurses, and even the psychiatrists actively avoided contact with the pseudo-patients. When the pseudo-patients intercepted staff members to ask them simple questions (such as when they might be discharged), the psychiatrists averted their eyes and walked away 71% of the time, as did 88% of the nurses and nursing attendants. Another reason, one emphasized by Rosenhan, is the power that a diagnosis of mental illness carries. He concluded that the initial "schizophrenic" label given upon admission to the hospitals provided staff with a **schema**, or a mental framework, which affected their interpretations of the pseudo-patients' behaviours; *all* behaviours then came to be interpreted as indicative of pathology. In contrast, those very same behaviours exhibited by someone who had not been diagnosed as mentally ill would not be perceived as indicative of pathology. What was Rosenhan's conclusion? The salient characteristics in the diagnosis of mental illness lie more within the social context, or the environment, than within the individual.

As you can imagine, the results of this research project caused quite a stir in the psychiatric community. An outcry from psychiatric hospitals throughout the United States claimed that something like that could certainly never happen at their hospital; they suggested that the hospitals utilized within Rosenhan's study were poorly run. Well, Rosenhan created a follow-up study to look into this possibility.

Rosenhan selected a well-known and very well-respected teaching hospital. He told administrators that within the next three months at least one pseudo-patient would attempt to be admitted as a psychiatric patient. Hospital staff, including the psychiatrists, were asked to rate each person admitted during that time as to the likelihood that this was one of the pseudo-patients. During that period of time, a total of 191 psychiatric patients were admitted to this hospital. Of these patients, the hospital staff identified 41 as having a high likelihood of being pseudo-patients. At least one psychiatrist identified as many as 23 patients, and both a psychiatrist and at least one additional staff member identified 19 patients as being likely pseudo-patients. How many pseudo-patients had Rosenhan actually sent in? None. Rosenhan concluded that even mental health professionals could not distinguish the sane from the insane.

While Rosenhan's first study certainly caused a stir, when combined with the results of the follow-up study it was as though a tornado had hit the entire field of psychiatry. His research seemed to present a resounding critique of the efficacy of mental health professions. First, by illustrating that people without mental disorders could be kept in hospitals and not have their "sanity" detected, it raised significant concerns about those patients who had been committed to psychiatric hospitals involuntarily. It was possible that some of these patients, being kept against their wills, did not have any mental disorder. As a result of these concerns, governments throughout the Western world created or intensified legislation governing involuntary psychiatric admissions. In Canada, all provinces have mental health legislation that outlines the conditions under which individuals can and cannot be admitted for psychiatric care against their wills, and sets procedural safeguards in place for reviewing such cases at regular periods following admission. Within the government, the role of Mental Patient Advocate is to advise involuntarily committed patients and their families of their rights in such situations.

Second, Rosenhan's research described the dehumanizing treatment that patients in psychiatric hospitals frequently faced, such as being ignored by staff when asking a question, being prescribed large numbers of pills (i.e., the pseudo-patients in the first study were given a total of 2,100 pills during their hospital stays), and being mistreated in many other ways. For example, in one instance a nurse unbuttoned her shirt to adjust her bra, right in front of a group of male patients; it was not a teasing or sexual demonstration, but rather reflected her view that it was no big deal, because these were "mental patients" rather than "real" men. These results also contributed to many changes in the practices within psychiatric hospitals, and to the growth of mental health advocacy groups.

Third, Rosenhan's first study illustrated important aspects of Edwin Lemert's labelling theory (discussed in Chapter 3), which emphasized the influence that labels have on the way people are subsequently treated. In the psychiatric hospitals, it was the label of "mentally ill" rather than the actual behaviour of the pseudo-patients that determined how staff would interact with them and interpret their behaviours. Given the stigma that people with mental disorders face in society, inaccurately attaching a label of mental illness to individuals can have a significant impact on the rest of their lives.

Finally, Rosenhan's research pointed to the precarious nature of psychiatric diagnosis, and the unintentional influence of social factors on diagnostic processes. Considering the awareness stimulated by Rosenhan's research, one might think that, since that time, the influence of social factors in diagnosis has declined. Is this the case?

The Role of Social Factors in Diagnosis and Treatment

Given the way that social factors permeate every aspect of our daily lives, and the subsequent influence they have over our thoughts, feelings, and behaviours, it should not be too surprising that social factors continue to influence diagnosis and treatment. Loring and Powell (1988) presented psychiatrists with case summaries, and manipulated the sex (male or female) and race (black or white) within the cases. They found that the sex and race both influenced the diagnoses and other aspects of the psychiatrists' perceptions of the individuals contained within the case summaries. For example, black persons within the case summaries were more likely to be described as "dangerous" and "suspicious" than were white persons, even when everything in the case summary (other than the race of the individual) was identical.

Other research has found that women are more likely to be diagnosed with depression than men are, even when they present the same symptoms (Stoppe, Sandholzer, & Huppertz, 1999). However, there is some debate over the influence of sex on diagnosis, as some other studies have not detected this pattern (Gater et al., 1998). Despite the continued debate about whether there are sex differences in diagnosis, the evidence is quite clear that there are sex differences in treatment; women are far more likely to be prescribed psychotropic drugs than men are (Simoni-Wastila, 2000).

In answering the above questions, you may have referred to something like stereotypes—assumptions about what people of different races and genders are like, or should be like. Because of prejudicial attitudes that continue to pervade society,

Ask Yourself:

Why do you think race and sex might influence the diagnosis and treatment of mental disorders? That is, why would black individuals be perceived as more "dangerous" than white individuals given the exact same case summaries? Why would women be more likely to be diagnosed with depression than men, even when they present the same symptoms? And why would women be more likely to be prescribed psychotropic drugs for their mental disorders?

blacks and whites are perceived in different ways. So are men and women. Indeed, researchers working within the various critical theories that we explored in Chapter 3 (e.g., feminist theories) explain these research results in precisely those terms (Loring & Powell, 1988; Simoni-Wastila, 2000).

Thus far, we have looked at resistance to the medicalization of mental disorder in three different ways. One form of resistance emphasizes the ways that some normal social behaviours have been deviantized within the *DSM*, such as homosexuality and attention-deficit hyperactivity disorder. A second form of resistance launches broader critiques against the *DSM*, showing us the political dimension of the document. The third form of resistance focuses on some of the inaccuracies and biases that occur in the daily practices of mental health professionals, revealing the power of the labelling process and the influence of social factors on diagnosis and treatment. There is one last form of resistance to the medicalization of mental illness that moves to a much broader, more abstract level, criticizing the concept of "mental illness" itself as being a false label that denies free will (Szasz, 1994). Thomas Szasz (a psychiatrist himself) acknowledges that there are physical diseases of the brain, but argues that virtually none of the disorders listed in the *DSM* have been proven beyond a doubt to be physical diseases of the brain; instead, people use the diagnostic categories of the *DSM* to involuntarily treat people who do not want treatment, and to avoid responsibility for criminal acts. Szasz's arguments have stimulated controversy since the 1950s, and continue to stimulate controversy today.

However, most people agree that mental disorders *do* exist, and that people with mental disorders do not have everything they need to successfully recover and/or achieve a high quality of functioning in daily life. The continued stigmatization of mental illness is one of the central obstacles to recovery and high functioning, and even influences the extent and quality of policies and programs available. Governments, the medical community, and self-help/advocacy groups continue to work toward improving the lives of people with mental disorders—reducing the stigma and increasing the available resources. At another level, people are bringing to the forefront the political nature of the process by which diagnostic categories are created, and the social factors that can influence or bias diagnosis and treatment.

TIME TO REVIEW:

- What happened in Rosenhan's famous study?
- How were the pseudo-patients in his study treated while hospitalized?
- What happened in his follow-up study?
- What were Rosenhan's conclusions?
  What were the four different impacts that Rosenhan's research had?
- What influence do sex and race have on the diagnosis and treatment of mental disorders, and why?
- What are Thomas Szasz's criticisms of the medicalization of mental disorder?

Chapter Summary

Mental illness refers to thoughts, moods, and behaviours that cause significant distress and/or significantly impair functioning of individuals. The nature of these impairments is further delineated in the diagnostic categories listed in the American Psychiatric Association's *Diagnostic and Statistical Manual of Mental Disorders*; it includes disorders such as depression, schizophrenia, antisocial personality disorder, and more.

The estimates of the proportion of people who experience mental disorders at some point in their lifetimes range from 20% to 50%. The most common disorders are depression, anxiety, and somatic complaints. Although mental disorders can strike anyone, some social groups face higher risks than others. Women and men show equivalent overall rates of mental disorder, but depression and anxiety are far more common in women, and antisocial personality disorder is far more common in men. People in low socioeconomic status groups show higher rates of mental illness, as do adolescents and young adults.

Considerable costs are associated with mental illness, for the individuals experiencing the illness, their families, and society as a whole. Five of the ten leading causes of disability in the world are mental disorders, and depression alone is expected to become the second leading cause of disability (behind heart disease) by the year 2020. Despite the costs associated with untreated mental disorders, most people with symptoms do not see mental health professionals.

One of the main reasons people do not seek medical help is because of the stigmatization of mental illness in society. Negative perceptions of people with mental disorders are found in media representations, attitudes of the general public, and even attitudes of health professionals. These negative attitudes hinder recovery of people with mental disorders, contribute to discrimination in many areas (e.g., employment, housing, health care), and result in mental health programs and policies not being seen as priorities.

Mental health policies and programs are embedded within two different paradigms—the *disease paradigm* and the *discrimination paradigm*. The first paradigm emphasizes the role of symptoms of the disorders themselves in people's experience of mental illness. The second paradigm emphasizes the role of stigmatization and prejudice in people's experience of mental illness.

Policies and programs that emerge from the disease paradigm constitute the medicalization of mental illness. Although mental illness has been treated in various ways throughout history, in the late 19th century it became *medicalized*, that is, seen as an illness and treated by medical means. Today, a wide range of therapeutic, pharmaceutical, and social support resources are available to assist in recovery and/or improved daily functioning. Over the last several decades, the *deinstitutionalization* movement has been a significant determinant of the nature of treatment available. Although treating people within communities rather than within hospitals has helped millions of individuals with mental disorders, there have also been unintended negative consequences that have resulted in harm to many people's lives.

A number of individuals and groups have become involved in fighting back against the stigmatization of mental illness, challenging the perceptions of people with mental disorders as dangerous and unreliable, and the resulting discrimination. Some of those same groups are also active in efforts to improve the treatments that are available, and to ensure that fewer people fall through the cracks of the mental health system. In both of these cases, efforts are undertaken to change the nature of the social typing process.

The medicalization of mental disorder is also being resisted and changed in a number of different ways. Critics express concerns about the diagnostic handbook, the *DSM* for (a) the inclusion of some normal behaviours as "disorders," such as homosexuality and ADHD, and (b) the political nature of the process by which disorders are included in the *DSM*, and the subsequent power the handbook has.

Other people have raised questions about the mental health professions themselves. Rosenhan's classic study concluded that the salient characteristics in diagnosis lie more within the social context than within the individual, and that when this was combined with the lasting power of a mentally ill label in society, we should be concerned. Decades later, researchers continue to find that social factors (e.g., sex, race) have an impact on psychiatric diagnosis and treatment. Thomas Szasz takes his criticisms of psychiatry the furthest, suggesting that mental illness is a "myth."

Recommended Readings

Caplan, P. J. (1995) *They say you're crazy: How the world's most powerful psychiatrists decide who's normal*. Reading, MA: Perseus Books.

* In this book, Paula Caplan elaborates upon the various criticisms of and concerns with the *DSM*, and what the consequences are.

Goffman, E. (1961). *Asylums: Essays on the social situation of mental patients and other inmates*. Garden City, NY: Anchor Books.

* Goffman focuses on the stigmatization of mental illness, both within and outside of institutions, as well as the experiences of people in psychiatric hospitals.

Health Canada (2002b). *A report on mental illness in Canada*. Ottawa: Health Canada.

* This report provides a detailed overview of the prevalence of different types of mental disorders, research on their causes, and policy, program, and treatment recommendations. Separate chapters address mood disorders, schizophrenia, eating disorders, suicide, and more. This document is available at no charge on the Canadian Mental Health Association's Website (**http://www.cmha.ca**).

Endnotes

1 Canadian Mental Health Association. Retrieved June 2, 2003 from World Wide Web: **http://www.cmha.ca**

Key Terms

mental disorder, **p. 206**
social causation hypothesis, **p. 209**
retreatism, **p. 209**
social selection hypothesis, **p. 209**
discrimination paradigm, **p. 214**
disease paradigm, **p. 214**
deinstitutionalization, **p. 216**
least restrictive alternative, **p. 217**
schema, **p. 228**

CHAPTER 8

What Do You Believe? Religion and Deviance

Learning Objectives

After reading this chapter, you should be able to:

- Explain how religion is related to the concept of "truth."
- Describe what is meant by *religion as deviance*.
- Describe the traditional typology that helps determine which religions are "deviant," and explain why sects and cults are considered "deviant," using examples.
- Describe the different levels of social control that are directed at "deviant" religions, as well as the various ways that deviant labels are resisted.
- Explain how religion serves as a social typer of deviance, using both historical and contemporary examples.
- Describe the witch persecutions, residential schooling, and the child-savers movement.

"The task of history...is to establish the truth of this world." (Karl Marx, 1975)[1]

In uttering this phrase, Karl Marx was condemning religion, saying that the only way to find "truth" is through the full abandonment of religion. He claimed that religion is the "opium of the masses," a mechanism by which society's masses are prevented from seeing the "truth" about the society they are living in. Because of religion, the proletariat is incapable of rising up to resist their bourgeoisie oppressors; religion serves as the obstacle between the people and the "truth." But, in another sense, we can look at religion as proclaiming "truth." Although Marx would not use the above phrase in this way, one of the ways in which people throughout the world attempt to determine the "truth" is via the religions that are part of their lives.

Anything that you personally think is true represents one of your **beliefs**, regardless of whether it is actually true or not. Some of your beliefs might be entirely unique to you, while other people might share some of your beliefs; that is, a group of people might accept the very same "truths" that you do. And, frequently, single beliefs are combined with other interrelated beliefs into organized sets, or **belief systems** (Stebbins, 1996). Religious doctrines (e.g., Christian, Islamic), the ideologies of specific political parties (e.g., Canadian Alliance, New Democrats), and the knowledge contained within particular disciplines of science (e.g., astronomy, zoology) are all belief systems that are shared among large groups of people. Both religion (the topic of this chapter) and science (the topic of the next chapter) are built upon a foundation of propositions about what the "truth" is. Religious belief systems are those based upon "truths" about "supreme beings," the "supernatural realm," "superhuman beings," or the "sacred cosmos"—a being or beings that are far more powerful and more knowing than humans are, and that are capable of influencing our lives in significant ways (McGuire, 1997, p. 10).

Just as Karl Marx worked towards establishing the "truth of this world," so does each religious belief system proclaim the "truth of this world." Various religious belief systems declare different truths; what Buddhism says is "true" is considerably distinct from what Islam says is "true" (although there are some overlapping beliefs as well). Many religions claim that their version of "truth" is the only correct one, such that individuals who fail to accept and adhere to those "truths" will face some type of negative consequence, either in this world/lifetime or another world/lifetime. That is, refusing to follow religious "truth" results in the individual being socially typed as "deviant" and made subject to forms of social control. This social typing process can be engaged when people reject the "right" belief system and instead adopt a "wrong" one, or when individuals fail to act in accordance with the moral code integrated within the belief system. But at times the social typing process can also be directed *at* a religious institution itself, or at actions taking place *within* religious institutions (Stark & Bainbridge, 1996).

The various ways that the social typing process can occur represent the two different ways that we can explore the concept of deviance within the context of religion. First, we can consider **religion as deviance**—acts of deviance that occur within religious groups, or religious groups themselves being considered "deviant" in their entirety. Second, we can look at **religion as a social typer of deviance**, wherein religious belief systems or the way those belief systems are applied dictate to us who should be considered deviant, and what the consequences should/will be.

In analyzing the relationship between religion and deviance, it is of the utmost importance to distinguish between the belief systems themselves (i.e., theological doctrine) and the way those belief systems are operationalized within sociocultural contexts. It is the latter that sociologists focus their analyses on. Sociological analyses of religion *do not* make value judgments about people's religious beliefs, nor do they attempt to prove or disprove anyone's religious beliefs; religious beliefs are a matter of *faith* (McGuire, 1997). Instead, sociological analyses of religion explore the social embeddedness of religious belief systems—the processes by which such belief systems emerge, the role that religion plays in people's lives within societies, and the relationships between religion and other social structures or processes (e.g., social stratification). Religious institutions are social organizations, just like any other social organization, and like any other social organization, religious institutions are composed of and run by people who have their own attitudes, desires, and interests; this is the aspect of religion that sociologists pay attention to. Thus, in this chapter we are not analyzing *beliefs*, we are analyzing *social organizations* that are based on religious belief systems.

Ask Yourself:

Think for a moment about your own religious beliefs, and what they consist of—the "truth about the world" that is encapsulated in your religious belief system. Now shift your focus to religion as a social organization, an institution. Do you attend some type of organized religious functions, such as those sponsored by a church, temple, or synagogue? Why or why not? What influences how often you attend? What role does your religious institution play within the community and world?

In answering the "Ask Yourself" questions at left, you made the transition from thinking about religion as a belief system to thinking about religion as a social organization that holds a particular place in the community and in the larger society, and that carries out specific types of activities within that environment. If you are like many people, you do have religious beliefs, but you do not necessarily attend a church, temple, or synagogue on a weekly basis. Perhaps it is because of other responsibilities at work, school, or home. Perhaps it is because you do not think attending such institutions is necessary for worship. Perhaps it is because you do not approve of what religious organizations have done in the past. If you do regularly attend a place of worship, it holds a particular role within the community, in terms of both the way it is perceived by other members of the community and the activities it may engage in within the community. For example, your place of worship might be highly regarded in your community, or conversely it might be looked upon with suspicion or disdain. Maybe your place of worship is very active within the community—raising money for charity, providing the homeless with a place to sleep, running a neighbourhood day care, hosting debates among political candidates at election time, or organizing extracurricular activities for neighbourhood youth. The larger religion of which your place of worship is a part, may be running a school in a Third World country, or helping to build a well that will provide clean water. Historically, perhaps it has participated in less admirable pursuits, such as the witch burnings of the Middle Ages or the abuses of Canada's Aboriginal peoples in residential schools. Sociologists look at all of these types of social issues—the factors that influence people to participate in organized religion, the perceptions that people have of specific religions, and the actions carried out by religious institutions. It is the sociocultural aspect of religious institutions, not religious belief systems themselves, that is the area under discussion when we explore the linkages between religion and deviance.

Religion as Deviance

When we think of religion and "deviance," many of you may initially think of abuses carried out by representatives of different religions, such as instances of child sexual abuse by priests, and allegations that churches tried to cover up those incidents. In addition to "deviant" acts carried out by religious institutions or representatives of those institutions, talking about *religion as deviance* also brings to mind those religious groups that are thought of as "deviant" in their entirety—religions that are considered "weird," "strange," or "bizarre." Which religions are considered "deviant" and which are considered "normal"? Traditionally, religious belief systems were categorized within various typologies, based on characteristics of the particular group in question; a religious group's location within the typology determined whether it was considered "deviant." More recently, these traditional typologies have been questioned and even abandoned by some researchers, resulting in quite a different view of "deviant religions."

"Deviant Religions" According to Traditional Typologies

Different scholars have proposed various typologies of religious groups (McGuire, 1997; Troeltsch, 1931; Johnson, 1963; Yinger, 1970; Stark & Bainbridge, 1996). Although the typologies can be somewhat distinct from each other, a review of the various frameworks reveals that four categories of religious groups are commonly utilized. Deviance is then determined by which category a religious group is situated in.

Ecclesia refers to state religions, where a specific religious belief system is adopted at the governmental level, and becomes that nation's "official" religion. As a result, every citizen in that nation is theoretically seen as a member of that religion. Islam is an ecclesia in Iran, as is the Anglican denomination of Christianity in England, and the Lutheran denomination of Christianity in Sweden. The extent to which other religions are practiced in these countries depends on the particular nation in question. Some nations identify an ecclesia, and yet declare freedom of religion for their citizens (e.g., England); in other cases, non-ecclesiastic religions are outlawed (e.g., in Europe during the Middle Ages). **Churches** are not "official" religions of an entire society, but they are large and powerful religious groups. Those religious groups that are commonly perceived as being the world's "major religions"—Islam, Judaism, Hinduism, Buddhism, and Christianity—are categorized as *churches*. They are well established in society, highly bureaucratized (having complex hierarchies of leadership and administration, as well as formalized rituals and practices), and have millions of members around the world. They are further subdivided into **denominations**, such that there are different types of Christianity (e.g., Catholic), Islam (e.g., Sunni), and Judaism (e.g., Orthodox); the same can be said of all of the other churches of the world. **Sects** are smaller religious groups that have usually broken away from larger churches at some point in their history. They are less established in society than churches are, have fewer members, have more rigid doctrine formed in reaction to the doctrine of the larger church, and require higher levels of commitment from their members (e.g., clothing, behaviour, food). The Amish and the Hutterites are examples of sects that are offshoots of the larger Christian church, while the Taliban represented a sect that had broken away from mainstream Islam. Scientology is usually categorized as a sect, but is not an offshoot of any of the world's major religions. **Cults** are usually smaller than sects (although not always), frequently having only a handful of members. Their doctrine is even more reactionary and oppositional, and intense levels of commitment are required of members. A single, charismatic leader serves as a source of inspiration (or some might say brainwashing), convincing followers that the secret to salvation can be found in that group. Examples of cults that you may be most familiar with include the Branch Davidians, Heaven's Gate, and the Children of God.

This framework has traditionally been used as the foundation for decisions about whether a particular religious group is "deviant" or not. Ecclesias, which are the state-approved "official" religions of their respective nations, and which declare the whole of the nation's citizens as members (at least on a theoretical level), are not considered deviant within those societies. Of course, there may be some groups in those societies that do attempt to deviantize that religion, as part of the "deviance dance." Churches, with millions of members worldwide and their high level of integration within many societies, are also perceived as "normal" or conventional religions. Sects and cults, having fewer members, being more isolated from mainstream society, and having doctrine that is more reactionary or

The Amish are a Christian-based sect that rejects modern technology and lives in communal settings.

oppositional, are the religious groups that are traditionally seen as "deviant" and in need of social control. In other words, those religious groups that are characterized by high levels of tension with the broader society are perceived as "deviant," while those that are characterized by low levels of tension are seen as "normal" (Stark & Bainbridge, 1996).

TIME TO REVIEW:

- What are beliefs and belief systems, and how are they related to "truth"? Give examples of belief systems.
- What are the two different ways that deviance can be explored within the context of religion?
- What is the difference between religions as beliefs systems and religions as social organizations? Where do sociological analyses of religion fit in?
- What are the four categories of religious groups that have been commonly recognized in traditional typologies? Which types are perceived as "deviant"?

The "Deviant" World of Sects and Cults

Although both sects and cults are perceived as deviant, existing in a state of tension with the wider society, the deviance of cults is of a greater magnitude than that of sects. Cults are based on novel beliefs, while sects tend to have more traditional belief systems as their foundation, creating some differences in the level of tension that exists with society and the level of social control exerted upon the religious groups (Stark & Bainbridge, 1996).

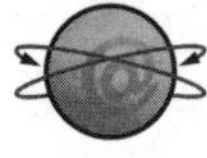

AN INTERNET MOMENT:

As you progress through the remainder of the chapter, you may want to go to "The Religious Movement Homepage at the University of Virginia" (http://religiousmovements.lib.Virginia.edu/). This is a reputable and highly respected academic Website that contains an abundance of information about religious groups, cults, religious freedom issues, research bibliographies, and more. You may find the site particularly useful for obtaining more information about specific religious groups that are mentioned in the remainder of this chapter. The "Profiles of Religious Groups" on the Website contains an alphabetical listing of almost every religious group (churches, sects, and cults) you can think of. The profiles include information on the groups' belief systems, origins, practices, history, and any controversies.

Sects

High levels of commitment are required of members of sects, and their beliefs and life habits are strictly controlled. Members who fail to think or act in accordance with the belief system are punished, and in many sects the most extreme punishment is being excommunicated from the group (Wilson, 1993; McGuire, 1997; Stark & Bainbridge, 1996). Along with the nature of the belief systems, these characteristics are what make many outsiders think of sects as somewhat peculiar. For those of us who are not a part of these types of groups, it can be difficult for us to understand why people adhere to such beliefs, and why they would be willing to tolerate such high levels of control exerted over their lives.

Although the levels of commitment required of members and the levels of control exerted over members' lives are higher in sects than in churches, there is considerable diversity among sects in these characteristics—that is, some sects have more rigid requirements than others. The degree of tension between sects and the wider society also varies, with some sects having more tension with society than others do. Such tension is fundamental to the deviantization and social control of sects within society. The level of tension experienced by a particular sect is determined by three factors: (a) the magnitude of the differences between the sect and society; (b) the level of antagonism that the sect feels for society; and (c) the extent to which the sect separates itself from the larger world (Stark & Bainbridge, 1996). Lawson (1995) illustrates this variation by comparing two sects, the Seventh Day Adventists and the Jehovah's Witnesses. Both sects formed in the 19th century, inspired by apocalyptic visions, and both can now be found in countries around the world. However, since their inception they have followed different trajectories, such that the Jehovah's Witnesses experience significantly higher levels of tension with their surrounding societies than do the Seventh Day Adventists.

Since their inception, greater degrees of difference, antagonism, and separation have characterized the Jehovah's Witnesses. They have persistently held to their original apocalyptic vision, although they have had to repeatedly revise their projected dates for the coming apocalypse (past failed dates have frequently resulted in a drop in membership due to disappointment and loss of faith). Members face rigid requirements for continued membership, such as attendance at many weekly meetings, meeting targets for hours spent witnessing (i.e., going door to door in an attempt to draw converts), and following behavioural guidelines (e.g., prohibitions against substance use and blood transfusions). These kinds of requirement make the daily lives of members considerably distinct from the general population's. Their belief system, as illustrated in their publications, is considerably antagonistic to other religious groups, the government, and patriotic symbols. Antagonisms toward governments and patriotic symbols in particular have placed them on the receiving end of social hostilities during conflicts like the American Civil War, World War I, and World War II. The antagonistic dimension of the belief system contributes to the perception that they are attacking everyone and everything outside of the sect. Because of their beliefs about the wider society, members of the Jehovah's Witnesses live in considerable isolation from it, other than their witnessing and their participation in the labour force. Labour force participation is frequently of a limited nature, because members are discouraged from pursuing higher education, and jobs are considered secondary to witnessing. The boundaries between the sect and the larger society are reinforced when members fail to adhere to behavioural requirements of membership. They are excommunicated from the group, and remaining members are directed to actively shun them in any public settings; for example, if an excommunicated member is seen in the supermarket, current members may even leave their full carts behind and exit the store. The magnitude of the tension created because of these differences, antagonisms, and separation has resulted in significant persecution in countries around the world. In various countries, members of the Jehovah's Witnesses have been physically attacked by mobs, arrested, and even put to death (e.g., for refusing to fight during wartime).

In contrast, the Seventh Day Adventists have undergone substantial changes over time, contributing to lesser degrees of tension with the larger society. The notion of a coming apocalypse maintains its presence within this sect's belief system, but it no longer holds the central position that it used to, and specific date projections have been abandoned. High levels of commitment are required of members, including not eating certain foods and not consuming certain substances. However, the requirements for membership have relaxed over time, as antagonisms and the separation from society have declined. Early in their history, leaders determined that compromise was necessary in order to avoid conflicts and gain acceptance in the wider society. The sect became deeply involved in creating schools, colleges, businesses, hospitals, and institutions for the elderly in the early 20th century, in their desire to "claim an increasing stake in society" (p. 375) and attract new members. Although members are encouraged to utilize these Seventh Day Adventist resources instead of those outside of the sect, the boundaries with the outside world are quite permeable. The pursuit of higher education is quite common, and members typically have high-status occupations in the labour force. The value placed on higher education has also indirectly contributed to the relaxing of requirements and the growing diversity of thought among members, further enhancing integration with the wider society. Members of this sect have frequently been persecuted in many countries in the world (e.g., for working on the traditional Christian Sabbath day of Sunday; refusing to fight during wartime); however, the extent of their persecution is less than that faced by Jehovah's Witnesses. As a result of the different trajectories the two groups have followed, they are seen as different types of sects. The Seventh Day Adventists are frequently labelled a *denominational sect*, suggesting that they are verging on being considered a conventional Christian denomination. The Jehovah's Witnesses are considered an *established sect* because of the magnitude of the tension that continues to exist between them and the societies in which they reside.

The Seventh Day Adventists and the Jehovah's Witnesses are just two of the thousands of sects that exist throughout the world. Because of the similarities in their origins, contrasting these two sects is particularly useful in demonstrating the diversity that exists among the sects of the world, as well as the variations in the degree of tension different sects have with the larger society. The belief system and the practices of the sects themselves contribute to that level of tension; however, the tension is not solely the result of characteristics of the sects. It is also a product of characteristics of the wider society, such as the way authorities have interacted with the sects and the public attitudes towards those sects. Tension emerges from *bi*-directional processes, in that sects may have certain levels of antagonism toward society, but society may have certain levels of antagonism toward particular sects. Furthermore, existing hostilities in society toward specific religious groups may actually contribute to greater polarization of a sect's belief system and even more separation from the outside world. When a "deviant" group becomes even more deviant as a response to hostilities or social control efforts from outsiders, this is referred to as **deviancy amplification** (Becker, 1963).

Although the tensions between different sects and the sociocultural environment vary considerably, some degree of tension must exist for a religious group to be considered a sect rather than a church. Tension is also characteristic of the types of religious groups known as *cults*. When looking at cults, the tensions with the wider society are typically of an even greater magnitude, especially in the realm of public attitudes. Simply mentioning the word "cult" fuels a flood of images in most people's minds, more so than when the word "sect" is mentioned.

TIME TO REVIEW:

- Does the level of tension between sects and the wider society vary? Explain.
- What three characteristics of sects determine the level of tension?
- In what way do those three characteristics differ for the Seventh Day Adventists and the Jehovah's Witnesses, and why?
- How are the two sects mentioned above differentially categorized now as a result of these differences?
- How is tension the product of a bi-directional relationship? How does "deviancy amplification" fit in?

Cults

Your thoughts about cults likely draw heavily upon the media, particularly news stories or documentaries about specific cults. When cults are covered in the media, it is usually because some sensationalistic incident has occurred, such as the mass suicides of the People's Temple cult in Guyana in 1978, the Solar Temple in Canada and Switzerland in 1994, and the Heaven's Gate in the United States in 1997. You might also recall the storming of the Branch Davidians' compound in Waco, Texas, by the American government in 1993, or the allegations of the sexual abuse of children in various cults throughout the late 1980s and early 1990s. These are the kind of cults that are typically represented in the media—doomsday suicide cults and cults that engage in various criminal activities, such as the sexual abuse of children. Wright (1997) explains the selective and distorted coverage of cults as the result of: (a) a lack of accurate or in-depth knowledge about cults and the groups in question; (b) the use of biased sources of information (e.g., ex-members of cults rather than social scientists who conduct research on cults); and (c) limited time or financial resources, resulting in the tendency to overreport sensationalistic stories in the beginning but then ignore later developments. Sensationalist language is used to attract an audience, language that frequently disparages cult members. For example, after the Heaven's Gate mass suicide in 1997, news stories referred to the leader as "loony" and "crazy," while headlines screamed, "UFO Wackos Blasted Off with Vodka and Pills" (Hoffman & Burke, 1997, p. 63). More than 2000 different groups exist in the United States alone, and, of these, only a handful have been involved with violence—but every single cult within this handful received abundant media coverage (Bromley & Melton, 2002). The thousands of other cults in the world, those that lead quiet, non-criminal lives, having little conflict with their sociocultural environment, never reach public attention to influence our images of what cults are like (Jenkins, 2000; Wright, 1997).

Ask Yourself:

When you think of "cults," what images or ideas come to mind? Whom do you see as belonging to cults? What do you imagine their leaders to be like? What actions are carried out within the cults you are thinking about?

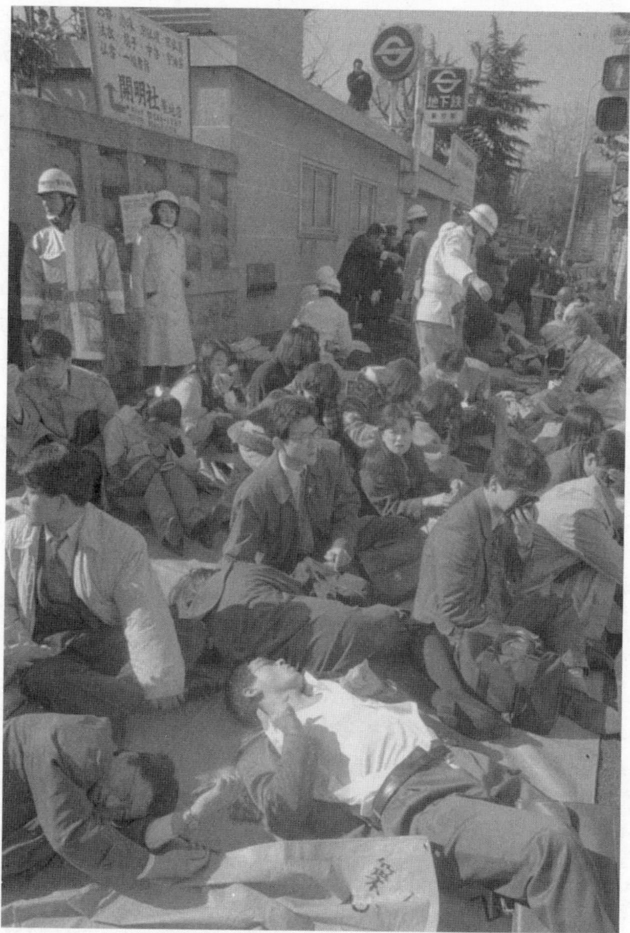

In 1995, 12 people were killed and thousands were injured when members of Aum Shinrikyô, a Japanese cult with Christian and Buddhist foundations, released Sarin nerve gas in the Tokyo subway. Incidents like this one strongly influence public perceptions about cults.

Consequently, public perceptions of cults are that they are dangerous to themselves, to other individuals, and to society (Melton & Bromley, 2002; Chryssides, 1996; Hoffman & Burke, 1997; Anthony & Robbins, 1994; Wright, 1997). In the public mind, cults are associated with mind control, violence, mental illness, sexual deviance, and the sexual abuse of children. People believe that cults effectively carry out mind control using secretive techniques unique to cults, and that as a result cult members may behave uncharacteristically during altered mental states, when they are incapable of rational thought (Anthony & Robbins, 1994). Violence is commonly perceived as pervasive in cults (Melton & Bromley,

2002), either against themselves, such as with mass suicides (e.g., Heaven's Gate), or against others (e.g., Aum Shinrikyô). They are also perceived as provoking opponents into acts of violence, such as in the Waco standoff between the Branch Davidians and American federal authorities. Sexual deviance has been considered characteristic of cults for more than a century, stimulated by groups advocating polygamous marriage and "free love" between all members of the group (Jenkins, 2000). Children have frequently been viewed as victims of cults. "Satanic" cults have been accused of sacrificing unbaptized babies, and cults of all forms have been associated with the ritual abuse of children, including sexual abuse (Nathan & Snedeker, 1995; deYoung, 1998; Richardson, Best, & Bromley, 1991).

Concerns over the ritual abuse of children emerged with the McMartin preschool case in California in 1984, when authorities charged that hundreds of children attending this preschool were sexually abused as part of the rituals of a Satanic cult. A moral panic followed, bringing forward more than 100 other cases of ritualistic abuse within schools and day cares in the ensuing months and years—all the way from California to Martensville, Saskatchewan. Almost all of these cases, including the McMartin preschool case, turned out to be unfounded. Investigators were accused of having posed extremely leading questions to very young children, and the various groups involved in the perpetuation of this moral panic were criticized for ignoring systematic, empirical studies, preferring to believe folklore (Jenkins, 2000; deYoung, 1998). By the end of the 1980s, the concept of pervasive Satanic abuse of children was debunked, and the moral panic ceased. However, concerns about sexual abuse and sexual deviance in cults today continue, as the description of the Family of Love in Box 8.1 illustrates (Lewis & Melton, 1994; Kent, 1994; Bainsbridge, 2002):

Box 8.1 The Family Of Love

The Family of Love, formerly known as the Children of God (and now calling itself "the Family" more generally), is a group that has been a target of attention for cult watchers and investigators for more than 30 years. Its founder, David "Moses" Berg, brought together a group of young hippies in the late 1960s, based on his revelation from God that he would be the prophet who would play the key role in the second coming of Jesus Christ. Members fully devoted themselves to the group by abandoning all ties with their families, giving up all personal possessions, and evangelizing. Although they first lived on several communes throughout the United States, a revelation that the nation would be destroyed for its impurity led Berg to disperse all of the group's members to countries around the world. There, they continued their attempts to recruit new converts.

Controversy surrounded many of Berg's teachings, such as his concept of *flirty fishing*. Because Jesus was referred to as a "fisher of men," Berg claimed that the women in the group should also be "fishers of men," seducing and offering sexual favours to men they would meet, in attempts to recruit new members. *Sexual sharing* was another component of Berg's doctrine; sex was to be freely shared among members of the group (except between two men). Whether sex was to be freely shared between adults and children within the group is a matter of debate. Analyses of the group's own newsletters, as well as the testimony of current and former members, points to pedophilia and incest between Berg, his daughters, and granddaughters. However, criminal investigations in a number of different countries have been unable to prove these allegations in court; some civil suits have been successful.

In 1987 Berg officially banned adult-child sex and decreed that offenders would be excommunicated from the group. Flirty fishing has also been officially abandoned, due to the danger of sexually transmitted diseases. However, some researchers suggest that these practices have been removed from the group's official documentation only to prevent further investigation by authorities, and that the practices actually continue (e.g., Kent, 1994). Although Berg died in 1994, the Family is alive and well, claiming more than 12 000 members worldwide. They present musical performances at youth shelters and women's shelters free of charge, and participate in humanitarian efforts following natural disasters and in Third World countries.

The public concerns that emerge as a consequence of popular images of cults are not entirely unfounded. Sexual behaviours that violate cultural norms do occur in some cults, as illustrated with the *sexual sharing* and *flirty fishing* that characterizes the Family (i.e., the Children of God). These practices violate the norms of many cultures, especially those having more conservative sexual cultures (e.g., India). Some former child members of certain cults were sexually or physically abused as children, although this is not as common as popular images may suggest. Violence can emerge with some cults that have apocalyptic or doomsday visions, especially when latent tensions between those groups and societal authorities intensify, their respective beliefs become more polarized, and third parties are unable or unwilling to mediate the conflict (Bromley, 2002; Hall, 2002). Within some groups, the leaders are able to effectively influence members' thoughts (Stark & Bainbridge, 1996), such that they are willing to engage in mass suicide. For example, an analysis of the mass suicides of the Solar Temple (1994), People's Temple (1978), and Heaven's Gate (1997) reveals parallels in the beliefs that came to permeate all of these groups, beliefs that the majority of members came to accept as the "truth" (Introvigne & Mayer, 2002). First, they believed that they did not belong in this world any longer, that they were destined to be somewhere else, somewhere better. Second, they felt increasingly isolated and estranged from the larger society, as though they did not fit in anywhere. Third, they thought society was persecuting them, denigrating their beliefs, and trying to destroy their groups; society consisted of hostile outsiders who were a threat to them and everything they believed in. Finally, the combination of these types of beliefs generated one final conviction—the rules of the hostile society and the increasingly distant world did not apply to them. These beliefs open the door for the kinds of mass suicides we hear about in the media.

Although there is some foundation to the images of cults that saturate popular images, such as mass suicide, violence, mind control, child abuse, and sexual deviance, these qualities are characteristic of only a small proportion of the thousands of groups in the world that are considered "cults." Cults are characterized by diversity in beliefs and practices, as well as the level of overt tension that exists with society, just as sects are. However, popular images of cults and the resulting public attitudes contribute to more of an overriding tension for cults. For both cults and sects, these tensions are played out in the "deviance dance"—the various means of social control of these deviant religions, and the corresponding resistance to those means of control.

TIME TO REVIEW:

- How are cults represented in the media, and what factors contribute to these representations?
- What are cults typically associated with in the public mind? Are these images accurate?
- Who are the Family, and what aspects of their belief system have been the most criticized?
- When is violence more likely to emerge with cults?
- What beliefs are shared among members of cults that commit mass suicides?

Cults, Sects, and the "Deviance Dance"

Controlling "Deviant" Religions

The international community has repeatedly declared the importance of religious freedom; many people see it as the foundation for all human rights. The *United Nations' Universal Declaration of Human Rights*, created in 1948 and signed by more than 100 countries around the world (including Canada), states that freedom of thought, conscience, and religious belief and practice are fundamental human rights. In the ensuing decades, that document was followed by numerous others that reiterated the same idea. Most notably, two decades after the United Nations declaration, the *International Covenant on Civil and Political Rights (CCPR)* made the guarantee of religious freedom legally binding upon all of its signatories. These international documents were the underpinning for changes to constitutional documents (or their equivalents) in countries around the world. The slogan of the group Forum 18, a worldwide network of non-governmental organizations focusing on religious freedom, captures the essence of this human right:

"The right to believe, to worship and witness. The right to change one's belief or religion. The right to join together and express one's belief." (Forum 18, 2001, p.1)

Despite the recognition of religious freedom as a fundamental human right, this right is not unbridled. Threats to public health, public order, and infringement on the rights of others constitute valid reasons for governments to violate religious freedom, according to the international declarations and the documents that mirror them in most individual nations. These caveats to freedom of religion serve as the basis for the various measures of social control that target sects and cults.

During the 20th century, a number of social organizations emerged in response to the perceived problems caused by "deviant" religions. Acting as *moral entrepreneurs* who have identified a significant social problem, they apply various measures in their efforts to control "deviant" religions. In particular, during the late 1960s and early 1970s, the **anti-cult movement** materialized (Jenkins, 2000; Bromley & Shupe, 1993; Shupe & Bromley, 1995). Initially, it consisted of parents whose hippie children had joined small, new religious groups that were part of the broader countercultural movement. Concerned about the way their children had severed ties with their families, the brainwashing that they thought was occurring, and the deviant behaviours they feared their children would be led into, parents coalesced into support groups. Media stories about violent activities carried out by some of these new cults, such as the infamous murders committed by members of the Manson "family," seemed to validate their concerns. These support groups later became information networks working towards making other parents aware of the dangers of these new religious groups. Over time numerous mental health, legal, and political professionals, along with academic researchers, became involved in many of the anti-cult groups, and representatives became the "experts" featured in media stories about cults. Some of these anti-cult groups offered services to parents, such as psychologists who would "de-program" their children who had left the cults; a few groups even provided services for kidnapping the children from the cult environments in order to forcibly de-program them. Anti-cult groups today, or what Barker (2001) calls **cult awareness groups**, engage in measures to warn everyone about the dangers of cults, and to control their activities through lobbying governments and other organizations. The anti-cult movement targets only certain religious groups, those considered to be "destructive cults"; in fact, the word "cult" is used within this movement to refer specifically to those religious groups that have dangerous or destructive characteristics. A summary of some of these "warning signs" can be found in Box 8.2 (American Family Foundation, 2003; Fight Against Coercive Tactics Network, 2003; Ontario Consultants for Religious Freedom, 2003).

Box 8.2 Characteristics of Destructive Cults

Although there is some disagreement over precisely what the characteristics of "dangerous" cults are, there are some common "warning signs" that are pointed out by various organizations:

- The leader of the cult places the group above the law, telling members that they are not bound by the same laws that outsiders are.

- The leader does not have to follow the same rules as the rest of the cult members.
- The leader exerts control beyond the realm of religious doctrine, extending control to members' personal lives, such as whom to marry and whether to go to college.
- "Mind control" techniques are used on members to facilitate indoctrination.
- The group follows a formal or informal policy of deceiving outsiders when recruiting, fundraising, or answering to societal authorities.
- The group is based on an apocalyptic vision in which the cult will play a key role. For example, the group may stockpile weapons to prepare for a battle with outsiders when Armageddon arrives.

Although the anti-cult movement is a relatively recent construction, the **counter-cult movement** is noticeably older, going back more than a century (Bromley & Shupe, 1993; Ontario Consultants for Religious Freedom, 2003; Cowan, 2001; Melton, 2000; Barker, 2001). Unlike the anti-cult movement, this movement does not base its philosophy on the internationally recognized legitimate limits to religious freedom discussed earlier. In fact, members of the counter-cult movement are overwhelmingly opposed to religious freedom itself. These groups primarily consist of conservative Christians drawn from evangelical and fundamentalist denominations. They are not concerned about the possibility of brainwashing or abuse in cults, but instead express a theological concern about groups utilizing the "wrong" interpretation of the Bible. Any religious group that does not follow fundamentalist, evangelical Christian doctrine is labelled a "cult." Thus, not only are the groups that are commonly categorized as sects or cults targets of the counter-cult movement's control efforts, so are mainstream Christian religions (e.g., Catholicism) and all Eastern religions (e.g., Hindu, Islam, Buddhism). Franklin Graham (son of the well-known evangelist Billy Graham) referred to Islam as a "wicked and evil" religion, Jerry Vines (former president of the Southern Baptist Convention) called Islam's prophet Muhammad "a demon-possessed pedophile" (Goodstein, 2003), and Pat Robertson blamed the poverty in nations like India and Bangledesh on the demonic cults of Islam, Buddhism, and Hinduism (Viujst, 1995). Counter-cult groups engage in measures to eliminate "deviant" religions, such as lobbying governments and law enforcement officials to enforce the law harshly against target religions, in a larger attempt to recruit converts to their own religious groups. However, due to some of the negative perceptions that fundamentalist and evangelical Christian religious groups themselves face in society, their lobbying efforts are not as successful as those of the secular anti-cult movement. Consequently, the counter-cult movement tends to operate on a less formal level, within communities. They also make extensive use of the Internet to spread the "truth" about deviant religions as they know it, something they share in common with anti-cult groups (Dawson & Henneby, 1999).

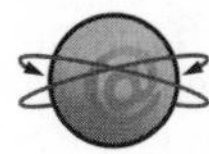

AN INTERNET MOMENT:

Websites for cult awareness groups (i.e., the anti-cult movement) and counter-cult groups are easily found on the Internet. The largest and most influential cult awareness group is the American Family Foundation (http://www.csj.org). Their Website is extensive, and includes information for professionals working with former cult members, support to family members, and access to the peer-reviewed, academic "Cultic Studies Journal." The largest counter-cult group is the Watchman Fellowship (http://watchman.org). Their Website provides information on which religious groups are actually "cults," in their eyes, and offers documents for individuals who would like to learn how to convince members of particular "cults" to leave. A comparison of these two Websites clearly illustrates the different ideological foundations of the anti-cult and counter-cult movements, as well as the activities they engage in as part of their social control of "deviant" religions. You will find these two Websites fascinating!

In addition to the Internet, the media is fundamental to many of the efforts of anti-cult and counter-cult groups. The relationship between these groups and the media is bi-directional. At times, these groups may use the media as tools for enhancing their control efforts, but the media also draw upon the "expertise" of members of these groups when covering news stories that may involve cults (Jenkins, 2000; Crouch & Damphousse, 1992; Bartowski, 1998). However, the "experts" that the media utilize are usually not the members of academia that study these religious groups, but rather former cult members, parents of cult members, and "cult cops" (Crouch & Damphousse, 1992, p. 15). Former cult members and parents of cult members lend additional drama to the story, while police experts (i.e., "cult cops") lend legitimacy. Unfortunately, at times the perspectives of these media "experts" may be uninformed, or even biased. Former cult members and parents of cult members may have only the narrow view of their own experiences, which may be contradicted by research. The training of "cult cops" is tremendously diverse; although some might have undergone in-depth training that includes knowledge of the research, others might not have any specialized training at all. Furthermore, research has found that some of these law enforcement officials who specialize in cults share the religious views of the counter-cult movement, scoring higher on measures of religiosity (and fundamentalist religiosity) than police officers as a whole (Crouch & Damphousse, 1991, 1992; Victor, 1990; Hicks, 1990). When law enforcement officials who have these kinds of beliefs are the "experts" utilized by the media, the counter-cult movement is able to indirectly widen the influence of its social control efforts.

Independent of the anti-cult and counter-cult movements, the media contains its own representations of "deviant" religions. The underlying profit motive of the media, with its corresponding need to attract larger audiences than competitors are able to, contributes to distorted and sensationalized coverage of news incidents involving cults or their slightly less "deviant" companions, sects (Wright, 1997). The role of the media in the creation of moral panics has been analyzed in the context of the Satanic scare of the 1980s (discussed earlier in this chapter) (deYoung, 1998; Jenkins, 2000; Crouch & Damphousse, 1992), the standoff between the Branch Davidians and federal authorities in Waco (Shupe & Hadden, 1996), and the deviantizing of voodoo (Bartowski, 1998).

In addition to a relationship with the media, anti-cult and counter-cult groups influence governments to create legislation, policies, and programs that will curb the destructive nature of "deviant" religions. When governments do enact legislation or alternative forms of policy, it is often under the rubric of the exceptions to religious freedom stated in international and constitutional types of documents—threats to public health, public order, and the rights of others (Forum 18, 2001; US Department of State, 2002). Determining at what point governmental measures of control can be enacted without violating the right to religious freedom is an especially gray area in those nations that declare an official separation of Church and State. Thus, in many Western nations, efforts are directed at those religious groups commonly recognized as sects and cults. For example, the Canadian Security Intelligence Service (CSIS) monitors doomsday/apocalyptic cults, those whose members may commit mass suicide (e.g., Solar Temple) or inflict mass harm (e.g., Aum Shinrikyô); in the United States, the FBI does the same thing. The actions of some nations, however, are not without controversy. In the late 1990s, the government of France formed the Interministerial Mission on the Fight against Sects/Cults (MILS) to monitor and control the 173 groups identified as sects or cults in a 1996 government report—groups like the Church of Scientology, the Jehovah's Witnesses, Latter Day Saints (i.e., "Mormons"), and doomsday cults. After certain groups were forced to disband, and members of other groups were arrested for violating the new related pieces of legislation, the European Court overturned many convictions upon appeal. Measures undertaken by the German government have also raised questions in the international community and among religious freedom advocates. Germany is in an ongoing struggle to make the Church of Scientology in particular an illegal organization. *Sect filters* are used by local governments in many areas, as well as by some private firms, in weeding out Scientologists in hiring and awarding contracts (US Department of State, 2002).

Concerns about violations of religious freedom at the hands of government are of considerable interest to the international community. The US Department of State (via the Bureau of Democracy, Human Rights and Labor) releases an annual report on the state of religious freedom in the world, as does the international advocacy group Forum 18 (which includes a wide range of groups, including the renowned Max Planck Institute in Germany). Each year, organizations like these document violations of religious freedom in specific countries, and the measures being taken to improve religious freedom in other countries. Five barriers to religious freedom throughout the world have been identified (US Department of State, 2002), barriers based on governmental measures that not only socially control those groups considered "sects" and "cults" according to academic definitions, but many other religious groups as well.

First, some governments exert *authoritarian measures to control religious beliefs and practices*. This is currently occurring in countries like China, Cuba, and Vietnam. For example, under China's Religious Affairs Bureau, religious beliefs and groups are divided into three categories (Forum 18, 2001). Communism is declared to be the only *orthodox and legal teaching* in China. Taoism, Buddhism, Islam, Protestantism, and Catholicism are *unorthodox but legal religious groups*. All other religious groups, including Christian sects, are categorized as *heterodox and illegal religious groups*; their members are subject to harassment, arrest, imprisonment, and even death. The politically active meditation-based group "Falun Gong" has had tens of thousands of its members arrested in the last few years, and thousands of them have died while in prison. The government monitors the "unorthodox but legal" religious groups; all of their activities are monitored, people who want to be baptized are kept track of, and their religious leaders must be approved or selected by the government. Despite the fact that they are recognized as legal groups, their presence is unwelcome in the officially atheist state, and several mosques and temples have been closed. Islam is the object of particular disdain, and the law states the government is the only one that can print Islam's religious literature. The Chinese constitution guarantees religious freedom, as international human rights documents do; however, it legitimizes its actions on the basis of threats to the public order and public health. The right to religious freedom does not extend to children under the age of 18, and anyone who teaches anything other than Communism to children is subject to arrest. Members of the Communist party are also not entitled to religious freedom, and any member who expresses a religious belief is kicked out of the party.

The second barrier to religious freedom is *hostility toward non-approved religious groups*. In these instances, governments try to intimidate members of these groups so that they will either covert to a state-approved religion, or leave the country altogether. Examples include Iraq under the leadership of Saddam Hussein, Iran, Saudi Arabia, and Uzbekistan. For instance, under the power of the Hussein government, Shi'a Muslims in Iraq were arrested, leaders were executed, mosques were desecrated, and their religious broadcasts were banned from national radio and television (US Department of State, 2002).

The third barrier emerges due to *state neglect of the problem of discrimination against non-approved religions*, such as in Guatemala, India, and Nigeria. In these kinds of countries, although laws may exist that prohibit discrimination based on religious beliefs and practices, the government does not actually enforce those laws. In Guatemala, the spiritual practices of the indigenous Mayan, Garifuna, and Xinca groups, although protected by law, continue to be persecuted due to a lack of policing (US Department of State, 2002).

The fourth barrier to religious freedom is *discriminatory legislation or policies disadvantaging certain religions*, for example in Israel and Russia (US Department of State, 2002). In Russia, seventy years of Communist rule made Russia an officially atheist state. Following the fall of Communism, Russian leaders feared that naïve citizens were at risk of being lured into "deviant" sects and cults, because of their lack of religious knowledge. Consequently, the government declared Christianity, Buddhism, Judaism, and Islam as the country's official religions, but gave local authorities control over which religious groups would be legal, and which would be labelled "cults." Those determined to be cults "must register with the government and meet a long list of requirements to win the right to meet, rent property or even hand out leaflets" (Webster, 2001, p. 28). Jehovah's Witnesses, the Church of Scientology, the Baptist church, the Pentecostal church, and even the Salvation Army have been labelled "cults," and made subject to strict controls (Webster, 2001).

The fifth barrier to religious freedom is the *stigmatization of certain religions by wrongfully associating them with dangerous "cults" or "sects"* (US Department of State, 2002). The controversial policies recently created in Belgium, France, and Germany are examples of this barrier. Human rights groups and cult defender groups, active in countries throughout the world (Barker, 2001), are just some of the many groups engaged in ongoing efforts to have these government policies revoked.

TIME TO REVIEW:

- How has the concept of religious freedom entered the international community, and what are the exceptions to religious freedom?
- In what ways do the anti-cult movement and counter-cult movement differ, in terms of (a) who their members are, (b) their ideologies, and (c) which religious groups they target in the efforts as moral entrepreneurs? What techniques do they use?
- In what ways does the media engage in the social control of deviant religions, both in terms of its relationship with anti-cult and counter-cult movements, as well as independently of those movements?
- What are some examples of governmental controls of "deviant" religions? Why are these governmental controls frequently monitored and questioned?
- What are the five barriers to religious freedom throughout the world?

Resisting a Deviant Label

Anti-cult groups, counter-cult groups, the media, and governments all act as social control agents in minimizing the perceived dangers of "deviant" religions. However, their efforts are counteracted, to some extent, by acts of resistance. The right to religious freedom is an international concept that serves as a nexus for many of these measures of resistance, but the social typing of "deviant" religions is resisted in numerous other ways as well. Individual religious groups defend themselves against accusations of deviance, both inside and outside of court. For example, individuals and groups targeted for control under France's new anti-sect laws have taken their cases all the way to the highest European Court, and have frequently won their cases (Forum 18, 2001; US Department of State, 2002). The Seventh Day Adventists hired public relations people during the standoff between the Branch Davidians and federal authorities in Waco, because they wanted to make it clear to the public (via the media) that the Branch Davidians were a "cult" that had distorted Seventh Day Adventist teachings, and were in no way representative of the larger group (Lawson, 1995). "The Family" not only defended itself in court cases and child custody hearings against allegations of sexual abuse, it also (a) changed its publications to remove any portions that might be perceived as indicating approval of pedophilia, (b) issued a statement declaring sexual relations between adults and children in the group was forbidden, and (c) tried to improve the group's image, by highlighting its humanitarian efforts on its Website and within the community (Lewis & Melton, 1994, Kent, 1994, Bainbridge, 2002). Individual groups also resist the social typing process by continuing to recruit new members. A number of religious groups make use of Internet Websites in this regard, although they are not as successful with their Internet use as the anti-cult and counter-cult movements are (Chryssides, 1996; Dawson & Henneby, 1999).

One of the most significant forms of resistance to the social typing of "deviant" religious groups comes, not from the groups themselves, but rather academia. The traditional distinction among ecclesia, churches, sects, and cults was used for most of the 20th century. The distinctions among these different types of religious groups were not questioned, although sometimes debates would emerge about how a specific religion should be categorized. However, as time progressed, questions about these distinctions were raised and criticisms grew. Ecclesias were easily recognized, in that "official" state religions are identified in legislation. By contrast, with continued discussion it became evident that the boundaries between churches, sects, and cults may not be as definitive as they seem.

What Are "Deviant" Religions? The Traditional Distinction Reconsidered

As you were reading through the chapter thus far, you might have already begun to feel somewhat confused about what "deviant" religions actually are. We began with academic definitions of "cults" and "sects," but then as the chapter progressed we saw that different kinds of religious groups were labelled in this way at various times. The anti-cult movement prefaces the term "cult" with the descriptor "destructive," emphasizing only those groups that have certain characteristics, such as mind control or "brainwashing." Critics now even question whether "brainwashing" is a scientific reality (e.g., Richardson, 1995; Richardson & Introvigne, 2001). The counter-cult movement uses the term "cult" to refer to the theology of certain religious groups—that which does not adhere to fundamentalist Christian doctrine. Thus, their use of the word "cult" can refer to mainstream Christian religious groups (e.g., Catholics), as well as all non-Western religions (e.g., Islam, Buddhism). When the media uses the word "cult," we saw that it usually does so in the context of a distorted image of cults—those religious groups involved in destructive events captured in the news, such as the Waco standoff, the Heaven's Gate mass suicide, or the release of poisonous gas in the Tokyo subway. Finally, we saw that in an international context any religious groups that a particular government does not approve of are categorized as "cults." This includes groups like the Family, Jehovah's Witnesses, and Scientology, but also groups that are typically seen as conventional and mainstream, such as the Salvation Army, Islam, and the Baptist church.

The boundaries between churches, sects, and cults become blurred even further when we incorporate a historical perspective. All of the world's major religions, now categorized as "churches," began as "cults"—a small group of highly committed members who were following a single-charismatic leader, and whose doctrine was an oppositional one in the context of a society's conventional belief system at the time (Jenkins, 2000; Hadden & Bromley, 1995). As these major religions became more established and attracted larger numbers of members they progressed from being "cults," to "sects," and finally to "churches." In fact, many "sects" become recognized as denominations of major churches over time, just as it appears the Seventh Day Adventists may be doing, as we saw earlier in the chapter. The Church of Jesus Christ of Latter Day Saints (frequently referred to as "Mormons") are usually categorized as a "sect." However, with almost 12 million members worldwide (more than many recognized "denominations" have), the Mormon church, many people would argue, should more logically be considered a denomination of the Christian church (Church of Jesus Christ of Latter Day Saints, 2003).

Even when we temporarily set aside the debates over which groups are "cults" or "sects," the notion of "deviant" religions crosses all boundaries. Every religious belief system in the world has been considered "deviant" at some time, in some place. There is no group of religious believers that has not been persecuted at some moment in history, perceived as "evil," dangerous, or a threat to the social order. This is most evident in looking at the former Soviet Union, where *all* religion was prohibited, but is also apparent when looking at the progression of history—the Crusades, the current Israel/Palestine conflicts, the bloodshed between Protestants and Catholics in Europe for hundreds of years, the religious dimension of European colonization of indigenous peoples throughout the world, and more.

For all of these reasons, many contemporary academics have abandoned the traditional terminology, and instead use more encompassing terms, such as "ideological groups." Some scholars who wish to distinguish the world's major religions from more recent religious groups that may exist in some tension with society use the term **new religious movements** (Chryssides, 1994; Jenkins, 2000). Although some scholars find the traditional typology valid and continue to use it for various reasons, a historical and global perspective shows us that *any* religion can be socially typed as "deviant" and made subject to measures of social control.

TIME TO REVIEW:

- In what ways have "deviant" religious groups themselves acted in resistance to social typing?
- What limitations are there in the traditional typology that distinguishes between churches, sects, and cults?
- Why can we say that any religion can be socially typed as deviant and made subject to social control efforts?

Religion as a Social Typer of Deviance

While various religions have been socially typed as deviant at different times and in different places, religious belief systems also play a role in the social typing *of* deviance. That is, their proclamations of "truth" incorporate moral "truths" as well, dictums of what is considered "right" and "wrong." At the individual level, the religious belief systems we adhere to present us with guidelines for our own behaviour. Some religious groups prohibit the use of caffeine, alcohol, tobacco, or drugs (e.g., Latter Day Saints). Others dictate rules about appropriate and inappropriate foods (e.g., Seventh Day Adventists; Judaism; Hinduism). Religious doctrine may dictate aspects of dress (e.g., Sikhism; Islam) or restrict the use of certain medical treatments (e.g., Jehovah's Witnesses). Behavioural guidelines may govern marriage, sexual relations, and parenting. These individual influences may be direct, such as through explicit directives contained within the doctrine, but may also be indirect, through a broad general influence that the belief system has. Empirically, religiosity has been found to influence behaviours as diverse as smoking (Bush et al., 2003) and use of contraception (Orji & Onwudiegwu, 2002) in many different cultures. Among American high school students, positive attitudes toward their religions and regular religious attendance are related to less drug use, fewer school attendance problems, positive attitudes toward parental involvement, better grades, and positive attitudes toward school (Trust & Watts, 1999). When shared religious beliefs contribute to the formation of a moral community, religiosity is related to lower rates of criminality (Stark, Doyle, & Kent, 1982).

Not only do the moral "truths" contained within religious beliefs systems influence the behaviour of followers, they also dictate to followers how they should evaluate and deal with the behaviours of others. For example, our earlier exploration of the Jehovah's Witnesses revealed that within the belief system other religions, the government, and patriotic symbols are evaluated negatively (Lawson, 1995). We also saw that leaders of the Christian Right have recently indicated that Islam is a "wicked and evil" religion, and the prophet Muhammad was a "demon-possessed pedophile" (Goodstein, 2003); followers of Islam have also had negative labels visibly attached by these religious leaders. The judgments of other people's behaviours and beliefs are not always as overtly stated as in the above examples. More indirectly, the same moral guidelines that influence our own behaviours have an impact on our evaluations of other people's behaviours. And even more broadly, our religious belief systems influence the way we approach the events of the day, and the way we interact with people. For example, if you adhere to a religious belief system that has the characteristics of love and kindness as its foundation, that will govern your interactions with others.

Beyond the individual level, religious belief systems may also serve as social typers of deviance at the societal level. This is of particular interest when the boundaries between religious and political belief systems become blurred; that is, when a particular religious belief system becomes institutionalized by the gov-

Its belief system established as "law," the Christian church was central to the persecution of witches from the 14th to the 17th centuries.

ernment, and serves as the foundation for the construction of governmental policy and law. Those people and behaviours considered "deviant" according to religious beliefs thereby become the people and behaviours considered "deviant" at the political level. Historically, the witch persecutions that occurred throughout much of Europe during the late Middle Ages and early Renaissance are a classic example of the lack of boundaries between religious and political belief systems.

Religion and Politics in History

The Witch Persecutions

During the Middle Ages and the Renaissance, the Christian church was essentially the core of government in Europe. It either served as the main governing body itself, or acted in a key advisory capacity for governing bodies (such as monarchs) in virtually all of Europe. Thus, its belief system was the foundation for law and governance. It was in this capacity that the "witchcraze" occurred (Anderson & Gordon, 1978; Barstow, 1994; Quaife, 1987).

It is estimated that from the 14th through the 17th centuries, more than 100 000 "witches" were persecuted, sometimes by being burned at the stake. One of the best known was Joan of Arc, who was convicted of witchcraft and burned at the stake in 1431. Witches were declared to be in league with Satan, and responsible for plagues, floods, stillborn children, infertility, crop failures, and more.

Those accused of witchcraft included a wide range of people, the list growing larger as the witchcraze snowballed and became more extreme. Followers of the pre-Christian religions (now frequently referred to as Paganism) were suspect in their refusal to convert to Christianity (although many people combined Christian and Pagan beliefs). Women who violated new cultural norms were suspect—those who were financially independent, those who met with other women after dark, those who outlived their husbands, and others. Midwives were suspect, because in their use of herbs and other natural techniques they eased the pain of childbirth; according to church doctrine at the time, this violated God's plan, because the pain of childbirth was women's punishment for Eve's sin in the Garden of Eden. Village "wisewomen," who used herbs in healing illness and injury, were frequently accused of witchcraft. In some regions laws were passed stating that no one who had not formally studied could practice medicine (such as in the use of herbs). Since women were prohibited from attending universities, this guaranteed prosecution for many village wisewomen. The majority of people prosecuted as witches were women (75–85%); however, some men, children, and even animals were prosecuted. At the peak of the witchcraze, *anyone* could potentially be accused of witchcraft (except for church leaders); all it would take was a report from a disgruntled neighbour.

Once arrested, torture was used to elicit confessions. The torture was so horrendous (e.g., having one's toenails pulled out, being stretched on "the rack"), many people did confess. The content of their confessions was virtually guaranteed, given that a handbook (the *Malleus Maleficarum*) had been written with approval by the Pope in 1486 about how to question and torture witches. The nature of the questions asked typically led to specific types of responses, and torture would progress until that point. Upon being found guilty, the witch was put to death via hanging, decapitation, burning at the stake, or other means. With the invention of the printing press, church documents about the "witch problem" flooded the educated classes. Various witch-hunting manuals, church sermons, and pamphlets made people aware of the extent of the problem, frequently exaggerating the magnitude of persecution in order to gain more support and strike more fear into the populace.

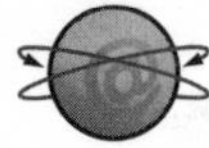

AN INTERNET MOMENT:

The Malleus Maleficarum (translated into English) can be found in its entirety as http://www.malleusmaleficarum.org. This book outlines the religious and pragmatic rationales for hunting witches, and the step-by-step process for arresting, trying, questioning, torturing, and killing the accused witches. The site contains a search engine for the document as well.

The witchcraze was not a uniform phenomenon throughout Europe. Witch trials occurred far more often in some countries (e.g., France, Germany) than in others. In some regions, the Christian church was directly responsible for the arrest and trial of the witches, while in other regions it was local authorities that hunted and tried them. In these latter instances, even though the church was not directly involved, church doctrine provided the theological foundation for persecution. Witch persecutions frequently followed peasant rebellions against the political elite, or preceded them in an attempt to distract peasants from rebellion. Witch hunts also occurred in regions where intense Protestant-Catholic conflicts emerged, as each side used the trials to demonstrate their religious dominance. The witch persecutions gradually removed the existing status and power of women as well, as female subordination to men was an essential component of the religious belief system at the time. As Quaife (1987, p. 208) concludes, the witch-hunts were the result "of either the godly zeal of the political and religious elite and their peasant allies or the furious rage of her discomforted and ill-fortuned neighbours." As political change progressed, as Christian doctrine was transformed, and as philosophical and scientific ideas grew, the witch hunts faded away. But for those few hundred years religious belief systems were the foundation of political belief systems, with the end result in this particular instance being the loss of more than 100 000 lives.

Residential Schooling

Following the colonization of North American by Europeans, the colonizing governments began to establish a long list of laws and policies designed to assimilate the Aboriginal people. An "apple" analogy was used, meaning that they would still be "red" on the outside, but would be "white" on the inside. An integral part of the assimilation process was "christianizing" natives (Miller, 1996; Milloy, 1999;

Fournier & Crey, 1998). Every aspect of Aboriginal cultures was perceived as "deviant" and in need of elimination. Efforts on this front began when, upon settlement, Christian missionaries were among the first Europeans sent to North America. At a later point, laws prohibiting various Aboriginal spiritual practices were enacted; spiritual leaders faced up to 30 years in prison for violating some of these laws. In 1879, the Canadian government adopted a **residential schooling** policy that it hoped would guarantee assimilation. Aboriginal children would be removed from their homes and families and taken to residential boarding schools, where they would be given an education—not only in reading, writing, and arithmetic, but also in Christianity and learning to act "white." Taking children from their homes would remove the "heathen" influence, and facilitate greater assimilation. Residential schools were a part of government policy, and were funded by the government, but were operated by Christian churches. Residential schooling occurred for more than a century, beginning in 1879; approximately 160 000 children went through these schools.

One of the mandates of the residential schools was to provide Aboriginal children with an education so that they would be equipped with the knowledge and skills necessary for success in the industrial economy. In fact, this was the main rationale provided to Aboriginal parents when they were approached to consent to having their children taken. However, consent was not necessary. In many instances, Aboriginal communities that refused to have their children removed were threatened with the loss of government-provided resources, and even arrest. In some instances, government and law enforcement authorities forcibly removed (or kidnapped) the children. Once in the schools, children had their long hair shaved off and their traditional clothes discarded. Although formal education was one of the mandates, in many of the schools the children received formal teaching for only half of the day; for the rest, the children had to engage in physical labour on school grounds or for nearby farmers. But even more important than learning to read, write, and do math was learning to adopt Euro-Canadian beliefs and practices. Any behaviours related to traditional Aboriginal spirituality or culture were prohibited, and children were punished if caught engaging in these behaviours. For many children, what was perceived as punishment was actually physical abuse; furthermore, thousands of children were sexually abused in some of these schools as well. Of the 160 000 children who went to residential schools, 91 000 have reported being physically and/or sexually abused. Psychological abuse is too great to even be estimated. Many children went years without being able to see their parents; some never saw their parents alive again. On a daily basis, many were told that their parents, having not found God, would burn in hell for eternity, as would they if they did not do as they were told.

One of my students told me about her grandfather, who only recently began to talk about his years at a residential school. He arrived there at the age of 8, and upon his arrival was slapped in the face by the minister who ran the school, for having dared to look him in the eye. At the school there were only two sizes of shoes, so that most of the children had to wear shoes that were far too big or far too small. It was more than two years before his mother was able to arrange to visit him, because the school was hundreds of miles away from his community. Before she arrived, he was given instructions for the visit. If he spoke anything other than English, the visit would be ended and he would be punished. His mother did not speak English, so she was unable to understand anything he said. If there was any physical contact between them, the visit would be ended and he would be punished. After more than two years of separation, his mother was unable to even hug her 10-year-old son. The school authorities supervised the entire visit to watch for violations.

In the 1990s government and religious authorities acknowledged the damage caused by the residential schooling initiative, recognizing the high rates of substance abuse, suicide, and family violence, as well as the loss of traditional cultures. The federal government, United Church of Canada, Anglican Church of Canada, and Presbyterian Church of Canada have all issued formal apologies to the Aboriginal people of Canada. The Roman Catholic Church (via the Pope) has apologized for the ethnic and racial injustices inflicted on some groups in the world by members of the Catholic church, but they have not mentioned residential schools specifically, and their apology is directed at God rather than the victims (Ontario Consultants for Religious Tolerance, 2003). The federal government issued a formal apology, stating, in part: "As a country, we are burdened by past actions that resulted in weakening the identity of aboriginal peoples, suppressing their languages and cultures, and outlawing spiritual practices. We must recognize the impact of these actions on the once self-sustaining nations that were disaggregated, disrupted, limited or even destroyed by the dispossession of traditional territory, by the relocation of aboriginal people, and by some provisions of the Indian Act."

The apologies issued by the various churches contain the following types of statements: "We are aware of some of the damage that this cruel and ill-conceived system of assimilation has perpetrated on Canada's First Nations peoples. For this we are truly and most humbly sorry….I am sorry, more than I can say, that we were part of a system which took you and your children from home and family….I am sorry, more than I can say, that we tried to remake you in our image, taking from you your language and the signs of your identity….I am sorry, more than I can say, that in our schools so many were abused physically, sexually, culturally and emotionally" (Ontario Consultants for Religious Tolerance, 2003).

Not only have the government and churches issued formal apologies for residential schooling, they are also offering financial restitution. A number of churches (e.g., the Anglican Church of Canada), in conjunction with Aboriginal communities, are also embarking upon various church and community programs designed to undo some of the damage that was done by residential schooling.

The Victorian Child-Savers

At the same time as residential schooling was being implemented in Canada, the Victorian **child-savers movement** was at its apex, another example of religious belief systems influencing political belief systems. During the late 19th and early 20th centuries, this movement played an essential role in child welfare reforms, compulsory education legislation, prohibition, and many other government policies in Canada, the United States, and Britain (Platt, 1977; Jordon, 1998; Valverde, 1993). An aspect of Protestant theology known as the Social Gospel largely informed the child-savers movement, whereby Christian principles were applied in real-world settings to solve social problems (providing humanitarian aid to the less fortunate in society was seen as one way of achieving salvation). The child-savers consisted primarily of ministers of local churches, and upstanding (primarily female) members of those congregations.

The child-savers were especially interested in the social problems that involved children. The Protestant belief system had recently changed, so that children were now perceived as pure and innocent instead of born in sin. Corruption occurred as a result of children growing up in immoral homes, leading to drunkenness, poverty, and vice. The child-savers thought that is was the state's responsibility to provide a moral environment for children whose parents were unwilling or unable to. Child abuse and neglect was deviantized, and over time, the efforts of the child-savers led to legislation dictating that children whose parents were abusive or neglectful should be removed from their homes. They were placed in foster homes—with morally upstanding families who could teach these children the path to good citizenship and to salvation.

What was the path to citizenship and salvation? It was based on the beliefs and norms of the Protestant middle class. Interpretations of Protestant doctrine at the time suggested that God rewarded strong morality with material success. Thus, the fact that people of the middle class had material success meant that whatever beliefs and norms they adhered to were the "moral" ones, those ordained by God. People who were members of the lower classes, or who lived in poverty, were automatically considered immoral—after all, if they were moral, they would be rewarded by God and would not be lower class! Consequently, simply being of a lower socioeconomic class was automatically considered deviant, and virtually all of the efforts of the child-savers were directed at lower-class families. Since parents of the lower classes were seen as inherently immoral, it was primarily their children who were removed to receive the care of the state. Single mothers, who violated middle-class norms by virtue of being unmarried, were also considered inherently deviant and targeted for social control efforts by the child-savers. Lower-class parents and single mothers were threatened with the removal of their children to motivate them to adopt middle-class beliefs and practices. For many child-saver groups, alcoholism was perceived as the foundation for lower-class immorality. Consequently, there was considerable overlap in membership between the child-savers and the social reformers who led the temperance movement; their efforts eventually resulted in prohibition (discussed in Chapter 1).

Conclusion

A historical perspective provides excellent examples of blurred boundaries between religious and political belief systems. With the witchcraze, residential schooling, and the Victorian child-savers, those behaviours, beliefs, and people that were considered deviant within specific religious belief systems came to be socially typed as deviant within political belief systems as well. As components of religious beliefs were incorporated into the political realm, social control shifted to legislation and other forms of government policy. Looking back, most of us consider what happened during the witch hunts and with residential schooling to be overwhelmingly negative examples of what can happen when religious beliefs serve as the foundation for governance of a society. Perhaps you believe that these two historical events are not only instances of religion serving as a social typer of deviance, but are also examples of *religion as deviance*, wherein religious institutions or their representatives have done something "deviant" themselves. The case of the Victorian child-savers is not as overwhelmingly negative in its outcomes, and instead combines positive and negative aspects. On one hand, part of the movement's foundation did lie in prejudice, based on social characteristics like class, race, and family structure. Movement activists did also attempt to impose their own middle-class norms and values on everyone in society, such as in their efforts at prohibition. On the other hand, they did provide assistance to children who were abused or neglected; their efforts underlie our modern-day child abuse and neglect laws, the child welfare and social assistance systems, and compulsory education for children.

TIME TO REVIEW:

- What role does religion play as a social typer of deviance in terms of individuals' own behaviours, and their evaluations of others?
- What happened during the witchcraze? How did religion serve as a social typer of deviance during this time?
- What was residential schooling? Why was it embarked upon?
- What happened in residential schools? How did religion serve as a social typer of deviance in residential schools?
- How have the federal government and various churches responded to the history of residential schooling?
- Who were the Victorian child-savers? What role did religion play as a social typer of deviance?
- In what way were both positive and negative aspects incorporated into the child-saver movement?

Religion and Politics Today

Perhaps you think that the blurring of religious and political belief systems is something relegated to the distant past, something that occurred when people were less educated, less aware, and less informed. In fact, the influence of religion and politics continues throughout the world today. It is most obvious in those societies we looked at earlier, where the government exerts authoritarian control over religious beliefs and practices, or attempts to intimidate members of non-approved religions (e.g., Vietnam, Iran, Saudi Arabia). Another example where the eradication of religious and political boundaries is obvious is Afghanistan under Taliban rule. During that time, the laws were based on the Taliban's fundamentalist interpretation of Islam. Behaviour considered "crimes" included the failure of women to be fully covered (including their faces) when outside of their homes, women allowing themselves to be seen through windows when inside of their homes, dancing, listening to music, and proselytizing (i.e., expressing any other religious beliefs to another person).

The blurring of religious and political boundaries is also evident in the United States today, in the influence of the Christian Coalition (Watson, 1997; Viujst, 1995; Ontario Consultants for Religious Tolerance, 2003; Boston, 1996). The precursor to the Christian coalition was the Moral Majority, a politically active religious group comprising ultra-right wing conservative fundamentalist Christians. Televangelist Pat Robertson founded it, and its symbolic leader was fellow televangelist Jerry Falwell. The Moral Majority's political efforts culminated in Pat Robertson's run for President of the United States in 1988. After his attempt at the Presidency failed, it appeared that the Moral Majority lost steam, leading Stebbins (1996) to conclude that the ultra-right wing Christian conservative political movement had essentially disappeared by the end of the 1980s. In fact, it did not disappear, but was simply reborn in 1990 as the Christian Coalition, with Pat Robertson as its founder. It registered as a "social welfare organization" that would provide assistance to the needy; on this basis, it received tax-exempt status. As a requirement for tax-exempt status, it could not be active in the political agenda of any single political party. Its members could express political beliefs, but the organization could not give money to any particular party, nor could it be active in lobbying for any specific party. In time, it became clear that the Christian Coalition was engaging in precisely these prohibited activities, and in 1999 its tax-exempt status was removed (MacDonald, 1999).

After Pat Robertson's failed attempts at the Presidency, the Christian Coalition determined that it would be more successful at a local level. Subsequently, it refocused its efforts on state politics and local politics (e.g., school boards, town councilors, etc.). Using what have been called **stealth tactics**, political candidates avoid religious agendas during election time, and focus on non-religious issues. The Christian Coalition makes ultra-right-wing fundamentalist Christian voters aware of who these candidates are by distributing voter guides, primarily through fundamentalist Christian churches, on the Sunday before election day. Prior to the 2000 Presidential election, they distributed more than 70 million voter guides through all 50 states (Christian Coalition, 2003). The voter guides list all of the candidates in that district, and evaluate them on the basis of the Coalition's "pro-family agenda"; in practice, the only candidates likely to be approved in the voter guide are the most conservative of Republicans. Rival political candidates and other critics have accused the Coalition of lying about rival candidates' positions on various issues in order to increase the likelihood of the one candidate they support being elected. The Coalition runs political training workshops for members who want to run for political office, as well as workshops teaching other members the most effective ways to convince voters whom to vote for. For example, a segment of the documentary *Onward Christian Soldiers* captures a meeting held for church ministers (Viujst, 1995). At this meeting, the Coalition representative tells the ministers that although he cannot tell them whom to vote for, he can tell them whom he is voting for. He then tells them they can do the same in front of their parishioners, and if they are good leaders, the parishioners will follow and vote for the same person.

These "stealth" efforts have been extremely successful for the Coalition. Scholars and political analysts suggest the Christian Coalition essentially controls the Republican Party, and that a Republican candidate cannot get elected without the support of the Coalition. Various groups have formed in opposition to the Christian Coalition (e.g., "Fight the Right"), and civil rights organizations (e.g., the American Civil Liberties Union) are involved in opposition as well. Their core concern is that, because of the power and influence of the Coalition, their religious belief system will come to be reflected in law and government policy—a belief system that many people think, if institutionalized within government, would violate human rights legislation, although this is disputed by the Coalition. Leaders of the Christian Coalition have stated that they are opposed to the separation of church and state, want to incorporate religion into the public school system (but only particular religious belief systems), want to prohibit the teaching of evolution in science classes, and are opposed to any forms of gun control. Concerned critics fear these beliefs will be turned into law if the Coalition fully succeeds. Given the influence the Coalition already holds, the possibility of their perceptions of "deviance" being institutionalized in American law is not as remote as one might think.

TIME TO REVIEW:

- What are some contemporary examples of the boundaries between religious and political belief systems becoming blurred?
- What is the Christian Coalition? What activities do they engage in?
- In what way is the Christian Coalition an example of religion influencing politics? Why are some critics and scholars concerned?

Exercise Your Mind:

Is the blurring of religious and political boundaries evident in Canadian politics in any way, or is it limited to the American context? You might find it interesting to explore this question in more detail. A good place to start your investigation is the Website of the Canadian Family Action Coalition at **http://www.familyaction.org**. This organization, located in Calgary, encourages Christians to be politically active, and their Website focuses on current political and legal issues. What themes are there in the type of influence this group is trying to have on Canadian politics? Does this group actually have any influence, in practice? Can you find other groups, perhaps associated with non-Christian religions, that also bring religious beliefs to bear on political attitudes and actions? Compare this organization, and any other organizations you find, with the Christian Coalition (**http://www.cc.org**). What similarities and differences can you detect between the groups? You also might want to consider the issue of religious and political belief systems during the next election held in your area. Who are the candidates? Do they declare religious agendas? Finally, what are the possible positive and negative outcomes that could occur if any of the religious belief systems you look at were to influence legislation and government policy?

Chapter Summary

Two types of relationship exist between religion and deviance. *Religion as deviance* refers to religious institutions (or their representatives) that commit deviant acts, and to religious groups that are considered deviant in their entirety. *Religion as a social typer of deviance* exists when religion serves to tell us who or what should be considered deviant.

Traditionally, the typology distinguishing between *ecclesia, churches, sects, and cults* has been used to determine which religions—in particular, which sects and cults—are deviant. Sects are perceived as deviant because of a combination of rigid belief systems and high levels of commitment required of members. However, sects vary on both of these measures, so that different sects experience varying levels of tension with the wider society.

The media presents distorted images of cults, which influence public attitudes towards those religious groups categorized as cults. Cults are considered deviant because of the brainwashing that they are presumed to employ, the sexual deviance often associated with them, and the presupposed dangers they present to members (e.g., mass suicide, pedophilia) and outsiders (e.g., releasing toxic gas). Although the cults that present dangers are extremely small in number, under certain conditions mass suicides or violence directed to outsiders does occur.

Deviant religions are subject to a wide range of social control measures. The *anti-cult movement* and *counter-cult movement* are active in reducing the threat they consider cults present. The media exerts control over cults, both in conjunction with these movements, and independently, in their representations of cults. Governments also control deviant religions, but precisely which religions are considered "deviant," and the manner in which they are controlled, vary across countries.

Numerous forms of resistance to the social typing of deviant religions occur as well, with the internationally recognized right to *freedom of religion* as the nexus. Individual religious groups defend themselves in court, try to demonstrate that they are not "deviant," and continue to recruit new members (e.g., via the Internet). Human rights groups and religious freedom groups also resist the social typing of "deviant" religions. Even the traditional distinction between churches, sects, and cults that serves as the foundation for the deviantizing of certain religious groups has been called into question; a global and historical perspective shows us that *all* religious groups have been socially typed as deviant.

In addition to being socially typed as deviant, religion can also serve as a social typer of deviance, telling us who or what is deviant. Individually, our religious beliefs provide guidelines for our own behaviour and how to evaluate the behaviour of others. At a societal level, religion can serve as a social typer of deviance when the boundaries between religious and political beliefs systems become blurred. Historically, this occurred during the witch persecutions, with residential schooling, and with the Victorian child-savers movement. In contemporary society, an example is the power held by the Christian Coalition in American politics.

Recommended Readings

Jenkins, P. (2000). *Mystics and messiahs: Cults and new religions in American history*. New York: Oxford University Press.

* This book touches upon problems with the distinctions between churches, sects, and cults, and explores the various religious groups that have been considered cults in American history. The author analyzes the social factors that contribute to the creation of moral panics about cults, as well as the roles played by different social institutions in these moral panics.

Boston, R. (1996). *The most dangerous man in America? Pat Robertson and the rise of the Christian Coalition*. Amherst, NY: Prometheus Books.

* This book is a detailed critique of the Christian Coalition, written by a leading member of Americans United for the Separation of Church and State.

Ontario Consultants for Religious Tolerance. *The religious tolerance Webpage*. URL: **www.religioustolerance.org**.

* This is a Website rather than a book or article, but I highly recommend you look at this Website. This site is an essential resource for information about dozens of specific religious groups, including doomsday cults (e.g., the Solar Temple), historically persecuted groups

(e.g., witches), and groups that act as social typers of deviance (e.g., the Christian Coalition). It also includes material about controversies different religious groups have been involved with, important social issues related to religion (e.g., debates over same-sex marriages), and links to other academic and popular resources. This is an outstanding site that you could spend hours looking through. It is also highly recommended by a number of academics specializing in the social analysis of religion (e.g., Jeffrey Hadden).

Endnotes

1 Karl Marx (1975). Retrieved June 15, 2003 from World Wide Web: **http://www.bartleby.com**

Key Terms

beliefs, **p. 236**
belief systems, **p. 236**
religion as deviance, **p. 237**
religion as a social type of deviance, **p. 237**
ecclesia, **p. 239**
churches, **p. 239**
denominations, **p. 239**
sects, **p. 239**
cults, **p. 239**
deviancy amplification, **p. 243**
anti-cult movement, **p. 249**
cult awareness groups, **p. 249**
counter-cult movement, **p. 250**
new religious movements, **p. 256**
residential schooling, **p. 261**
child-savers movement, **p. 262**
stealth tactics, **p. 265**

CHAPTER 9

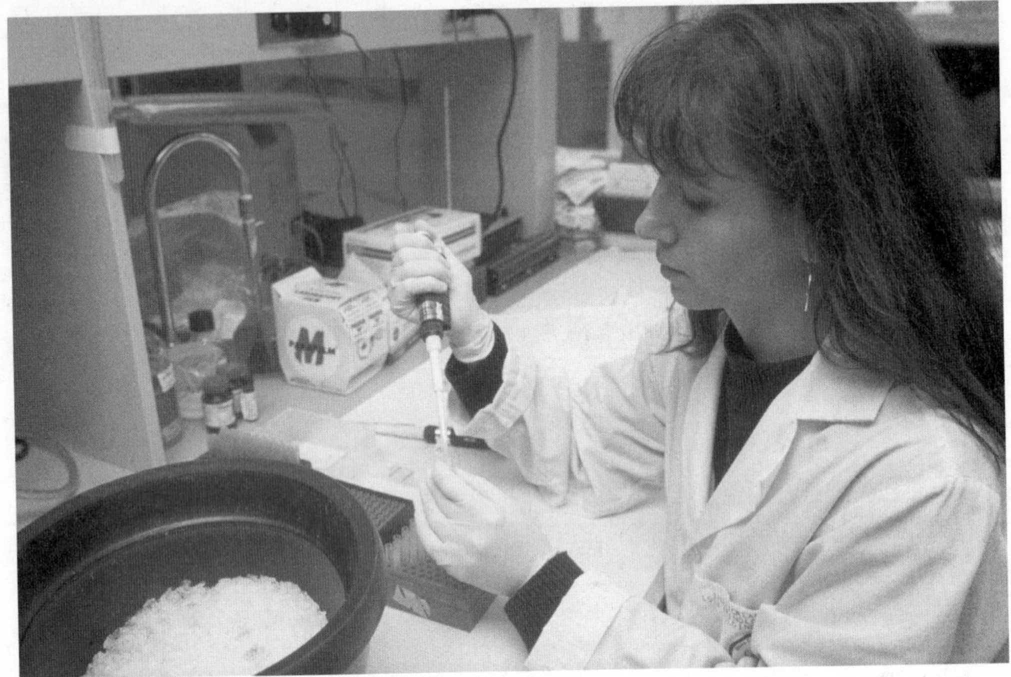

Scientific Belief Systems

Learning Objectives

After reading this chapter, you should be able to:

- Describe the components of science.
- List the different forms of "deviance in science," and provide examples.
- Describe the contrasting explanations for "deviance in science."
- Define "deviant" science, and provide examples.
- Explain what makes a science appear "deviant."
- Describe the power science holds as a social typer of deviance, and give historical and contemporary examples of science acting as a social typer.
- Describe the contemporary debates over the science of genetics.

"The wise man regulates his conduct by the theories both of religion and science. But he regards these theories not as statements of ultimate fact but as art-forms." (J.B.S. Haldane (1892–1964)[1]

Religion Compared to Science

The above quotation indicates that both religious and scientific belief systems are vital parts of our daily lives. It also suggests that these belief systems can, and indeed should, serve social control functions; if we are "wise," we will act on the basis of religion and science. In the above quote, Haldane also points to the subjectivity of religious and scientific belief systems. Although these beliefs systems proclaim "truths," they emerge through processes of social construction or creation, just as art does. In the preceding chapter, we saw that religion does act as a social control agent for individuals, and also for the larger society when religious belief systems come to influence political belief systems. But we saw that religion is a recipient of social control as well. "Deviant" religions are controlled by groups of activists, the media, and government; precisely which religions are considered "deviant" varies across cultures, over time, and even among different groups of people in the same society.

In this chapter, we will see the same is true for scientific belief systems. Science serves a social control function, dictating to us what is "deviant" and providing means for controlling that deviance. Like religion, science is also made subject to social control itself, in order to prevent and resolve deviance. "Deviant" sciences and scientists are regulated, although precisely which sciences are considered to be "deviant" varies across cultures, over time, and even among different groups of people in the same society. However, the extent of debate over what is "deviant" within the realm of science is somewhat less than is the case with religion, because of the greater level of legitimacy that society grants to scientific belief systems and methods. As with religion, when it comes to science and deviance, we can speak of two different relationships—**science as deviance** (i.e., when deviance occurs within science) and **science as a social typer of deviance** (i.e., when science tells us what is, or should be considered, deviant).

Ask Yourself:

In your own life, what roles are played by the "truths" proclaimed by the religious belief system you adhere to (or do not adhere to) and scientific beliefs systems? How do religion and science each affect your daily life—the way you act, the thoughts you have, and the way you evaluate other people? Does one of those beliefs systems play a larger role in your life than others? If so, why?

What is "science"? It can be broadly defined as "knowledge or a system of knowledge covering *general truths* of the operation of general laws especially as obtained and tested through *scientific method*" [italics added] (Merriam Webster Collegiate Dictionary, 2003). Looking at this definition, we can see that science consists of both **scientific belief systems** (i.e., the proclaimed "truths") and **technologies** (i.e., the techniques and methods used to obtain that knowledge) (Ben-Yehuda, 1990). As with religion, the belief systems contained within science are twofold. First, there are claims about the nature of reality—the way the world works. Second, there are ethical and moral claims embedded within the scientific belief system. For example, in psychiatry not only are claims being made about the "truths" of how the brain and the mind work, but also ethical and moral claims are implicit in the creation of diagnostic categories of mental illness (e.g., gender identity dysphoria, ADHD, sexual addiction). Similarly, in the forms of science involved in cloning, claims are being made about both the biological or genetic foundations and the implicit morality of carrying out cloning. Some beliefs are characteristic of science as a whole (e.g., that the "truths" about nature can be discovered), but other beliefs are specific to each of the disciplines or sub-disciplines of science. For instance, biology and physics each have their own distinct "truths" as well, based on the specific objects of study. The same can be said for the technologies. The technology known as the *scientific method* is broadly shared among sciences, but then specific techniques and methods are also used within each sub-discipline of science, such as physics and genetics.

Science as Deviance

"Science's major effort is to find, describe, and analyze…the truth." (Ben-Yehuda, 1990, p. 196)

In the pursuit of this ultimate goal, scientists can be thought of as "deviant" in two instances. First, scientists may be socially typed when they engage in fraud or violate ethical guidelines; this is **deviance in science**. Second, scientists my be considered "deviant" when they are part of a discipline that is not recognized by the scientific community as being "real" science; this can be called **deviant science**.

Deviance in Science

Forms of Deviant Science

Precisely what does *deviance in science* consists of? Babbage (cited in Ben-Yehuda, 1986) identifies three forms of behaviour that are commonly considered "deviant" within the scientific community, although other scholars describe and categorize deviant behavioiurs in different ways. First is **forging**, which refers to scientists who falsify their data, reporting observations that never really occurred; this is similar to what Park (2000) calls **fraudulent science** (although Park includes honest mistakes as part of this "deviant" behaviour). Second is **trimming**, which means manipulating the real observations so that they will support the theory in question. Third is **cooking**, that is selectively reporting only that data that supports the theory in question, and suppressing the remaining data. Exactly how common these data-related deviant behaviours are is not quite clear, and is a matter of debate. Some scholars claim that these actions are quite rare in the scientific community due to the search for "truth" that most scientists pursue in their work. However, other researchers suggest these behaviours are far more frequent that empirical studies can capture (Ben-Yehuda, 1986; Bechtel & Pearson, 1985; Park 2000). It has become frequent enough, and considered of enough importance, that the journal *Nature* now publishes an annual review of cases of scientific fraud (e.g., Dalton, 2002).

A number of recent examples have been publicly revealed. A British cardiologist was suspended from practice for one year because of his fraudulent research claims. He falsely claimed that, following a first heart attack, men of Indian descent had a higher risk of death than men not of Indian descent (Kerr, 2003). A neurologist was reprimanded for falsifying data about the effectiveness of a particular drug in the treatment of diabetes; the drug's manufacturer had promised the neurologist 0.5% of the profits from the drug if it became marketable (Dyer, 2003). A physicist who had published several high-profile articles on his research was found to have falsified data when two fellow researchers were unable to reproduce his findings (Ball, 2003). A well-known environmental scientist who published a book that was far more optimistic about the environmental future than other research was determined to have falsified data, distorted data, plagiarized other people's work, and deliberately misrepresented research findings (White, 2003). And all of these instances are from the first six months of 2003! Something these cases have in common is that they are all based on research that was fairly high profile. Ben-Yehuda (1986, p. 18) suggests that deviance is far more likely to be detected in research on "hot" issues and in "breakthrough" research, because of the interest that is generated. Research having a lower profile is less likely to raise questions and create controversy, so that deviance within that research is less likely to be detected.

Deviance in science is also represented by **hoaxes**, which Babbage (cited in Ben-Yehuda, 1986) describes as similar to practical jokes, although some creators of hoaxes may have less humourous motives. A scientific hoax with Canadian origins was discovered in 2000. In 1999, the curator of the Royal Tyrell Museum, Philip Currie, had brought a paleontological find to the attention of *National Geographic*. A fossil had been found in China, purported to be a new species that bridged birds and dinosaurs; a photograph of the fossil was published in the magazine. It did not take long for fellow scientists to declare that the fossil had to be a hoax, and an investigation determined that it was, indeed. The fossil had been created by placing pieces of fossils from various different species together. The curator, knowing this (via x-rays of the fossil), reported the "finding" to *National Geographic* anyway (Parker, 2000). Representatives of the museum declared this to be a "mistake," and the curator was able to keep his position; however, his reputation has been significantly sullied. More recently, another alleged scientific hoax has been brought to public attention. Scientists working for the company "Clonaid" recently contacted the media, claiming that they had successfully cloned a human being; the rest of the scientific community has declared this to be a hoax, and the Clonaid scientists have refused to come forward to offer evidence of their cloning success.

AN INTERNET MOMENT:

The Clonaid controversy is also an interesting example of the blending of religion and science. Clonaid is a company established by a religious group, the Raelians (commonly labelled a "sect" by the media). The Raelians claim that human life on Earth is the result of cloning by extraterrestrials. You can learn more about the Raelian religious group, its beliefs, and the research allegedly being carried out by its scientists, at http://www.clonaid.com.

A form of hoax that you may be more familiar with are email hoaxes, particularly those that make health claims. For example, over the last few years tens of thousands of people have received emails claiming that antiperspirant causes breast cancer. The email cites scientific experts as saying that antiperspirant blocks the skin's pores, which prevents the release of toxins from those areas of the body, and ultimately leads to breast cancer. The email goes on to say that the reason women are more likely than men to get breast cancer is because men do not shave their armpits, so less antiperspirant touches their skin. Other rationales have been offered in different versions of the email message. In fact, no research has ever linked the use of antiperspirants or deodorants to an increased risk of breast cancer. Although this email hoax cites the work of scientists, scientists are not involved in the hoax, which means that these email hoaxes are not truly examples of *deviance in science.* However, because of the widespread nature of this hoax, scientists have had to become involved in disputing the claims made in the hoax. Medical organizations have had to issue press releases stating the fraudulent nature of this claim (e.g., National Cancer Institute, 2003).

TIME TO REVIEW:

- In what ways are religion and science similar?
- What is "science"? What components does it consist of?
- What are the possible relationships between science and deviance?
- What are the two aspects of "science as deviance"?
- What are some of the forms of "deviance in science," and what are some examples?

In addition to using data fraudulently in some way, and constructing hoaxes, other behaviours can constitute *deviance in science* as well. Park (2000) refers to *pathological science* and *junk science.* **Pathological science** refers to scientists seeing what they expect (or want) to see, regardless of what data is actually there. **Junk science** refers to people with little or no scientific background making scientific claims, or people using their scientific credentials alone to try to convince people of the validity of their claims. Huber (1991) discusses how *junk science* is frequently utilized in courtrooms and in front of other legislative bodies, as lawyers and junk scientists form a coalition in the joint pursuit of profit. One frequent target of *junk science* accusations, as well as other forms of *deviance in science,* is the tobacco industry.

The Tobacco Industry. One has only to think of the scientists that have worked for tobacco companies for many years, claiming that their research showed that smoking was neither addictive nor harmful, to see many possible forms of *deviance in science* (Ramsey, 2002; Rampton & Stauber, 2000b; Rampton & Stauber, 2001). Were they using research data fraudulently? Were they seeing what they wanted to see in the data, either intentionally or unintentionally? Were they simply using their scientific credentials to convince people of the truth of their claims? Were public relations firms simply using scientific credentials to convince people of the tobacco companies' claims? It is possible to say that forging, trimming, cooking, pathological science, and junk science have all characterized the scientific claims of the tobacco industry, "which has arguably done more to corrupt science than any other industry in history" (Rampton & Stauber, 2000a). The tobacco industry did not finally admit that smoking is harmful until 1999. Critics say then they turned their sights on the research that was showing a link between second-hand smoke and health problems. In their efforts to discredit that research, they had their own scientific experts label it *junk science*, and even established "The Advancement of Sound Science Coalition (TASSC) to explain to people the different between invalid *junk science* and valid **sound science** (Rampton & Stauber, 2000a, 2000b, 2001; Ong & Glantz, 2001). Initially, the fact that this coalition was created and funded by Philip Morris (a leading tobacco firm) was hidden. Of course, the scientists from the TASSC consistently showed that the research linking second-hand smoke with physical harm was invalid science. The scientific claims made by TASSC typically conclude that research showing evidence of harm due to any environmental toxins (e.g., arsenic in water supplies, airborne pollutants) is all *junk science*. Critics of the TASSC comment on how its research always comes down in favour of the tobacco industry, and opposed to any environmental legislation that would regulate that industry. So although claims of *junk science* are frequently directed at the tobacco industry, similar claims are directed by the tobacco industry at its critics.

When looking at *junk science*, where people misuse scientific credentials in some way, media and popular culture are not exempt from criticisms. In recent years, media figure Dr. Laura Schlessinger has become the target of critics for allegedly misusing her scientific credentials (Presley, 2000; Epstein, 2001; Solomon, 2000; Small, 1994; Buzzard, 2002). Relationship guru John Gray has faced similar criticisms, but has escaped relatively unscathed in comparison.

Laura Schlessinger & John Gray. Popular author and radio show host Laura Schlessinger does have a PhD. However, Laura Schlessinger's PhD is not in any scientific discipline associated with the relationship advice she gives in her syndicated radio show or in her books as *Dr.* Laura; rather, it is in Physiology. By referring to herself as someone with a doctorate, people are left with the impression that she is scientifically trained in the area in which she gives advice. A survey of adult New Yorkers found that, of those people who had heard of Dr. Laura, 40% were certain that she was either a psychologist or a psychiatrist; only 30% were quite sure she was neither (cited in Epstein, 2001). Furthermore, scholars say that a psychologist or psychiatrist would never give the kind of advice that she does. First, critics say that she models and advocates abusive behaviour, for example, by calling people "evil" and "whores" (Epstein, 2001, p. 5). Second, her advice is not supported by scientific research; in fact, it frequently contradicts the findings of science (Solomon, 2000; Presley, 2000). Third, it divides families rather than providing them with ways of working out problems (Epstein, 2001; Presley, 2000). Epstein (2001) cites an example, a father who phoned Dr. Laura because he and his wife were disagreeing over whether their young adult son should be paying rent while living at home. Her advice to the father was to throw the son out of the house before the weekend. Fourth, the statements she has used to refer to gays and lesbians in her public venue are discriminatory (Presley, 2000) to the point where legal consultants suggested that her statements could be effectively argued as "spreading hate" against an identifiable social group. As a result, her television show was first cancelled in Canada, and shortly thereafter was cancelled in the United States (**http://stopdrlaura.com**). Finally, critics say that she uses her scientific credentials as a spurious validation of the religious belief system that she promotes in her radio shows and books (Presley, 2000; Epstein, 2001).

Some similar criticisms have been directed at John Gray, author of the *Men are from Mars, Women are from Venus* (see **http://www.marsvenus.com**). His background is theological, and he spent many years as a monk. His PhD is from Columbia Pacific University, a non-accredited university that offers doctoral degrees via correspondence courses in extremely short periods of time (Small, 1994). Although these credentials caused considerable criticism in the early years of his popularity, criticisms have died down in recent years. Despite his non-accredited doctoral credentials, he has become quite an accepted member of the psychological and counselling communities, and currently sits on various international boards involved with marriage and family therapy. This leaves one to wonder how John Gray has been able to legitimize his work in the scientific community to a greater extent than Laura Schlessinger has. One reason may be that, while Laura Schlessinger anchors her work firmly within a particular religious and moral belief system, John Gray's work has distanced itself from religion and makes more use of scientific belief systems. Although scientists, of course, may have their own personal religious belief systems, the scientific community considers it "deviant" to use that belief system as the foundation for scientific work.

Explanations for Deviance in Science

Scientific deviance may come from various sources. With popular media scientists, there may be the desire to truly help people, but the pursuit of fame and material success cannot be discounted. The pursuit of profit also drives the actions of the *junk scientists* Huber (1991) refers to, those who align themselves with lawyers in court cases in the hope of making money, and those aligned with certain industries (Ramsey, 2002). However, outside of media and industry, the causes of *deviance in science* are a matter of some debate. The essence of the debate lies in whether the **bad apple/bad person theory** or the **iceberg theory** is best able to explain these diverse acts of deviance (Ben-Yehuda, 1986; Bechtel & Pearson, 1985; James, 1995)

For many years, deviant acts committed by scientists were explained on the basis of individual factors—the *bad apple/bad person theory* of scientific deviance (Ben-Yehuda, 1986; Bechtel & Pearson, 1985). Just as some people commit crimes because of psychological disturbances, personality factors, or free choice, some scientists commit deviant acts in their work for these same reasons. In contrast, the *iceberg theory* of scientific deviance claims that the structure within which scientists work actually encourages deviance, making it likely to occur (James, 1995; Bechtel & Pearson, 1985; Ben-Yehuda, 1986). First, scientists today face an incredible amount of "pressure to publish." The number of publications that a scientist has can determine hiring, increases in salary, promotion, likelihood of receiving monetary research grants, and the degree of respect received within the scientific community. All of these pressures increase the chance that scientists will use deviant means of getting these publications. Second, scientific deviance is unlikely to be detected. Unless research is controversial or about a particularly "hot" issue, it is unlikely to stimulate questions and efforts at replication, because replicating someone else's research, which is viewed as non-innovative, does not add much to the prestige of scientists. Because the chances of being caught are remote, there is little motivation not to engage in deviant acts. Third, although organizational structures and committees have been put in place to investigate reports of *deviance in science*, their investigations are often fraught with controversy themselves (e.g., White, 2003), and even if scientists' deviance is detected, sanctions are not likely to be of sufficient severity to deter other potential offenders. For example, the curator at the Royal Tyrell Museum may have had his reputation tarnished for his participation in the hoax described earlier, but he was able to keep his position as curator of this prestigious museum. These three characteristics of the scientific community combine to create a structure that actually encourages rather deters *deviance in science*.

Within the approach known as the *iceberg theory* of scientific deviance (so labelled because the known cases are seen as representing just the tip of the iceberg), different scholars have applied various specific theories that we addressed in Chapter 2 to explain this form of deviance. For example, Ben-Yehuda (1986) proposes that *techniques of neutralization* (Sykes & Matza, 1957) play an important role in scientific deviance. Techniques like *denial of injury* or *denial of responsibility* help scientists to justify their actions, convincing themselves or others that what they are doing is not *really* wrong. Bechtel & Pearson (1985) discuss the usefulness of Robert Merton's *anomie theory*. They point out that scientific deviance can be considered an example of the mode of adaptation called *innovation*; the gap between legitimized goals and access to the legitimate means of attaining those goals leads some people to pursue those goals in "innovative" ways. Just as some people who want fancy cars will steal them instead of purchase them, some scientists who want career success will achieve it by falsifying data (or other forms of deviance) rather than by obtaining it legitimately. Gottfredson and Hirschi's (1990) *general theory of crime* has not been used to study scientific deviance specifically, but has been applied to occupational more generally. Research has found that *self-control* plays a role in occupational deviance, particularly when low self-control is combined with an environment in which co-workers are engaging in deviance (Gibson & Wright, 2001). If co-workers appear to be rewarded for their deviance, such as by receiving promotions or large research grants for their productivity in publishing, the pull towards deviance may be even greater.

Exercise Your Mind:

Go back to the various theories discussed in Chapters 2 and 3. Which of these theories could be used to help you understand the forms of "deviance in science" that we have addressed? This could be an interesting classroom exercise, with different groups of students exploring the applicability of different theories.

Ethics in Science

Deviance in science includes the numerous behaviours we have explored thus far—fraudulently using data in some way (e.g., forging, cooking), creating hoaxes, and misusing scientific credentials (either by not actually having any, or by using real credentials in an inappropriate way). However, this list is not exclusive. Other actions may also be considered *deviance in science*. For example, some scholars mention **ethical violations** as instances of scientific deviance as well. The various disciplines of science are governed by various codes of ethics. The code of ethics you may be most familiar with is that used by some medical doctors, the Hippocratic Oath, whereby doctors vow to balance the protection of their patients with the pursuit of science and the practice of the art of medicine. But all scientific disciplines are governed by codes of ethics. For example, the Canadian Psychological Association has a code of ethics that governs both research and clinical practice with clients. The Canadian Sociology and Anthropology Association has a code of ethics as well (see Box 9.2).

Box 9.2 Canadian Sociology and Anthropology Associations' *Statement of Professional Ethics*

In June 1994, the CSAA approved their *Statement of Professional Ethics.* Its intention is "to serve as a set of issues to be considered in the design and implementation of research and in professional practice in sociology and anthropology," by offering "a resource in the professional training of students and faculty in these disciplines; and to enter into dialogue with the communities we research, with other professions, and with university ethics committees on sociological and anthropological visions of professional ethics" (CSAA, 1994).

The statement lists a number of guidelines governing several different areas. Some of these areas include:

- the way research is done
- protecting human research participants from harm
- relationships with academic peers, and with the discipline of sociology
- relationships with students in postsecondary settings
- harassment and exploitation

The *Statement of Professional Ethics* can be viewed in its entirety at the following URL: **http://alcor.Concordia.ca/~csaa1/.**

Although each scientific discipline may have its own specific code of ethics, all scientists working within academic institutions are subject to the research ethics committees of their institutions. These committees must approve the research proposal before scientists may begin any research project that involves human subjects. That is, before any faculty member at a university begins a research project, if that research project directly involves people (e.g., observations, interviews, surveys), the faculty member must submit a research proposal to the research ethics committee. The proposal must describe the research project, its rationale, the research methods that will be used, and the efforts being undertaken to protect any vulnerable populations that will be affected by the research project. Committee approval is required before the faculty member may begin the research.

TIME TO REVIEW:

- What are "pathological science," "junk science," and "sound science"?
- How has the concept of "junk science" been used in relation to the tobacco industry?
- What criticisms have been launched against popular media scientists Laura Schlessinger and John Gray?
- How is "deviance in science" explained by the "bad apple theory" and the "iceberg theory"?
- What are some of the specific theories that have been used with the "iceberg" approach?
- What are ethical violations, and what role do codes of ethics play in preventing "deviance in science"?

"Deviant" Science

As we have seen thus far, deviance can occur within science when scientists engage in particular behaviours that are deemed "deviant" by fellow members of the scientific community (i.e., *deviance in science*). This is one form that *science as deviance* can take, paralleling one of the ideas we explored in the previous chapter, wherein religious institutions or their representative engage in deviant actions (e.g., sexual abuse of children by priests, and the alleged cover-up by churches). Another form that *science as deviance* can take is when an entire discipline of science is perceived as "deviant" in its entirety—the notion of *"deviant" science* (Ben-Yehuda, 1990). This serves as a parallel to the "deviant" religions discussed in the previous chapter; there we saw that traditionally, *sects* and *cults* have been the religious groups socially typed as deviant and made subject to social control.

An entire science may be socially typed as "deviant" when its belief system and/or technologies are significantly called into question. If subject to enough doubt, the belief system and/or technologies may be determined to not be a "science" as all; instead, they may be labelled a "non-science" (or "nonsense"). Particular combinations of belief systems and technologies can be thought of as falling along a continuum.

Figure 9.1 THE DEVIANT SCIENCE/REAL SCIENCE CONTINUUM

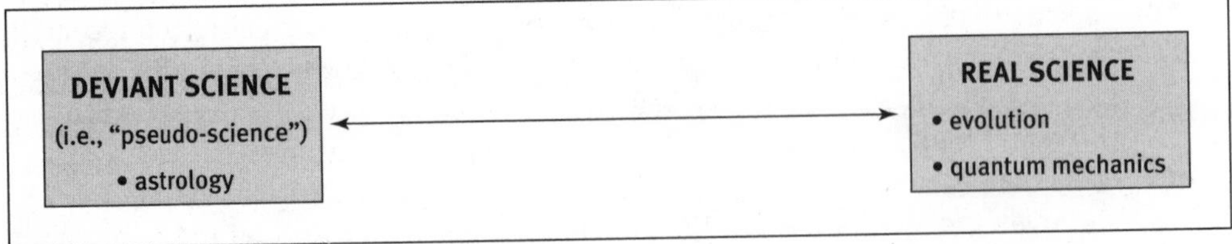

Source: Adapted from Shermer's (2001a) model of the science/pseudo-science continuum.

At one end of the continuum lie those belief systems that have not been supported by empirical research using scientific methods, such as astrology, magnetic therapy, and Bible codes; these are labelled *pseudo-science*. At the other end of the continuum are those belief systems that have consistently supported by an abundance of research evidence, such as evolution and quantum mechanics; these are labelled *science*. Falling at various points between these two polar ends of the continuum are the bulk of other belief systems/technologies, such as those involved with human cloning (Shermer, 2001a).

Astrology is an interesting example of a "deviant" science. Its belief system proposes that people's personalities, interests, strengths, and weaknesses are determined by the position of the various planets at the time of birth. The solar system is divided into different sections, or "houses" (and correspondingly labelled Leo, Aquarius, etc.). Astrology's techniques include complex mathematical calculations and some techniques borrowed from astronomy. Based on the date and time of people's births, astrologists determine where each planet was (i.e., which "house") at the moment of birth. The position of various planets is claimed to determine personality, abilities, and life events. Some ancient scientists and philosophers, such as Aristotle and Ptolemy, were proponents of astrology, but today astrology is perceived as a pseudo-science or anti-science (Saliba, 2001/2002; Emery, 2001; *Skeptical Inquirer*, 1999; Clark & Gabriels, 1996; Maddox, 1994). However, recently scientists have begun using scientific methods to study whether some of the claims of astrology might actually be valid. For example, Clarke and Gabriels (1996) investigated whether personality traits like extroversion and emotionality were associated with astrological signs; they found no relationship between these variables. However, other research has found support for astrological claims. One research study compared scientists who had won Nobel prizes in medicine and physiology with scientists who had not won such prizes, but who worked in reputable academic institutions. This study found a statistically significant relationship between astrological sign and Nobel laureate status: the Nobel-winning scientists were likely to have had the sun sign of Gemini, while scientists with the sun sign of Leo were the least likely to have won Nobel prizes in medicine and science (Pollex, Hegels, & Ban, 2001). Despite the fact that astrology has tried to establish itself as a science for hundreds (or even thousands) of years (Pruzhinin & Scanlan, 1995), it continues to be viewed as a pseudo-science. The question of its scientific nature aside, many non-scientists continue to subscribe to some of the claims of astrology. Feher's (1992) study of believers in astrology finds them to be very mainstream people, with even higher levels of education than average. A number of cultures also overwhelmingly believe in astrology, having the common cultural practice of consulting astrological charts prior to arranging marriages, for example. While astrology continues to be widely viewed as a "deviant" science by the scientific community, the nature of its belief system is studied in other ways, that is, as a religious belief system and as philosophy. For example, the Sophia Project, whose aim is to promote the development of skilled and prestigious contemporary philosophers in the British post-secondary system, includes the study of astrological beliefs.

The media plays an important role in reproducing pseudo-scientific beliefs (Yam, 1997). Newspapers and magazines throughout North America frequently include horoscopes in every issue. The "stranger" the scientific claims, the more likely it seems the media is to present a story on those claims; unusual scientific claims are sensationalistic, and can reliably attract an audience. The media ties into commercialization as well. Belief systems that are frequently labelled as "deviant" science are often linked to companies that are selling a marketable product or service related to those claims (Yam, 1997). Astrological charts, magnetic insoles for your shoes, and homeopathic remedies are just some of the services and products available.

Determining what is a "deviant" science, or a pseudo-science, may initially appear to be quite straightforward. However, as with religious belief systems, determining which ones are "deviant" presents a rather gray area. Something

Astrology has been considered a "deviant" science for many years. However, some scientists are now finding support for some of astrology's claims.

that may be perceived as a "deviant" science at one time may become an accepted science at a later point. This is what happened with radio astronomy in the early 20th century (Ben-Yehuda, 1986, 1990). Although I am certainly oversimplifying the science somewhat, radio astronomy makes the claims that scientists can identify events that are occurring in the solar system by measuring the radio waves the events emit. Those of you who are familiar with astronomy may be asking how radio astronomy can be an example of a "deviant" science, when its claims are entirely accepted within the scientific community. Well, this was not always the case. The scientists who initially proposed that this way of conducting astronomy was possible and valid faced considerable censure. They had tremendous difficulty in finding a research journal that was willing to publish their article. For a number of years, they were effectively stigmatized, made "outsiders" in the scientific community. Thereafter, other astronomers conducted research and concluded that these claims were, in fact, valid; radio astronomy entered the realm of mainstream science.

Because of instances where the claims made by a "deviant" science eventually came to be adopted within the scientific community, proponents of "deviant" sciences today frequently claim that the same might eventually become true of their belief systems. They argue that the methods for investigation within mainstream science have not evolved sufficiently to properly evaluate the claims being made (Shermer, 2001a). Ben-Yehuda (1986, 1990) points out that one of the reasons that something may be considered a "deviant" science at one point but later become an accepted science is the conservative character of the scientific community. Although scientists pursue innovation via their research efforts, the tendency to resist change can sometimes prevail. Senior scientists who have become well established are usually the members of the scientific community who determine whether new ideas are viewed as valid or not—whether new claims being made are characteristic of "science" or "pseudo-science." The cynical view they have developed as part of the scientific worldview (i.e., presuming that something is *not* true until it is proven beyond a doubt), which to some degree is necessary to evaluate competing claims, contributes to this conservative dimension. The conservative aspect of science then increases the likelihood that any claim outside of the mainstream will, at least initially, be looked upon with suspicion.

Some disciplines are considered "deviant" science because the claims they make about the nature of reality are questioned, or empirical support cannot be found for them. But at other times disciplines may be considered "deviant" even when their claims about the nature of reality are considered to be true. In these cases, it can be the ethical and moral claims with which the discipline is intertwined that lead to a deviant label. For example, some groups within the scientific community accept the claims about the nature of reality that are made by scientists involved in cloning research, that is, the claims that cloning is possible by certain means. But the claims made by scientists about *human* cloning in particular are presently more subject to questioning (Mayor, 2003). The aspects of the belief system more widely considered deviant are the ethical and moral claims that serve as the foundation for cloning research, those claims that suggest cloning is morally appropriate. The dubiousness of the underlying ethics is such that a number of governments have begun to explore legislation to exert tight control over human cloning research, or to even prohibit it.

Pseudo-science surrounds us in our daily lives, whether in the form of the horoscope in the newspaper each morning, the magazine advertisement for magnetic insoles that will heal our illnesses, or the "new" remedies on the drugstore shelves. The prevalence of scientific claims we see being made, especially in the media, makes it important that we be able to distinguish between "true" scientific claims and pseudo-scientific claims. Shermer (2001b) points to several criteria that people should use to determine whether they are being subjected to pseudo-scientific claims. The criteria include:

- reliability of the source
- method used to reach conclusions

- methodological reliability (i.e., whether other scientists could verify the research results by using the same method)
- presence of personal biases, such as political, economic, or religious agendas
- extent to which the claims to truth are supported or contradicted within the rest of the scientific community

Because scientific claims are frequently utilized by destructive or doomsday cults within their belief systems, cult scholars also address the importance of being able to distinguish a science from a pseudo-science. The American Family Foundation, the creators of the *Cultic Studies Journal*, suggest that the best tool for detecting a pseudo-science is knowledge about science itself, particularly knowledge of the methods, checks, and balances utilized within the various disciplines of science. By knowing how science actually works, people can more easily detect claims that fall short of scientific requirements. (**http://www.csj.org/studyindex/studycrthk/study_pseddoscience/study_factpseudo.htm**).

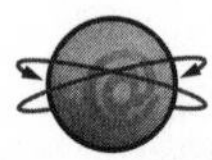

AN INTERNET MOMENT:

There are a number of Websites that address the issue of pseudo-science. An informative, but fun, site is http://physics.syr.edu/courses/modules/PSEUDO/pseudo_main.html. It provides links to material from advocates of various pseudo-sciences, as well as skeptics and critics. On this site you can learn more about astrology, UFOology, crop circles, and much more!

Conclusion

In the last chapter we saw how religions can be socially typed as deviant and made subject to social control. In this chapter, we have explored how science can also be socially typed as deviant and made subject to social control. Sometimes this occurs when scientists engage in specific actions that are considered "deviant" within the scientific community, such as using data fraudulently, intentionally stimulating hoaxes, and violating codes of ethics. At other times, the claims being made about the nature of reality, or the ethical and moral claims being made within a discipline, are called into question themselves; in these instances, the entire science is labelled "deviant" and made subject to control.

TIME TO REVIEW:

- What is a "deviant" science?
- What is the nature of the continuum that describes "sciences" and "pseudo-sciences"?
- What is astrology? Why is astrology called a "deviant" science? What have scientists investigating the claims of astrology found?
- Who determines whether a science is "deviant"?
- Why is the science involved in cloning considered a "deviant" science by some people?

Science as a Social Typer of Deviance

The Power of Scientific Social Typing

For most of history, religious belief systems have been the foundation for the dominant moral codes for societies. The "truths" proclaimed within religion dictated to followers who or what should be considered "deviant," and the nature of social controls to be exerted. Following the Renaissance and the scientific revolution, religion began to slowly lose some of its grip as a legitimate claims-maker for the "truth." In contemporary Western societies, science has replaced religion as the creator of society's dominant moral code, by which "deviance" and "normality" are judged (Conrad, 1992). Anything or anyone that can claim to be "scientific" is automatically granted additional legitimacy.

In his book *Power/Knowledge*, Michel Foucault (1980) proposed that a relationship exists among knowledge claims, the power of people making those knowledge claims, and the resulting influence those knowledge claims have. Thus, when claims to "truth" come from individuals or groups in society that have high levels of institutionalized power, those claims also become institutionalized; people believe the claims being made, simply because those claims are coming from "experts." This is the position that that science holds in our culture today. Science holds a tremendous degree of institutionalized power, so that the knowledge claims made by scientists also typically become institutionalized. If a "scientist" makes a claim, most of us will believe it, because the scientist is perceived as the "expert." The social typing of deviance is more effective when the social typer is in a position of power (Rubington & Weinberg, 2002). Given the preeminent power that science holds in society, the social typing done by scientists tends to be quite effective. Our tendency not to question scientists more closely establishes the social typing that scientists engage in, making them highly resistant to change. "Laypeople generally hesitate to question those who seem to be experts in a mystifying or highly technical field; to do such questioning can feel like asking the clergy if there really is a God. It can also feel presumptuous: 'Who am I to question someone who went to school for so many years and learned about all of this stuff? My questions will probably be stupid.'" (Caplan, 1995, p. xxii)

The legitimacy of science today is such that scientists are placed upon a pedestal of "truth," where no one but other scientists dares to question them.

ASK YOURSELF:

- What are some examples of times when you have believed something, simply because an "expert" claimed it to be true?
- Have there been times when you have not believed something, because there was no "expert" to support the claim being made?

Earlier in this chapter, we explored the controversy surrounding Dr. Laura Schlessinger. Critics say that she is misusing her scientific credentials, providing people with relationship advice even though her PhD is in physiology. In her work, Schlessinger is very clear on precisely who or what is "deviant"—gays and lesbians, mothers who work outside the home, parents who allow their adult children to live with them, and people who engage in premarital sex, to name only a few. In the advice she gives to callers and the statements she makes on international radio, she attempts to exert social control over society's "deviants." The reason that critics are bothered by her work is because of the power they know that a scientific credential holds. Their concern is that calling herself *Dr. Laura* makes people more likely to follow her advice, advice that is viewed by many as unethical, discriminatory, and in opposition to what scientific research has found (Presley, 2000; Epstein, 2001).

In response, gay and lesbian activist groups have lobbied against Laura Schlessinger's radio show and former television show (e.g., **http://stopdrlaura.com**). The magnitude of reaction to her power has been massive, utilizing both the Internet and television. In the late 1990s, an anonymous letter to Laura Schlessinger was emailed to tens of thousands of people (see Box 9.3). Then, in 2000, the popular television show *The West Wing* incorporated the content of that anonymous Internet letter into an episode of the show (October 18, 2000). On this show, the President of the United States (played by Martin Sheen) confronts popular radio advice guru "Dr. Jacobs."

Box 9.3 Letter to Dr. Laura

The following anonymous letter was sent via email to a mass of people during the late 1990s, criticizing the foundation for Laura Schlessinger's advice. In the context of this textbook, we can look at this letter as a form of resistance against the social typing of deviance that Schlessinger engages in on her international radio show and in her books; her social typing is based on a particular religious belief system, but critics argue that she expresses it under the guise of "science."

"Dear Dr. Laura:

Thank you for doing so much to educate people regarding God's law. I have learned a great deal from your show, and I try to share that knowledge with as many people as I can. When someone tries to defend the homosexual lifestyle, for example, I simply remind them that Leviticus 18:22 clearly states it to be an abomination. End of debate.

I do need some advice from you, however, regarding some specific laws and how to follow them:

> When I burn a bull on the alter as a sacrifice, I know it creates a pleasing odor for the Lord (Lev. 1:9). The problem is my neighbors. They claim the odor is not pleasing to them. Should I smite them?
>
> I would like to sell my daughter into slavery, as sanctioned in Exodus 21:7. In this day and age, what do you think would be a fair price for her?

I know that I am allowed no contact with a woman while she is in her period of menstrual uncleanliness (Lev. 15:19-24). The problem is, how do I tell? I have tried asking, but most women take offence.

Lev. 25:44 states that I may indeed possess slaves, both male and female, provided they are purchased from neighboring nations. A friend of mine claims that this applies to Mexicans but not Canadians. Can you clarify? Why can't I own Canadians?

I have a neighbor who insists on working on the Sabbath. Exodus 35:2 clearly states that he should be put to death. Am I morally obligated to kill him myself?

A friend of mine feels that even through eating shellfish is an abomination (Lev. 11:10), it is a lesser abomination than homosexuality. I don't agree. Can you settle this?

Lev. 21:20 states that I may not approach the altar of God if I have a defect in my sight. I have to admit that I wear reading glasses. Does my vision have to be 20/20, or is there some wiggle room here?

Most of my male friends get their hair trimmed, including the hair around their temples, even though this is expressly forbidden by Lev. 19:27. How should they die?

I know from Lev. 11:6-8 that touching the skin of a dead pig makes me unclean, but may I still play football if I wear gloves?

My uncle has a farm. He violates Lev. 19:19 by planting two different crops in the same field, as does his wife by wearing garments made of two different kinds of thread (cotton/polyester blend). He also tends to curse and blaspheme a lot. Is it really necessary that we go to all the trouble of getting the whole town together to stone them? (Lev. 24:10-16) Couldn't we just burn them to death at a private family affair like we do with people who sleep with their in-laws? (Lev. 20:14).

I know you have studied these things extensively, so I am confident you can help. Thank you again for reminding us that God's word is eternal and unchanging.

Your devoted disciple and adoring fan."

Not all scientific claims of deviance are as controversial as those of Laura Schlessinger. The social typing of deviance is associated with *all* science, not just questionable science. The examples of science serving as a social typer of deviance are so numerous that it is not possible to address them all; however, we can look at a few examples, both historical and contemporary.

TIME TO REVIEW:

- How does science serve as a social typer of deviance? Why is the social typing done by science so effective?
- Why do concerns about the power of science as a social typer of deviance sometimes emerge?
- What type of resistance emerged in response to the social typing being done by popular radio scientist Laura Schlessinger?

Scientific Social Typing in History: Social Darwinism, Eugenics, and the Nazis

In the previous chapter, we briefly explored the European colonization of North America, and the role that religious belief systems played in the government initiative for residential schooling, a policy that caused long-term damage to Aboriginal individuals, their families, and their cultures. European colonization did not just occur in North America, but throughout most of the world—Africa, Asia, Australia, Central America, and South America—missing only Japan, Korea, Turkey, Iran, Thailand, Saudi Arabia, and (to some extent) China. What all of these instances of colonization have in common is that indigenous populations were encouraged, and usually coerced, into abandoning traditional beliefs and cultural norms, and adopting the European beliefs and norms of their colonizers (e.g., Abernathy, 2001; Jaimes, 1992). Religious beliefs were central to the push toward colonization, serving as the primary rationalization for several centuries. However, by the end of the 19th century the nature of scientific theory provided both a rationale for the last several centuries of European colonization, and a justification for government policies regarding indigenous peoples for years to come. (It also served to legitimize the social status quo within European societies themselves.) **Social Darwinism**, exemplified by the work of sociologist Herbert Spencer, applied the Darwinian concept of *evolution* to an understanding of history and society (Asma, 1993; Jones, 1998). The theory proposed that, just as biological species evolve over time, so do human societies, from "primitive" to "civilized." Although ancient Athenian society was seen by many social Darwinists as the most evolved in history, European societies were seen as the most evolved societies in the 19th century. Thus, the earlier colonization of more "primitive" societies was justified as being for the benefit of their indigenous peoples; the European colonizers were seen as helping these cultures to evolve at a more rapid rate than they were doing on their own. Government policies based on the principle of assimilation were also justified in moving the evolution of indigenous cultures forward.

Social Darwinism was soon popularized as the science of **eugenics** (Asma, 1993; Jones, 1998; Jones, 1986; Kevles, 1995); similar principles were applied, but to various individuals and groups within particular societies rather than to all societies as a whole. Recent biological developments were used to support the argument that some social groups were more evolved, and therefore biologically "superior" to other groups. Although eugenics is most often associated with Nazi Germany (Kuhl, 1994), governments in Britain (Jones, 1986), the United States (Seldon & Montagu, 1999), Australia (Jones, 1998) and Canada (McLaren, 1990) also pursued eugenic ideals. The science of eugenics had multiple related purposes, as the following excerpt from a 1922 sociology textbook on eugenics illustrates: "The problems of eugenics is to make such legal, social and economic adjustments that (1) a larger proportion of superior persons will have children than at present, (2) that the average number of offspring of each superior person will be greater than at present, (3) that the most inferior persons will have no children, and finally that (4) other inferior persons will have fewer children than now." (Popenoe & Johnson, 1922)

Over time, "inferior" persons came to include non-whites, Eastern and Southern Europeans, "mental defectives," criminals, the poor, and the morally suspect (Dennis, 1995; Beaud & Prevost, 1996; McLaren, 1990; Kevles, 1985; Buchanan, 1997). Social activists drawn primarily from the scientific and social reform communities engaged in a number of measures to increase reproduction in "superior" people and decrease reproduction in "inferior" people. Local fairs held "family fitness competitions" (Whiting, 1996; Seldon, 1999), referring not to physical fitness, but to genetic and evolutionary fitness. In many colleges and universities, biology and sociology students studied from eugenics textbooks, just like the one quoted above. In churches, ministers presented sermons on eugenic ideals, and competed for awards from local eugenics societies (Seldon, 1999). Eugenics societies influenced restrictions on immigration policies, legislation enforcing racial segregation and prohibiting interracial marriages, and involuntary sterilization (Seldon, 1999; Dennis, 1995; McLaren, 1990).

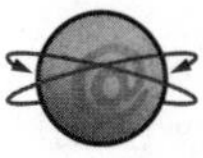

AN INTERNET MOMENT:

This is a Website you cannot miss! The Eugenics Archive at *http://eugenicsarchive.org* is an award-winning Website that documents the history of eugenics, emphasizing the United States. It includes material on the social origins of eugenics, its scientific foundations, its popularization, and the various forms of its implementation. The text is complemented by images of actual eugenics documentation from the time, such as photographs of winners of family fitness contests, posters advertising the local eugenics boards, and scientific figures and charts explaining the necessity for eugenics. Not only is this the best Website I have found on the history of eugenics, it is one of the best Websites on any topic I have seen!

The history of involuntary sterilization and the eugenics movement reached widespread public attention in Canada in the 1990s, when Leilani Muir launched a lawsuit against the Alberta government for wrongful sterilization. In 1928, the Alberta government set up a Eugenics Board and instituted the *Sexual Sterilization Act*. The Board would evaluate suspected "mental defectives" when they reached puberty, and after an interview of only a few minutes, would determine if they should be sterilized. Leilani Muir was one of the young women who were sterilized, without her knowledge. As a pre-teen, her alcoholic and abusive mother dropped Muir off at the Provincial Training School in Red Deer. Shortly thereafter, she was classified as a "mental defective" and sterilized. After leaving the training school and embarking upon a completely normal life, she discovered that she had been sterilized when she went to a doctor to determine why she was unable to become pregnant. "The doctor described her insides as 'being as if she'd been through a slaughterhouse.' Then, when she tried to adopt, she was refused because of the stigma of being a former inmate of Red Deer"(Buchanan, 1997, p. 46). She won her lawsuit, being awarded an undisclosed amount of money for the pain and suffering she had endured (Whiting, 1996; Buchanan, 1997; Grekul, 2002).

The Eugenics Board attached the label "mental defective" to an extremely wide range of people—those with low IQs, those who had lifestyles deemed to be "immoral" (presuming that only a "mental defective" would live an immoral lifestyle), immigrants unable to speak English, those who were considered burdens because of their poverty, and poverty-stricken women who dared to have children. In a significant proportion of cases, the "mental defectives" that were sterilized were really people who simply violated social norms (Grekul, 2002). For example, one young woman had been gang-raped by local boys, and as a result was labelled "sexually immoral" and entered into the juvenile justice system herself. Her father, unable to live with what had happened, placed her in the Provincial Training School, where she was sterilized (Buchanan, 1997). The act was not repealed until 1978, lasting far longer than in other countries that used sterilization in pursuit of eugenic ideals. Even following World War II, at a time when "Nazis were being hung for their eugenic programs, 'lessons from this dark period of human history appeared to have little or no impact on the operation of the Alberta Eugenics Board'" (Wahlstein, cited in Buchanan, 1997, p. 46). Thus, even though governments throughout the world (including Canada's) considered the way that the Nazis pursued eugenic ideals "deviant" (Proctor, 1988; Weiss, 1988), the continued pursuit of those ideals through sterilization continued to be practiced in Canada.

Of course, the Nazis in Germany went much further in their application of eugenics (Proctor, 1988; Weiss, 1988). They sterilized between 350 000 and 400 000 between the time Hitler was elected in 1933 and the beginnings of World War II in the late 1930s. Initially, the world community viewed the size of the Nazi sterilization program in a positive light, setting it as a standard that they could attempt to approximate themselves (Proctor, 1988). However, as the drive for "racial purity" progressed under the Nazis, genocidal measures were implemented, including the killing of millions of people in concentration camps—those who were Jewish, "Gypsies," trade unionists, homosexuals, "mental defectives," and the physically disabled. An immense science program was established as well, with significant strides made in the area of genetics; torturous medical experimentation (e.g., on twins) served as the basis for these scientific advancements (Proctor, 1988).

The history of social Darwinism and eugenics demonstrates the power that science has held as a social typer of deviance. The science of the time proclaimed a "truth" that had widespread implications. The "truth" according to these scientists was that certain social groups were biologically "superior," while others were "inferior." This rationalized a diversity of measures that ranged from laws prohibiting interracial marriage, to restrictive immigration policies, to involuntary sexual sterilization, to the horrors of the Holocaust. These historical events are a rather dramatic illustration of the power of science. However, the role that science plays in the social typing of deviance is not limited to the past. We can explore many contemporary examples as well.

The eugenics movement reached its historical apex in Nazi Germany, with the millions of people killed in concentration camps. However, eugenic ideals were also being pursued to lesser degrees in Canada, Britain, Australia, and the United States.

TIME TO REVIEW:

- What is "social Darwinism," and how is it related to the social typing of deviance?
- What is "eugenics," and when was it popular?
- What were the goals of the eugenics movements?
- In what countries were eugenic ideals pursued, and how were they pursued? Provide specific examples.

Scientific Social Typing Today: Medicine, Psychiatry, and Genetics

Medicalization

Science continues to play a role in the determination and control of deviance. Medical science, in particular, plays a central role; in fact, some scholars claim that medicine is *the* form of science that underlies our culture's dominant moral codes (Conrad, 1992; Turner, 1987). As you have progressed through this textbook, the medicalization of deviance has been one of the central themes. In the chapter on physical appearance, we addressed the role that medical science plays in defining "too fat" and "too thin," and then the various ways that doctors exert social control over those "deviant" populations. Gentle suggestions to their patients about losing weight, handing out material on healthy eating and physical fitness, provision of medically-supervised weight loss programs, hospital-based programs for treating people with anorexia, weight-loss pills, gastric bypass surgery, and liposuction are different ways that medical science treats people who are "too fat" or "too thin."

In the chapter on mental disorders, the role of the psychiatric community in the medicalization of deviance was evident. Members of the psychiatric community determine the symptoms that constitute "deviance," through their creation of the *Diagnostic and Statistical Manual of Mental Disorders* (American Psychiatric Association, 1994). They then diagnose people with those disorders, and provide treatment in the amelioration of symptoms. The categories of mental disorder bring us back to the chapter on sexuality, wherein the psychiatric community determines that certain sexual behaviours constitute mental disorders (e.g., transvestic fetishism). Precisely what mental "deviance" consists of varies over time, as some characteristics are removed from the diagnostic manual (e.g., homosexuality), and new ones are added (e.g., ADHD, gender identity disorder). Debates over the diagnostic categories, the absolute guardianship that psychiatrists have over the determination of what constitutes mental "deviance," and the political nature of how it is determined are all ongoing (Caplan, 1995).

Earlier in this chapter, we briefly looked at the tobacco industry and the "science wars" that have occurred surrounding it. The scientists of note in these "wars" are medical scientists. As a consequence of the research done by the anti-smoking medical activists, smoking has become successfully medicalized. Direct smoking was the first to be medicalized, and with medical research as the foundation, anti-smoking activists (including a large number of doctors) have had a tremendous impact on society. Their efforts have resulted in getting warning labels on cigarette packages, banning cigarette commercials on television, restricting events that can be sponsored by tobacco companies, and instituting anti-smoking programs in schools. More recently, second-hand smoking has been effectively medicalized, and has resulted in many communities instituting bylaws prohibiting smoking in various places—shopping malls, restaurants, workplaces, government buildings, and bars. The ongoing struggles between anti-smoking activists and groups defending smokers' rights continue to hold a central place in the media and government (Tuggle & Holmes, 1997); you may have even been following these struggles in your own local newspaper.

There is no doubt that medicine is of tremendous importance to people's health throughout the world. Being overweight or underweight *does* increase health risks. Advances in psychopharmaceuticals *have* cured many people of mental disorders such as depression and have enabled many people with ongoing mental disorders to lead high-quality, high-functioning lives. Smoking *is* dangerous to smokers and to people around them. However, the primacy that is given to medical science in determining deviance has led to numerous questions and concerns (Conrad, 1992), not the least of which is whether *social* characteristics are being medicalized. This concern in particular is illustrated by the practice of giving liposuction to patients solely for the purpose of physical appearance, by the categorization of social groups (e.g., immigrants, people who did not follow social norms) as "mental defectives" under the science of eugenics, and by the individualization of social problems in the widespread diagnosis of ADHD in North America. Concerns about the possible implications of the social nature of medicalization are especially widespread today with questions surrounding genetic testing and genetic manipulation.

Genetic Testing and Genetic Manipulation

The Human Genome Project, an international effort involving governments, universities, and private industry, has created the first map of the human genome. The success of this project has generated almost limitless hopes among scientists. They are making almost science-fiction-like promises (Carlson & Stimeling, 2002) that the science of genetics will be able to prevent and cure illness, increase longevity and intelligence, and allow us to ensure that our children begin life with the best possible chance in the world (Carlson & Stimeling, 2002; Stock, 2002). Some proponents have even suggested that social problems, such as homelessness, will be solved (Koshland, cited in Beckwith, 1993). At the same time, ethicists are raising questions about whether this science is simply eugenics in 21st-century clothing (Ward, 1993).

There are several different positions involved in the debates over genetic testing and genetic manipulation (Sinsheimer, 1990): (a) those who advocate the complete abandonment of the Human Genome Project; (b) those who claim that beneficial gains can be made through this science, but because of the great danger also involved, scientists should select only a handful of areas in which to make use of the science; (c) those who do want to give science freedom to advance, but advocate caution on the part of scientists, and a slow pace of implementation; and (d) those who would set no limits on the science of genetics or its implementation.

Arguments for the complete abandonment of this science are frequently based on religious or other stringent moral belief systems. The human genetic structure, and the genes possessed by specific individuals, are perceived as a matter of "divine will" (Sinsheimer, 1990, para. 4). Humanity, and particularly science, has no place in altering the will of God (or the will of nature, depending on the fundamental belief system).

Awareness of the potential social dangers of the misuse of genetic science serves as the foundation for advocates of strict controls or extreme cautions. Memories of the Nazi genetic program serve as a reminder of where ranking some biological characteristics as "superior" to or more desirable than others can potentially lead a society (Beckwith, 1993; Proctor, 1988). Although what happened in Nazi Germany may not happen again, the fact that "Nazi racial policy...was played out, at least in part, in the spheres of science and medicine [has] forever taint[ed] genetic research, at least in the public mind, with a sinister aspect" (*Wilson Quarterly*, 1992, para. 7). The complex intertwining of science with both politics and commerce today creates a structure wherein the misuse of genetic science is possible, and of concern (Sinsheimer, 1990; Stock, 2002; Carlson & Stimeling, 2002).

More abstract and more specific questions about the possible implications of this science abound. Who will decide which genes are "desirable" and which are "undesirable" (Stock, 1992; Carlson & Stimeling, 2001)? For example, will being short, brown-eyed, and dark-skinned be considered problematic? Will having artistic abilities be seen as inferior to having scientific abilities? Will people with Down syndrome, or other genetic disorders, simply no longer be born? The issue of power is central to answering these questions. The decisions are likely to be made by medical scientists themselves, given the degree of power that medical science holds in society today, as we have seen. But then, what safeguards will control the decisions made by these scientists?

Of course, the hope is that genetic research will eventually be able to cure disease rather than eliminate individuals. However, the lag between the ability to diagnose genetic problems and the ability to treat those genetic problems is significant, and likely to grow even larger (Ward, 1993). The Human Genome Project was extraordinarily expensive for numerous corporate entities; the quickest and most profitable means of recouping these costs is through the mass marketing of tests for specific genetic conditions, rather than through continued research into finding "cures" (Stikeman & Fraticelli, 1992). Furthermore, critics point out that very few diseases and conditions are purely genetic in origin. In most cases, disease emerges from the interaction between biology, environment, and lifestyle. Thus, they claim that genetic science will *not* be able to significantly alter the presence of disease and disability in society (Stikeman & Fraticelli, 1992; Beckwith, 1993; Dunne & Warren, 1998).

The suggestion that social problems, such as homelessness, can be solved by genetic science (because of the prevalence of mental illness among the homeless) is criticized as being ignorant and uninformed (Beckwith, 1993). As we saw in the chapter on mental disorders, homelessness is not caused by mental illness, but rather by the structure of the health care system, wherein people with mental illnesses fall through the cracks. This has happened due to the unintended consequences of deinstitutionalization, and a lack of sufficient funding for community-based treatment programs. By suggesting that genetic manipulation is the solution, attention is drawn away from the non-biological factors that are involved in social problems, and changes that would make society a better place are not given a priority (Beckwith, 1993). Some critics have even indicated that the trillions of dollars that have been spent on the Human Genome Project would have been better spent on social improvements throughout the world.

The largest issues that are raised in relation to genetic testing and genetic manipulation emphasize human rights. Some nations (e.g., Iceland) are trying to implement national banks of genetic information, wherein citizens will have no choice but to undergo genetic testing (Jones, 2001). Voluntary genetic testing is considered an important human rights issue, yet the results of Dunne and Warren's (1998) research questions whether "voluntary" testing is even "voluntary." Genetic counsellors advise certain groups of pregnant women about potential genetic defects in their fetuses; the counsellors are expected to provide women with enough information, coming from all sides of the issue, to decide whether or not they want genetic testing to be done. All too often, the genetic counsellors only provide the negative information about the specific disease or condition involved, rather than all of the information (Dunne & Warren, 1998). That is, instead of telling women about the resources that are available to them if they do decide to have a child that has a genetic condition (e.g., support groups, educational programs, medical treatments), they may only provide information on the negative aspects of the condition.

Thus, the "deviant" label that is attached to genetic conditions within parts of the medical community means that the information provided to patients may be biased, unduly influencing the nature of decisions they make about whether to get tested, and if tested, whether or not to continue with a pregnancy.

The possibility that the results of genetic testing could be used for the purposes of discrimination in insurance and employment is realistic as well (Ward, 1993; Beckwith, 1993; Carlson & Stimeling, 2002). A 1996 study of 332 people who had undergone or refused to undergo genetic testing reveals the potential for discriminatory use of genetic information (Lapham et al., cited in Dunne & Warren, 1998) (see Table 9.1).

Table 9.1 GENETIC INFORMATION DISCRIMINATION SURVEY

FORMS OF DISCRIMINATION	% OF RESPONDENTS
Denied or fired from employment	13%
Denied life insurance coverage	25%
Denied health insurance coverage	22%
Refused to be tested for fear of discrimination	9%
Would not reveal information to employers	17%
Would not reveal information to insurance companies	18%

The various concerns involving the possible implications of genetic testing have resulted in social control measures being directed at the scientific community itself. Groups of scientists have come together to raise issues, ask questions, and issue guidelines for scientific work—"Science for the People," "The Council for Responsible Genetics," and "The Union of Concerned Scientists" (Beckwith, 1993). For example, the "Council for Responsible Genetics" has adopted a *Genetic Bill of Rights,* which outlines what they see as fundamental principles that genetic research and implementation should be based on. It includes "the right to a world in which living organisms cannot be patented," "the right to protection against eugenic measures such as forced sterilization or mandatory screening aimed at aborting or manipulating selected embryos or fetuses," and "the right to be free from genetic discrimination" (The Council for Responsible Genetics, 2000).

International coalitions of governments are also addressing the issues, and having discussions about appropriate control measures. In 1997, the United Nations Educational, Scientific, and Cultural Organization (UNESCO) adopted the *Universal Declaration on the Human Genome and Human Rights,* which makes similar declarations as those made by The Council on Responsible Genetics. Significant aspects of the declaration include prohibitions against human cloning, guidelines for scientists declaring that "they should seek to ensure that research results are not used for non-peaceful purposes," and the statement that the "uniqueness and diversity" of individuals must be respected (UNESCO, 1997). Individual governments have also developed guidelines for genetic research and its application. What most of these organizational, international, and national guidelines share are the fundamental principles that underlie their policies (Jones, 2001):

- respect for human dignity
- the right to genetic privacy
- health protection and promotion
- genetic equality
- public participation in decision-making processes

Given the rapid pace at which this science is developing, and the expansion of discussion surrounding ethical and legal issues involved with the science, policy and law is in a constant state of change. New genetic advances continue to be made, new ethical issues emerge, and lawsuits involving some aspect of genetic testing, research, or manipulation are ongoing in countries throughout the world. It can be difficult to keep up with these developments. However Health Canada, the World Health Organization, UNESCO, and organizations like the Council for Responsible Genetics are all reliable sources of information about the current state of affairs with respect to ethical, scientific, and legal issues involving the science of genetics. All of these organizations have extensive Websites with vast amounts of documentation and publications available on-site at no charge.

Like religious belief systems, scientific belief systems also have extensive relationships with the concept of deviance. Certain practices that occur within science can be considered "deviant," and entire bodies of science can be considered "deviant." However, science also serves as a powerful social typer of deviance, perhaps the most powerful social typer in society today. That power does not go unquestioned, and controls are being exerted on the social typing that occurs within science. Religious and scientific belief systems are both governing forces in the lives of billions of people in the world. The "truths" that they proclaim are a foundation for our own behaviours, as well as our judgments of others. But as the quote at the beginning of this chapter suggests, both types of belief systems are socially constructed. The subjective dimension of religious and scientific belief systems means that neither should operate unbridled and without questioning.

TIME TO REVIEW:

- What are some contemporary examples of how science serves as a social typer of deviance?
- What is the Human Genome Project, and how does its application related to the social typing of deviance?
- What are the different positions involved in the debate over genetic testing and genetic manipulation?
- What benefits could the science of genetics bring?
- What are the potential dangers of the science of genetics?
- How have scientific organizations, governments, and the international community responded to the potential dangers of the science of genetics?

CHAPTER SUMMARY

Science consists of *belief systems* and *technologies*. Like religious belief systems, science also exists in different types of relationships with deviance: *science as deviance* and *science as a social typer of deviance*.

Science as deviance occurs in two different ways: *deviance in science* and *"deviant" sciences*. Various forms of behaviour characterize *deviance in science*. Fraudulent use of data, creating hoaxes, misusing scientific credentials, and violating codes of ethics are all actions that are negatively sanctioned within the scientific community. *Bad apple theories* propose that individual characteristics are the cause of *deviance in science*; some people are simply more prone to deviance than others. The *iceberg theory* claims that the structure of the scientific community itself sets the stage for deviance to occur.

"Deviant" sciences are those in which the claims being made about the nature of reality (e.g., astrology), or the implicit ethical/moral claims (e.g., cloning), are questioned in their entirety. As a result, the entire science is labelled "deviant," a "pseudo-science," or a "non-science." What is considered to be a *"deviant" science* can change over time, as illustrated by the case of radio astronomy.

Science also *serves as a social typer of deviance*. Historical examples of the social typing in which science has been involved include social Darwinism, the eugenics movement, and certain scientific pursuits in Nazi Germany. Instances of contemporary social typing are evident in a number of topics addressed in earlier chapters (e.g., mental disorder; body size; sexuality). An especially controversial issue today is the actual and potential social typing that occurs within the science of genetics.

Recommended Readings

Pruzhinin, B. I. & Scanlon, J. P. (1995). Astrology. *Russian Social Science Review, 36*(5), 75-94.

* This article is one of the most thorough academic treatments of astrology I have read. The claims made by astrology, its social history, and its efforts to be treated as a "real" science are reviewed. Its continued status as a "deviant" science is also documented.

McLaren, A. (1990). *Our own master race: Eugenics in Canada 1885-1945.* Toronto: McClelland and Stewart.

* McLaren provides an in-depth analysis of the pursuit of eugenic ideals in Canadian history.

Carlson, R. J. & Stimeling, G. (2002). *The terrible gift: The brave new world of genetic medicine.* New York: PublicAffairs.

* The authors of this book review the promises and the dangers of genetic medicine; however, they emphasize the dangers.

Endnotes

1 J. B. S. Haldane. Retrieved June 13, 2003 from World Wide Web: **http://www.quotationspage.com**.

Key Terms

science as deviance, **p. 271**
science as a social typer of deviance, **p. 271**
scientific belief systems, **p. 272**
technologies, **p. 272**
deviance in science, **p. 272**
deviant science, **p. 272**
forging, **p. 272**
fraudulent science, **p. 273**
trimming, **p. 273**
cooking, **p. 273**
hoaxes, **p. 273**
pathological science, **p. 274**
junk science, **p. 275**
sound science, **p. 275**
bad apple/bad person theory, **p. 277**
iceberg theory, **p. 277**
ethical violations, **p. 278**
social Darwinism, **p. 288**
eugenics, **p. 288**

CHAPTER 10

The "Deviance Dance" Continues

Learning Objectives

After reading this chapter, you should be able to:

- Describe how more objective and more subjective approaches to studying deviance have been reflected in the chapters in this textbook.
- Describe how the notion of the social typing process has been reflected in the topics explored in this textbook.
- Explain how the importance of *power* has been addressed within the chapters in this textbook.
- Explain how the concept of the "deviance dance" has been integrated into the topics explored in this textbook.
- Cite examples of human rights legislation, and explain how these documents can determine when it is, and is not, appropriate to attach a deviant label to people, behaviours, or characteristics.

"Conformity makes everything easier, if you can still breathe." (Mason Cooley)[1]

"You have to be deviant if you're going to do anything new." (David Lee)[2]

Ask Yourself:

In the first chapter, I asked the following questions: Who are the conformists in our society and in our world? Is life easier for them? Are their thoughts, behaviours, and identities limited by their conformity? Who are the deviants? Are they really the deviants of our world, or do they represent some type of problem that we need to control? What is it that differentiates a "deviant" from a "conformist"? How can we distinguish between them? Given what you have learned during the course, and the ideas that the course material has stimulated, spend some time thinking about how you would answer these questions now.

These are the two quotations that this textbook began with. The first quotation suggests that conforming will make our lives run more smoothly; at the same time, it points out that **conformity** is restricting. The second quotation suggests that we can only achieve innovation and change if we're willing to risk being thought of as **deviant**. Now that you have reached the last chapter, this is a good time to reflect upon these ideas. In this chapter, we will look back at some of the main ideas that were introduced in the first chapter, and explore how those ideas have been reflected in the various substantive topics that have been addressed—sexuality, youth, physical appearance (and especially body size), mental disorder, religion, and science. As you read through this chapter, you will be asked to do a lot of thinking on your own. This is the time when you can reflect on the topics you have learned about and the ideas you had during this course.

The Objective-Subjective Continuum

Various researchers approach the study of deviance differently. Although the differences among researchers have traditionally been characterized as a dichotomy or dualism (Adler & Adler, 2003; Ben-Yehuda, 1990), most deviance specialists today combine some aspects of both objective and subjective (e.g., Evans, 2001). Even looking back at earlier research reveals that the distinctions between these approaches were not as clear-cut as has been suggested (e.g., Becker, 1963). Thus, we can think of deviance research as falling along a continuum, wherein virtually all scholars fit somewhere between the two extreme polar ends. Some deviance specialists lean to the more objective side of the continuum, while others lean to the more subjective side of the continuum.

Scholars who lean to the more **objective** side of the continuum focus their analytical spotlight on the deviant act itself. The "deviant" act exists a priori to the analysis, and can be recognized by specific characteristics such as a negative societal reaction, social harm, statistical rarity, or a violation of norms. With an overarching interest in explaining the variation in human behaviour, they focus on causation—what makes people act in deviant ways. Although this **positivist** interest is one shared with the natural sciences, the search for causation in the social sciences emphasizes statistical probabilities rather than causation in its pure sense (Ashley & Orenstein, 2001). Due to their focus on explaining the deviant act, they find particular types of theories are more useful to them than to the scholars that lean toward the more subjective side of the research continuum. These were the theories addressed in Chapter 2—functionalist theories, social learning theories, and social control theories.

Deviance specialists who lean to the more **subjective** side of the continuum focus their analytical spotlight on the social processes by which certain people, actions, or characteristics come to be perceived as deviant. They suggest that we cannot recognize deviance in any objective sense, but instead must be taught that certain people, actions, and characteristics are deviant (Becker, 1963). Power is perceived as central to determining what is deviant. Due to their emphasis on explaining the social processes that underlie deviant labels, particular types of theories are more useful to them than to scholars that lean toward the more objective side of the research continuum. These were the theories addressed in Chapter 3—**interpretive** theories and **critical** theories (Ashley & Orenstein, 2001).

Combining the results of both the more objective and the more subjective research provides us with the most comprehensive understanding of deviance, wherein we learn something about the deviant act (i.e., why, when, and how it occurs) and the processes by which that act has come to be perceived and treated as deviant. Throughout this textbook you have seen many instances of each of these areas of emphasis.

In the chapter on sexuality (Chapter 4), a historical context surrounded our exploration. In looking at the sexual cultures of 5th century B.C. Athens (Arkins, 1994), the Sambia of New Guinea (Herdt, 1984), traditional Aboriginal cultures (Newhouse, 1998), and North America before, during, and after industrialization (D'Emilio & Freedman, 1997; Razack, 2002; Valverde, 1991), we saw the various norms that shaped people's sexual behaviours. For example, we saw that the reason why ritualized homosexual acts with young boys occur in Sambian society is because of cultural norms emerging out of their spiritual belief system (Herdt, 1984). In contemporary society, we explored the cultural norms that, if violated, are considered deviant (e.g., age of the sexual partner). An historical context also enabled us to look at the culturally specific processes by which certain people, acts, or characteristics come to be labelled deviant. In the sexuality chapter as a whole, the tremendous diversity in sexual cultures around the world and throughout history illustrated that what is considered sexually "deviant" lies not in the acts themselves, but in the evaluations of particular acts based on the dominant moral codes in society at the time.

In the chapter on youth (Chapter 5), the objective and subjective dimensions were reflected in the various topics of youthful deviance that we addressed—crime, gangs, substance use, and the nature of adolescence itself. An abundance of research has been conducted on the causes of youth crime (e.g., Davies, 1994), gang emergence and involvement (e.g., Jankowski, 1991; Gordon, 1995), smoking, alcohol use, and drug use (e.g., Roberts et al., 2001). We explored some of the theoretical and empirical research that explains these "deviant" behaviours. Differential association theory, social control theories, and social learning theories have been applied to understandings of many of these acts, and empirical research reveals the complex web of factors that contributes to them as well. For instance, characteristics of family life (especially the balance of parental expectations and parent-child affection) are consistently found to play an important role in youth crime (Milan, 2000; Brook et al., 1999). Because these behaviours emerge from the interaction of personal, family, school, and community factors, programs and policies to reduce the frequency of these behaviours must address these multilevel factors. Shifting our focus to the social processes that underlie the deviantization of youth, we explored how the gap between the perceptions of youth crime or the "gang problem" and their prevalence contribute to particular ways of trying to control these problems (Tanner, 2001; Fasiolo & Leckie, 1993). In looking at the way that youth itself, as a stage in the life cycle, is considered deviant, we saw that adolescents live the lives that we, as adults, create for them. The exaggerated "generation gap" of the past may become a reality in the future; however, it is not because of the "deviant" nature of adolescence, but rather the structure of society as created by adults. However, the continued misperception of all youth as "deviant" influences the ways that youth are treated in society.

Body size was the emphasis for the chapter on physical appearance (Chapter 6)—"too fat," "too thin," and "ideal." Certain body sizes are, indeed, associated with significantly higher risks of health problems (World Health Organization, 2002; Health Canada, 2002); scholars have analyzed various biological, psychological, and social factors in their attempts to determine why people become obese or anorexic, and what treatments will help them (Caldwell, 2001; McLorg & Taub, 1987). However, popular social perceptions of "too fat," "too thin," and "ideal" have little to do with health risks, and much to do with current cultural standards of beauty, standards that critics say have reached alarmingly thin proportions (Owen & Laurel-Seller, 2000; Spitzer, Henderson, & Zivian, 1999). These standards of beauty vary considerable across cultures and over time, so that what is seen as being a "deviant" body size in 21st-century Canada is very different than in 21st-century Ghana, or 19th-century Canada (Shuriquie, 1999).

Mental disorders are medicalized forms of deviance. In the chapter on mental disorders (Chapter 7), the more objective approach was reflected in the material on prevalence, causes, and treatments of mental illness. We saw that mental illness affects most Canadians, either directly (through their own experiences of mental illness) or indirectly (having a friend, family member, or co-worker with a mental illness) (Health Canada, 2002). The social and economic costs of mental disorders are tremendous, not only in Canada but throughout the world (Ettner, Frank, & Kessler, 1998; Murray & Lopez, 1996; Stephans & Jorbert, 2001). Therefore, a wide range of therapeutic techniques—counselling, medication, and family supports—treat the combined biological and social aspects of mental disorders (World Health Organization, 2002). The more subjective approach is reflected in the research that emphasizes the political and social aspects of diagnosis and treatment. Although there is considerable overlap between North American and international diagnostic tools, scholars point out that there is a political aspect to determining what constitutes psychological "deviance" (Caplan, 1995). For example, homosexuality is no longer categorized as a mental disorder, but other behaviours (e.g., gender identity dysphoria) now are. Some critics suggest that *social* problems are being medicalized, and treated as illnesses. For example, the high rate of ADHD diagnosis in North America may have more to do with the multi-tasking that characterizes modern life rather than with a psychological disorder of particular children (McConnell, 1997; Shute, 2000).

The objective and subjective dimensions of deviance research are reflected in the chapter on religious belief systems as well (Chapter 8). More objective research is reflected in the search to understand sects and cults. Researchers have explored

Marshall Applewhite, founder of the Heaven's Gate cult. Deviance scholars with a more objective approach to research try to explain why mass suicides occur in some cults.

why "deviant" religious groups form, what conditions foster acts like mass suicides, and what factors contribute to sect or cult violence (Lewis & Melton, 1994; Bromley, 2002; Hall, 2002). Specialists in the study of cults have investigated specific groups (e.g., "the Family"), testified in court as expert witnesses, and created guidelines for people to use in determining whether a specific religious group may be dangerous (Barker, 2001). Scholars with more subjective interests have questioned the traditional distinction between churches, sects, and cults, and have demonstrated that political factors frequently determine which groups are treated as "deviant" within a particular society (Jenkins, 2000; Chryssides, 1994). They have also pointed out the power that religion has frequently had as a social typer of deviance—it dictated to us who or what should be considered deviant—and the potential dangers of the boundaries between religion and politics becoming blurred (Boston, 1996).

Researchers with more objective research interests have studied "deviant" acts that occur within science, such as the fraudulent use of data (e.g., Park, 2000). Many of them have concluded that these acts are more common than might be suspected. Some explanations of "deviant" scientific acts focus on individual factors (i.e., **bad apple theory**), but others emphasize that the characteristics of the scientific community itself set the stage for "deviant" acts (i.e., **iceberg theory**) (Ben-Yehuda, 1986; Bechtel & Pearson, 1985; Jammes, 1995). Within the latter approach, a number of specific theories have been applied, such as differential association theory, Merton's anomie theory, and social control theories. The subjective dimension of deviance is explored in the analysis of science as a powerful social typer of deviance, telling us who or what should be considered deviant. When scientists make claims to "truth," many of us automatically believe them and, in any instance, would not likely dare to question them. These tendencies underlie some of the criticisms that have been directed at popular radio scientist Dr. Laura Schlessinger for misusing her scientific credentials. Although in many cases the efforts of scientists benefit us all (e.g., regarding the health dangers of obesity), we must also remember the central role that science played in the eugenics movement and the horrors of what occurred in Nazi Germany.

Social Typing, Social Control, and Powerful Groups

The notion of deviance emerges out of the **social typing process** (Rubington & Weinberg, 2002). The first component of social typing is **description**, wherein a label is attached to a person, behaviour, or characteristic. The second component is **evaluation**, in which a judgment is attached to the person, behaviour, or characteristic because of the initial label. The last component is **prescription**, where the person is treated in specific ways only because of the label and the judgment that have been attached. This last component of the social typing process refers to measures of **social control** or **regulation**. Deviance can be controlled **informally** (i.e., through everyday social interactions) or **formally** (i.e., at the hands of an institution or organization) (Rubington & Weinberg, 2002). The social control of deviance may be **preventative** (i.e., preventing a deviant act in the first place, such as through socialization) or **retroactive** (i.e., following a deviant act) (Edwards, 1988). **Self-control** is another form of regulation, wherein we all monitor our own behaviours to prevent and fix our own deviance (Edwards, 1988; Foucault, 1995).

The social typing of deviance is the most effective when someone who has some institutionalized power in society does it (Rubington & Weinberg, 2002). Five different groups in society are especially powerful, able to influence our decisions about who or what is "deviant," and able to exert potent measures of social control: the media, commercial enterprise, government, religion, and science. At times these powerful groups act as **moral entrepreneurs** themselves, by trying to influence or change society's dominant moral code in relation to a particular issue. At other times, these powerful groups serve as tools used by other groups of moral entrepreneurs in their efforts. The central role that the media plays in the daily lives of billions of people makes it the locus of claims-making in the struggles over moral codes and deviance. Commercial enterprise is another powerful group involved in the social typing process. Its efforts are also intertwined with the media, in two different ways. First, although there is a small non-profit element in Canadian broadcasting, the media is predominantly a form of commercial enterprise, an industry that is driven by the profit motive. Second, commercial enterprise uses the media as a tool for selling its products, via advertising, commercials, and product placement in television shows or movies. Politicians and governments are the group in whom ultimate power is vested. In their hands lies the power to create or revoke legislation, to construct social policies that will be implemented through various means, and to influence the enforcement of society's dominant moral codes. Politicians may act as moral entrepreneurs, or may be lobbied by interest groups acting as moral entrepreneurs. The work of politicians also exists in a bi-directional relationship with the media, where the media follows the work of politicians, and politicians use the media as a tool to spread their influence over the public mind. Religious institutions have played a vital role in the creation of dominant moral codes throughout history, maybe more so in the past than today. Finally, the power of scientists in the social typing process is perhaps granted more legitimacy than any other group. Science is seen by many people as a purely "objective" discipline, such that the claims to "truth" that are made by scientists are frequently considered unaffected by political, religious, or commercial interests.

Ask Yourself:

Social typers frequently rationalize the labelling of certain people, actions, or characteristics as deviant on the basis of notions of statistical rarity, social harm, negative societal reaction, or normative violation. As you read through the review of how social typing was addressed within the substantive topics in this textbook, consider the rationales that were used for the social typing of deviance in each of the various instances.

The chapter on sexuality revealed that in any given culture at any particular time in history, certain sexual behaviours are socially typed as deviant and made subject to social control measures. In 5th century B.C. Athens, sexual relationships between males were accepted, but only if the males were of different social statuses; if two males of equal status had a sexual relationship, they would be subject to informal sanctions. Males that received money for engaging in anal intercourse had their citizenship revoked, and lost their right to participate in political life (Arkins, 1994). Following European colonization, Aboriginal sexuality was socially controlled through religion (e.g., the teachings of local missionaries) and government (e.g., through legislation banning polygamy) (Newhouse, 1988; Razack, 2002). Over the last several hundred years, what has been socially typed as "deviant" sexuality has varied, based upon the cultural norms of the time (D'Emilio & Freedman, 1997). When sexuality was perceived as solely for the purpose of procreation, any non-procreative sexual acts (e.g., heterosexual coitus involving contraceptive use; homosexuality; masturbation) were socially typed as deviant. This is considerably different from society today, wherein personal pleasure is perceived as the purpose of sexuality. Although there is more freedom in sexual norms today than in the past, certain sexual acts are still socially typed as "deviant" (e.g., sex with a minor; having sex "too frequently"; being "kinky") (Goode, 1997). The way that sexuality is socially controlled has changed as well. During the 16th and 17th centuries, sexual "deviance" was primarily a religious and familial concern; for example, sexual deviance could result in excommunication from the church, and fathers would enforce "shotgun" weddings following premarital pregnancy. Today, religion has lost its hold over sexuality, succeeded by a diversity of social control measures. We have legislation that governs certain aspects of sexuality (e.g., degree of consent; age), medicalization (e.g., encouraging "safer" sex; "sexual disorders" as mental disorders), social organizations that try to encourage abstinence and contraceptive use in adolescents, and the pervasiveness of sexuality in all forms of the media.

In the chapter on youth, we saw that certain behaviours and characteristics of youth are socially typed as deviant and made subject to social control. Youth crime is defined and controlled by government and the criminal justice system. Youth gangs are considered a widespread social concern, which is reflected in media reports of youth street gangs, specialized law enforcement units to monitor gang members, as well as various educational programs that discourage gang membership (Fasiolo & Leckie, 1993; Tanner, 2001). The science of "risk management" attempts to intervene with youth who are seen as "at risk" of gang membership, criminal involvement, homelessness, substance abuse, teen pregnancy, and more. Law enforcement, social workers, psychologists, educators, health professionals, governments, and social organizations all participate in such "risk management" (Bessant, 2001). Youth substance use is socially typed as deviant, being seen as both a medical and a social problem. Public service campaigns via the media, education and intervention programs within various social organizations, and medical treatment are all means by which substance use is controlled (Roberts et al., 2001). Binge drinking in college is controlled through diverse programs that include peer education and support, college policies, and in some cases even "dry" campuses (Keeling, 2000; 2002).

Certain types of voluntary and involuntary physical appearances are socially typed as deviant. Those who choose particular hairstyles, makeup, and clothing (e.g., "goths") may find it difficult to find employment, because of employers' attitudes and biases. People who stray beyond the "ideal" body size are socially typed as "too fat" or "too thin," although there is much more leeway for thinness before a deviant label is attached. Body size is regulated in the realms of medicine for health reasons, but is controlled in other arenas as well. The media is a powerful social typing and social control agent for "too fat," with media imagery having a significant influence on people's perceptions of body size, feelings about themselves, and efforts at weight loss (Stice & Shaw, 1998; Garner, 1997). Commercial industry permeates social control over "too fat." Books, magazines, videos, pills, potions, and patches all promise to help us lose weight and look great. In the realm of everyday interaction, people who are considered "too fat" are controlled through stigmatization (e.g., name-calling), prejudicial attitudes, and overt discrimination (e.g., in employment) (Puhl & Brownell, 2001). Government programs target people who are overweight and/or out of shape, trying to encourage people to adopt healthier lifestyles (e.g., Health Canada, 2003). Even some schools are attempting to reduce the proportion of children who are overweight, by instituting daily fitness activities (Demont, 2002).

The social typing of psychological deviance as mental disorder occurs at both formal and informal levels. Mental disorder today is highly medicalized. The fields of psychiatry and psychology are intimately involved in social typing, determining what the "descriptions" are (e.g., "depression"), what the evaluation is (i.e., "ill"), and what the treatments should be (e.g., therapy, medication, hospitalization). In the past, mental illness was perceived quite differently. For example, for several centuries people who are now seen as "mentally ill" were instead perceived as possessed by the devil or guilty of witchcraft. Control measures included religious rituals to exorcise the devil (in the case possession) or, in the case of witchcraft, executions carried out by religious or governmental authorities. Over the last several decades the **deinstitutionalization** movement has characterized most Western nations, with a shift from hospital-based treatments to community-based treatments. Deinstitutionalization has worked very well for those people who have strong support networks and who live in communities with sufficient resources. However, for people lacking support networks and community resources, deinstitutionalization has meant a lack of medical treatment (Krieg, 2001; Sullivan, Jackson, & Spritzer, 1996). People with mental illnesses who do not receive medical treatment frequently end up being socially controlled as homeless persons or criminals (Belcher, 1989; Hodgins, 1995).

In the religion chapter, we saw that many different religious groups are socially typed as deviant by governments, scientific "experts," or other religious groups. For example, the government of Germany labels Scientology as deviant, and does

Ask Yourself:

An important aspect of social typing is who benefits from the social typing process—the social typers themselves, particular groups in society, society as a whole, or sometimes even the people who have been socially typed. Select one specific issue from each of the substantive topics covered in the textbook—sexuality, youth, physical appearance, mental disorder, religion, and science—and ask yourself who has benefitted from the social typing in that instance.

not hire its adherents (Forum 18, 2001). The Chinese government closely monitors and controls the few legalized religions in that country: adults are legally prohibited from teaching any religion to children, members of the Communist Party are not permitted to hold any religious beliefs, and religious leaders are frequently appointed by the government (Forum 18, 2001). The **anti-cult movement** socially types certain religious groups as "deviant," emphasizing those groups thought to use mind control techniques and authoritarian leadership. Organizations that are part of this movement provide information on cult awareness, support groups for parents of cult members, and in some cases, deprogramming services for former cult members (Barker, 2001). The **counter-cult movement** consists of certain fundamentalist Christian groups that identify all non-fundamentalist Christians and all non-Christian religions as "deviant"; they spread their messages via the Internet, at church meetings, and through publications that teach members how to convince adherents of specific cults to leave those groups (Bromley & Shupe, 1993).

In the science chapter, one of the ways that social typing, social control, and power made themselves evident was in the concept of "deviant" sciences or pseudo-sciences (Shermer, 2001a). The scientific community itself determines which belief systems are not "real" sciences, such as astrology. Although the scientific community is the most qualified entity to evaluate the scientific claims being made by others, some scholars suggest that its inherent conservatism often leads it to automatically reject anything that is new or too different from the status quo (Ben-Yehuda, 1990). This is particularly apparent in those instances where claims that were initially rejected as "deviant" come to be accepted at a later point. The astronomy community socially typed the first radio astronomers as "deviant"; consequently, they had difficulty getting their work published and became outcasts in the astronomy community. At a later point, that same scientific community determined that radio astronomy was a "real" science after all (Ben-Yehuda, 1990).

The "Deviance Dance"

Another theme throughout this textbook is the notion of the "**deviance dance**." This refers to the idea that, with any particular person, action, or characteristic that has been socially typed as "deviant," there will be differing points of view, debate, and resistance. The "dance" surrounding deviance is sometimes uniform (like a country line dance), with virtually everyone agreeing on the issue and what should

At times, the struggle over deviance is characterized by intense debate and conflict.

be done with it; everyone moves in the same direction in pursuit of the same goal. At other times, the "dance" is more waltz-like, where various groups work toward the same goal, but everyone is not taking the same steps to reach that goal. At yet other times, the "dance" is more like a mosh pit, with groups pushing, shoving, and slamming into each other in order to reach their own particular goals.

Every substantive topic we have looked at involves the "deviance dance." With sexuality, our historical review revealed that although a dominant sexual culture exists in any given society, there are always differences, resistance, and disagreement within such sexual cultures. For example, although sexual relationships between aristocratic men and adolescent boys was normative within the dominant sexual culture of 5th B.C. century Athens, there were groups of people within Athenian society who considered such relationships inappropriate and dangerous for the boys involved. They implemented efforts to regulate these relationships, such as legislation barring contact between the hours of dusk and dawn (Arkins, 1994). In contemporary society, we see debate over various aspects of sexuality, such as how often is "too often" or "not often enough," whether pornography is harmful, and how old is "too creepy" for sexual activity (Goode, 1997). We can even see resistance to legislation that prohibits sexual contact between adults and children; despite the fact that such behaviours are widely abhorred in Canadian society, the North America Man/Boy Love Association tries to convince people that consensual sexual relationships between adults and children are not harmful (NAMBLA, 2002).

In the chapter on youth, different opinions, debates, and resistance are evident also. For example, critics say that the virtually every adolescent ends up being perceived as "at risk" within the knowledge and practices of "risk management" (Bessant, 2001; Ericson & Haggerty, 2001). That is, adolescence itself has become defined as a time of inherent "risk." The "deviance dance" is also apparent in the debates that occur between politicians or interest groups that proclaim youth crime to be out of control and in need of tougher legislation, and those groups that point out the public image of youth crime is tremendously overblown. Differing points of view are present with regard to problems that *are* generally recognized, as well. For example, although most college administrators see binge drinking among students as problematic, they can have very different approaches to controlling it (Weschler et al., 2000). The most controversial approach has been the "dry campus," where all alcohol is prohibited. This has met with resistance from students, who oppose college alcohol programs or policies that are directed *at* them rather than created *with* them. It has also been criticized by a number of substance abuse experts, who claim that prohibitionist approaches are ineffective and simply move binge drinking off campus (Keeling, 2002).

The topic of body size embodies differing views and resistance as well. Although the cultural ideal of thinness continues to be perpetuated in the media and public opinion, various organizations are trying to change cultural ideals to accommodate a wider range of body sizes, and are lobbying the media to integrate more realistic representations of the female body. Anorexia is an extremely dangerous disorder that frequently requires immediate medical intervention. However, recent media images (e.g., of *Playboy* centerfolds) actually promote anorexic ideals, and "Ana" Websites even provide tips to people with anorexia to enable them to continue their pursuit of weight loss.

In the chapter on mental disorders, the "deviance dance" is most apparent in debates surrounding specific diagnostic categories contained in the American Psychiatric Association's *Diagnostic and Statistical Manual of Mental Disorders* (e.g., Caplan, 1995). For example, in contemporary society, debates over the extent to which ADHD is being diagnosed within North America are common. However, some groups have even gone a step further, suing the American Psychiatric Association for "manufacturing" a mental illness (Shute, 2000; Peck, 2001). Debates over whether gender identity disorder is a mental illness are also common today. Some scholars resist the medicalization of mental disorders even more profoundly, arguing that the concept of mental illness itself is a "myth" (Szasz, 1994).

The "deviance dance" is perhaps at its most obvious in the chapter on religion, where various groups socially typed as "sects" or "cults" must then defend themselves against the accusations. In France, more than one hundred groups have been socially typed in this way by the French government. Some members of these groups have taken their cases all the way to the European Court, where the judges' decisions have frequently opposed the claims made by the French government (United States Department of State, 2002). Throughout the world, as the Jehovah's Witnesses resist the "deviant" label that has been attached to them (and the discriminatory actions they have faced as a result, including arrest), they claim that all religious groups other than their own are "deviant" (Lawson, 1995). In the United States, the Christian Coalition attempts to influence government policy on the basis of their own beliefs about the people, actions, and characteristics that are "deviant." Conversely, various individuals and groups that are concerned about the Coalition's influence on the Republican party and the blurring of religious and political boundaries oppose the Coalition's actions (e.g., Boston, 1996).

Difference, debate, and resistance are even evident in the world of science. Ongoing debates have characterized scientific claims in relation to the tobacco industry. For example, the industry's scientists label the work of their opposition as "junk science," while scientists whose research shows the dangers of smoking launch similar claims at the industry (Rampton & Stauber, 2000a; Ong & Glantz, 2001). Historically, although the eugenics movement had considerable influence in Canada, the United States, Britain, and Germany, there were also scientists and social organizations within each of those societies that were critical of eugenic ideals. In contemporary society, while some groups of scientists proclaim the benefits that genetic testing and manipulation will bring to the world, other groups of scientists disagree, and some claim that modern genetics is nothing more than eugenics in 21st century clothing (Ward, 1993; Carlson & Stimeling, 2002).

Exercise Your Mind:

The examples that are included in this chapter barely scratch the surface of how certain themes that were introduced in the first chapter have been embodied within the rest of this textbook. You may want to look back at a particular chapter, or small segments of several chapters to look for the numerous other instances of these themes: the objective-subjective continuum; social typing, social control, and power; and the "deviance dance."

TIME TO REVIEW:

- How have more objective research interests been reflected in the chapters in this textbook?
- How have more subjective research interests been reflected in the chapters in this book?
- What are some examples of how social typing and social control are evident with each of the substantive topics explored in the textbook?
- How are notions of power embedded in the chapters in the textbook?
- In what way is the "deviance dance" apparent in the topics we have looked at?

The Search for Standards

Throughout this textbook we have seen that, to some extent, "deviance" is in the eye of the beholder. That is, there is far more to the concept of deviance than the inherent nature of the person, act, or characteristic. The cross-cultural and historical examples that we have looked at show us that power is fundamental to determining what or who will be considered deviant in society. Actions considered criminal in certain cultures at specific historical moments are seen as acceptable actions in other cultures and at other historical moments. For example, homosexual acts were seen as criminal throughout North America a century ago, but today they are not considered criminal in Canada or the United States. Conversely, during most of the 19th century child abuse and spousal abuse were seen as legally, socially, and morally acceptable, but today are considered crimes in much of the world. The sexual relationships between boys and adult men in Sambian society would constitute pedophilia according to Canadian standards. Adultery, while merely frowned upon in North America, is considered criminal in other nations (Mackay, 2000). A half-century ago, youth (but not adults) could run afoul of the criminal justice system for misbehaviours like truancy, sexual promiscuity, and incorrigibility; today, the list of offences is identical for youth and adults.

Historically, acts that were carried out by societal authorities with wide support from the rest of the community would now be considered "deviant" by contemporary standards. The witch persecutions that swept much of Europe for centuries are now looked upon, with disdain, as an instance of religious and political authorities preying upon the superstitious populace in order to further their own goals of power. Residential schooling is perceived as a regrettable event in Canadian history, even by those societal institutions that participated in it, the federal government and several church bodies. Formal apologies have been given, reparations are underway, and programs have been instituted to assist Aboriginal communities in beginning the healing process (Ontario Consultants for Religious Tolerance, 2003). Social Darwinism and the subsequent eugenics movement, popular in Canada, the United States, Britain, and other nations during the late 19th and early 20th centuries, targetted numerous social groups for forced sterilization; the eugenics movement itself is now looked upon as a "deviant" use of science and politics. The apex the eugenics movement reached in the Holocaust is widely perceived as one of the most horrific events in human history; however, it is important to remember that for several years during the 1930s, the rest of the world (including Canada) looked upon the success of Nazi eugenics with admiration.

After exploring cross-cultural and historical variations, as well as the debate and differing points of view that exist within a single society at any given time, some people understandably may begin to think that there are no transcendent

The United Nations is one international body that develops universal human rights standards.

standards by which people, behaviours, or characteristics can be evaluated—and that no group has the right to impose its subjective standards of behaviour on any other group. Because deviance is in the eye of the beholder, "anything goes." Of course, if that belief were fully realized, anarchy would reign in society. So how can balance be achieved? How can we determine whether it is appropriate to socially type specific groups of people as "deviant," and subject them to measures of social control?

To some extent, subjectivity will always be involved in the social typing of deviance. Regardless of what norms, policies, programs, or legislation exist, there will always be some people (no matter how few) who will be in opposition. However, one place to begin in a search for possible universal standards is with documents that emphasize the notion of human rights.

The *Universal Declaration of Human Rights*, adopted by the member states of the United Nations on December 10, 1948, is the foundational document for other modern human rights policies, programs, and legislation throughout the world (including the *Canadian Charter of Rights and Freedoms*). A larger sample of human rights documents can be found in Box 10.1.

Box 10.1 A Sample of Human Rights Documents

- The Magna Carta (On the British Library Website you can look at the actual pages from the original Magna Carta, and can read a translation. The Website is **http://www.bl.uk/collections/treasures/magna.html**)
- Declaration of the Rights of Man and Citizens (from the French Revolution)
- Universal Declaration of Human Rights
- Canadian Charter of Rights and Freedoms
- Convention on the Rights of the Child
- International Covenant on Civil and Political Rights
- International Covenant on Economic, Social, and Cultural Rights
- European Convention on Human Rights
- Universal Declaration on Sexual Rights
- Universal Declaration on the Human Genome and Human Rights
- Declaration on the Elimination of All Forms of Intolerance and of Discrimination Based on Religion and Belief
- Declaration on the Rights of Disabled Persons
- Principles for the Protection of Persons with Mental Illness and the Improvement of Mental Health Care
- Convention Concerning Indigenous and Tribal Peoples in Independent Countries

All of these documents can be found, in their entirety, on the Internet. A good source of information for human rights documents is the National Center for Human Rights Education, at **http://www.nchre.org**.

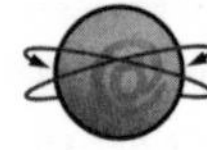

AN INTERNET MOMENT:

Go to the British Library's Website, as listed in Box 10.1, and look at the Magna Carta, which was written back in the 13th century. Then select a handful of the other human rights documents listed in Box 10.1, and find them on the Internet. Look for some of the ideas that these human rights documents share, as well as some of the distinct components of specific documents.

A number of themes run through the range of human rights documents that can be found in countries around the world. One of these is the right to **human dignity**, which is the right to be treated with respect. Numerous issues that have been addressed in this textbook can be considered in relation to this human right. The way that certain social groups were targeted by the eugenics movement can certainly be considered a violation of human dignity, as can the Nazi's racial hygiene program. European colonization and residential schooling also involved infringements on the dignity of Aboriginal people. The notion of human dignity underlies other international documents as well, such as the *Universal Declaration of Sexual Rights* (World Association for Sexology, 1999), and UNESCO's *Universal Declaration on the Human Genome and Human Rights* (UNESCO, 1997). The former document emphasizes that consensual adult sexual activities should not be deviantized, and that the freedom to sexual expression must prevail. The latter document suggests that certain genetic traits should not be considered superior or inferior to other traits; that is, individuals with specific genetic traits should not be deviantized.

Another theme in human rights documents is the prohibiting of differential treatment on the basis of group membership (i.e., **discrimination**). The characteristics that are commonly listed in relation to this right are race, sex, ethnicity, colour, nation of origin, religion, political membership, and language; however, other groups (e.g., sexual orientation) are included in some human rights documents as well. The *Canadian Charter of Rights and Freedoms* and various pieces of provincial human rights legislation address the notion of discrimination in Canadian society. The World Health Organization's constitution declares that the right to physical, mental, and social health applies to all social groups, such as those just listed (World Health Organization, 2003). The *Universal Declaration on the Human Genome and Human Rights* prohibits discrimination on the basis of genetic characteristics (UNESCO, 1997). Historically, the right to freedom from discrimination was infringed upon in the eugenics movement and during European colonization. In contemporary society, people who are considered "too fat" face discrimination in employment, housing, health care, and education (Puhl & Brownell, 2001). Members of certain religious groups are discriminated against in several countries, such as the groups identified by the government of France as "cults" (e.g., Jehovah's Witnesses; Scientology) (United States Department of State, 2002). Members of the Christian Coalition have voiced narrow views of a number of different social groups, including non-whites, members of other religious groups, and immigrants; their influence in the political realm has the potential to turn those prejudicial beliefs into overt discrimination (Boston, 1996; Viujst, 1995).

Security of person and property are also prevalent in human rights documents. Violent crimes (e.g., assault) and property crimes (e.g., theft) violate security of the person and property. The World Health Organization's constitution declares that the universal right to physical, mental, and social health is necessary for peace and security, not specifically for individuals, but within societies and throughout the world (World Health Organization, 2003); thus, the failure to provide the necessary means for achieving health for any group is seen as unacceptable. The involuntary sterilization of "mental defectives," the torture and death involved in the Holocaust, the abuse suffered by tens of thousands of Aboriginal children in residential schools, and the witch persecutions (wherein witches were not only executed, but also had their property seized to pay for their arrest, torture, trial, and execution) can all be seen as infringements upon the right to security of the person and of property. When the Canadian government defined Japanese-Canadians as "enemy aliens" during World War II, it placed thousands of Japanese-Canadian citizens in internment camps, and subsequently seized their property and auctioned it to the highest bidder. Security of person and security of property were again violated by the Canadian government.

Human dignity, freedom from discrimination, and security of person and property are three of the core themes that are integrated into various types of human rights policies and legislation. Given the influence of subjectivity and power that has been involved in the social typing of deviance across cultures and throughout history, human rights policies represent some basic standards that we may be able to apply in determining whether it is appropriate to label anyone or anything as "deviant." However, a level of subjectivity also exists in determining whether human rights have been violated in any particular instance. Human rights documents themselves state that there are circumstances where someone's human rights may legitimately be violated; typically this is when there are threats to social order, morality, or other people's human rights. For example, although freedom of religion is a basic human right, many governments monitor, regulate, and even ban specific religious groups that are perceived as a threat to social order or morality (Forum 18, 2001; United States Department of State, 2002). Although freedom of expression is a universal human right, Canada, the United States, and numerous other countries have hate crime legislation that prohibits the spreading of hatred or advocating the genocide of identifiable social groups that are protected by human rights legislation. For instance, some leaders and members of white supremacist groups have been charged with spreading hatred, even though charging them with that offence is a violation of their right to freedom of expression. International human rights documents condone this as a legitimate violation of that freedom, based on threats to the social order and violations of others people's human rights.

Box 10.2 Are You Interested in Human Rights?

If you want to learn more about human rights, or wish to become active in the pursuit of human rights, you may find the following organizations and information centers useful:

- Human Rights Watch (**http://www.hrw.org**)
- Amnesty International (**http://www.amnesty.org**)
- International Gay and Lesbian Human Rights Commission (**http://www.iglhrc.site/iglhrc/**)
- Women's Human Rights Resources (**http://www.law-lib.utoronto.ca/diana/**)
- African Human Rights Resource Center (**http://www1.umn.edu/humanrts/africa/**)

"Never doubt that a small group of thoughtful committed citizens can change the world. Indeed, it's the only thing that ever has." (Margaret Mead)[3]

Chapter Summary

Certain ideas that were introduced in Chapter 1 represent themes that have been carried through the various chapters in the textbook. One of these themes is the blending of *objective* and *subjective* approaches to the study of deviance. In various chapters, the *positivist* interest in causation that characterizes more objective approaches was explored; we looked at explanations of youth crime, substance use, mental illness, mass suicides in cults, and fraudulent research in science.

The *interpretive* and *critical* interests in the social processes by which "deviance" is assigned that characterized more subjective approaches was addressed throughout the chapters as well. We looked at the *moral panics* surrounding youth crime and gangs, the social standards that define "too fat," the criticisms directed at the mental health professions, the ambiguity in determining which religious groups are "cults," and the absolute power we tend to grant the claims made by scientists.

A second theme throughout this book is the notion of the *social typing process*. Power plays a critical role in determining who or what will be considered deviant, and what social control measures are directed at them. Governments, the media, religious institutions, scientists, and commercial industry are all intimately involved in the social typing and social control of various aspects of deviance.

The "*deviance dance*" can be seen throughout this book as well. Regardless of the specific issue in question, various individuals and groups have differing points of view on whether something or someone is "deviant," how "deviant" they are, and what the most effective means of social control will be. Even those issues that have extraordinarily high levels of consensus (e.g., sexual relationships between adults and children) are characterized by debate, disagreement, and resistance.

Given the role of subjectivity in understanding deviance, does that mean "anything goes"? Does it mean that we cannot legitimately socially type anyone or anything as deviant? The concept of *human rights* is one place where we can begin looking at whether any standards can be applied. Numerous international human rights documents exist, and they give some indication of criteria that may be used to determine who should and should not be deviantized.

Recommended Readings

Sweet, W. (2003). *Philosophical theory and the Universal Declaration of Human Rights*. Ottawa: University of Ottawa Press.

* This book is an excellent overview of the theoretical, philosophical, and social issues involved with the creation of this human rights document, its application in contemporary society, and what the future may hold.

Schulz, W. (2003). *Tainted legacy: 9-11 and the ruins of human rights*. New York: Thunder's Mouth Press.

* This book is written by the Executive Director of the American branch of Amnesty International. It critically explores how international terrorism and human rights violations are intimately intertwined.

British Medical Association (2000). *The medical profession and human rights: Handbook for a changing agenda*. London: Zed Books.

* Medical ethics and the potential human rights abuses in our rapidly changing world are issues that are central to discussions of deviance. This book explores numerous issues, such as the organ trade, patient abuse, and more.

Endnotes

1 Mason Cooley. Retrieved August 28, 2001 from World Wide Web: **http://www.bartleby.com**

2 David Lee. Retrieved August 28, 2001 from World Wide Web: **http://www.quotationspage.com**

3 Margaret Mead. Retrieved July 4, 2003 from World Wide Web: **http://www.quotationspage.com**

Key Terms

conformity, **p. 300**
deviant, **p. 300**
objective, **p. 300**
subjective, **p. 301**
positivist, **p. 301**
interpretive, **p. 301**
critical, **p. 301**
bad apple theory, **p. 304**
iceberg theory, **p. 304**
social typing process, **p. 304**
description, **p. 304**
evaluation, **p. 304**
prescription, **p. 304**
social control, **p. 304**
regulation, **p. 304**
informal control, **p. 304**
formal control, **p. 305**
preventative control, **p. 305**
retroactive control, **p. 305**
self-control, **p. 305**
moral entrepreneurs, **p. 305**
deviantization, **p. 306**
deinstitutionalization, **p. 307**
anti-cult movement, **p. 308**
counter-cult movement, **p. 308**
deviance dance, **p. 308**
human dignity, **p. 314**
discrimination, **p. 315**
security of person and property, **p. 315**

References

ABC News (2001). Trying to be ex-gay. Retrieved March 24, 2002, from **http://abcnews.com**

Abernethy, D. B. (2001). *The dynamics of global dominance: European overseas empires, 1415-1980.* New Haven, CT: Yale University Press.

Accordino, M. P., Porter, D. F., & Morse, T. (2001). Deinstitutionalization of persons with severe mental illness: Context and consequences. *Journal of Rehabilitation Medicine, 67*(2), 16-21.

Adlaf, E. M., Gliksman, L., Demers, A., & Newton-Taylor, B. (2001). The prevalence of elevated psychological distress among Canadian undergraduates. *Journal of American College Health, 50*(2), 67-72.

Adler, P. A., & Adler, P. (1997). *Constructions of deviance: Social power, context, and interaction* (2nd ed.). Belmont, CA: Wadsworth.

Adler, P. A., & Adler, P. (2003). *Constructions of deviance: Social power, context, and interaction* (4th edition). Belmont, CA: Wadsworth.

Agnew, R. (1992). A foundation for a general strain theory of crime and delinquency. *Criminology, 30*, 47-87.

Agnew, R. (1998). A general strain theory of crime and delinquency. In F. T. Cullen & R. Agnew (Eds.), *Criminological theory: Past to present* (pp. 152-156). Los Angeles, CA: Roxbury.

Akers, R. L. (1977). *Deviant behavior: A social learning approach.* Belmont, CA: Wadsworth.

Akers, R. L. (2000). *Criminological theories: Introduction, evaluation, and application* (3rd ed.). Los Angeles, CA: Roxbury.

Alberta Alliance on Mental Illness & Mental Health (2003). Home page. Retrieved April 19, 2003, from **http://www.aamimh.ca**

Alberta Medical Association (1991). *Go ahead...ask me: Physician's guide to teen sexuality counselling.* Edmonton, AB: Author.

Alberta Mental Health Act (n.d.). Retrieved June 1, 2003, from **http://qp.gov.ab.ca/Documents/acts/M13.CFM**

American Family Foundation (2003). Home page. Retrieved June 1 to July 3, 2003, from **http://www.aff.org**

American Psychiatric Association (1994). *Diagnostic and statistical manual of mental disorders-IV.* Washington, DC: Author.

American Psychiatric Association (2000). *American Psychiatric Association practice guidelines for the treatment of psychiatric disorders: Compendium 2000.* Washington, DC: Author.

Andersen, A. E. (1995). Eating disorders in males. In K. D. Brownell and C. G. Fairburn (Eds.), *Eating disorders and obesity* (pp. 177-182). New York: Guilford Press.

Andersen, A. E., & DiDomenico, L. (1992). Diet vs. shape content of popular male and female magazines: A dose-response relationship to the incidence of eating disorders? *International Journal of Eating Disorders, 11*(3), 283-287.

Anderson, A., & Gordon, R. (1978). Witchcraft and the status of women—the case of England. *British Journal of Sociology, 29*, 171-184.

Anthony, D. & Robbins, T. (1994). Brainwashing and totalitarian influence. In S. Ramachandran (Ed.), *Encyclopedia of Human Behavior* (Vol. 1) (pp. 457-471). San Diego, CA: Academic Press.

Arkins, B. (1994). Sexuality in fifth-century Athens. *Classics Ireland, 1*, 1-8.

Arnett, J. (1992). Reckless behavior in adolescence: A developmental perspective. *Developmental Review, 12*, 339-373.

Arnett, J. J. (1999). Adolescent storm and stress reconsidered. *American Psychologist, 54*(5), 317-326.

Aseltine, R. (1995). A reconsideration of parental and peer influences on adolescent deviance. *Journal of Health and Social Behavior, 3*(6), 103-121.

Asma, S. T. (1993). The new social Darwinism. *Humanist, 53*(5), 10-12.

Ashley, D., & Orenstein, D. M. (2001). *Sociological theory: Classical statements* (5th ed.). Boston: Allyn & Bacon.

Atkinson, M. (2003). The civilizing of resistance: Straightedge tattooing. *Deviant Behavior: An Interdisciplinary Journal, 24*, 197-220.

Bader, C., Becker, P. J., & Desmond, S. (1996). Reclaiming deviance as a unique course from criminology. *Teaching Sociology, 24*, 3316-320.

Bagley, C., & Trembley, P. (1998). On the prevalence of homosexuality and bisexuality, in a random community survey of 750 men aged 18 to 27. *Journal of Homosexuality, 36*(2), 1-18.

Bainsbridge, W. S. (2002). *The endtime family: Children of God*. New York: State University of New York Press.

Ball, P. (2003). Physicists fail to find saving grace for falsified research. *Nature, 421*(6926), 878.

Bandura, A. (1986). *Social foundations of thought and action: A social cognitive theory*. Englewood Cliffs, NJ: Prentice Hall.

Barker, E. (2001). Watching for violence: A comparative analysis of the roles of five types of cult-watching groups. Paper presented at the annual meeting of the Center for Studies in New Religions.

Baron, S. W. (1989). Canadian West Coast punk subculture: A field study. *Canadian Journal of Sociology, 14*(3), 289-316.

Barsley, M. (1967). *The other hand; an investigation into the sinister history of left-handedness*. New York: Hawthorn Books.

Barstow, A. L. (1994). *Witchcraze*. San Francisco: Pandora.

Bartowski, J. P. (1998). Claimsmaking and typifications of voodoo as a deviant religion: Hex, lies, and videotape. *Journal for the Scientific Study of Religion, 37*(4), 559-579.

Baumrind, D. (1991). Parenting styles and adolescent development. In R. Lerner, A. Peterson, & J. Brooks-Gunn (Eds.), *Encyclopedia of adolescence*. New York: Garland Publishing.

Beaman, L. G. (2000). *New perspectives on deviance: The construction of deviance in everyday life*. Scarborough, ON: Prentice Hall.

Beaud, J-P, & Prevost, J-G (1996). Immigration, eugenics, and statistics; Measuring racial origins in Canada, 1921-1941. *Canadian Ethnic Studies, 28*(2), 1-23.

Bechtel, K., & Pearson, W. (1985). Deviant scientists and scientific deviance. *Deviant Behavior: An Interdisciplinary Journal, 6*, 237-252.

Beck, M. (2001, November). Embracing your inner brat. *O Magazine*, p. 69.

Beck, U. (1992). *Risk society: Towards a new modernity*. London: Sage.

Beck, U. (1999). *World risk*. Cambridge: Polity Press.

Becker, H. (1963). *Outsiders: Studies in the sociology of deviance*. New York: Free Press.

Beckwith, J. (1993). A historical view of social responsibility in genetics. *Bioscience, 43*(5), 327-333.

Beggan, J., & Allison, S. (2003). "What sort of man reads *Playboy*?" The self-reported influence of *Playboy* on the construction of masculinity. *Journal of Men's Studies, 11*(2), 189-206.

Belcher, J. R. (1989). On becoming homeless: A study of chronically mentally ill persons. *Journal of Community Psychology, 17*, 173-185.

Bell, S., Cossman, B., Ross, B. L., Gottell, L., & Janovicek, N. 1998). Bad attitude/s on trial: Feminism, pornography & the Butler decision. *Journal of Canadian Studies, 33*(1), 163-172.

Bell, S. J. (2002). *Young offenders and juvenile justice: A century after the fact* (2nd ed.). Scarborough, ON: Nelson Thomson.

Benard, R. (1991). *Fostering resilience in kids: Protective factors in the family, school, and community.* Portland, OR: Weston Center for Drug Free Schools and Communities.

Ben-Yehuda, N. (1986). Deviance in science. *British Journal of Criminology, 26*(1), 1-27.

Ben-Yehuda, N. (1990). *The politics and morality of deviance: Moral panics, drug abuse, deviant science, and reversed stigmatization.* Albany, NY: State University of New York Press.

Bereska, T. (2003). The changing boys' world in the 20th century: Reality and "fiction". *Journal of Men's Studies, 11*(2), 157-174.

Bessant, J. (2001). From sociology of deviance to sociology of risk: Youth homelessness and the problem of empiricism. *Journal of Criminal Justice, 29,* 31-43.

Bibby, R. W. (2001). *Canada's teens: Today, yesterday, and tomorrow.* Toronto, ON: Stoddart.

Block, E. (2001). Sex between men and boys in classical Greece: Was it education for citizenship of child abuse? *Journal of Men's Studies, 9*(2). Retrieved October 2, 2001, from Expanded Academic ASAP database.

Blumer, H. (1986). *Symbolic interactionism: Perspective and method.* Berkeley, CA: University of California Press.

Bochenek, M., & Brown, A. W., (2001). *Hatred in the hallways: Violence and discrimination against lesbian, gay, bisexual, and transgender students in U. S. schools.* New York: Human Rights Watch.

Bogdan, R., & Taylor, S. (1987). Toward a sociology of acceptance: The other side of the study of deviance. *Social Policy, 18*(2), 34-39.

Bortner, M. (1988). *Delinquency and justice: An age of crisis.* Toronto, ON: McGraw Hill.

Boston, R. (1996). *The most dangerous man in America? Pat Robertson and the rise of the Christian Coalition.* Amherst, NY: Prometheus Books.

Braithwaite, J. (2000). Shame and criminal justice. *Canadian Journal of Criminology, 42*(3), 281-298.

British Columbia Eating Disorders Association (2003). Home page. Retrieved May 17, 2003, from **http://preventingdisorderedeating.org**

Broidy, L. M., & Agnew, R. (1997). Gender and crime: A general strain theory perspective. *Journal of Research in Crime and Delinquency, 34,* 275-306.

Bromley, D. G. (2002). Dramatic denouement. In D. G. Bromley & J. G. Melton (Eds.), *Cults, religion, and violence* (pp. 11-41). Cambridge, UK: Cambridge University Press.

Bromley, D. G., & Melton, J. G. (Eds.) (2002). *Cults, religion, and violence.* Cambridge, UK: Cambridge University Press.

Bromley, D. G., & Shupe, A. D. (1993). Organized opposition to new religious movements. In D. G. Bromley & J. K. Hadden (Eds.), *The handbook of cults and sects* (pp. 177-198). Greenwich, CT: JAI Press.

Brook, J. S., Brook, D. W., De La Rosa, M., Whiteman, M., & Montoya, I. D. (1999). The role of parents in protecting Colombian adolescents from delinquency and marijuana use. *Archives of Pediatrics & Adolescent Medicine, 153*(5). Retrieved October 7, 2002, from Expanded Academic ASAP database.

Brounstein, P. J., & Zweig, J. M. (1999). *Understanding substance abuse prevention: Toward the 21st century: A primer on effective programs.* Rockville, MD: U. S. Department of Health and Human Services.

Brower, A. M. (2002). Are college students alcoholics? *Journal of American College Health, 50*(5), 253-255.

Brower, R. (1999). Dangerous minds: Eminently creative people who spent time in jail. *Creative Research Journal, 12*(1). Retrieved August 6, 2001, from Academic Search Premier database.

Brownfield, D., & Thompson, K. (1991). Attachment to peers and delinquent behaviour. *Canadian Journal of Criminology, 33*, 46-60.

Buchanan, C. M., & Holmbeck, G. N. (1998). Measuring beliefs about adolescent personality and behavior. *Journal of Youth & Adolescence, 27*, 609-629.

Buchanan, E. (1997). A school for sterilization. *World Press Review, June*, 46.

Bush, J., White, M., Kai, J., Rankin, J., & Bhopal, R. (2003). Understanding influences on smoking in Bangladeshi and Pakistani adults: Community based qualitative study. *British Medical Journal, 326*, 962-965.

Buzzard, R. F. (2002). The Coca-Cola of self-help: The branding of John Gray's *Men are from Mars, Women are from Venus*. *Journal of Popular Culture, 35*(4), 89-102.

Caldwell, W. (2001). *Obesity sourcebook*. Detroit, MI: Omnigraphics.

Canadian Medical Association (1999). Canada's tipplers cutting back. *CMAJ: Canadian Medical Association Journal, 160*(7), 979.

Canadian Medical Association (2001). Is Canada smoked out? *CMAJ: Canadian Medical Association Journal, 164*(13), 1881.

Canadian Press (2001, July 16). 75% back full rights for gays, poll finds. *Edmonton Journal*.

Canadian Sociology and Anthropology Association (1994). *Statement of Professional Ethics*. Retrieved June 17, 2003, from **http://alcor.concordia.ca/~csaa1/**

Caplan, P. J. (1995). *They say you're crazy: How the world's more powerful psychiatrists decide who's normal*. Reading, MA: Perseus Books.

Caputo, T., Weiler, R., & Anderson, J. (1996). *The street lifestyle study*. Ottawa, ON: Health Canada.

Carlson, R. J., & Stimeling, G. (2002). *The terrible gift: The brave new world of genetic medicine*. New York: PublicAffairs.

Carol, A. (1994). *Nudes, prudes and attitudes: Pornography and censorship*. Chettenham, UK: New Clarion Press.

Chambliss, W. J., & Seidman, R. (1982). *Law, order and power* (2nd ed.). Reading, MA: Addison-Wesley.

Childress, S. A. (1991). Reel "rape speech": Violent pornography and the politics of harm. *Law & Society Review, 25*(1), 177-214.

Chryssides, G. D. (1994). New religious movements—some problems with definition. *Diskus: Web Edition, 2*(2). Retrieved February 19, 2003, from **http://www.uni-marburg-edu**

Chryssides, G. D. (1996). New religions and the Internet. *Diskus: Web Edition, 4*(2). Retrieved February 19, 2003, from **http://www.uni-marburg-edu**

Clarke, D., & Gabriels, T. (1996). Astrological signs as determinants of extroversion and emotionality: An empirical study. *Journal of Psychology, 130*(2), 131-140.

Clinard, M. B., & Meier, R. F. (2001). *Sociology of deviant behavior* (11th ed.). Fort Worth, TX: Harcourt College Publishers.

Cloward, R. A., & Ohlin, L. E. (1960). *Delinquency and opportunity: A theory of delinquent gangs*. New York: Free Press.

Cohen, A. J. (1955). *Delinquent boys*. New York: Free Press.

Cohen, R. (1996, March 7). The girl friend. *Rolling Stone, 729*(34). Retrieved July 31, 2001, from MasterFILE database.

Cohen, S. (1973). *Folk devils and moral panics*. London: MacGibbons and Kee.

Connell, R. W. (1995). *Masculinities*. Berkeley, CA: University of California Press.

Conrad, P. (1992). Medicalization and social control. *Annual Review of Sociology, 18*, 209-232.

Coontz, S. (1992). *The way we never were: American families and the nostalgia trap*. New York: Basis Books.

Cooper, A. (Ed.). (2002). *Sex and the Internet*. New York: Brunner-Routledge.

Costin, C. (1999). *The eating disorder sourcebook*. Los Angeles, CA: Lowell House.

Council for Responsible Genetics (2003). Home page. Retrieved July 5, 2003, from **http://www.gene-watch.org**

Cowan, D. E. (2001). From parchment to pixels: The Christian countercult on the Internet. Paper presented at the 2001 conference of the Center for Studies on New Religions, April 20, London.

Crisp, A. H. (1999). The stigmatization of sufferers with mental disorders. *British Journal of General Practice, 49*, 3-4.

Crouch, A., & Degelman, D. (1998). Influence of female body images in printed advertising on self-ratings of physical attractiveness by adolescent girls. *Perceptual & Motor Skills, 87*(2), 585-586.

Crouch, B., & Damphousse, K. (1991). Law enforcement and the Satanism-crime connection: A survey of "cult-cops". In J. T. Richardson, J. Best, & D. Bromley (Eds.), *The Satanism Scare* (pp. 191-204). New York: Aldine de Gruyter.

Crouch, B. M. & Damphousse, K. R. (1992). Newspapers and the anti-Satanism movement. *Sociological Spectrum, 12*, 1-20.

Cullen, F. T., & Agnew, R. (1998). *Criminological theory: Past to present*. Los Angeles, CA: Roxbury.

Czikszentmihalyi, M., & Larsen, R. W. (1984). *Being adolescent: Conflict and growth in the teenage years*. New York: Basic Books.

Dalton, R. (2002). Misconduct: The stars who fell to Earth. *Nature, 420*(6917), 728-729.

Das Gupta, T. (2000). Families of Native people, immigrants, and people of colour. In N. Mandell & A. Duffy (Eds.), *Canadian families: Diversity, conflict, and change* (2nd ed.) (pp. 146-187). Scarborough, ON: Nelson Thomson.

Davidson, L., Hoge, M. A., Godleski, L., Rakfeldt, J., & Griffith, E. I. H. (1996). Hospital or community living? Examining consumer perspectives on deinstitutionalization. *Psychiatric Rehabilitation Journal, 19*(3), 49-58.

Davies, J. (1996). The future of "no future:" Punk rock and postmodern theory. *Journal of Popular Culture, 29*(4), 3-25.

Davies, K. A. (1997). Voluntary exposure to pornography and men's attitudes toward feminism and rape. *Journal of Sex Research, 34*(2), 131-137.

Davies, L. (1994). In search of resistance and rebellion among high school drop-outs. *Canadian Journal of Sociology, 19*(3), 331-350.

Dawson, L. L., & Henneby, J. (1999). New religions and the Internet: Recruiting in new public space. *Journal of Contemporary Religion, 14*(1), 17-39.

Degher, D. & Hughes, G. (2003). The adoption and management of a "fat" identity. In P. A. Adler & P. Adler (Eds.), *Constructions of deviance: Social power, context, and interaction* (pp. 211-221). Belmont, CA: Wadsworth.

DeMello, M. (2000). *Bodies of inscription: A cultural history of the modern tattoo community*. Durham, NC: Duke University Press.

D'Emilio, J., & Freedman, E. B. (1997). *Intimate matters: A history of sexuality in America* (2nd ed.). Chicago: University of Chicago Press.

DeMont, J. (2002, August 5). Growing up large. *Maclean's, 115*(31), 20-26.

Dennis, R. M. (1995). Social Darwinism, scientific racism and the metaphysics of race. *Journal of Negro Education, 64*(3), 243-252.

Deutschmann, L. B. (2002). *Deviance and social control* (3rd ed.). Scarbourough, ON: Nelson Thomson Learning.

de Young, M. (1998). Another look at moral panics: The case of satanic day care centers. *Deviant Behavior: An Interdisciplinary Journal, 19*, 257-278.

Dobson, R. (1996, November 30). Mentally ill people face discrimination. *British Medical Journal, 313*(7069), 1352.

Doherty, J. (2000). The social construction of welfare recipients as "lazy". In L. G. Beaman (Ed.), *New perspectives on deviance* (pp. 150-162). Scarborough, ON: Prentice Hall.

Doherty, T. (1988). *Teenagers & teenpics: The juvenilization of American movies in the 1950s*. Boston: Unwin Hyman.

Doherwend, B. P., & Levav, I.. (1992, February 21). Socioeconomic status and psychiatric disorders: The causation-selection issue. *Science, 255*(5047), 946-952.

Dunleavey, M. P. (2001, April). Would you have surgery to lose weight? *Self*, pp. 172-175, 199-200.

Dunne, C. & Warren, C. (1998). Lethal autonomy: The malfunction of informed consent mechanism within the context of prenatal diagnosis of genetic variants. *Issues in Law & Medicine, 14*(2), 165-202.

Durex (2002). *Global sex survey 2002*. Author.

Durkheim, E. (1933). *The division of labour in society*. New York: Free Press.

Durkheim, E. (1951). *Suicide*. New York: Free Press.

Dyer, O. (2003). GMC reprimands doctor for research fraud. *British Medical Journal, 326*(7392), 730.

Edmonton Police Service (2003). *Who are your children hanging with? A resource guide on youth & gangs*. Edmonton: Author.

Edwards, A. R. (1988). *Regulation and repression: The study of social control*. Sydney, Australia: Allen & Unwin.

Eliason, S. L., & Dodder, R. A. (2000). Neutralization among deer poachers. *Journal of Social Psychology, 140*(4), 536-539.

Elliot, D., Huizinga, D., & Ageton, S. (1985). *Explaining delinquency and substance use*. Beverly Hills, CA: Sage.

Emery, J. R. (2001). Cracked crystal balls? Psychics' predictions for past year a litany of prognostive failures. *Skeptical Inquirer, 25*(1), 8.

Epstein, R. E. (2001, July/August). Physiologist Laura: She's not a psychologist, and we don't want her. *Psychology Today*, 5.

Erickson, K. G., Crosnoe, R., & Dornbusch, S. M. (2000). A social process model of adolescent deviance: Combining social control and differential association perspectives. *Journal of Youth and Adolescence, 29*(4), 395-425.

Ericson, R. V., & Haggerty, K. D. (2001). Governing the young. In R. C. Smandych (Ed.), *Youth justice: History, legislation, and reform* (pp. 104-123). Toronto, ON: Harcourt.

Erikson, K. (1966). *Wayward puritans*. New York: Wiley.

Erwin, R. (1998). Scrawny chic. *North American Review, 283*(1), 30-31.

Ettner, S. L., Frank, R. G., & Kessler, R. C. (1997). The impact of psychiatric disorders on labor market outcomes. *Industrial and Labor Relations Review, 51*(1), 64-83.

Evans, R. D. (2001). Examining the informal sanctioning of deviance in a chat room culture. *Deviant Behavior: An Interdisciplinary Journal, 22*, 195-210.

Fasiolo, R., & Leckie, S. (1993). *Canadian media coverage of gangs: A content analysis*. Ottawa, ON: Solicitor-General Canada.

Feher, S. (1992). Who looks to the stars? Astrology and its constituency. *Journal for the Scientific Study of Religion, 31*(1), 88-93.

Ferguson, S. (2001, June 25). Tale of a witch hunt. *Maclean's*, pp. 34-36.

Fernea, E. W. (1990). *In search of Islamic feminism*. New York: Anchor Books.

Fight Against Coercive Tactics Network (2003). Home page. Retrieved July 8, 2003, from **http://www.factnet.org**

Fink, M. (1999, August). Jennifer in love. *Redbook, 193*(3). Retrieved July 31, 2001 from MasterFILE database.

First for Women (2001, September 17). How much sex is normal? *First for Women*, p. 39.

Flannery, D. J., Huff, C. R., & Manos, M. (2001). Youth gangs: A developmental perspective. In R. C. Smandych (Ed.), *Youth crime: Varieties, theories, and prevention* (pp. 206-229). Toronto, ON: Harcourt.

Fleming, A. T. (1999, January). The new ideal: What makes a body beautiful? *Women's Sports and Fitness, 2*(2). Retrieved August 1, 2001, from Expanded Academic ASAP database.

Ford, C. (2001, July 24). Chretien and Klein, take a hike. *National Post*, p. A16.

Forum 18 (2001). *Freedom of Religion: A report with special emphasis on the right to choose religion and registration systems*. Retrieved June 2, 2003, from **http://www.forum18.org**

Foucault, M. (1980). *Power/knowledge: Selected interviews and other writings 1972-1977* (1st American ed.). Translated by C. Gordon, L. Marshall, J. Mepham, & K. Super. New York: Pantheon Books.

Foucault, M. (1995 [1977]). *Discipline and punish: The birth of the prison* (2nd ed.). New York: Vintage Books.

Fournier, S., & Crey, E. (1998). *Stolen from our embrace*. Berkeley, CA: Roundhouse Publishing.

Franklin, K. (2000). Antigay behaviors among young adults: Prevalence, patterns, and motivators in a noncriminal population. *Journal of Interpersonal Violence, 15*(4), 339-362.

Freud, S. (1999). The social construction of normality. *Families in Society: The Journal of Contemporary Human Services, 80*(4), 333-339.

Gardner, C. B. (1991). Stigma and the public self: Notes on communication, self, and others. *Journal of Contemporary Ethnography, 20*(3), 251-252.

Garner, D. M. (1997, January/February). The 1997 body image survey results. *Psychology Today*, 31-44, 75-84.

Gater, R., Tnasella, M., Korten, A., Mavreas, V. G., & Olatawura, M. O. (1998). Sex differences in the prevalence and detection of depressive and anxiety disorders in general health care settings. *Archives of General Psychiatry, 55*, 405-413.

Gibson, C., & Wright, J. (2001). Low self-control and coworker delinquency: A research note. *Journal of Criminal Justice, 29*(6), 483-492.

Goffman, E. (1959). *The presentation of self in everyday life*. Garden City, NY: Doubleday-Anchor.

Goffman, E. (1963). *Stigma: Notes on the management of spoiled identity*. Englewood Cliffs, NJ: Prentice Hall.

Gomme, I. M. (1985). Predictors of status and criminal offences among male and female adolescents in an Ontario community. *Canadian Journal of Criminology, 27*, 157-159.

Goode, E. (1997). *Deviant behavior* (5th ed.). Upper Saddle River, NJ: Prentice Hall.

Goodstein, L. (2003, May 27). Seeing Islam as an evil faith, evangelicals seek converts. *New York Times*. Retrieved June 20, 2003, from **http//nytimes.com**

Gordon, R. A. (2000). *Eating disorders: Anatomy of a social epidemic*. Malden, MA: Blackwell.

Gordon, R. M. (1993). *Incarcerated gang members in British Columbia: A preliminary study*. Victoria: Ministry of Attorney-General.

Gordon, R. M. (1995). Street gangs in Vancouver. In J. Creechan & R. Silverman (Eds.), *Canadian delinquency* (pp. 311-320). Scarborough, ON: Prentice Hall.

Gordon, R. M. (2001). Street gangs and criminal business organizations: A Canadian perspective. In R. C. Smandych (Ed.), *Youth crime: Varieties, theories, and prevention* (pp. 248-265). Toronto, ON: Harcourt.

Gottfredson, M. R., & Hirschi, T. (1990). *A general theory of crime*. Stanford, CT: Stanford University Press.

Greco, A. N. (1995/96). The First Amendment, freedom of the press, and the issues of "harm": A conundrum for publishers. *Publishing Research Quarterly, 11*(4), 39-57.

Green, K. L., & Cameron, R.. (1997). Weight dissatisfaction and weight loss attempts among Canadian adults. *Canadian Medical Journal Association, 157*, 517-525.

Grekul, J. M. (2002). *The social construction of the feebleminded threat: Implementation of the Sexual Sterilization Act in Alberta, 1929-1972*. Unpublished doctoral dissertation, University of Alberta, Edmonton, AB.

Grob, G. N. (1994). *The mad among us: A history of the care of America's mentally ill*. New York: Free Press.

Hackler, J. C. (2000). Strain theories. In R. Linden (Ed.), *Criminology: A Canadian perspective* (4th ed.) (pp. 270-300). Toronto, ON: Harcourt Canada.

Hadden, J., & Bromley, D. (Eds.) (1995). *The handbook of cults and sects in America*. Greenwich, CT: JAI Press.

Hall, G. S. (1904). *Adolescence* (Vol. I). Englewood Cliffs, NJ: Prentice Hall.

Hall, J. (2002). Mass suicide and the Branch Davidians. In D. G. Bromley & J. G. Melton (Eds.), *Cults, religion, and violence* (pp. 149-169). Cambridge, UK: Cambridge University Press.

Hannigan, B. (1999). Mental health care in the community: An analysis of contemporary public attitudes towards, and public representations of, mental illness. *Journal of Mental Health, 8*(5), 431-440.

Harkin, A. M., Anderson, P., & Goos, C. (1997). *Smoking, drinking and drug taking in the European region*. Copenhagen, DK: World Health Organization.

Harrison, K. (2000). Television viewing, fat stereotyping, body shape standards and eating disorder symptomatology in grade school children. *Communications Research, 27*(5), 617-640.

Hathaway, A. D., & Atkinson, M. F. (2001). Tolerable differences revisited: Crossroads in theory on the social construction of deviance. *Deviant Behavior: An Interdisciplinary Journal, 22*, 353-377.

Hawdon, J. E. (1996). Deviant lifestyles: The social control of daily routines. *Youth & Society, 28*(2), 162-188.

Health Canada (1999). *Trends in the health of Canadian children*. Ottawa: Author.

Health Canada (2002a). *A review of weight guidelines*. Ottawa, ON: Author.

Health Canada (2002b). *A report on mental illness in Canada*. Ottawa, ON: Author.

Health Canada (2003). Physical activity. Retrieved June 1, 2003, from **http://www.hc-sc.gc.ca**

Heltsley, M., & Calhoun, T. C. (2003). The good mother: Neutralization techniques used by pageant mothers. *Deviant Behavior: An Interdisciplinary Journal, 24*, 81-100.

Herek, G. M., Gillis, J. R., Cogan, J. C., & Glunt, E. K. (1997). Hate crime victimization among lesbian, gay, and bisexual adults: Prevalence, psychological correlates, and methodological issues. *Journal of Interpersonal Violence, 12*(2), 195-215.

Herdt, G. (1984). Ritualized homosexuality in the male cults of Melanesia, 1862-1982: An introduction. In G. Herdt, (Ed.), *Ritualized homosexuality in Melanesia*, (pp. 1-81). Berkeley, CA: University of California Press.

Herdt, G. (1999). Clinical ethnography and sexual culture. *Annual Review of Sex Research, 10*, 100-119.

Hersch, P. (1998). *A tribe apart: A journey into the heart of American adolescence*. New York: Ballantine Books.

Hicks, R. (1990). Police pursuit of satanic crime. *Skeptical Inquirer, 14*, 276-286.

Hirschi, T. C. (1969). *Causes of delinquency*. Berkeley, CA: University of California Press.

Hodgins, S. (1993). The criminality of mentally disordered persons. In S. Hodgins (Ed.), *Mental disorder and crime*. Newbury Park, CA: Sage.

Hoffman, A. (1999, March 1). Boogie rights: An immodest proposal. *The Globe and Mail*, p. C1.

Hoffman, B., & Burke, c. (1997). *Heaven's Gate cult: Suicide in San Diego*. New York: Harper Collins.

Huber, P. W. (1991). *Galileo's revenge: Junk science in the courtroom*. New York: Basic Books.

Hunt, A. (1998). The great masturbation panic and the discourses of moral regulation in nineteenth- and early twentieth-century Britain. *Journal of the History of Sexuality, 8*(4), 575-615.

Intercamp (2001, October 11). The censorship issue. Edmonton, AB: Grant MacEwan Students' Association.

International Obesity Task Force (2003). Home page. Retrieved April 3, 2003, from **http://www.iotf.org**

International Size Acceptance Association (2003). Home page. Retrieved April 3, 2003, from **http://size-acceptance.org**

Introvigne, M., & Mayer, J.-F. (2002). Occult masters and the temple of doom: The fiery end of the Solar Temple. In D. G. Bromley & J. G. Melton (Eds.), *Cults, religion, and violence* (pp. 170-188). Cambridge, UK: Cambridge University Press.

Irwin, D. (1999). The straight edge subculture: Examining the youths' drug-free way. *Journal of Drug Issues, 29*, 365-380.

Jaimes, M. A. (1992). *The state of Native America: Genocide, colonization, and resistance*. Cambridge, MA: South End Press.

James, W. H. (1995). Frauds and hoaxes in science. *Nature, 377*(6549), 474.

Jang, S. J., & Smith, C. A. (1997). A test of reciprocal causal relationships among parental supervision, affective ties, and delinquency. *Journal of Research in Crime and Delinquency, 34*(3), 307-336.

Jankowski, M. S. (1991). *Islands in the street: Gangs and American urban society*. Berkeley, CA: University of California Press.

Jenkins, P. (2000). *Mystics and messiahs: Cults and new religions in American history*. New York: Oxford University Press.

Johnson, B. (1963). On church and sect. *American Sociological Review, 28*, 539-549.

Jones, D. J. (2001). *Selected legal issues in genetic testing: Guidance from human rights*. Ottawa: Health Canada.

Jones, G. (1986). *Social hygiene in twentieth-century Britain*. London: Croom Helm.

Jones, L. (1998). Social Darwinism revisited. *History Today, 48*(8). Retrieved October 16, 2001, from Expanded Academic ASAP database.

Jordon, T. E. (1998). *Victorian child savers and their culture: A thematic evaluation* (Mellon Studies in Sociology, Vol. 19). Lewiston, NY: Edwin Mellon Press.

Kaiser Family Foundation (1997). *Reflections of girls in the media*. Retrieved March 29, 2003, from **http://www.kff.org**

Keeling, R. P. (2000). The political, social, and public health problems of binge drinking in college. *Journal of American College Health, 48*(5), 195-198.

Keeling, R. P. (20020. Binge drinking and the college environment. *Journal of American College Health, 50*(5), 197-201.

Kendall, D., Murray, J. L., & Linden, R. (2000). *Sociology in our times* (2nd Canadian ed.). Scarborough, ON: Nelson Thomson Learning.

Kennedy, D. B., & Homant, R. J. (1984). Personnel managers and the stigmatized employee. *Journal of Employment Counseling, 21*, 89-94.

Kent, S. A. (1994). Lustful prophet: A psychosexual history of the Children of God's leader, David Berg. *Cultic Studies Journal, 11*(2), 135-188.

Kerr, C. (2003). Phony research earns 1-year suspension. *Canadian Medical Association Journal, 168*(8), 1032.

Kessler, R. C., McGonagle, K. A., Zhao, S., Nelson, C. B., Hughes, M., Eshleman, S. et al. (1994). Lifetime and 12-month prevalence of DSM-III-R psychiatric disorders in the United States. *Archives of General Psychiatry, 51*, 8-19.

Kevles, D. (1995). *In the name of eugenics: Genetics and the uses of human heredity*. Berkeley, CA: University of California Press.

Kimmel, M. (1996). *Manhood in America: A cultural history*. New York: Free Press.

Kimmel, M. S. & Messner, M. A. (1989). *Men's lives* (1st ed.). Boston: Allyn & Bacon.

Kimmel, M. S., & Messner, M. A. (1998). *Men's lives* (4th ed.). Boston: Allyn & Bacon.

Kitsuse, J. I. (1980). Coming out all over: Deviants and the politics of social problems. *Social Problems, 28*(1), 1-12.

Kitsuse, J. I., & Dietrick, D. C. (1979). Delinquent boys: A critique. In H. L. Voss (Ed.), *Society, delinquency, and delinquent behavior* (pp. 238-245). Boston: Little, Brown.

Krieg, R. G. (2001). An interdisciplinary look at the deinstitutionalization of the mentally ill. *Social Science Journal, 38*, 367-380.

Krucoff, C. (2003, July). Move! *Prevention, 55*(7), 140-144.

Kuhl, S. (1994). *The Nazi Connection*. New York: Oxford University Press.

LaGrange, T. C., & Silverman, R. A. (1999). Low self-control and opportunity: Testing the general theory of crime as an explanation for gender differences in delinquency. *Criminology, 37*(1), 41-72.

Larsen, N. (2000). Prostitution: Deviant activity or legitimate occupation? In L. G. Beaman (Ed.), *New perspectives on deviance: The construction of deviance in everyday life* (pp. 50-66). Scarborough, ON: Prentice Hall.

Larsen, R., & Richards, M. H. (1994). *Divergent realities: The emotional lives of mothers, fathers, and adolescents*. New York: Basic Books.

Latner, J., & Stunkard, A. (2003). Stigmatization of obese children. *Nutrition Research Newsletter, 22*(4), 12.

Laursen, B. (1995). Conflict and social interaction in adolescent relationships. *Journal of Research on Adolescence, 5*, 55-70.

Laursen, B., Coy, K. C., & Collins, W. A. (1998). Reconsidering changes in parent-child conflict across adolescence: A meta-analysis. *Child Development, 69*, 817-832.

Lawrie, S. M., Martin, K., McNeill, G., Drife, J., Chrystie, P., Reid, A. et al. (1998). General practitioners' attitudes to psychiatric and medical illness. *Psychiatric Medicine, 28*, 1463-1467.

Lawson, R. (1995). Sect-state relations: Accounting for the differing trajectories of Seventh-Day Adventists and Jehovah's Witnesses. *Sociology of Religion, 56*(4), 351-378.

Lemert, E. M. (1951). *Social pathology: A systematic approach to the study of sociopathic behavior*. New York: McGraw Hill.

Leon, J. S. (1977). The development of Canadian juvenile justice: A background for reform. *Osgoode Hall Law Journal, 15*, 71-106.

Levenkron, S. (2000). *Anatomy of anorexia*. New York: WW Norton.

Levine, M., & Maine, M. (2003). Eating disorders can be prevented. *National Eating Disorders Association*. Retrieved July 7, 2003, from **http://www.nationaleatingdisorders.org**

Levy, L. D. (2000). *Conquering obesity*. Toronto, ON: Key Porter Books.

Lewis, G., & Bebbington, P. (1998). Socioeconomic status, standard of living, and neurotic disorder. *Lancet, 352*(9128), 605-609.

Lewis, J., & Melton, J. G. (1994). *Sex, slander, and salvation: Investigating the Family/Children of God*. Stanford, CA: Center for Academic Publication.

Lianos, M., with Douglas, M. (2000). Dangerization and the end of deviance. *British Journal of Criminology, 40*, 261-278.

Liazos, A. (1972). The poverty of the sociology of deviance: Nuts, sluts, and perverts. *Social Problems, 20*, 102-120.

Linden, R. (Ed.) (2000). *Criminology: A Canadian perspective* (4th ed.). Toronto, ON: Harcourt Canada.

Lipkin, L. (2001, April 3). Hurried parents, harried kids. *Family Circle*, 112.

Liska, A., & Reid, M. (1985). Ties to conventional institutions and delinquency. *American Sociological Review, 50*, 547-560.

Liska, A. E., & Warner, B. D. (1991). Functions of crime: A paradoxical process. *The American Journal of Sociology, 96*(6), 1441-1463.

Lock, J. (2001). *Treatment manual for anorexia nervosa: A family based approach*. New York: Guilford Press.

Loring, M., & Powell, B. (1988). Gender, race and DSM-III. *Journal of Health and Social Behavior, 29*, 1-22.

Mackay, J. (2000). Global sex: Sexuality and sexual practices around the world. Paper presented at the 5th Congress of the European Federation of Sexology, June 29-July 2, 2000, Berlin.

Maddox, J. (1994). Defending science against anti-science. *Nature, 368*, 185.

Mandell, N., & Momirov, J. (2000). Family histories. In N. Mandell & A. Duffy (Eds.), *Canadian families: Diversity, conflict, and change* (2nd ed.) (pp. 17-47). Scarborough, ON: Nelson Thomson.

Marble, M. (1995, February 1). Eating disorders awareness week: February 6-12. *Women's Health Weekly, February 1*, 7-8.

March, P. A. (1999). Ethical responses to media depictions of mental illness: An advocacy approach. *Journal of Humanistic Counseling, Education, & Development, 38*(2), 70-79.

Marcos, A. C., Bahr, S. J., & Johnson, R. E. (1986). Test of a bonding/association theory of adolescent drug use. *Social Forces, 65*, 135-161.

Mason, A., & Palmer, A. (1996). *Queer bashing: A national survey of hate crimes against lesbians and gay men*. London: Stonewall.

Mason, G., & Tomsen, S. (Eds.) (1997). *Homophobic violence*. Annandale, AUS: Hawkins Press.

Massey, J. L., & Krohn, M. D. (1986). A longitudinal examination of an integrated social process model of deviant behavior. *Social Forces, 65*, 106-134.

Matthews, B. J. (2000). The body beautiful: Adolescent girls and images of beauty. In L. G. Beaman (Ed.), *New perspectives on deviance: The construction of deviance in everyday life* (pp. 208-219). Scarbourough, ON: Prentice Hall.

Matthews, D. D. (2001). *Eating disorders sourcebook*. Detroit, MI: Omnigraphics.

Mattson, K. (2001). Did punk matter? Analyzing the practices of a youth subculture. *American Studies, 42*(1), 69-97.

Mayor, S. (2003). Human cloning may be impossible. *BMJ: British Medical Journal, 326*(7394), 838.

McCabe, M. P., & Ricciardelli, L. A. (2003). Socioculture influences on body image and body changes among adolescent boys and girls. *Journal of Social Psychology, 143*(1), 5-26.

McCaghy, C. H., Capron, T. A., & Jamieson, J. D. (2003). *Deviant behavior: Crime, conflict, and interest groups* (6th ed). Boston: Allyn & Bacon.

McConnell, H. (1997, January 21). ADHD just doesn't add up to Brit Psych society. *Medical Post*. Retrieved August 20, 2002, from **http://mentalhealth.com**

McGovern, C. M. (1985). *Masters of madness: Social origins of the American psychiatric profession*. Hanover, NH: University Press of New England.

McGuire, M. B. (1997). *Religion: The social context* (4th ed.). Belmont, CA: Wadsworth.

McLaren, A. (1990). *Our own master race: Eugenics in Canada 1885-1945*. Toronto, ON: McClelland & Stewart.

McLorg, P. A., & Taub, D. E. (1987). Anorexia, bulimia, and developing a deviant identity. *Deviant Behavior: An Interdisciplinary Journal, 8*, 177-189.

Mead, M. (1927). *Coming of age in Samoa*. New York: Dutton.

Mellin, L. M., Scully, S., & Irwin, C. E. (1986). Disordered eating characteristics in preadolescent girls. Paper presented at the annual meeting of the American Dietetic Association, October, Las Vegas, NV.

Melton, D. E. (2000). Emerging religious movements in North America: Some missiological reflections. *Missiology: An international review*, 27(1), 85-98.

Melton, J. G., & Bromley, D. (2002). Challenging misconceptions about the new religion-violence connection. In D. G. Bromley & J. G. Melton (Eds.), *Cults, religion, and violence* (pp. 42-56). Cambridge, UK: Cambridge University Press.

Merriam-Webster (2002). *Merriam-Webster's Online Dictionary*. Retrieved January 4, 2002, from **http://www.merriam-webster.com**

Merriam-Webster (2003). *Merriam-Webster's Online Dictionary*. Retrieved June 17, 2003, from **http://www.merriam-webster.com**

Merton, R. K. (1938). Social structure and anomie. *American Sociological Review, 3*, 672-682.

Merton, R. K. (1968). *Social theory and social structure*. New York: Free Press.

Messner, M. (1990). Boyhood, organized sports, and the construction of masculinities. *Journal of Contemporary Ethnography, 18*(4), 416-444.

Miech, R. A., Caspi, A., Moffitt, T. E., Wright, B. R. E., & Silva, P. A. (1999). Low socioeconomic status and mental disorders: A longitudinal study of selection and causation during young adulthood. *American Journal of Sociology, 104*(4). Retrieved October 23, 2001, from Expanded Academic ASAP database.

Miller, J. (1996). *Shingwauk's vision*. Toronto, ON: University of Toronto Press.

Miller, J. M., Wright, R. A., & Dannels, D. (2001). Is deviance "dead"? The decline of a sociological research specialization. *American Sociologist, 32*(3), 43-59.

Milloy, J. S. (1999). *A national crime: The Canadian government and the residential school system, 1879-1986*. Winnipeg, MB: University of Manitoba Press.

Milne, C. (1998, January 12). Pressures to conform: The thin, shapely look can be dangerously unrealistic. *Maclean's*, 60-62.

Monahan, J. (1992). Mental disorder and violent behavior: Perceptions and evidence. *American Psychologist, 47*, 511-521.

Mosher, C. E. (2002). Impact of gender and problem severity upon intervention selection. *Sex Roles, 46*(3/4), 113-119.

Mostert, M. P. (2002). Useless eaters: Disability as genocidal marker in Nazi Germany. *Journal of Special Education, 36*(3), 155-168.

Mulgrew, I. (2001). Sex in space. *Homemakers Magazine, Feb./Mar.*, 33-39.

Murphy, E. F. (1973 [1922]). *The black candle*. Toronto, ON: Coles Publishing Co.

Murphy, S., Waldorf, D., & Reinarman, C. (1990). Drifting into dealing: Becoming a cocaine seller. *Qualitative Sociology, 13*(4), 487-507.

Murray, J. L., & Lopez, A. D. (1996). *The global burden of disease: A comprehensive assessment of mortality and disability from diseases, injuries, and risk factors in 1990 and projected to 2020: Summary*. Boston: Harvard School of Public Health/World Health Organization.

NAMBLA Home Page. Retrieved January 7, 2002, from **http://www.nambla1.de**

Nathan, D., & Snedeker, M. (1995). *Satan's silence: Ritual abuse and the making of a modern American witchhunt*. New York: Basic Books.

National Cancer Institute (2003). Antiperspirants/deodorants and breast cancer—Fact sheet. Retrieved June 29, 2003, from **http://www.cis.nih.gov**

National Eating Disorders Association (2003). Home page. Retrieved July 8, 2003, from **http://nationaleatingdisorders.org**

National Eating Disorder Information Centre (2003). Home page. Retrieved May 4, 2003, from **http://www.nedic.ca**

National Institute on Drug Abuse (1997). *Preventing drug abuse among children and adolescents*. Rockville, MD: U. S. National Institutes of Health.

National Institute on Drug Abuse (2002). *National survey results on drug use from the Monitoring the Future study, 1975-2001, Volume I, Secondary school students*. Rockville, MD: U. S. National Institutes of Health.

Nelson, E. D., & Robinson, B. W. (1999). *Gender in Canada*. Scarborough, ON: Prentice Hall.

Network World Canada (2002). Sex drive down on net. *Network World Canada, 12*(9). Retrieved October 7, 2002, from Canadian Business and Current Affairs database.

Neumark-Sztainer, D., & Sherwood, N. (1998). Dieting status among US adolescents. *Nutrition Research Newsletter, 17*(11), 12.

Neumark-Sztainer, D., Story, M., & Faibisch, L. (1998). Perceived stigmatization among overweight African-American and Caucasian adolescent girls. *Journal of Adolescent Health, 33*(5), 264-270.

Newhouse, D. (1998). Magic and joy: Traditional aboriginal views of human sexuality. *Canadian Journal of Human Sexuality, 7*(2), 183-187.

Obesity Association (2003). Home page. Retrieved April 4, 2003, from **http://www.obesity.org**

Ontario Consultants for Religous Tolerance (2003). Home page. Retrieved October 7, 2002, to July 2, 2003, from **http://www.religioustolerance.org**

Ong, E. K., & Glantz, S. A. (2001). Constructing "sound science" and "good epidemiology": Tobacco, lawyers, and public relations firms. *American Journal of Public Health, 91*, 1749-1757.

Owen, P. R., & Laurel-Seller, E. (2000). Weight and shape ideals: Thin is dangerously in. *Journal of Applied Social Psychology, 30*(5), 979-990.

Orji, E. O., & Onwudiegwu, U. (2002). Prevalence and determinants of contraceptive practice in a defined Nigerian population. *Journal of Obstetrics and Gynaecology, 22*(5), 540-543.

Padilla, F. W. (1992). *The gang as an American enterprise: Puerto Rican youth and the American dream*. New Brunswick, NJ: Rutgers University Press.

Parents Television Council (2001). The sour family hour: 8 to 9 goes from bad to worse. *Special Report*. Retrieved August 2, 2001, from **http://www.parentstv.org**

Park, R. (2000). *Voodoo science: The road from foolishness to fraud*. New York: Oxford University Press.

Parker, S. (2000). The tail wagging the bird. *Report/Newsmagazine (National Edition), 27*(12), 36-37.

Parsons, T., & Bales, R. F. (1955). *Family, socialization, and interaction process*. Glencoe, IL: Free Press.

Patel, V., Araya, R., deLima, M., Ludermir, A., & Todd, C. (1999). Women, poverty and common mental disorders in four restructuring societies. *Social Science & Medicine, 49*, 1461-1471.

Paxton, S. J., Wertheim, E. H., Gibbons, K., Szmukler, G. I., Hillier L., Petrovich, J.L. et al. (1991). Body image satisfaction, dieting beliefs, and weight loss behaviors in adolescent girls and boys. *Journal of Youth & Adolescence, 20*(3), 361-370.

Peace, K. A., Beaman, L. G., & Sneddon, K. (2000). Theoretical approaches to the study of deviance. In L. G. Beaman (Ed.), *New perspectives on deviance: The construction of deviance in everyday life* (pp. 2-17). Scarborough, ON: Prentice Hall.

Pearson, G. (1983). *Hooligan: A history of respectable fears*. London: MacMillan Press.

Peck, R. L., (2001). What's new with ADHD? *Behavioral Health Management, November/December*, 26-29.

Petrie, T. A., Austin, L. J., Crowley, B. J., Helmcamp, A., Johnson, C. E., Lester, R.et al. (1996). Sociocultural expectations of attractiveness for males. *Sex Roles, 35*(9/10), 581-602.

PFLAG (2001). Anti-gay harassment & abuse at school: What we know. *Families & Educators Partnering for Safe Schools*. Retrieved March 19, 2001, from **http://pflag.org**

Pfohl, S. (1994). *Images of deviance and social control: A sociological history*. New York: McGraw-Hill.

Piccinelli, M., & Homen, F. G. (1997). *Gender differences in the epidemiology of affective disorders and schizophrenia.* Geneva, Switzerland: World Health Organization.

Pingetore, R., Dugoni, B. L., Tindale, R. S., & Spring, B. C. (1994). Bias against overweight job applicants in a simulated employment interaction. *Journal of Applied Psychology, 79*, 909-917.

Platt, A. M. (1977). *The child savers: The invention of delinquency*. Chicago: University of Chicago Press.

Pollack, W. (1998). *Real boys: Rescuing our sons from the myths of boyhood*. New York: Henry Holt.

Pollex, R., Hegels, B., & Ban, M. R. (2001). Celestial determinants of success in research. *Canadian Medical Association Journal, 165*, 12.

Pongonis, A., & Snyder, R. (1998). Links between body size, food, and perceptions of morality. Paper presented at the annual meeting of the American Psychological Association, August 14-18, San Francisco.

Poponoe, P., & Johnson, R. H. (1922). *Applied eugenics*. New York: MacMillan.

Presley, S. (2000). Don't listen to Dr. Laura. *Free Inquiry, 21*(1). Retrieved June 18, 2001, from Expanded Academic ASAP database.

Price, J. H., Desmond, S. M., Krol, R. A., Snyder, F. F., & O'Connell, J. K. (1987). Family practice physicians' beliefs, attitudes, and practices regarding obesity. *American Journal of Preventative Medicine, 3*(6), 339-345.

Proctor, R. N. (1988). *Racial hygiene: Medicine under the Nazis*. Cambridge, MA: Harvard University Press.

Pruzhinin, B. I., & Scanlon, J. P. (1995). Astrology has tried to establish itself as a science for more than 2000 years. *Russian Social Science Review, 36*(5), 75-94.

Puhl, R., & Brownell, K. D. (2001). Bias, discrimination, and obesity. *Obesity Research, 9*, 788-805.

Quaife, G. R. (1987). *Godly zeal and furious rage: The witch craze in early modern Europe*. New York: St. Martin's Press.

Quinney, R. (1977). *The problem of crime: A critical introduction to criminology* (2nd ed.). New York: Harper & Row.

R. vs. Butler (1992). Canadian Legal Information Institute. Retrieved May 19, 2002, from **http://canlil.org**

R. vs. Sharpe (2001). Canadian Legal Information Institute. Retrieved May 18, 2002, from **http://canlil.org**

Raback-Wagener, J., Eickhoff-Shemek, J., & Kelly-Vance, L. (1998). The effect of media analysis on attitudes and behaviors regarding body image among college students. *Journal of American College Health, 47*(1). Retrieved August 14, 2002, from Expanded Academic ASAP database.

Rampton, S., & Stauber, J. (2000a). How big tobacco helped create "the junkman". *PR Watch, 7*(3), 5-9.

Rampton, S., & Stauber, J. (2000b). Tobacco's secondhand science of smoke-filled rooms. *PR Watch, 7*(3), 10-11.

Rampton, S., & Stauber, J. (2001). *Trust us, we're experts: How industry manipulates science and gambles with your future*. New York: Tarcher/Putnam.

Ramsey, S. (2002). PAHO exposes tobacco-industry tactics in Latin America. *Lancet, 360*(9350), 2057.

Razack, S. H. (2002). *Race, space, and the law: Unmapping a white settler society*. Toronto, ON: Between the Lines.

Read, D. (Director), Armstrong, M., Pettigrew, M., & Johansson, S. (Producers) (1994). *Burning Times* [videorecording]. Available from the National Film Board of Canada.

Read, J., & Harre, N. (2001). The role of biological and genetic causal beliefs in the stigmatisation of 'mental patients'. *Journal of Mental Health, 10*(2), 223-235.

Regioli, R., & Hewitt, J. (1994). *Delinquency in society: A child-centered approach*. New York: McGraw Hill.

Reitsma-Street, M. (1989-90). More control than care: A critique of historical and contemporary laws for delinquency and neglect of children in Ontario. *Canadian Journal of Women and the Law, 3*(2), 510-530.

Richardson, J. T. (1995). A social psychological critique of "brainwashing" claims made about recruitment to new religions. In J. Hadden & D. Bromley (Eds.), *The handbook of cults and sects in America* (Vol. 3, Part B) (pp. 75-97). Greenwich, CT: JAI Press.

Richardson, J. T., Best, J., & Bromley, D. G. (1991). *The satanism scare*. New York: Aldine de Gruyter.

Richardson, J. T., & Introvigne, M. (2001). "Brainwashing" theories in European and administrative reports on "cults" and "sects". *Journal for the Scientific Study of Religion, 40*(2), 143-168.

Roberts, G., McCall, D., Stevens-Lavigne, A., Anderson, J., Paglia, A., Bollenbach, S., Weibe, J., & Gliksman, L. (2001). *Preventing substance abuse problems among young people: A compendium of best practices*. Ottawa: Health Canada.

Roberts, G. L., Lawrence, J. M., Williams, G. M., & Raphael, B. (1998). The impact of domestic violence on women's health. *Australia and New Zealand Journal of Public Health, 22*, 796-801.

Roehling, M. (1999). Weight based discrimination in employment: Psychological and legal aspects. *Personnel Psychology, 52*(4). Retrieved March 23, 2003, from Expanded Academic ASAP database.

Rosenhan, D. L. (1973). Being sane in insane places. *Science, 179*(1973), 250-258.

Rossol, J. (2001). The medicalization of deviance as an interactive achievement: The construction of compulsive gambling. *Symbolic Interaction*, 24(3), 315-341.

Rothman, D. J. (1971). *The discovery of the asylum: Social order & disorder in the New Republic*. Baltimore, MD: Johns Hopkins University Press.

Rubington, E., & Weinberg, M. S. (2002). *Deviance: The interactionist perspective* (8th ed.). Boston: Allyn & Bacon.

Sacco, V. F. (1992). *Deviance, conformity and control in Canadian society*. Scarborough, ON: Prentice Hall.

Saliba, G. (2001/2002). Reading the heavens. *Natural History, 110*(10), 80-81.

Salusso-Deonier, C. J., Markee, N. L., & Pedersen, E. L. (1993). Gender differences in the evaluation of physical attractiveness for male and female body builds. *Perceptual & Motor Skills, 76*, 1155-1167.

Sandbek, T. J. (1993). *The deadly diet: Recovering from anorexia & bulimia* (2nd ed.). Oakland, CA: New Harbinger Publications.

Sayce, L. (1998). Stigma, discrimination and social exclusion. What's in a word? *Journal of Mental Health, 7*, 331-343.

Sayce, L. (2000). *From psychiatric patient to citizen: Overcoming discrimination and social exclusion*. New York: St. Martin's Press.

Schissel, B. (1997). Youth crime, moral panics, and the politics of hate. Halifax, NS: Fernwood.

Schissel, B. (2001). Youth crime, moral panics, and the news: The conspiracy against the marginalized in Canada. In R. C. Smandych (Ed.), *Youth justice: History, legislation, and reform* (pp. 84-103). Toronto, ON: Harcourt.

Schlenker, J. A., Caron, S. L., & Halteman, W. A. (1998). A feminist analysis of *Seventeen* magazine: Content analysis from 1945-1995. *Sex Roles, 38*(1/2), 135-149.

Schlosser, E. (1997, February 10). The business of pornography. *U. S. New & World Report*, p. 42-50.

Schneider, K. S., Levitt, S., Morton, D., Yoo, P., Skolnick, S., Brooks, A.et al. (1996, June 3). Mission impossible. *People, 45*(22). Retrieved August 1, 2001, from Canadian MAS Fulltext Elite database.

Seldon, S., & Montagu, A. (1999). *Inheriting shame: The story of eugenics and racism in America*. New York: Teachers College Press.

Sellin, T. (1938). *Culture conflict and crime*. New York: Social Science Research Council.

Sharp, S. F., Terling-Watt, T. L., Atkins, L. A., & Gilliam, J. T. (2001). Purging behavior in a sample of college females: A research note on general strain theory and female deviance. *Deviant Behavior: An Interdisciplinary Journal, 22,* 171-188.

Shermer, M. (2001a). *The borderlands of science: Where sense meets nonsense.* New York: Oxford University Press.

Shermer, M. (2001b). Baloney detection. *Scientific American, 285*(6), 34.

Shupe, A. D., & Bromley, D. G. (1995). The evolution of modern American anti-cult ideology. In T. Miller (Ed.), *America's alternative religions* (pp. 401-409). Albany, NY: State University Press.

Shupe, A., & Hadden, J. K. (1996). Copes, new copy and public opinion: Legitimacy and the social construction of evil in Waco. In S. Wright (Ed.), *Armageddon in Waco* (pp. 177-202). Chicago, IL: University of Chicago Press.

Shuriquie, N. (1999). Eating disorders: A transcultural perspective. *Eastern Mediterranean Health Journal, 5*(2), 354-360.

Shute, N. (2002, October 2). Pushing pills on kids? *U. S. News & World Report, 129*(13), 60.

Siegal, L. J., & McCormick, C. (2003). *Criminology in Canada: Theories, patterns, and typologies* (2nd ed.). Scarborough, ON: Nelson Thomson.

Silverstein, B., Perdue, L., Peterson, B., & Kelly, E. (1986). The role of the mass media in promoting a thin standard of bodily attractiveness for women. *Sex Roles, 14*(9/10), 519-532.

Simon, R. W. (2002). Revisiting the relationships among gender, marital status, and mental health. *American Journal of Sociology, 107*(4), 1065-1098.

Simoni-Wastila, L. (2000). The use of abusable prescription drugs: The role of gender. *Journal of Women's Health and Gender Based Medicine, 9,* 289-297.

Sinsheimer, R. L. (1990). Whither the Genome Project? *Hastings Center Report, 20*(4), 5.

Skeptical Inquirer (1999). Science needs to combat pseudo-science. *Skeptical Inquirer, 23*(1), 37-38.

Small, M. (1994, May 30). His favorite Martians. *People Weekly, 41*(20), 57-59.

Smandych, R. C. (Ed.) (2001). *Youth crime: varieties, theories, and prevention.* Toronto, ON: Harcourt.

Smart, R., Adlaf, E., Walsh, G., & Zdanowicz, Y. (1992). *Drifting and doing: Changes in drug use among Toronto street youth, 1990-1992.* Toronto, ON: Addiction Research Foundation.

Solomon, N. (2000). Dr. Laura goes TV—but at what cost? *Humanist, 60*(6), 3.

Spector, M. (1981). Beyond crime: Seven methods to control troublesome rascals. In L. Ross (Ed.), *Law and deviance* (pp. 127-148). Beverly Hills, CA: Sage Publications.

Spitzer, R. L. (1975). On pseudoscience in science, logic in remission, and psychiatric diagnosis. *Journal of Abnormal Psychology, 84*(1975), 442-452.

Stark, C. A. (1997). Is pornography an action?: The causal vs. the conceptual view of pornography's harm. *Social Theory & Practice, 23*(2), 277-306.

Stark, R., Doyle, D. P., & Kent, L. (1992). Rediscovering moral communities: Church membership and crime. In T. Hirschi & M. Gottfredson (Eds.), *Understanding crime: Current theory and research* (pp. 43-52). Beverly Hills, CA: Sage.

Stark, R., & Bainbridge, W. S. (1996). *A theory of religion.* New Brunswick, NJ: Rutgers University Press.

Statistics Canada (1992). Crime trends in Canada, 1962-1990. *Juristat, 12*(7). Catalogue No: 85002XIE.

Statistics Canada (2001a). *Children and youth in Canada.* Canadian Centre for Justice Statistics Profile Series. Catalogue No: 85F0033MIE.

Statistics Canada (2001b). *Juristat, 21*(8). Catalogue No: 85002XIE.

Statistics Canada (2002a). *Juristat, 22*(6). Catalogue No. 85002XIE.

Statistics Canada (2002b). *The Daily, October 18.* Retrieved February 17, 2003, from **http://www.statcan.ca**

Statistics Canada (2003). *Health Indicators, 2003*(1). Catalogue No. 82221XIE.

Stebbins, R. A. (1996). *Tolerable differences: Living with deviance.* Toronto, ON: McGraw Hill Ryerson.

Stephans, T., & Jorbert, N. (2001). The economic burden of mental health problems in Canada. *Chronic Diseases in Canada, 22*(1), 18-23.

Stice, E., & Shaw, H. E. (1994). Adverse effects of the media portrayed thin-ideal on women and linkages to bulimic symptomatology. *Journal of Social and Clinical Psychology, 13*(3). Retrieved April 18, 2003, from Expanded Academic ASAP database.

Stip, E., Caron, J., & Lane, L. J. (2001). Schizophrenia: People's perceptions in Quebec. *Canadian Medical Association Journal, 164*(9), 1299-1300.

Stock, G. (2002). *Redesigning humans: Our inevitable genetic future.* Boston: Houghton Mifflin.

Stoppe, G., Sandholzer, H., & Huppertz, C. (1999). Gender differences in the recognition of depression in old age. *Maturitas, 32,* 205-212.

Story, M., Neumark-Sztainer, D., & Sherwood, N. (1998). Dieting status among U. S. adolescents. *Nutrition Research Newsletter, 17*(11), 12.

Streigel-Moore, R. (2001). *Eating disorders: Innovative directions for research and practice.* Washington, DC: American Psychological Association.

Stylianou, S. (2002). Control attitudes toward drug use as a function of paternalistic and moralistic principles. *Journal of Drug Use, 32*(1), 119-152.

Sullivan, G., Jackson, C. A., & Spritzer, K. L. (1996). Characteristics and service use of seriously mentally ill persons living in rural areas. *Psychiatric Services, 47*(1), 57-61.

Sumner, C. (1994). *The sociology of deviance: An obituary.* New York: Continuum.

Sutherland, E. H. (1947). *Principles of criminology.* Philadelphia, PA: J. B. Lippincott.

Sutherland, N. (1976). *Children in English-Canadian society: Framing the twentieth-century consensus.* Toronto, ON: University of Toronto Press.

Sydie, R. (1994). *Natural women, cultured men: A feminist perspective on sociological theory.* Vancouver, BC: UBC Press.

Sykes, G., & Matza, D. (1957). Techniques of neutralization: A theory of delinquency. *American Sociological Review, 22,* 664-670.

Szasz, T. (1994). Mental illness is still a myth. *Society, 31*(4), 34-39.

Tait, G. (1999). Rethinking youth cultures: The case of the Gothics. *Social Alternatives, 18*(2), 15-20.

Tannenbaum, F. (1938). *Crime and the community.* New York: Ginn.

Tanner, J. (1992). Youthful deviance. In V. Sacco (Ed.), *Deviance, conformity and control in Canadian society* (2nd ed.). Scarborough, ON: Prentice Hall.

Tanner, J. (2001). *Teenage troubles: Youth and deviance in Canada* (2nd ed.). Scarborough, ON: Nelson Thomson.

Tanzman, B. (1993). An overview of surveys of mental health consumers' preferences for housing and support services. *Hospital and Community Psychiatry, 44*(5), 450-455.

Tauber, M., Norman, P., Brailsford, K., Gee, A., Grant, M., Laudadio, N. F.et al. (2001, April 2). Hollywood's healthy bodies are back. *People, April,* 92-101.

Teevan, J. J., & Dryburgh, H. B. (2000). First person accounts and sociological explanations of delinquency. *Canadian Review of Sociology and Anthropology, 37*(1), 77-94.

Thelen, M. H., & Cormier, J. F. (1995). Desire to be thinner and weight control among children and their parents. *Behavior Therapy, 26*, 85-99.

Thio, A. (1983). *Deviant behavior* (2nd ed.). Boston: Houghton Mifflin.

Thomson, G., & Reid, M. (2001, July 24). Klein warns thugs, punks away from Kananaskis. *Victoria Times Colonist*, p. A3.

Thornberry, T., Lizotte, A., Krohm, M., Farnworth, M., & Jang, S. (1991). Testing interactional theory: An examination of reciprocal causal relationships among family, school and delinquency. *Journal of Criminal Law and Criminology, 82*(1), 3-33.

Tittle, C. R., & Paternoster, R. (2000). *Social deviance and crime*. Los Angeles, CA: Roxbury.

Todd, P. (2001, October). Veiled threats? *Homemakers, October*, 45-53.

Troeltsch, E. ([1931] 1960). *The social teachings of the Christian churches* (Vols. 1 and 2). Translated by O. Wyon. New York: Harper & Row.

Trust, J., & Watts, R. E. (1999). Relationship of high school seniors' religious participation and behavior to educational, career, and leisure variables. *Counseling Values, 44*(1), 30-39.

Tuggle, J. L., & Holmes, M. D. (1997). Blowing smoke: Status politics and the smoking ban. In P. A. Adler & P. Adler (Eds.), *Constructions of deviance: Social power, context, and interaction* (pp. 149-159). Belmont, CA: Wadsworth.

Turk, A. (1969). *Criminality and legal order*. Chicago: Rand McNally.

Turner, R. J., Wheaton, B., & Lloyd, D. A. (1995). The epidemiology of social stress. *American Sociological Review, 60*(1), 104-127.

Ullman, S. R. (1997). *Sex seen: The emergence of modern sexuality in America*. Berkeley, CA: University of California Press.

UNESCO (1997). *Universal declaration on the human genome and human rights*. Paris: Author.

U. S. Department of State (2002). *International religious freedom report 2002*. Washington, DC: Bureau of Democracy, Human Rights, and Labor.

Valpy, M. (1998, March 7). Cleaning out the cuckoo's nest. *Globe and Mail*, p. D1.

Valverde, M. (1991). *The age of light, soap, and water: Moral reform in English Canada, 1885-1925*. Toronto, ON: McClelland & Stewart.

Vandereycken, W. (1998). *Treating eating disorders: Ethical, legal, and personal issues*. New York: New York University Press.

Victor, J. (1992). The search for scapegoat deviants. *Humanist, 52*(5), 10-13.

Victor, J. (1993). *Satanic panic: The creation of a contemporary legend*. Chicago, IL: Open Court.

Vold, G. (1958). *Theoretical criminology*. New York: Oxford University Press.

Vuijst, F. (narrator, director) (1995). *Onward Christian Soldiers* [videorecording]. Available from Filmakers' Library, New York.

Wachholz, S. (2000). The good mother. In L. G. Beaman (Ed.), *New perspectives on deviance* (pp. 180-191). Scarborough, ON: Prentice Hall.

Wahl, O. F. (1992). Mass media images of mental illness: A review of the literature. *Journal of Community Psychology, 15*, 285-291.

Wahl, O. F. (1999). Mental health consumers' experience of stigma. *Schizophrenia Bulletin, 25*, 467-478.

Ward, D. E. (1993). Gene therapy: The splice of life. *USA Today Magazine, 121*(2572), 63-66.

Ward, D. A., Carter, T. J., & Perrin, R. D. (1994). *Social deviance: Being, behaving, and branding*. Boston: Allyn & Bacon.

Watson, J. (1997). *The Christian Coalition: Dreams of restoration and demands for recognition*. New York: St. Martin's Press.

Weber, T. (1999). Raving in Toronto: Peace, love, unity, and respect in transition. *Journal of Youth Studies, 2*(3), 317-336.

Webster, P. (2001, March 26). Defending the faith. *Maclean's*, 28-29.

Wegs, R. (1999). Youth delinquency & "crime": The perception and the reality. *Journal of Social History, 32*(3). Retrieved December 20, 2002, from Expanded Academic ASAP database.

Weinberg, M. S. (1967). Nudist camp: Way of life and social structure. *Human Organization, 26*, 91-99.

Weiss, S. F. (1988). *Race hygiene and national efficiency: The eugenics of Wilhelm Schallmayer*. Berkeley, CA: University of California Press.

Wells, E., & Rankin, J. (1991). Families and delinquency: A meta-analysis of the impact of broken homes. *Social Problems, 38*, 71-93.

Wertheim, E. H., Paxton, S. J., Schutz, H. K., & Muir, S. L. (1997). Why do adolescent girls watch their weight? An interview study examining sociocultural pressures to be thin. *Journal of Psychosomatic Research, 42*(4), 345-355.

Weschler, H., Kelley, K., Weitzman, E. R., San Giovanni, J. P., & Seibring, M. (2000). What colleges are doing about student binge drinking. *Journal of American College Health, 48*(5), 219-226.

Weschler, H., & Kuo, M. (2000). College students define binge drinking and estimate its prevalence: Results of a national survey. *Journal of American College Health, 49*(2), 57-64.

West, G. (1991). Towards a more socially informed understanding of Canadian delinquency legislation. In A. Leschied, P. Jaffe, & W. Willis (Eds.), *The Young Offenders Act: A revolution in Canadian juvenile justice*. Toronto, ON: University of Toronto Press.

West, W. G. (1984). *Young offenders and the state: A Canadian perspective on delinquency*. Toronto, ON: Butterworths.

Westbrook, M. T., Legge, V., & Pennay, M. (1993). Attitudes towards disabilities in a multicultural society. *Social Science & Medicine, 36*(5), 615-623.

Wheeler, S. (1960). Sex offenses: A sociological critique. *Law and Contemporary Society, 25* (Spring), 258-278.

White, C. (2003). Environmentalist accused of scientific dishonesty. *British Medical Journal, 326*(7381), 120.

Whiting, G. (1996). *The sterilization of Leilani Muir* [videorecording]. Available from the National Film Board of Canada.

Whorton, J. (2001). The solitary vice. *The Western Journal of Medicine, 175*(1). Retrieved January 24, 2002, from Expanded Academic ASAP database.

Williams, D. R., & Takeuchi, D. T. (1992). Socioeconomic status and psychiatric disorder among blacks and whites. *Social Forces, 70*(5), 179-194.

Wilson, B. (2002). The Canadian rave scene and five theses on youth resistance. *Canadian Journal of Sociology, 27*(3), 373-412.

Wilson, B. R. (1993). Historical lessons in the study of sects and cults. *Religion and the Social Order, 3A*, 53-73.

Wilson Quarterly (1992). The fateful code. *Wilson Quarterly, 16*(2), 85-86.

Wiseman, C. V., Gray, J. J., Mosimann, J. E., & Ahrens, A. H. (1992). Cultural expectations of thinness in women: An update. *International Journal of Eating Disorders, 11*, 85-89.

Women's Sports and Fitness (2000, July). Which body do you want? *Women's Sports and Fitness, 3*(7). Retrieved August 1, 2001, from Expanded Academic ASAP database.

Wood, R. (1999). Nailed to the X: A lyrical history of the straightedge youth subculture. *Journal of Youth Studies, 2*, 133-151.

Wood, R. (2000). *Straightedge youth: Subculture, genesis, permutation, and identity formation.* Unpublished doctoral dissertation, University of Alberta, Edmonton, AB.

World Association for Sexology (1999). *The universal declaration of sexual rights.* Retrieved August 8, 2002, from **http://www.tc.umn.edu/~coleman001/was/wasindex.htm**

World Health Organization (2001). Costs of mental illness. *Fact Sheet No. 218.* Retrieved May 7, 2002, from **http://www.who.int**

World Health Organization (2002a). Home page. Retrieved April 15, 2003, from **http://www.who.int**

World Health Organization (2002b). *Mental health global action programme.* Geneva, Switzerland: Author.

World Health Organization (2003). *The global strategy on diet, physical activity and health.* Geneva, Switzerland: Author.

World Health Organization (2003). World Health Assembly adopts historic tobacco control pact. Retrieved March 3, 2003, from **http://www.who.int**

World Psychiatric Association (2003). Program against stigmatization and discrimination because of schizophrenia. Retrieved May 17, 2003, from **http://www.wpanet.org**

Wright, S. A. (1997). Media coverage of unconventional religion: Any "good news" for minority faiths? *Review of Religious Research, 39*(2), 101-115.

Wroblewska, A. M. (1997). Androgenic anabolic steroids and body dysmorphia in young men. *Journal of Psychosomatic Research, 42*, 225-234.

Yam, P. (1997). The media's eerie fascination. *Scientific American, 276*(1), 100-101.

Yinger, J. M. (1970). *The scientific study of religion.* New York: Macmillan.

Young, M. (1993). *The history of Vancouver youth gangs, 1900-1985.* Unpublished M. A. thesis, School of Criminology, Simon Fraser University, Vancouver, BC.

Index

N

O

P

R

S

Photo Credits

Page 1: Toby Canham, The Image Works; page 9: from Museum of Questionable Medical Devices; page 27: © Bettman/CORBIS/Magmaphoto.com; page 40: DK; page 53: © Greg Smith/Maxximages.com; page 64: photo by Ho, © Reuters 2000; page 73: Pearson Education/PH College Archives; page 86: The Granger Collection; page 99: © Masterfile, www.masterfile.com; page 138: © Michael Newman/Photo Edit; page 143: © Myrleen Ferguson Cate/Photo Edit; page 156: © Joel W. Rogers/CORBIS/Magmaphoto.com; page 161: © Chuck Savage/CORBIS/Magmaphoto.com; page 175: image courtesy of Circus World Museum, Baraboo, Wisconsin, with permission from Ringling Bros. and Barnum & Bailey® THE GREATEST SHOW ON EARTH®; page 184, left: AP Photo/Stephen Chernin; page 184, right: photo by Jose Breton; page 205: © Peter Turnley/CORBIS/Magmaphoto.com; page 215: Chuck Savage/CORBIS/Magmaphoto.com; page 227: Ed Souza/Stanford News Service; page 235: AP/Wide World Photos; page 240: © Esbin-Anderson/Omni-Photo Communications; page 245: AP Photo/Asahi, Eiji Hori; page 258: © Bettmann/CORBIS; page 270: COREL; page 282: © Denis Scott/CORGIS; page 291: AP Photo; page 299: © Clive Newton; The Military Picture Library/CORGIS; page 303: AP Photo; page 309: © Henry Diltz/CORBIS/MagmaPhoto.com; page 313: AP Photo/Richard Drew.